WRITING BORDERLESS HISTORIES OF ART

Writing Borderless Histories of Art is an aspirational, historical, and critical project that offers a fundamental rethinking of the relationship of humans to the rest of nature.

Social justice, Indigeneity, abuses of power, and the environmental crisis are the burning issues of today. A transcultural approach calls for abandoning structures of domination that are built into the academic disciplines, regardless of the scale or extent of interpretation. Drawing upon writings from a wide range of fields, Claire Farago argues that art history can play a role in advancing the public's interconnectedness with the planetary life-support system that so urgently needs to be restored. Studying the discourse on art at the intersection of global capitalism, environmental degradation, and human subjection over four centuries, *Writing Borderless Histories of Art* advocates ontologies that do not distinguish between the sentience of humans and other animals and go beyond the dualistic metaphysics of the nature/culture divide.

While this book is addressed to a wide audience, its multilayered approach also reaches out to art historians for whom chronology, canons, and style are structures fundamental to the organization and operation of the discipline. The book is neither a history of ideas nor a search for the origins of art history, but a recognition of the structures that drive its narratives.

Claire Farago is Professor Emerita at the University of Colorado Boulder, currently living in Los Angeles. She has written extensively on processes of transculturation, the epistemological foundations of art history, art theory, and museums. Her anthology, *Reframing the Renaissance* (1995) was a groundbreaking contribution to transcultural studies in art history.

"*Writing Borderless Histories of Art* is an extraordinary book, as bold as it is erudite. Claire Farago brings to light formative connections that have always existed between art making, climate theory, and transcultural relationships, but which have been overlooked by scholarship in art history. Eloquently written and incisively argued, this is a book of vital contemporary relevance that will transform the field. It deserves to be read by every art historian."

Monica Juneja, *Senior Professor at the Heidelberg Centre for Transcultural Studies, University of Heidelberg, Germany, and Distinguished Professor of Humanities & Social Sciences, Shiv Nadar University, India*

"Eurocentrism has a cost far beyond the obvious power asymmetries we see damaging the world today. Claire Farago's erudite and readable book makes that point forcefully in relation to climate transformation and art discourse. She powerfully combines her deep knowledge of European ancient to early modern thought with an expansive view of contemporary global society and its brutal extractive methods, tracing the origins of human exceptionalism in European thought to the present. Demonstrating the interrelations among globalization, colonization, disciplinary formations, and the traffic in art objects, she offers refreshing counter arguments that are collective, relational, and 'borderless.' A tour-de-force!"

Amelia Jones, *Robert A. Day Professor of Art and Design and Professor of Art and Design, Art History and American Studies & Ethnicity, University of Southern California, USA*

WRITING BORDERLESS HISTORIES OF ART

Human Exceptionalism and the Climate Crisis

five fugues on the future of the past

Claire Farago

Routledge
Taylor & Francis Group
LONDON AND NEW YORK

Designed cover image: © Getty Images/ Digital Vision

First published 2025
by Routledge
4 Park Square, Milton Park, Abingdon, Oxon OX14 4RN

and by Routledge
605 Third Avenue, New York, NY 10158

Routledge is an imprint of the Taylor & Francis Group, an informa business

British Library Cataloguing-in-Publication Data
A catalogue record for this book is available from the British Library

ISBN: 978-1-138-49581-4 (hbk)
ISBN: 978-1-138-49582-1 (pbk)
ISBN: 978-1-351-02342-9 (ebk)

DOI: 10.4324/9781351023429

Typeset in Times New Roman
by Apex CoVantage, LLC

For Mia and Reed
with love and hope for the future

ABOUT THE COVER

On December 24, 1968, Apollo 8 astronauts Frank Borman, Jim Lovell, and Bill Anders became the first humans to orbit the Moon, and the first to witness the magnificent sight later called "Earthrise." As the spacecraft was in the process of rotating, Anders took this iconic picture showing Earth rising over the Moon's horizon. Image credit: NASA. See recreation of the event with original voice recordings here: https://science.nasa.gov/resource/the-story-behind-apollo-8s-famous-earthrise-photo/. See discussion, pp. 7–8.

CONTENTS

ACKNOWLEDGMENTS

Many colleagues contributed their energy, ideas, and expertise to this project as it evolved over the past six years, many more than I can thank by name in these brief Acknowledgments. Most of the actual writing took place in Los Angeles, so I would like to begin by acknowledging the Gabrielino/Tongva peoples as the traditional land caretakers of Tovaangar (the Los Angeles basin and Southern Channel Islands) whose descendants are maintaining deeply rooted connections to their cultural traditions to ensure that their heritage is passed on to future generations. Indigenous knowledge is valuable in restoring the environment, but not in the sense of the colonizer's literary trope that the "native informant" is "one with nature." To the contrary, the premise of *this* book is that all societies are heterogeneous. The implications of this claim are far-reaching because it problematizes the notion of purity at every scale. What's at stake in being pure? In being heterogeneous? Humans are composites at every scale. My ideas were germinating along these lines when I held the inaugural Fulbright Fellowship at the University of York, U.K., in 2011–2012. I gave talks and participated in workshops there and at the University of East Anglia, the University of Leeds, and the University of Birmingham. The main outlines of the chapters took shape in fall 2021 when I was invited to give a series of public lectures on my current research as Ruth and Clarence Kennedy Professor in Renaissance Studies at Smith College in Northampton, Massachusetts. I am deeply grateful to Dana Leibsohn and her colleagues and staff in the Art Department for initiating the invitation and to the College for offering such a congenial welcome and an excellent working environment with exceptional library resources and an art museum with a wonderful teaching collection and staff. Laila Smith and Diem Nguyen were superb research assistants. It was an honor to teach such amazing strong women – thank you all, I found each of you remarkable and my hat's off for your perseverance and creativity coming out of lockdown still during the pandemic.

I warmly thank Dana Leibsohn for stimulating conversations in Northampton. Her candid reading of the very first draft encouraged me to focus on the idea of human exceptionalism. I am profoundly grateful to Amelia Jones, dear friend and consummate critic, who has encouraged this book since the proposal stage and offered astute feedback at many points along the way. Karin Frei, Research Professor of Archaeometry at the National Museum of Denmark, invited me to meet her colleagues in Copenhagen, including the archaeologist Flemming Kaul and Matthew Walsh, who introduced me to important research on animal intelligence. Further down the line, I am happily indebted to Steven Stowell for his careful reading of my interpretation of Paleotti. I am also fortunate for the intellectual generosity of Tomasz Grusiecki, whose knowledge of early modern state formations has been invaluable. Matthew Vollgraff generously shared his work and offered incisive comments on what became Chapter 3. I thank Roger Crum for his honed editorial expertise on an earlier draft. My thanks also to Kamini Vellodi for her excellent suggestions on the Introduction. Thanks as well to Janis Bell who reviewed my discussion of Mannerism. I am grateful to Friedrich von Bose for his careful review of the section on the Benin Bronzes. I also benefited from reading and discussing Catholic Reformation history with two of the finest scholars in the field, Simon Ditchfield and Pamela Jones. My knowledge of Indigenous Australian art and art history has been enriched through recent exchanges with Jennifer Green and Susan Lowish. I extend my profound thanks to Jen for reviewing my discussion of Arandic sand stories, to Jeanette Favrot Peterson for sharing her deep knowledge of visual culture in sixteenth-century Mexico, to Lisa Pon for consulting on a difficult Latin inscription, to Daniela Bleichmar for expert advice on the Codex Mendoza, and many others: I am grateful to you all.

For the past four years, I have had many stimulating conversations with my co-editors from the Global South, Susan Lowish at the University of Melbourne and Jens Baumgarten at the Federal University of São Paulo, as we collaborated with each other and our contributors on the anthology that complements this publication, *Transcultural Histories of Art and Artisanal Epistemologies: Knowledge to Be Made* (Routledge 2025). My final chapter is indebted to their intellectual generosity and particularly Susan's expertise in Australian Aboriginal art and the critical discourse on Indigeneity.

Monica Juneja is really the midwife of this book. Monica read numerous drafts of chapters critically and reviewed the entire final manuscript in detail. Her own rigorous scholarship has been inspiring and her friendship means more than I can say. Through her invitations to conferences and workshops at the University of Heidelberg's Centre of Transcultural Studies (HCTS), and the transatlantic research initiative, "Worlding Public Culture: The Arts and Social Innovation" (WPC), I have met many other scholars and her students at all levels. I single out

Jo Ziebritzki and her team for facilitating my most recent visit in 2024 to celebrate Monica's career. Monica has produced a phalanx of energetic PhDs committed to transcultural approaches. I am especially grateful to Birgit Hopfener and Franziska Koch for their inspiring work, their intellectual generosity, and their friendship. A special note of thanks to the Heidelberg WPC team and to Birgit Hopfener, Ming Tiampo, and Kelly Tialiou at Carleton University in Ottowa, Canada.

Another international network of scholars whose important work and collegiality have been instrumental in developing this project are centered in South America. My warmest thanks to Jens Baumgarten, Maria Berbara, Claudia Mattos, Flavia Galli Tatsch, and Patricia Zalamea for including me in conferences and collaborative projects. In the process of working out my ideas, I presented papers at numerous other national and international conferences and universities over the past decade, too many to enumerate here. My enthusiastic thanks to lively discussions with many audiences: your responsiveness has informed my thinking. I was fortunate to meet Renja Suominen-Kokkonen who arranged lectures on several occasions at the University of Helsinki, Finland. I also happily acknowledge Tristan Weddigen and his staff, notably Charlotte Matter, for the opportunity to teach a seminar in the Art History in Global Context Specialized Master of Arts program at the University of Zurich, Switzerland, in 2018. I warmly thank Bill Sherman, Director of the Warburg Institute, London, for the opportunity to present a working paper there in 2021. There are many more wonderful scholars and artists to thank that I met and learned a great deal from along this journey including Mari-Tere Álvare, the late Frederick "Rick" Asher, Sussan Baabaie, Clara Bargellini, Philip Batty, Erin Benay, Barbara Berrie, Charlene Villaseñor Black, Dan Bridgman, Peter Brunt, Amy Buono, Brigitte Buettner, Rex Butler, Nanne Buurman, Danielle Carabino, Paul Carter, Brian Catlos and the Mediterranean Studies Group at CU-Boulder, Ananda Cohen-Aponte, Roberto Conduru, James Córdova, Jane Chin Davidson, Rebecca Davis, Jae Emerling, Sandy Esslinger, Noéme Étienne, Lucretia and Peter Farago, Ksenia Federova, Dario Gamboni, Christine Göttler, Charles Green, Maria Fabricius Hansen, Grace Harpster, Helen Hills and the Department of the History of Art at the University of York, UK; Çiğdem Kafescioğlu, the late Eloise Quiñones Keber, Barbara Kellum, Henry Keazor, Ryszard Kluszczynski, Jeanette Kohl, Matthew Landrus, Stephanie Leitch, Jenny Lin, Virginia Marano, David Maskill, Marsha Meskimmon, Kylie Message, Barbara Mittler, Mia Mochizuki, Howard Morphy, Julia Murray, Jessica Nicoll, John Onians and the World Art Studies program at UEA, Nikos Papastergiadis, Ruth Phillips, Donna Pierce, Kathleen Pierce, Griselda Pollock, Lisa Pon and the research group, Collaborations in History, Art, Religion, and Museum (CHARM) at the University of Southern California, Los Angeles; Matthew Rampley, Dorothee Richter, James Saslow, Daniel Savoy, Mona Schieren, Pamela H. Smith, Terry Smith, Jutta Sperling, Zrinka Stahuljak and the UCLA CMRS Center for Early Global Studies, David Summers, Lisbet Tarp, Caroline Turner, Nancy Um, Angela Vanhalen, Victoria Vesna, Hélène Visentin, Frazer Ward, Gregory de Wet, Bronwen Wilson, Kathy Woyda, Kitty Zijlmans, and Rob

Zwijnenberg. I warmly thank the staff in Special Collections at the Getty Research Institute Library for accommodating me on numerous occasions and the Institute for their generous reader privileges and welcoming staff.

At Routledge Press, my heartfelt thanks go to Natalie Foster, who has been a tremendously warm and supportive editor; Deanna Waistell and Ann-Kathrin Klein, who efficiently ushered the manuscript through the production process; Maire Harris, copyeditor; and the excellent team who put it all together. Emma Brown worked numerous miracles securing the pictures and rights. My thanks also to all the institutions and copyright holders who provided images, and to the Press and the University of Southern California for supporting the costs.

Dear colleagues, family, and friends: I could not have written this book without you. Thanks to Zoom technology and occasional reunions, a group of steadfast friends from childhood who reconnected in 2016 provided essential emotional support and good company. My warmest thanks to Susie DiMaina, Sally Forb, Jane Goldman, Carol Hooper, Harriet Meader, and Anne Rainey O'Toole. I am indebted beyond measure to my husband, soulmate, and intellectual partner Donald Preziosi who has supported this project at every step along the way. This book is the latest chapter that our longstanding collaboration has made possible. *Writing Borderless Histories of Art* is above all about the futurity of our planet and all its creatures. My amazing daughter Mia Chunling, who was studying veterinary medicine when I began this book and is now a practicing emergency room veterinarian, has been my greatest inspiration in no small measure because of her lifelong love of animals. I dedicate this writing to Dr. Mia Woyda and Dr. Reed Woyda, my joyful, animal-loving son-in-law.

The present format does not permit a full scholarly apparatus acknowledging my colleagues individually who shared bibliography, expertise, and advice. Nor could I document all the research that went into writing this book, a challenging circumstance but also an opportunity that led me to concentrate on making the primary texts and intergenerational issues accessible to a broad academic audience. I have included other voices and traditions directly in sidebars sprinkled throughout the text to complement and add counterpoint to these arguments. I remain solely responsible for the views expressed here.

INTRODUCTION

Taking Responsibility in the Age of Capital

Writing Borderless Histories of Art is an aspirational, historical, and critical project drawing upon writings from a wide range of fields to offer a fundamental rethinking of the relationship of humans to the rest of nature. The main focus of *Writing Borderless Histories of Art* concerns the historical relationship between European assumptions about art and society and the degradation of the environment on a global scale. It is important to pursue this subject now because human exceptionalism is a leading topic on the minds of those who study and comment on climate change and the degradation of the planet's ecosystems. The Oxford *Dictionary of Environment and Conservation* defines human exceptionalism as a paradigm based on the view that humans are different from all other organisms, that all human behavior is controlled by culture and free will, and that all problems can be solved by human ingenuity and technology. Between 1900 and 2015, humans destroyed more than 80% of major mammal *species* populations on the planet.[1] Given that about 70% of wild animal *populations* have also been wiped out since 1970, with another million species of plants and animals under threat of extinction and the unprecedented rate of decline accelerating, discussions of the sustainability of life on our planet cannot be limited to what is presumed best for humanity.[2]

Imagine how an ecological account of the history of culture that included all life could support efforts to create conditions of sustainability on the planet we share. This book adopts the concept of "post-human" and "more than human" to broaden the scope of what it means to be treated as a valued life form. The advantages of such an ecological approach to conceptualizing the study of culture stem from its ability to institute a more pluralistic historical vision at any scale of study that considers different signifying systems, worldviews, and contexts of use on equal footing. Efforts to bring the social and the biological together in numerous fields are moving beyond the inherited dichotomy between nature and culture.

DOI: 10.4324/9781351023429-1

Today, the ontological divisions between the domains of the human and all other animals, and between the social and the biological, are fluid. Some kinds of animals pass on their learned behavior, mourn their dead, nurture and teach their children, even use human language to communicate (not just to parrot words), and engage in many other remarkable behaviors that research scientists and other careful observers of animals have recorded. Octopuses are sentient; insects feel, respond to pain, learn from experience, and share their learned knowledge with others. Plants, with no apparent nervous system, make the same chemicals – serotonin, dopamine, and glutamate – that serve as neurotransmitters and help create mood in animals [Figure 0.1].

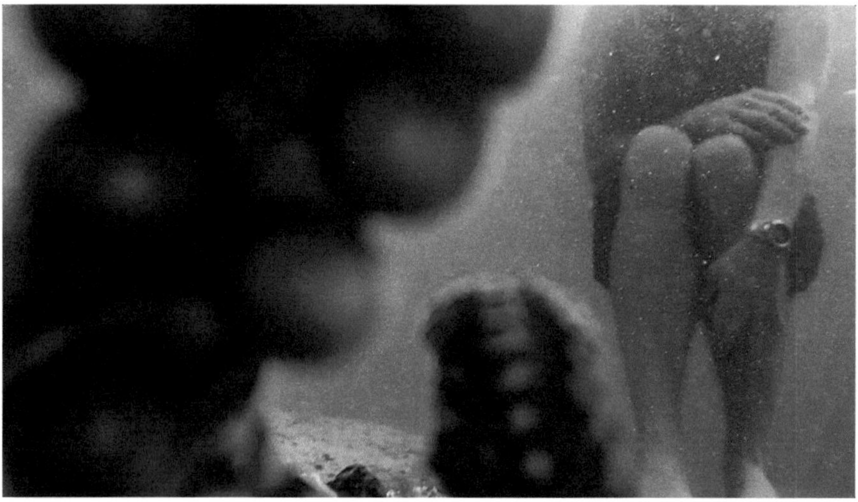

FIGURE 0.1 Photograph taken by an octopus of Craig Foster, whose film, *My Octopus Teacher,* won the Academy Award for best documentary feature in 2021. Foster was filming creatures living in the Great African Sea Forest off the coast of South Africa in 2023 when a young octopus grabbed his camera, zoomed backward across the ocean floor, and began filming videos of her own graceful arms draped over the camera lens with his awkward body, all limbs, in the background. Photo © Craig Foster/Sea Change Project.

What if this understanding of connectivity, rather than human exceptionalism, were taught as part of a general education curriculum in the humanities? Indigenous ontologies, once a marker distinguishing savages from civilized peoples, offer promising paradigms for questioning the division between the biological and social realms, "arriving at a place where the line between human and nonhuman becomes nonsensical," to cite Kim Tallbear, Canada Research Chair in Indigenous Peoples, Technoscience, and Society.[3] The Inka view certain rocks as both transubstantial and transformational. Andean oral culture is filled with instances of animate beings converting to stone, as well as rock coming to life. To the Inka and other Andeans, past and present, writes Andeanist Carolyn Dean, "certain rocks were perceived to be quite literally alive."[4] As far-fetched as it may seem for scientists to think of rocks as alive, alternative ontologies are also encouraged by the recent discovery of communities of microbes that are up to 104 million years old living in cold oceanic crust 330 feet below the sea in the middle of the South Pacific floor, living under 580 atmospheres of pressure. These hyper-dense communities of microbes are dominated by bacteria known as heterotrophs that synthesize their own food either from the remains of marine life or from the non-biological breakdown of the crust itself. Such methane-eating microbial life might be present throughout the ocean crust, a layer of rock as thick as Mount Everest is tall that extends over three-fifths of the planet's surface and is similar to volcanic bands on Mars and very possibly other places in the universe.[5]

Social anthropologist Tim Ingold similarly advocates re-drawing the opposition between innate capacity (biology) and acquired content (culture) to achieve a new "sociobiological synthesis" that describes how all creatures learn through processes of growth and discovery forged "in the crucible of their common life."[6] Physicist and feminist philosopher Karen Barad proposes "intra-activity" as a new "ontoepistemological" framework that focuses on the "performative" context in which signification takes place in direct material engagement with the world. Barad's conceptions and language provide another useful post-human framework, one that can map onto the real-time generation of the live media event. She argues that entanglements between matter and agency, between performer and "apparatus," are the primary means by which "relationalities" and "(re)articulations" are produced.[7] Dipesh Chakrabarty, one of the first humanists to urge collective, interdisciplinary attention to the climate crisis, offers the "emergent humanist category" of *planetarity* for studying the "habitability" of the planet. Planetarity includes "all multicellular life," unlike the term "globe" which for Chakrabarty is limited to the "anthropocentric and anthropological practice of representation."[8]

Earth Systems Science (ESS) scientists also avoid setting humans apart from nature by defining the Earth system in terms of integrating physical, chemical, and biological processes, including human society, in the "critical zone" of the planet's habitability. In a matter of centuries, humans are destroying billions of years of accumulated resources and destabilizing the biosphere. For such a civilization to survive, ESS scientists argue that humans must sustain and foster planetary habitability by viewing themselves as an integral and responsible part of a planetary system.[9] Resources for reversing global warming through interlocking initiatives that rely on people acting together to change the world include youth activist Greta Thunberg's *The Climate Book: The Facts and the Solutions* and environmentalist writer and entrepreneur Paul Hawken's *Drawdown* and *Regeneration*. Hawken advocates comprehensive approaches that combine scientific studies with "justice, climate, biodiversity, and human dignity into a tapestry of action, policy, and transformation that can end the climate crisis in one generation."[10] "Drawdown" refers to the moment when the concentration of greenhouse gases in the Earth's atmosphere begins to decline on a year-to-year basis.

I intend this book for a broad academic audience including just about anyone with an interest in art and material culture who is concerned about their future in an uncertain world increasingly preoccupied with managing unprecedented environmental and humanitarian crises. In *The Future We Choose: Surviving the Climate Crisis* (2020), the architects of the 2015 Paris Climate Agreement, Christiana Figueres and Tom Rivett-Carnac, warn that "we have almost extinguished nature's capacity for self-renewal." Yet they say there is hope: well-planned regenerative practices will restore ecosystems "to a new state of regained health with enhanced resilience."[11] However, there is also a catch: "in an imaginary world, [if] we stopped using all fossil fuels in an instant, if we denied people what they are used to – we would have a global revolution in a matter of weeks if not days."[12]

The good news is that the impossibility of a rapid global response to catastrophe has been proven false. Figueres and Rivett-Carnac published their book shortly before the World Health Organization declared the SARS novel corona virus known as Covid-19 a global pandemic on 11 March 2020. In response to this killer, the vast majority of the world's people and governments demonstrated that, contrary to expectations, we *can* act together on short notice to avert even greater catastrophe. Unfortunately, the coronavirus pandemic has since been unscrupulously politicized, the economic and humanitarian effects of the disease as well as the vaccine are distributed across the planet unevenly, climate emergencies and new wars of aggression have destroyed countless lives and habitats, and pollution is worse than ever. By 2023, speaking on the occasion of a United Nations' climate summit involving more than 100 national governments, Figueres had run out of patience with the fossil fuel industry: companies should *not* be included in the next summit if they continue to be obstructors.[13] Global capitalism has made the depletion of resources so rapid, convenient, and barrier-free, writes journalist Naomi Klein, that earth–human systems are becoming dangerously unstable in response.[14] In the wake of human-induced environmental disaster, we also witness demographic shifts on an unprecedented scale accompanied by the rise of populism and totalitarianism worldwide. Whose life is worth recording? Remembering? Whose rights are restricted to "bare life," and treated as disposable?

Conflicting interests are at the center of ongoing discussions about unregulated eco-catastrophes, their proposed cures, and the complexity of environmental data and visual media. Who will regulate the media, evaluate the science, and address the ethical implications of projects competing with one another for resources and profit? Historian of contemporary art and visual culture, T. J. Demos, one of most articulate and well-informed voices, has raised the alarm against the position that, since humans have mastered nature, technocrats and scientists are the ones who can fix the problem via geoengineering: there is no international environmental governance, much less a democratic process to counter the practices of corporations, wealthy nations, and private individuals, to regulate the use of such technology.[15]

Juxtapose this precarious situation with the two most pressing realities for the humanities in higher education: the need to educate students to meet today's challenges (unfortunately, a goal that is often reduced to succeeding in today's job market) and the need to rethink how and what is taught, especially at the undergraduate level. In 2001, Sam Weber, an eminent professor of comparative literature and philosophy, speculated on the university's diminishing role in the present era of transnational corporate capitalism that much will depend on the ways in which the established humanistic disciplines define their future practices. Disciplines that continue to conceive of their activity in terms of self-contained and sovereign "fields" will find themselves faced with increasing difficulties, both in terms of their attractiveness to outside donors, and in terms of finding an internal constituency among incoming students.[16] Two decades later, a US federal survey, *The Economic Well-Being of U.S. Households in 2020*, appears to confirm Weber's dire prediction. It found that "nearly half of humanities and arts majors" regret their choice of major, and nearly the same percentage of regret exists for majors in the social and behavioral sciences. Part of what journalist Andrew Van Dam calls the "bonfire of the humanities" is due in the United States to the exorbitant cost of higher education and consequent repayment of educational loans, a situation that is creating even more social inequality.[17]

Who will teach how to analyze arguments and visual evidence critically, traditionally the strength of the arts and humanities? This is not a rhetorical question but an important consideration in nurturing resilient societies and competitive knowledge-based economies at a time when neither democracy nor prosperity can be taken for granted. Ultimately, Demos emphasizes in *Against the Anthropocene* (2017), "mainstream media images form part of the technological apparatus of advanced capitalism that created the environmental problems in the first place."[18] With the transformation of the public sphere, including the impacts of unregulated social media and the emergence of AI, the visual has gained even greater primacy. The visual has always been capable of multiple interpretations. It takes a lot of effort, involving acquired skills and introspection, to identify the values that get dragged along with images.

What matters crucially are the values that we instill along with the subject matter. What kinds of political implications are there to the knowledge we produce? Our work can seem apolitical when we produce it, but at the same time it excludes other work from taking place or relegates that work to the margins. One of the primary vulnerabilities faced by the humanities is the fragmentation of knowledge into highly specialized disciplinary formations. The line of argument pursued here is that the discourse on art became entangled with notions of human exceptionalism in the sixteenth century, during the initial phase of economic globalization that accompanied European expansionism. Colonialism, the policy and practice of domination in the socioeconomic and political sphere, includes imposing religion, language, and other cultural practices over other peoples and resources. European states are not the only ones that created colonizing empires, a practice known since ancient times all over the world, but European colonial practices hold a unique place in the history of the modern, initially European idea of art. Contemporary art and its modes of history, criticism, curating, and institutionalization are "structurally European," write the co-editors of an ambitious new anthology conceived in a global framework for discussing contemporary art. The editors Jane Chin Davidson and Amelia Jones emphasize that European art and aesthetics developed in relation to other cultural systems of belief and ways of making and doing creatively.[19]

Attention to the migration of visual culture and the conditions of its circulation has opened up a vast interdisciplinary field of research concerned with the function, reception, and power of specific kinds of images and other objects of human manufacture. The emphasis has been on the essentially heterogeneous character of the many kinds of objects and activities associated with the category art. *Writing Borderless Histories of Art* provides tools to recognize and reflect critically on systems, standards, hierarchies, and other "structuring structures" in the European discourse on art.[20] Instead of searching for origins or engaging in taxonomic exercises, it investigates how things operate in an economy of forces. It investigates the "epistemic violence" caused by "sanctioned ignorance" within the orders and distinctions of the hegemonic European legacy, to cite the widely quoted words of Gayatri Chakravorty Spivak over two decades ago.[21]

Why would a broadly conceived, inclusive history of planetary culture be desirable now? To understand the European discourse on art in a more-than-human framework, it is necessary to consider a much broader trajectory than the modern discipline of art history professionalized in the nineteenth century. The discourse on art was involved in debates on the humanity of Indigenous peoples that began with the European conquest/invasion of the Americas in the early sixteenth century. Art was held to be a distinguishing feature of humanity based on a parallel between human reasoning and nature established 2,500 years ago in ancient Greek philosophy. In the long Western tradition of writing about art, Aristotle's biological account of the body and soul set the terms for later discussions. According to Aristotle, the differences between human and animal intelligence, and also between human and animal art, are based on the difference between human powers of cognition, associated with reason and reminiscence, and those of animals, associated with instinct and a retentive memory. This account of humans as exceptions to the rest of nature runs through the entire Western tradition, but it was particularly important in establishing the idea that mentality and cultural production are directly linked – that one represents the other.

Expanding applications of ancient authority for classifying humans developed alongside the extraction of raw materials and degradation of the environment in the Americas since the beginning of the sixteenth century. European colonizers moved from one commodity frontier to the next as human and material resources reduced profitability or were exhausted. The following chapters will develop the argument in detail, but the main lesson to be learned is that supply chain economics continues to degrade vast numbers of people and the environment in our interdependent, global capitalist economy today. In a series of resolutions issued by the Human Rights Council of the United Nations since 2008, the Council for the first time recognized that the impact of climate change must be addressed in the framework of human rights and the environment. In July 2021, the Council officially recognized that the rights of people in vulnerable situations were disproportionally affected by the negative impact of climate change and requested a report and panel discussion on related themes beginning in 2023.[22]

The 1990s were a decade of resistance to free trade and US hegemony that foreshadowed the global spread of populisms, writes Chilean-based sociologist Martín Arboleda, in *Planetary Mine: Territories of Extracting under Late Capitalism* (2020). In short, Arboleda argues, minerals feed the machines and human labor functions as an appendage to the technical apparatus. Shifts in class structure are interrelated across the supply chain network: the reproduction of the Chinese working class hinges on the dispossession of Latin American small farmers – and along with it come the deforestation, contamination, and cancer epidemics that the extraction of raw minerals and mega-agriculture entail. The role of banks and multilateral corporations in expanding the extractive frontier is likewise the expression of the same unequal global process. From a planetary perspective, "core" and "periphery" do not correspond to nationally bounded entities in supply chain economics. Instead, writes Arboleda, core and periphery exist in a fractal relationship that repeats itself across scales. The mineral supply chain, engineers, domestic workers, and truck drivers who reside in segregated landscapes of gleaming urban towers and polluted shantytowns link landscapes and labor together. The flipside of the smooth flow of goods is the relentless precarization of workers. The task today is to grasp the brutal reality of planetary interdependency *and* its emancipatory possibilities.

Grasping Emancipatory Possibilities: Methodological Considerations

I adopt the category "planet" as offering a productive alternative to the more frequently encountered choice between world and globe. Gayatri Spivak introduced the term "planetarity" in 2003 to signal efforts in Comparative Literature that counter the destructive effects of economic globalization. "Mondialisation" or "worldmaking" are similar designations for an active counterforce to the leveling processes of global capitalism. "Pluriverse" is yet another term to designate "the coexistence of a multipolar world order" as a universal project that counters the hegemonic effects of global capitalism. Donna Haraway proposes "Chthulucene" (derived from science fiction) that does not have self-defined spatial or temporal boundaries. Others, such as Bruno Latour (1947–2022), who was a major contributor to the ecocritical literature long known for his science and technology studies, object to holistic, cartographical views of planet earth but agree with the resistance to capitalism and hegemony (and with the impossibility of separating science from politics). They prefer the term "Critical Zone" taken from the geosciences, referring to the surface and near-surface environment that sustains nearly all terrestrial life, because it "complicates and interrupts the legal and political unity of any global view." They specifically object to the "attraction of the too-famous Blue Marble" captured by astronauts for this reason: they associate the iconic photograph with models of the Earth as unified and homogeneous, belying the complexity of the legal and political work required for "unifying the planet for good." Critical Zones are, by contrast, "patchy, heterogeneous, discontinuous." [23]

Obviously, I disagree with their take on the Blue Marble or I would not have selected the photograph known as "Earthrise" from the Apollo 8 mission (1968) as the cover of this book. The same view can inspire hope or prompt sober reflection on the need to act in concert. Every image, by its nature, is capable of more than one interpretation. Totalizing master narratives and unlocatable relativism, no matter where they come from, are "god tricks" writes Haraway because they promise "vision from everywhere and nowhere equally and fully." Visualizing technologies may present the illusion of infinite vision, but all actual vision is embodied and partial. [24] Even astronauts circling the moon some 250,000 miles away photographed the Earth from a particular point of view at a specific moment in time. ESS scientists urge *joining* our many partial perspectives and knowledges to act together. Caution is also advisable in applying the findings of climate scientists and other writers on environmental issues directly to complex questions of legal and political unity. In most cases, they lack an adequate understanding of the history of European expansionism involved in generating the environmental degradation that now poses an existential threat to all life on Earth. Macarena Gómez-Barris, Professor of Modern Culture and Media, responds to the argument that the investigation of the Anthropocene should *not* examine the beginning of the era of European colonial expansion in her widely cited book, *The Extractive Zone* (2017):

> We use the term ["Anthropocene"] too generally, addressing "humanity" as a whole without understanding histories of racial thought and settler colonialism that are imposed upon categorizations of biodiversity, spaces where the biotechnologies of capitalism accelerate.
>
> In reality, the problem is far more specific: colonial capitalism has been the main catastrophic event that has gobbled up the planet's resources, discursively constructing racialized bodies within geographies of difference . . . [The Anthropocene] demarcates the temporalities and spatial catastrophe of the planetary through a universalizing idiom and viewpoint that hides the political geographies embedded within the conversion of complex life.[25]

How colonial capitalism "discursively constructs racialized bodies within geographies of difference" is what led to *Writing Borderless Histories of Art*. The role of art is far more complicated than it sounds or that I had imagined beforehand. The word and concept of art have a complex history that will be discussed throughout the Fugues but let's begin with the controversial term Anthropocene. It was coined in the early 1980s by ecologist Eugene Stoermer, an expert in freshwater diatoms, and adopted in discourses on globalization after 2000. Stoermer joined the Nobel laureate atmospheric chemist Paul Crutzen to propose that evidence for the transformative effects of human activities on the earth signaled by the steam engine and exploding use of coal in the eighteenth century, merited the use of a new geological term for a new epoch. This by-now conventional view of economic globalization has been called into question in recent economic literature on globalization. There is extensive empirical evidence that I will discuss below and in the following chapters to support the claim that extractive capitalism first practiced on a global scale has driven the climate crisis continuously since the sixteenth century.

Objections to the term focus on the ways that the universalizing logic of the Anthropocene rhetoric including its visualizations enables the military–state–corporate apparatus to disavow responsibility and accountability for the eco-catastrophe by making everyone equally complicit in its destructive effects. When the "Anthropocene" era began is another bone of contention. After fifteen years of debate, in 2024, an international committee of geologists rejected the Anthropocene as the designation of a new era beginning in the mid-twentieth century (sometimes referred to as the "great acceleration").[26] Maybe the geologists should invite some historians and atmospheric scientists to weigh in, but there are other reasons not to use the term. One is that "Anthropocene" has been seized upon and politicized by the fossil fuel industry. ESS scientists and environmental humanists identify the strategic and representational challenge of understanding spatial and temporal scales that exceed human comprehension. The discussion that follows here considers the implications of situating the emergence of an economic system based on capital accumulation, competitive markets, international forms of currency, the recognition of property rights, the manufacture of luxury goods, the destruction of the environment, and abusive labor practices on a planetary scale in the *sixteenth* century.

The conventional organization of art history by nation-states, continents, religions, period styles, and other such monolithic entities is part of the same historical process and therefore requires historical explanation just as much as the materials that are the primary subject of study. Transcultural frameworks, by contrast, exert analytical pressure on these established approaches by destabilizing "the nexus between the entities of nature and culture" while signaling "the tension between the nation as a ground of emancipation in cultural memory, and as a constricting ideological frame," writes Monica Juneja in a powerful new book focused on the question of how art history can grow from its European roots into a global project.[27] I use the term "transculturation" in the sense that Juneja and Christian Kravagna have reintroduced it from the work of Cuban anthropologist Fernando Ortiz (1881–1961) who studied sugar and tobacco cultures in colonial and postcolonial Cuba (1940). Transculturation can refer to a concrete object or an analytic method, and in both cases "trans" contests the discursive category of "culture" as it has been used to designate the life world of groups as internally cohesive and linguistically homogenous spheres. Instead, "transcultural" focuses on the dialogical processes through which forms emerge in local contexts within circuits of exchange. Their pathways are often recursive and braided in complex ways. No longer restricted to modernity, the concept of "transculturation" attends to the "dynamics of those formations past and present constituted through regimes of circulation and exchange . . . to investigate the multiple ways in which difference is negotiated within contacts and encounters."[28]

Ortiz introduced the term transculturation as a neologism to describe changes that alter societies as they adapt foreign cultural forms into their way of life.

He described the sugar industry in terms similar to the current economies of transnational corporations, while the tobacco trade brought a simple, rural cultural environment with it. Over the course of his career, Ortiz came to adamantly reject scientific theories of race that were still dominant in anthropology and other social sciences, including art history.[29] Taking issue with the terms acculturation and deculturation for their assumption of a cultural gradient between dominant and subaltern populations – a lingering artifact of racial thinking – Ortiz proposed a dialectical vision of complexly entangled processes affecting all sectors of societies in the post-Columbian Atlantic. On the one hand, Ortiz set out to recover the agency of those who remained unheard, and on the other, he wanted to recover the processes of transculturation that followed from migration, multilingualism, and ethnic plurality, while avoiding the trap of thinking in binaries.[30] He saw transculturation as a long-term process taking place through extended contact between cultures.

In 1992, Mary Louise Pratt introduced Ortiz's term "transculturation" to analyze the phenomenon of what she famously named a "contact zone" through the study of travel literature. Pratt raised fundamental questions about subjugated people on the receiving end of empire: how do they appropriate metropolitan modes of representation, how do they talk back, what do they say, what materials are available to answer such questions? Pratt's "de-colonizing" transcultural approach has been relevant far beyond literary studies in denouncing structures of domination that are built into many academic disciplines established during the formative period of modern nation-states in the nineteenth century. As subsequently theorized by James Clifford, an interdisciplinary scholar specialized in the intellectual history of anthropology, museum collections are also potentially "contact zones."[31]

Ortiz's anti-racist interest in transcultural processes associated with sugar plantation colonialism based on African slave labor evolved through his longstanding interest in Afro-Cuban culture. Today Ortiz is considered one of the earliest theorists of heterogeneous societies from the Global South who understood that the Caribbean region as a unit of analysis must proceed from the history of enslavement and agro-industrialization. Another axis of connections facilitated by Ortiz's notion of transculturation is between the Caribbean and the Mediterranean.[32] What Ortiz understood as a unidirectional process, in its present usage reconceptualizes processes of adaptation as transformation with general methodological applicability. Juneja and Kravagna use the term to analyze "historical forms of mobility and connectedness that have been characteristic of cultures over centuries . . . that unfold through extended contacts and relationships between cultures."[33] Transculturation reconceptualizes processes of adaptation as active transformation in many kinds of situations.

A transcultural approach calls for abandoning structures of domination that are built into the academic disciplines, regardless of the scale or extent of interpretation, by identifying epistemological and ontological assumptions and accounting for one's authorial position in relation to institutional authority. It is crucial to avoid oppositional binomial categories by rethinking the agency of individuals in *relational* terms (people, institutions, material things all share agency in creating the work of art). Ortiz's term was widely adopted by cultural anthropologists, so it also has the advantage of not separating cultural objects into two separate disciplines historically defined on European terms. Another advantage of transcultural approaches is that they do not isolate objects artificially and retrospectively from the rest of the world, writes art historian Mia Mochizuki, but such relational approaches to art history will only become fully operational "when the analysis of every object assumes an architecture of systemic connectivity and relative agency on the cellular level."[34] Such histories in the making are among the most promising ways in which old Eurocentric hierarches and narratives are being reconceptualized by historians in ways that change the large-scale narratives to a more pluralistic history.[35] Mochizuki studies Jesuit artistic workshops that set up the first system for the worldwide production of Christian images [Figure 0.2].[36] Her most recent project treats South and Southeast Asia in a single forum, not simply inter-Asian currents but in dialogue with America and Europe, to initiate a virtual conversation among scholars with very different views working around the world.[37]

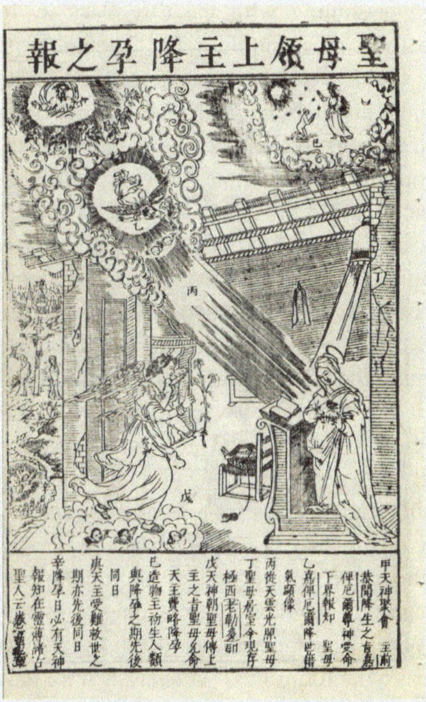

FIGURE 0.2 Chinese artist. *Annunciation* in Giulio Aleni, *Tian zhu jiang sheng chu xiang jing jie* (Jinjiang: Jing Kiao Tang, 1637), fol. 6r, woodcut. Harvard, Houghton Library, hyde_52_1049-METS

The signal achievement of the first Jesuits was their vision of an interconnected world. Gerome Nadal's *Evangelicae historiae imagines* (Antwerp, 1593), undertaken at the request of Ignatius of Loyola, founder of the Jesuits, provided visualizations of places for individual meditation. The *Annunciation* is the first devotional image in Nadal's book, the most popular print source circulating among Jesuit missions around the world. Jesuit efforts to cultivate a global audience resulted in the appearance of Nadal's imagery in Africa, East Asia, South America. In China, direct compositional borrowing was tweaked with local stylistic modifications.

Mia M. Mochizuki, *Jesuit Art* (Leiden: Brill, 2022)

There is no doubt that the relationship of humans to the rest of nature urgently needs to change. Throughout this book, I argue that the cutting edge of research in many subdisciplines of art history engaged with transcultural processes have direct bearing on climate change and other forms of environmental degradation. Mapped as structures of connectivity, the deep history of human development and migration, on the one hand, and the circulation of cultural artifacts, on the other hand, are open-ended branching structures spreading in many directions without top or bottom or boundaries. This connectivity forms the basis for a new topological approach in which biological development and cultural history operate in *separate* domains. When they overlap, the connections are historically constituted, not biologically determined as was considered to be the case when art history and anthropology were established as modern disciplines in the nineteenth century.

Beyond *Homo sapiens*

A very different model of biological identity from the one built into the foundational texts of art history and the other social sciences has been established by the genetic science of genomics, beginning with the discovery in 1953 that the DNA molecule exists in the form of a double helix. The subsequent sequencing of entire human genomes, the first of which was published in 2001, changed the way modern science thinks about biological identity individually and collectively. There are many valid reasons to criticize how genome analysis emerged on the problematic foundation that a white male individual (or a composite of individual white male subjects) could provide a "universal model."[38] In recent years, Indigenous scholars and policy advocates have articulated a host of ethical issues regarding exploitation and objectification by more powerful groups (scientists, colonial universities, federally funded researchers) of less powerful humans (Indigenous peoples), which maintains a colonial structure of knowledge production.[39] A key document, the United Nations Declaration on the Rights of Indigenous Peoples (UNDRIP), adopted by various countries where Indigenous peoples have been subjected to genetic and genomic research for decades, builds on existing human rights.[40]

With this caveat in mind, there are still other reasons for referring to genetic science in thinking about cultural memory on a planetary scale. Where the Darwinian model of evolution originally stressed the interconnectedness of life in terms of the anatomy of individual organisms, the current scientific understanding of evolution defines identity at the molecular level. Whole genome analysis identifies both paternal and maternal lines of descent, whereas older forms of DNA analysis were limited to the maternal DNA known as "mitochondrial DNA." Analyzing collective identity in terms of the complete set of genetic material present in an organism has created the possibility of addressing previously unapproachable questions to write the deep history of human populations, their movements, and their mixing throughout the planet.

The new DNA evidence of ancient human populations irrefutably shows that there was never a single trunk population in the human past. The implications of ongoing ancient DNA analysis are far from settled and some claims are deeply controversial, but the new science of ancient genetics is currently able to demonstrate that we are all blends of past populations. There is no "pure" lineage of *Homo sapiens*: humans from different populations interbred extensively with each other. Modern humans also bred successfully with Neanderthals, and Neanderthals interbred with other archaic humans, as the 2018 report of an offspring of a Neanderthal mother and a Denisovan father confirms.[41] Given the indisputable findings of intermixing populations, where and how should the boundaries of human culture be drawn in our histories? The analysis of ancient DNA adds considerable complexity to the question of how human traits have evolved. *Homo sapiens* interbred with other humans that produced fertile offspring. This new understanding of human evolution puts into question the modern category "species" used to distinguish *Homo sapiens* from archaic humans. Archaic humans made stone tools, cared for the sick and elderly, made jewelry with symbolic associations 130,000 years ago, constructed stone circles in caves 180,000 years ago, and left other material evidence of their cultural activities before and after they interacted with *Homo sapiens*.[42] At sites in southwestern Europe and southern Italy, modern human-style tools have been found in the midst of Neanderthal remains dated 44,000–39,000 years ago, suggesting some kind of direct cultural interaction took place. The analysis of whole genomes also shows that the people who live in a particular place today almost never exclusively descend from the people who lived there in the past.

Apart from genomic evidence, there has been a marked shift in the humanities over the past several decades to move away from questions of fixed identity to a multi-faceted understanding of the dynamic processes of collective identity formation. In the 1980s, Homi K. Bhabha introduced the concept of culturally hybrid literature, and since then the term "hybrid" has been applied to images and artifacts of all kinds to designate certain types of culturally complex objects. Bhabha re-purposed the nineteenth-century racial term "hybridity" as a "problematic of colonial representation" that results when colonial subjects mimic the forms of the dominant culture but articulate those forms with differential knowledges and positionalities that threaten "normalized" knowledge and disciplinary power.[43] Now, with the unprecedented findings of ancient genome sequencing, science provides a model of collective identity that *supports the critique* introduced by postcolonial theorists in the 1980s: *Homo sapiens* are mixtures all the way through the record of human existence and into the proto-human past.

However, as others have pointed out, there are many problems with the term "hybrid" ranging from its overemphasis on visual appearances (the visual occludes as much as it reveals) to the implication that some prior "purity" exists, a hangover from its past as a racial designation. How material things come to have significance, and how the same object or concrete manifestation can have multiple meanings for its users, is one of the main ways that the study of art can make significant theoretical contributions to the ongoing debates on the climate crisis. Works of art and other cultural artifacts are irreducibly multivalent – that is, all images and all material things, by their nature refuse absolute meaning. Images and objects with multiple cultural resonances are not necessarily synthetic products of cultural interaction either. In fact, they often mean one thing to one person or group and something quite different to other users. New methods of analysis and different horizons of interpretation are required to understand the complex interactions involved. There is no basis for a one-to-one relationship between cultural and biological identity. Biological identity operates at the molecular level of DNA while cultural identity operates at the level of objects and practices located in networks of exchange. The DNA model of biological identity and the materialist, circulation model for studying cultural artifacts are both fundamentally *relational rather than representational.* It is now possible to conceive the artifactual history of the planet in terms that are radically different from the taxonomic efforts of nineteenth-century scholars who isolated objects from their contexts of making and use and redefined them on European terms – a process already evident in the earliest responses to extra-European cultural belongings in the sixteenth century.

The principle of "affordance," a term coined by perceptual psychologist James Gibson in 1966, refers to the complementarity of the individual animal and the environment.[44] An affordance is what an environment offers to an animal in pursuit of its tasks of life, and one cannot exist without the other. Ingold objects to Gibson's ecological approach to perception because his principle of "affordance" still treats the environment as offering "objective properties" that do not, after all, "depend on the presence of the animal for their existence."[45] Ingold argues that, for the same reasons, modern evolutionary biology does not offer an adequate account of the "role of ontogenesis, that is, of the growth and development of the organism in its environment in the evolution of forms of life." For Ingold, form and matter, genes and the environment, are emergent properties "within a matrix of environmental resources." Life is forged in the collaboration of overlapping generations within the matrix, not successive generations isolated like sheets in a stack of papers.[46] It takes generations working together to produce the conditions on which the continued existence of a given lineage collectively depends. The concept of genetic replication (inheritance) must be discarded in favor of a "concept of perdurance that binds generations longitudinally into a continuous evolutionary braid" through learning. The material world is neither formed nor formless, but always in the process of formation – matter, as Barad puts it, does not consist of "little bits of nature . . . passively awaiting signification": matter is always in the process of becoming.[47]

An adequate ecological approach to the history of planetary culture needs to be framed with this collaborative, intergenerational process in mind without setting humans apart from the rest of the natural world or conflating biological identity with cultural identity on a one-to-one basis as racial theories of cultural evolution have in the past. With recent developments in animal behavioral science, the importance of social learning stressed by Ingold – inventiveness, innovation, adaptation, and other patterns of behavior resulting from interactions between animals and their environment – are once again the focus of evolutionary theory. Behavioral scientists are contributing to genetic theory in studying how learned behavior has a genetic impact through natural selection. When studied in detail, many patterns of behavior in other animals are found to be complex products of several types of learning rather than inherited traits. Summarizing recent work on animal intelligence in 2000, behavioral scientists Eytan Avital and Eva Jabonka make a case for animal culture by highlighting important general differences between genetic and cultural transmission: cultural offspring are not necessarily genetic offspring; cultural variations are acquired by learning; genes are transmitted according to "stable laws of genetic segregation"; and the more easily behaviors are learned, the more likely they are to be acquired and transmitted.[48] They define "culture" to mean social traditions and the transmission of social traditions. As long as we refrain from defining consciousness on exclusively human terms, marine biologist and ecologist Carl Safina argues, extensive evidence indicates widespread consciousness in the animal kingdom and in some cases the overlap between animal and human intelligence is astounding.[49] Elephants, for example, recognize hundreds of individuals and live in vast social networks of families and friendships, forming deep social bonds developed through many years. Abilities said to make us human exist to varying degrees among other minds sharing the world with us: all animals with backbones share the same basic skeleton, organs, nervous systems, hormones, and behaviors. The latest research shows that bees are also profoundly intelligent creatures that can memorize flowers and human faces, solve problems by thinking rather than simply by trial and error, learn to use tools by observing skilled bees, and experience basic emotions something like optimism and pessimism.[50] Ants have been shown amputating nest mates' legs to save their lives, seeming to know which injuries can be treated.[51]

In July 2012, during the "Consciousness in Human and Nonhuman Animals" conference in Cambridge a group of scientists signed a declaration with the following conclusions:

> Convergent evidence indicates that non-human animals have the neuroanatomical, neurochemical, and neurophysiological substrates of conscious states along with the capacity to exhibit intentional behaviors. Consequently, the weight of evidence indicates that humans are not unique in possessing the neurological substrates that generate consciousness. Non-human animals, including all mammals and birds, and many other forms of life, including plants, also possess these neurological substrates.[52]

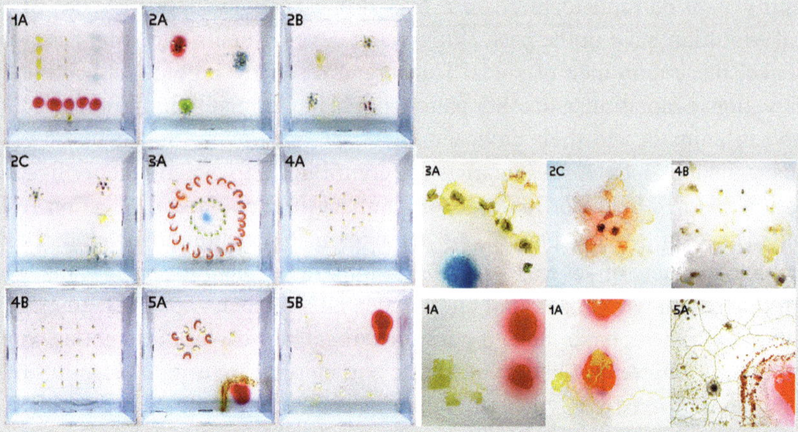

FIGURE 0.3 Nonconscious cognition and interspecies collaboration. Experimentation with slime mold. Initial set up and slime mold behavior in the same scenarios. Selena Savić and Sarah Grant, "Slime Mold Network Imaginaries," 2022. Photo Sarah Grant and Selena Savić.

The capacity of matter to make choices is a sign of cognitive activity broadly defined. Slime mold can transport information distributed and shared within a network. Pieces of food painted with natural food coloring work as attractants (honey, oats, pasta) and repellants (hot spices and salt). It took longer than expected to overcome the "wall" of spice to reach the honey – the slime mold provides a productive ground for embracing the importance of ecological relations and adaptive systems.

Ksenia Federova, "In Dialogue with Nonconscious Cognition and Expressions of the Commons," in *After Human*, ed. Kerstin Borchhardt (Berlin: De Gruyter 2025), citing Selena Savić and Sarah Grant, "Slime Mold and Network Imaginaries: An Experimental Approach to Communication," *Leonardo* 55 (2022): 462–467.

The position of mutual interdependence is taken by many Indigenous cosmologies or knowledge systems that do not distinguish between the sentience of humans and other animals and conceive of both within the environment. I will articulate these claims in greater detail but at the present juncture, I want to emphasize that relational thinking has direct implications for current efforts launched from many different starting points to think about the ways that humans are entailed with their environments. As I discuss throughout *Writing Borderless Histories of Art*, it is important to understand the epistemological categories and their ontological premises in our thinking because they shape thought almost without our knowing it. *Writing Borderless Histories of Art* makes the historical schemes and categories of the past part of the subject of study. My argument grows from two convictions. One is that parallel narratives that represent the same events from mutually exclusive points of view do not adequately address the issues that created these boundaries. Exclusionary narratives are co-constructions because one position would not exist without the other. Integrated attempts to define the historical issues that produced mutually exclusive narratives in the past and keep reproducing them in the present are still needed.

The other conviction is that we can get past our past only by confronting the epistemological structures and ontological framework of the nature/culture divide of European (or "Western" or Euro-Mediterranean) origin. The categories on which claims are premised are historical and culturally specific constructs about universals. They are not universal truths in themselves. Their pathways to the present are far from linear and to recreate their itineraries requires considerable historical knowledge of the European literature on art.

Organization of this Book

Writing Borderless Histories of Art offers a de-territorialized model for organizing artifactual history. The argument is organized into five fugues and three connecting "intermezzos" in keeping with the musical metaphor of "fugues." I named the chapter essays "fugues" for two reasons. First, because a "fugue" is a de-centered European musical form in which the subject is introduced in one part and then repeated and explored in the others, until all the parts are interwoven. That describes the organization of my chapters, individually and collectively.

My second reason for naming the chapters "fugues" derives from its other, much darker meaning, in psychiatry, to define "a state or period of loss of awareness of one's identity, often coupled with flight from one's usual environment." The utterly devastating psychological condition of fugue describes metaphorically and in many cases literally, the widespread and ever-growing humanitarian crisis. In today's world, refugees fleeing destruction of their besieged homelands correspond to the sacrificial victim in the fatal and exclusionary sense described by philosopher Giorgio Agamben as those whom the State defines as excluded from the human world.[53] Non-human animals are also excluded from the world increasingly reserved only for certain, privileged humans and their domesticated pets and food animals. What justifies such blatant disregard for life on our planet? If the short answer is unregulated capitalism in bed with feckless government officials and inadequate national and international laws and regulations, the longer answer is rooted in the Western metaphysical theory of knowledge that distinguishes between humans and all other animals for their ability to think, their ability to invent, their ability to master nature. The concept of human exceptionalism urgently deserves to be rethought. Who qualifies as fully "human"? Who is in a position of authority to judge?

I join ongoing efforts worldwide to decolonize art historical knowledge by replacing binary epistemological models with more relational approaches focusing on contacts, flows, and circulations, as well as on global relations of production, without falling back on problematic essentializing categories. Following this Introduction, the first Intermezzo engages with current widespread discussions of "temporality" ranging from critiques of periodization among art historians to Marxian refusals of "linear time" introduced by Chakrabarty (2000) to theoretical discussions that draw on non-linear models (Bergson, Deleuze and Guattari, Derrida). The first Fugue offers a historical account of human exceptionalism in the sixteenth century as it was entangled with debates over the humanity of Indigenous people in the Americas and global capitalism as they together bear on contemporary discussions of climate science. The second Fugue pursues the question of how accounts of human exceptionalism shaped modern European concepts of art. It identifies a previously unrecognized watershed moment in late sixteenth-century Italy when two longstanding approaches to composing works of art split. One led to the institutionalized understanding of the fine arts of painting and sculpture as founded on rational principles, the hallmark of Western representation. The other extolled artistic license and the powers of the human imagination to invent things beyond nature. In connection with Church reform in the late sixteenth century, artistic license that did not conform to an idealized imitation of natural appearances on scientific principles was excised from new, institutionally supported methods for training artists and associated instead with the supposedly irrational imaginations of makers who produce idols, the grotesque, and all kinds of images held to be lacking in rational principles.

We currently identify this split in the framework of modern ideas about art with a process that began during the eighteenth century when European philosophers interested in establishing the origins of culture constructed the idea of "primitive" art and distinguished it from art of the classical tradition institutionalized in academies of art throughout Europe and beyond. I argue that focusing on the eighteenth century misses crucial historical connections between the discourse on art and the exclusionary discourse on human exceptionalism that are necessary to understand for developing an ecological, decolonial approach to the history of art and material culture. An Intermezzo follows Fugue 2, briefly reviewing concepts of "national" identity during this era before the formation of modern nation-states.

The third Fugue breaks new ground in bringing together the two different strands of argumentation in earlier chapters by proposing that climate theory played a key role in the European discourse on art before "Art" was defined in modern terms as the object of individual, secular aesthetic contemplation. The argument focuses on the role of ingenuity in historical climate theory (the term itself dates from the nineteenth century) which held that where you were born and live largely determined your capabilities. My argument unpacks important continuities as well as crucial differences between the sixteenth and twenty-first centuries in which climate theory played a significant role. The discussion turns to Kant's account of aesthetic judgment in Fugue 3 and continues with Darwin's account of human evolution in Fugue 4 to locate their ideas in relation to the long history of climate theory. I argue that what has not been studied and is crucial to conceiving an ecological approach to the history of art and material culture is the significant role played by the concept of inventiveness and moral character in accounts of human difference at the collective level. The discussion in Fugue 4 takes a deeper dive into the foundational texts of European art history by examining their persistent concepts of visuality, form, universalism, and cosmopolitanism through a de-colonial lens. A short Intermezzo follows, looking at current understandings of genetic identity based on genome structure to imagine an approach to the history of the planet's material culture that does not treat modern humans as separate from the rest of the animal kingdom.

Taking counter examples from Indigenous ontologies and epistemologies, the fifth Fugue draws this book to a close by advocating a topological network or "diagrammatic" model of distributed agency to steer clear of the Western dualistic metaphysical ontology built into the foundation of the modern discipline of art history. I suggest a non-totalizing approach to the study of material culture beyond the parameters of any single discipline to consider "planetary" habitability. I suggest how considering global connectivity in a longer historical trajectory effectively de-centers the dominant role attributed to Europe and the West. In general, I try to avoid terms such as the West and Modernity whenever possible because they reinsert conventional geographic, stylistic, and temporal designations that undercut a non-totalizing, critical global framework. The argument throughout this book calls attention to one of the main challenges facing critical global approaches to the history of art and material culture: the entrenched idea that art *represents* something absent from but implied in the material object. Instead, we can imagine a non-totalizing approach to the planetary history of all material artifacts in their performative context, broadly conceived to focus on process rather than taxonomy, to think in concrete detail at any scale of study on any subject according to the porous, dynamic connectivities that historically developed on our planet.

The insistence on non-essentializing, dynamic transcultural approaches also makes it possible to de-familiarize European conceptions of art, to think its history anew. What is most important to scholarship and pedagogy, and ultimately to the ways in which scholars contribute to society beyond the academy, is the shared initiative of resisting notions of fixed, universal "truths" in favor of understanding knowledge as something that remains relative and particular, tied to evidence and the subject position of the speaker – a redemptive but also always a provisional project that cannot be coopted by specious and misleading "alternative facts." Truth in this telling is always tied to concrete situations and subject positions, including our own as part of the same historical continuum (with all its fractures, switchbacks, unexplored potentialities) as the subjects we study. The impact of poststructuralist theory on art history since the 1970s destabilized earlier, positivistic assumptions about what constitutes a valid interpretation. Even if those disruptive effects have now been tamed, *Writing Borderless Histories of Art* reflects on their usefulness in connecting the past with the present using a transcultural approach.

This book is addressed to a wide audience, but I also reach out to my fellow art historians for whom chronology, canons, and style are structures fundamental to the organization and operation of the discipline. We are today witnessing the expansion of the discourse of art history to encompass many kinds of cultural artifacts and activities. The global turn also inevitably means uniting the world's cultural productions which have been historically sorted into the separate disciplinary and sub-disciplinary practices of art history, archaeology, and anthropology. A practical problem arises because everything and anything manufactured by humans potentially becomes a legitimate object of study. How is this immense object domain to be organized in the art history of the future? The process of classifying itself is a challenging activity.

What follows here is neither a history of ideas nor a search for the origins of art history, but a recognition of the structures that drive its narratives. I offer a thought experiment in the form of an intra-disciplinary collaborative project aimed at conceiving a history of planetary culture that all living creatures and their environments share. Not to replace art history, but as a contribution to a dynamic discipline that is constantly reworking its foundations. *Writing Borderless Histories of Art* adds a new wing to the existing sprawling edifice capacious enough to embrace archaeologists, anthropologists, musicologists, scientists, philosophers, those who study media and performance — in short, all who study cultural artifacts and practices – without imposing a teleological framework.

Longstanding sub-disciplinary specializations are one of the main obstacles to re-envisioning the history of material culture in terms of cultural interaction. Periodization is essential to thinking historically, the notable literary critic and political philosopher Frederic Jameson once famously argued, because without borders marking off points of temporal difference, it would be impossible to conceive or express historical change. However, as many self-critical historians have also observed, periodization is a template for dividing up time and place that is *always* ideologically loaded.[54] The Intermezzo that follows this Introduction discusses ways in which historians structure temporality, a leading concern for those who attempt to revise disciplinary practices at an epistemological level. There is still a pressing need to promote an integrated study of art and culture in places that are routinely separated, spatially and temporally, by inherited categories. These divisions are founded on hierarchies of knowledge whose rationales are far from transparent or obvious.

Art history's traditional categories make assumptions that cannot be understood simply by interrogating the field of our disciplinary knowledge because the field "answers to a finite system of constraints," as the philosopher Jacques Derrida aptly put it.[55] In opening the arguments that comprise the rest of *Writing Borderless Histories of Art*, I want to stress how differently science understands biological identity now from the epistemological model on which the discipline of art history was built and still largely operates. Aristotle's distinction between humans and non-human animals based on cognitive differences is the theory of human exceptionalism at the root of Western metaphysics, but it is not upheld by recent science – in fact, just the opposite. Our understanding of both cultural and biological identity has changed significantly since the professionalization of art history in the nineteenth century.

Notes

1 According to a survey of 177 mammal species conducted by Gerardo Ceballos at Universidad Nacional Autónoma de México, reported in www.relativelyinteresting.com/36-extinct-animals-due-human-activity/, accessed 30 May 2018.
2 According to major reports issued by the World Wildlife Fund in 2019, 2020, and 2022.
3 Kim Tallbear, "An Indigenous Reflection on Working Beyond the Human/Not Human," *GLQ: A Journal of Lesbian and Gay Studies* 21/2–3 (2015): 231; Tallbear, *Native American DNA: Tribal Belonging and the False Promise of Genetic Science* (Minneapolis: University of Minnesota Press, 2013).
4 Carolyn Dean, "Reviewing Representation: The Subject-object in Pre-Hispanic and Colonial Inka Visual Culture." *Colonial Latin American Review* 23/3 (2014): 298–319, at 299.
5 Robin George Andrews, "Bizarre Life-forms Found Thriving in Ancient Rocks Beneath the Seafloor," *Science News*, 2 April 2020, reporting on the findings of geoscientist Yohey Suzuki, University of Tokyo, whose new study was published same day in *Communications Biology*.
6 Tim Ingold, "Prospect," in *Biosocial Becomings: Intregrating Social and Biological Anthropology*, ed. Tim Ingold and Gisli Palsson (Cambridge: Cambridge University Press, 2013), 1–21, at 8. Not to be confused with Edward O. Wilson's problematic evolutionary theory, *Sociobiology: The New Synthesis*, 1975, linking genetics directly with social behavior. See Ullica Segerstra, *Defenders of the Truth: The Battle for Science in the Sociobiology Debate and Beyond* (New York: Oxford University Press, 2001).
7 Jo Scott, "Matter Mattering: 'Intra-activity' in Live Media Performance," *Parallax*, 11 June 2014.
8 Dipesh Chakrabarty, "The Planet: An Emergent Humanist Category," *Critical Inquiry* 46/1 (2019): 20.
9 Charles H. Langmuir and Wally Broecker, *How to Build a Habitable Planet: The Story of the Earth from the Big Bang to Humankind* (Princeton: Princeton University Press, 2012), 599–600.
10 Greta Thunberg, *The Climate Book: The Facts and the Solutions* (New York: Penguin Books, 2023); Paul Hawken, *Regeneration: Ending the Climate Crisis in One Generation* (New York: Penguin Books, 2021); *Drawdown: The Most Comprehensive Plan Ever Proposed to Reverse Global Warming*, ed. Paul Hawken (New York: Penguin Books, 2017).
11 Christiana Figueres and Tom Rivett-Carnac, *The Future We Choose: Surviving the Climate Crisis* (New York: Alfred A. Knopf, 2020), 71–72.
12 Figueres and Rivett-Carnac, *The Future We Choose*, 84.
13 Darna Noor, "Exclude fossil fuel firms from Cop28 if they only want to obstruct, says ex-UN chief," *The Guardian*, Thursday 21 September 2023.

14 Reporting on a meeting of the American Geophysical Union in 2012, Naomi Klein, "Why Science Is Telling All of Us to Revolt and Change Our Lives Before We Destroy the Planet," *Alternet*, 30 October 2013. http://admin.alternet.org/print/environment/naomi-klein-why-science-telling-all-us-revolt-and-change-our-lives-we-destroy-planet, accessed on 28 February 2019. Klein has been addressing the globalization of disaster capitalism and the role of media for many years, most recently *Doppelganger: A Trip into the Mirror World* (UK: Penguin/Random House, 2023).

15 T. J. Demos, *Against the Anthropocene: Visual Culture and Environment Today* (Berlin: Sternberg Press, 2–17), 19 and 28–29. See further discussion of Demos on the role of art, p. 252. My thanks to Peter Farago for the following information. Climate scientists build and refine climate models using vast raw data from satellites, weather stations, ice cores, and ocean buoys. They use these models and data to project future climate conditions based on key variables such as greenhouse gas levels. They assess the impact of climate projections on ecosystems, including food and water supplies, human migration, plant and animal extinction, and disease. Accurate projections are necessary to inform international climate agreements and national policies to mitigate the destructive effects of climate change. Climate models require a lot of storage, fast data transfer, and computational power. Unsupervised AI learning models are being used to compress the essential elements of raw data and develop neural network-based climate models. These models significantly reduce storage requirements and improve computational efficiencies. See Geert De Paepe and Lesley De Cruz, "DIRESA, a distance-preserving nonlinear reduction technique based on regularized autoencoders," *arXiv*:2404.18314v1 [cs.LG] 28 Apr 2024. These efficiencies allow scientists to refine their climate models and test hypotheses more quickly, including simulating the effects of bioengineered climate interventions. Since bioengineered climate interventions could have disastrous unintended consequences in the real world, it is essential to develop an effective and international governing body that enforces mitigation measures and controls the deployment of climate interventions.

16 Samuel Weber, *Institution and Interpretation*, rev. ed. (Stanford: Stanford University Press, 2001), 229–230.

17 Andrew Van Dam, "The most regretted (and lowest-paying) college majors," *The Washington Post*, 2 September 2022, citing Board of Governors of the Federal Reserve, *The Economic Well-Being of U.S. Households in 2020* - May 2021, accessed on 2 September, 2022, at www.federalreserve.gov/publications/files/2020-report-economic-well-being-us-households-202105.pdf.

18 Demos, *Against the Anthropocene*, 27.

19 Jane Chin Davidson and Amelia Jones, "Introduction: The Eurocentrism of Contemporary Art, Staging the Project," in *A Companion to Contemporary Art in a Global Framework*, ed. Jane Chin Davidson and Amelia Jones (West Sussex: Wiley Blackwell, 2024), 6.

20 I lift the term "structuring structures" from sociologist Pierre Bourdieu's notion of *habitus* to describe schemata that "generate and organize practices and representations . . . without presupposing a conscious aiming at ends or an express mastery of the operations necessary in order to attain them" (Bourdieu, *Outline of a Theory of Practice* [1972], trans. Richard Nice [Cambridge: Cambridge University Press, 1977], 72).

21 Gayatri Chakravorty Spivak, *A Critique of Postcolonial Reason: Toward a History of the Vanishing Present* (Cambridge, MA: Harvard University Press, 1999).

22 Resolution 47/24, panel held at the 50th Council session 13 June–8 July 2022). In July 2022, the Human Rights Council issued a resolution (Resolution 50/9) that recognized the unequal impact of climate change on the "realization of the right to food." www.ohchr.org/en/climate-change/human-rights-council-resolutions-human-rights-and-climate-change, accessed on 25 October 2022.

23 Bruno Latour and Peter Weibel, ed., *Critical Zones: The Science and Politics of Landing on Earth*, ZKM, exh cat. (Karlsruhe–London: MIT Press distribution, 2020), 14.

24 Donna Haraway, "Situated Knowledges: The Science Question in Feminism and the Privilege of Partial Perspective," *Feminist Studies* 14, n. 3 (Autumn 1988): 575–599.
25 Macarena Gómez-Barris, *The Extractive Zone: Social Ecologies and Decolonial Perspectives* (Durham–London: Duke University Press, 2017), 4.
26 Raymond Zhong, "Are We in the 'Anthropocene,' the Human Age? Nope, Scientists Say," *The New York Times*, 5 and 8 March 2024, accessed 30 June. 2024, www.nytimes.com/2024/03/05/climate/anthropocene-epoch-vote-rejected.html.
27 Monica Juneja, *Can Art History Be Made Global? Meditations from the Periphery* (Berlin: De Gruyter, 2023), 281.
28 Monica Juneja and Christian Kravagna, "Understanding Transculturalism," in *Transcultural Modernisms: Model House Research Group*, ed. Fahim Amir et al. (Berlin: Sternberg Press, 2013), 25.
29 Anke Burkenmaier, "Fernando Ortiz and the Meanings of Raza," in *The Specter of Races: Latin American Anthropology and Literature between the Wars* (Charlottesville: University of Virginia Press, 2013), 19–46.
30 Fernando Coronil, "Introduction," in Fernando Ortiz, *Cuban Counterpoint: Tobacco and Sugar* (1940 Spanish ed), trans. Harriet Onis (1947), reprinted with an Introduction by Fernando Coronil (Durham, NC: Duke University Press, 1995), 97–98.
31 James Clifford, "Museums as Contact Zones," *Routes: Travel and Translation in the Late Twentieth Century* (Cambridge, MA: Harvard University Press, 1997), 188–219.
32 *Fernando Ortiz: Caribbean and Mediterranean Counterpoints*, ed. Stephan Palmié (Chicago: Hau Books, 2023).
33 Juneja and Kravagna, "Understanding Transculturalism," 23–24.
34 Mia M. Mochizuki, "Connected Worlds – The World, the Worldly, and the Otherworldly: An Introduction," in *The Nomadic Object: The Challenge of World for Early Modern Religious Art*, ed. Christine Göttler and Mia M. Mochizuki (Leiden–Boston: Brill, 2018), 14.
35 An excellent overview with extensive bibliography is *Making Worlds: Global Invention in the Early Modern Period*, ed. Angela Vanhaelen and Bronwen Wilson (University of Toronto Press in association with the UCLA Center for Seventeenth- and Eighteenth-Century Studies and the William, Andrews Clark Memorial Library, 2022).
36 Mochizuki, *Jesuit Art* (Leiden: Brill, 2022), is a preview of a longer work in progress.
37 *Palimpsests of Religious Encounter in Asia, 1500–1800*, ed. Mia Mochizuki and Ines G. Županov (Leiden–Boston: Brill, 2025).
38 Anne Fausto-Sterling, *Sexing the Body: Gender Politics and the Construction of Sexuality* (New York: Basic Books, 2000).
39 Kim Tallbear, "An Indigenous Reflection on Working Beyond the Human/Non-Human," *Glo: Journal of Lesbian and Gay Studies* 2015: *230–235*; Tallbear, *Native American Belonging and the False Promise of DNA* (U. Minnesota Press, 2013).
40 Nanibaa A. Garrison et al., "Genomic Research Through an Indigenous Lens: Understanding the Expectations," *Annual Review of Genomics and Human Genetics*, March 20, 2019.
41 Carl Zimmer, *The New York Times*, 22 August 2018.
42 David Reich, *Who We Are and How We Got Here: Ancient DNA and the New Science of the Human Past* (New York: Pantheon Books, 2018), 26–27.
43 Homi Bhabha, "Of Mimicry and Man: The Ambivalence of Colonial Discourse," *October* 28 (Spring 1984): 125–33.
44 James J. Gibson, *The Senses Considered as Perceptual Systems* (Boston: Houghton Mifflin, 1966); and *The Ecological Approach to Visual Perception* (Boston: Houghton Mifflin, 1979).
45 Tim Ingold, "Evolution without Inheritance: Steps to an Ecology of Learning," *Current Anthropology* 63, Supplement 25 (December 2022): S32–S55, at S35; https://doi.org/

10.1086/722437. This is a relationship between behaviors and environmental conditions ("descent with modification") that Darwin discovered but did not pursue.
46 Tim Ingold, *The Rise and Fall of Generation Now* (Cambridge, UK: Polity Press, 2024).
47 Karen Barad, "Posthumanist Performativity," 821, cited along with philosophers Alfred North Whitehead (1929), Susan Oyama (1986), and others by Ingold, "Evolution without Inheritance," 540. See further, Karen Barad, *Meeting the Universe Halfway: Quantum Physics and the Entanglement of Matter and Meaning* (Durham–London: Duke University Press, 2007).
48 Eytan Avital and Eva Jablonka, *Animal Traditions: Behavioral Inheritance in Evolution* (Cambridge: Cambridge University Press, 2000).
49 Carl Safina, *Beyond Words: What Animals Think and Feel* (NY: Picador, 2015).
50 Lars Chittka, *The Mind of a Bee* (Princeton: Princeton University Press, 2022).
51 Annie Roth, "Videos Show Ants Amputating Nest Mates' Legs to Save Their Lives," *The New York Times*, 2 July 2024.
52 Philip Low et al., *The Cambridge Declaration of Consciousness: Proceedings of the Francis Crick Memorial Conference on Human and Non-Human Consciousness*, Churchill College, Cambridge University, 1–2 publicly proclaimed and signed on 7 July 2012. A literature review is beyond the scope of the present study, but see David M. Peña-Guzmán, *When Animals Dream: The Hidden World of Animal Consciousness* (Princeton–Oxford: Princeton University Press, 2022), with further references.
53 Giorgio Agamben, *Homo Sacer: Sovereign Power and Bare Life* (1997), trans. Daniel Heller-Roazen (Stanford: Stanford University Press, 1998), 8–9.
54 Jennifer Summit and David Wallace, "Rethinking Periodization," *Journal of Medieval and Early Modern Studies* 37/3 (fall 2007): 447–451, citing Frederic Jameson, *A Singular Modernity: Essays on the Ontology of the Present* (New York: Verso, 2002), 29.
55 Jacques Derrida, *The Truth in Painting* (1978), trans. Geoff Bennington (Chicago: Chicago University Press, 1987), 7–8.

Intermezzo I

TIME AS A HEALER

What is at stake in moving beyond art history to the broader conceptual realm that the prospect of writing a history of planetary culture opens up? Circulation/ flow/process/ entanglements/ worldmaking /translatability /temporality/the problematics of representation/Indigeneity and native traditions/interlocking and overlapping economic zones and trade networks: these are some of the most popular topics animating current critical approaches to art history and contemporary art in a global framework. Many of the terms were introduced in the 1990s, a productive decade for theorizing cultural interaction and disciplinary reform. The notion of the world as a space to be filled with objects and people was rightly criticized as an inadequate way to ground the relationships that constitute meaningful connections in which selves exist with others. This book is published at a time of productive experimentation when there is no consensus on issues or methodologies, let alone content. Nor would it be desirable to create a unified body of knowledge given the many locations and perspectives from which to view the world.

With the global turn, "time" has become a topic of broad theoretical interest in reconceptualizing art history without teleology. While there has been an explosion of interest in cross-cultural studies, what Byzantinist Robert Nelson in 1997 called the "gerrymandered divisions of art history" has commanded considerably less intellectual attention than it has in other fields that deal with the same centuries and period designations.[1] Rethinking history and historiography as an emancipatory project of hope for the future is a useful way to intervene in the conventionalized linear chronological narratives that still operate as the dominant framework in art history. The idea of "art" is itself a modern and initially a European concept that evolved over several centuries, therefore also in need of historical explication. Our inherited monocultural and oppositional categories, like the historical idea of art itself, need to be unpacked - they are bound up with the matrices of imperialism and colonialism and embroiled

DOI: 10.4324/9781351023429-2

in the neo-colonialism that thrives in today's world of transnational corporate capitalism. A "pluritope" model of interchange, to cite Islamicist Eva Hoffman, involves more complex notions of causality because it proceeds in many directions, continuously changing and connecting objects with makers and users in dynamic networks extending over vast areas of space and time.[2]

The strongest critique of time has come from the Global South: the capitalist concept of labor as the common measure of human activity divides the twenty-four-hour day into units of equal exchange value, thereby reducing the value of human life to the living labor power they supply (Marx's "abstract labor"). Capitalist modes of production destroy human life-worlds that value time in other ways: different times of the day and the calendar are ordered according to shared beliefs/customs/social practices that are not interchangeable. Thus, argues Dipesh Chakrabarty, examining the idea of abstract labor (and abstract time) enables us to see what is politically and intellectually at stake today in the universalist humanism of the Enlightenment. To organize life under the sign of capital is to act as if labor could be abstracted from all the social issues in which it is always already embedded, but that is never actually the case.[3]

The living quality of labor also makes labor a potential source of resistance to capitalist abstraction. This idea of an alternate history is meant to provide a ground on which to situate our thoughts about multiple ways of being human and their relationship to the global logic of capital. Chakrabarty gives an example from Marx's *Grundrisse* – the distinction between the piano maker, who reproduces or services capital, and the pianist whose relationship to his tools are critical to the process of making a world out of this earth. Chakrabarty imagines music as part of how we make our "worlds" while interrupting the grinding process of servicing capital and alienating human life.

Pheng Cheah understands the study of world literature from the Global South ("postcolonial peripheries") as a worldmaking activity along similar lines. He also takes up the theme of alternate temporalities, drawing on Gayatri Spivak's critique of Heidegger's essay, *The Origin of the Work of Art*, as the source of the idea that only the rational subject defined on European terms is capable of "worlding the world." Whereas Heidegger viewed the destruction of the world in capitalist modernity as a fall from an authentic condition, free subjects have the power to begin something new, to fabricate the world through action. Citing Derrida's response to Heidegger (discussed in a different context in Fugue 5) that worlding carries the irreducible risk of unworlding, Cheah argues that every (un)worlding also points to the irreducible possibility of opening another world: "the incalculable gift of time is a principle of real messianic hope immanent to the world."[4] The devastating consequences of capitalist globalization makes the opening of other worlds imperative. There is an urgent need to remake the world as a place that is open to peoples deprived of their worlds by economic globalization.

Homi Bhabha emphasizes that migrants and refugees do not circulate as an "emancipatory ideal" in a borderless, global world: there are fixities, new borders, new pockets of polity. (Im)migrants need to settle, receive housing and education, assert their economic and cultural rights, and seek the status of some form of citizenship.[5] In *The Origins of Totalitarianism* (1951), Hannah Arendt argued in terms that appear prophetic to many today, that human rights are universal and inalienable but their enforcement is difficult because there is no political authority higher than that of sovereign nations, as seen most clearly in the treatment of refugees and other stateless people isolated from civil rights. Writing in Cold War America, Arendt had escaped from the French Vichy government's concentration camp and entered the US on a stateless person's passport in 1941, was then active in the German-Jewish community, and became a naturalized US citizen in 1950. Arendt identified two potential solutions, assimilation and repatriation, both of which are incapable of solving the crisis due to the sheer numbers of refugees and due to the nation's exercise of sovereignty through control over its national borders.[6]

In the book that followed, *The Human Condition* (1958), often considered her most influential work, Arendt pursued the roots of modern alienation from the world to ask what agency individuals *can* have in the social realm. The main outlines of her argument rest on a distinction between labor and work – again, with uncanny resonances today. She ties her argument to a critique of Marx and grounds it in ancient Greek philosophy. Labor corresponds to the biological process of the human body and provides for necessities. Labor is continuously consumed while, in contrast, work provides an enduring "artificial" world of things – the human condition of work is worldliness. Two senses of the human condition operate in tension in her text – the human ability to construct worldliness through the fabrication of artifice, and the consequences due to a plurality of human agents who are pursuing differing ends. Arendt laments that work has nearly disappeared from society in the current era of industrial capitalism: this disappearance is a major cause of alienation from the world.

In *The Human Condition*, Arendt discusses Plato's idea of the ideal state as the work of *homo faber* and contrasts it with her own view that action is fundamental to maintaining democracy, whereas understanding the state as a static work of art is not. When "people act in concert," that is, when people "make and keep promises," they can retreat from harmful regimes.[7] The Platonic separation of knowing from doing, Arendt continues, is at the root of all theories of domination. This division is alien to the realm of action, *the validity of which is destroyed when knowing and doing part company* (whereas it is an everyday and necessary occurrence in the fabrication of works). Humans have always been capable of destroying whatever was the product of human hands, Arendt observes, but today they have become capable of potentially destroying what humans did not make: the earth and earthly nature. Arendt wrote during the height of the Cold War, when nuclear disaster seemed an imminent threat (as it does again now): humans "have carried irreversibility and human unpredictability into the natural realm, where no remedy can be found to undo what has been done." Her grim observation has even greater urgency now when we are faced as never before with saving our shared home on planet Earth from premature and senseless destruction: nuclear holocaust and climate disaster have become competing threats.

We all share the ethical responsibility as producers of knowledge to understand how our knowledge shapes society. Marx's explanation of value was based on what he saw as the essential contradiction between "variable capital," that is, labor-power, which adds more than it costs in the production process, and "constant capital" which refers to the objective factors (such as the machinery needed to produce more commodities at a faster rate in order to compete successfully in the marketplace). Teresa Brennan concluded in an analysis of the role of time in Marx's theory of the political economy, that profit ultimately "depends on the difference a living subject makes to a dead object."[8] By definition, art historians are the labor-power (the living subject) in the production process of art history, just as artists are the labor-power in the production of art. The responsibilities of academics, artists, curators, journalists, and other intellectuals to link museology, history, theory, and criticism to contemporary social conditions is an urgent and painfully obvious question. Nineteenth-century European historians believed, as Hayden White famously argued in a 1978 essay entitled "The Fictions of Factual Representation," that "if one only eschewed ideology and remained true to the facts, history would produce a knowledge as certain as anything offered by the physical sciences and as objective as a mathematical exercise."[9] The problem with this assumption is in separating facts from the structures in which they reside in our texts and thinking. White directly confronts the fiction that history could be written without employing any "fictional" techniques – itself a reflection of the nineteenth-century ideology that a value-neutral description of the facts prior to interpretation or analysis was possible.

As White observes, "What is at issue here is not, what are the facts? But rather, how are the facts to be described in order to sanction one mode of explaining them rather than another?" What is at stake is the belief that a "scientific" or "objective" foundation – the true facts of History – could escape the shifting sands of interpretative controversy. History buries its conceptual apparatus in the interior of its narratives, whereas philosophy brings that apparatus to the surface of the text. Factual (re)presentation is grounded in an implicit philosophy which claims that a chain of causes and effects selected by an author is merely temporal succession and not narration. Chronology as a structure for narrating history is, for these reasons, a powerful and seductive rhetorical apparatus, a literary construct used to structure an argument so that it masks its persuasive power under the guise of "natural time."

The historian in the European tradition established by Renaissance/Early Modern humanists is a moral philosopher, a person of good character like the ideal orator of Antiquity described by Cicero and Quintilian. The historian's mode of judgment is based on particulars, that is to say, justified by the experienced evaluation of concrete evidence and dependent on the historian's upstanding moral character. Fast-forwarding to the nineteenth century, "positivism," refers to a philosophical system which holds that every rationally justifiable assertion can be scientifically verified or be capable of logical or mathematical proof. The advantage of positive science was its rejection of metaphysics and theism, but the adaptation of positivist methods to the humanities leaves open the fundamental question of what constitutes a historical "fact" on a par with hard scientific evidence. Hayden White's critique of established conventions in historical writing questioned not only the neutrality of chronology as an ordering device but also the objective status accorded to historical "facts" understood as what "actually" or "essentially happened" ("*wie es eigentlich gewesen*"), to cite the famous formulation of the nineteenth-century German positivist historian Leopold von Ranke (1795–1886), who emphasized reliance on primary sources (empirical evidence) and narrative history and rejected teleological approaches to history.[10] White argued that what counts as a fact also unavoidably involves selection and therefore interpretation. What is sayable, when and where, as critics of Eurocentric practices frequently point out, is always determined by someone or some institution with the power to do so.

What constitutes a valid "fact" depends on what counts as empirical evidence for the historian, and this is also open to debate. Joan Wallach Scott offers the following observations on the historian's access to experience:

> When experience is taken as the origin of knowledge, the vision of the individual subject (the person who had the experience or the historian who recounts it) becomes the bedrock of evidence on which explanation is built. Questions about the constructed nature of experience, about how subjects are constituted as different in the first place, about how one's vision is structured – about language (or discourse) and history – are left aside. The evidence of experience then becomes evidence for the fact of difference, rather than a way of exploring how difference is established, how it operates, how and in what ways it constitutes subjects who see and act in the world.[11]

White's famous critique of chronology as a narrative structure and the constructed nature of experience discussed by Scott and others are rarely mentioned in art historical writings. Decolonial approaches critique the Eurocentric episteme of temporality from the standpoint of the Global South. Yet the colonial matrix of power is not a universal condition either. It is not applicable to all places and cultures adversely affected by such universalist claims. On the other hand, the rigid, Eurocentric episteme that decolonial studies seek to identify and revise *is* of concern to the whole field. Chief among these are cultural beliefs about the space–time continuum that comprise an incommensurable array of strategies, of great value in writing about artifacts because they provide context, as long as it is recognized that all cultural systems of structuring space/time involve relations of knowledge and power. They are modes of distributing memory, methods for formatting the relation between past and present at the collective level, to cite philosopher Michel de Certeau. De Certeau defines history-writing as a relationship of succession (one thing after another), in which cause and effect, and separation from the present are key features. He contrasts this with a "psychoanalytic" approach defined as one of imbrication (one thing in place of the other) and repetition (one thing reproduces the other in another form). Both modes give the past explanatory value and/or make the present capable of explaining the past, but the latter looks critically at chronology as an explanatory mechanism because:

> History is "cannibalistic," and memory becomes the closed arena of conflict between two contradictory operations: forgetting, which is not something passive, a loss, but an action directed against the past; and the mnemic trace, the return of what was forgotten, in other words, an action by a past that is now forced to disguise itself.[12]

We might re-imagine a history that pivots the scholar's ethical responsibility toward the future of the discipline. For Walter Benjamin, the manner in which art and cultural history are to be integrated is the subject of investigation rather than its methodological premise. Benjamin argued that the work of art is never complete because it is by virtue of its after-history that the work of art's fore-history is recognizable. Since the process of embodying and distinguishing itself from the world is continued in the interpretations of the work, the work of art is never completed. Consequently, objects of the past cannot be fully possessed and they will always disrupt the efforts of the present to contain them within its categories or forms of narrative. This condition, of the artwork's dynamic ongoing production, makes the work of art an exemplary case of the impossibility of ever definitively reconstructing or "owning" the past. For Benjamin, the possibility of a dialectical cultural history depends on utilizing the "destructive element" of the past's effect on the present. The "reserve of the past" enables the past to destroy aspects of the present and open it to the future.[13]

The Emancipatory Potential of Time Conceptualized as Duration

Benjamin's analyses of how history "decomposes into images," is related directly to his famous concept of the "dialectical image" of the past that becomes readable (*Lesbarkeit*) in certain future contexts when it "bears to the highest degree the imprint of the perilous critical moment on which all reading is founded."[14] The concept of duration developed by philosopher Henri Bergson (1859–1941), writes Gilles Deleuze echoing De Certeau's "psychoanalytic" approach to history writing, is defined less by succession than by coexistence. The paradox is that what coexists with each present is the whole of the past on various interdependent levels.[15] Bergson's spatialized concept of the "pure past" is that the entirety of all that has happened coexists with each present.[16] In an outstanding article on "paramnesia" (false recognition), Deleuze writes, Bergson invoked metaphysics to show how a memory is not constituted after present perception, but "is strictly contemporaneous with it."[17] In each instant, duration divides into two simultaneous streams, one going toward the future and the other falling back into the past. The past is imagined as a "searchable" terrain for the investigator animated by the desire to understand its relevance for our times.[18] Deleuze took as his point of departure the structure defined by the baroque "fold" considered independent of a particular time and place. He understood the artwork as an "event" enfolded in time, a "futural force" enabling us to rethink the past in all its complex, fluid temporalities. The Deleuzian "transmissibility" of art shares key features with Walter Benjamin's idea of a dialectical cultural history that depends on utilizing the "destructive element" of the past's effect on the present. Conceptualizing the present as laden with repressed "mnemic traces" of the past is also how de Certeau described his "psychoanalytic" approach to history conceived along Bergsonian lines. Memory is the arena of conflict between active forgetting and the return of what was forgotten and forced to disguise itself: History is "cannibalistic," and memory becomes the closed arena of conflict between two contradictory operations: forgetting, which is not something passive, a loss, but an action directed against the past; and the mnemic trace, the return of what was forgotten, in other words, an action by a past that is now forced to disguise itself.[19]

There is nothing "natural" about European theories of cultural progress, and when has institutional memory *not* been an arena of conflict? The implications of Bergson's account that the past is immanent in the present are far-reaching. It means that all history is in the present and that action in the present is ignorant without historical knowledge. Bergson's "cone of time," first published in 1896 at the height of debates on cultural evolutionism, was a strategic intervention because it undercut linear accounts of cultural progress that conflate chronology and teleology [Figure i. 1].[20]

Not only does the past (AB) coexist with the present (S) but as the present passes, it is the whole, integral past that coexists with each present. The cone implies that in the past itself there appear all kinds of levels of profundity. Duration is virtual coexistence involving the repetition of "planes." The illusion about the essence of Time is that it makes us believe we can reconstitute the past gradually, distinguishing a before and an after that the mind carries out by adding individual elements, rather than by changing levels.

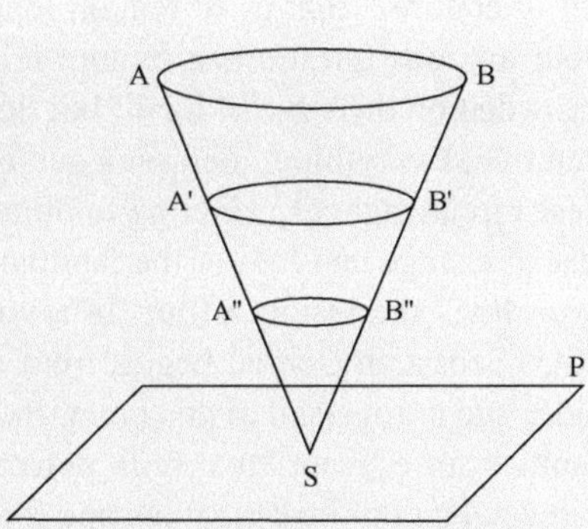

FIGURE I.1 Henri Bergson, cone of memory, *Matter and Memory*, 1896, representing the complete state of coexistence: all of our past coexists with each present. From Henri Bergson, *Matter and Memory*, trans. N.M. Paul and W. S. Palmer (New York: Zone Books, 1988), 162.

Gilles Deleuze, *Bergsonism* (New York: Zone Books, 1991), 59–62.

The writings of Walter Benjamin and Gilles Deleuze have encouraged the baroque to free itself from the anchor of chronological periodization, writes Helen Hills moderating a trans-continental discussion of the term "baroque," descriptive terms such as "provincial," "late," and "periphery" that ultimately have meaning only within a system of values based on an evolutionary theory of progress and normative standards.[21] The prospect of employing a Bergsonian concept of time instead of a linear chronology for recuperating the histories of the culturally dispossessed is promising: what occupies the hidden dimensions in the intricate folds of time, what has been intentionally repressed in past accounts that still haunts the present? Critical historiography by definition stands on the edge of a struggle – at the precipice of whatever discipline whose epistemological foundations it questions, revises, demolishes, or at least refines. Here's the double bind for rethinking our histories of art in an institutional setting: if our historical narratives change nothing in the "actual world," then are we not reproducing at the meta-critical level the very configurations that, research confirms, need to change? Consider, Sam Weber argues, that we professionals draw our value from the specific social needs we claim to fulfill. Professionalism may therefore be understood as the effort of a group "seeking to define and maintain a certain identity in the face of an extremely dynamic, unsettling, and powerful reorganization and transformation of society."[22] Weber compares the motivations of professionalism with the mechanism described by Freud as anxiety, a reaction of the ego to danger: the essence of danger for the ego is separation and object-loss associated with its helplessness; the ego forms a stable cathexis by investing perceptions and representations with a relative power to endure – that is, to remain identical to themselves. The implication is that our anxious questions are more telling than the answers we seek. We are not crowded on the edge of a cliff but floating on blocks of ice that have already broken free. Everything, including ourselves, is changing: no small wonder that, in these circumstances, we cling to objects as we leave them behind.

Fear of change and loss of the familiar, beloved art history is certainly a factor in "worlding" the history of art. In a volume entitled, *What Is Global History?* (2016),[23] Sebastian Conrad begins from a premise that most art historians would consider uncontroversial at this point. In his view, the modern social sciences and humanities suffer from "two birth defects": presupposing the nation-state as the fundamental unit of investigation; and foregrounding Europe as the central driving force of world history. Conrad rightly emphasizes that global studies do not necessarily encompass the entire globe. One can write a far more limited history with an awareness of global connections and structural conditions.

Time is not the only historical category that deserves careful thought, but it is certainly an important consideration. History itself is necessarily a form of literature no matter what its aspirations and pretentions to scientific status are. Modern historical writing was explicitly distinguished from the chronicle by sixteenth-century humanists who acknowledged the higher status of history due to its moral purpose, which justified the use of rhetorical artifices (elements of style, *elocutio*, as they were known in rhetorical theory) that historians employ to persuade their readers. Beginning a story in the middle, *in medias res*, for example, is the historian's prerogative because the historian's responsibility and the purpose of history writing are to teach moral values. Historians have the responsibility to interpret the significance of events and persuade their readers. A chronicle, by contrast, is an account of events presented chronologically.

When Georges Didi-Huberman posited that art history was an "anachronistic" discipline, he meant that, in practice, art historians impose a modern notion of art on evidence that came before this understanding of art developed. Understood as an active interrogation of the limiting conditions of art historical writing and research in general, Didi-Huberman conceived the pictorial sign as a material imprint, the symptom of a culturally and historically specific kind of figurability.[24] The critical concept of anachrony (as opposed to anachronism, the mispositioning of events within a stable temporal sequence), was introduced to art history from the philosophical writings of Jacques Rancière and Jacques Derrida by Alexander Nagel and Christopher Wood (2010) to destabilize the naturalized temporal frameworks on which the discipline was built in the nineteenth century.[25] Wood and Nagel position themselves in relation to existing discussions of anachronism by locating a different sense of historical time, one that existed prior to the development of the hegemonic chronological narratives of modern nation-states. Historical time conceived as a chain of replicas somewhat resembles the structure of typological exegesis, Wood and Nagel observe, and both resemble the structure of "dialectical anachronism" defined as the strategic juxtaposition of heterogeneous moments in time.

Yet the substitution of an "ana-chronic" structure for a "chronological" one does not eliminate the need to legitimize the reality of the historical account. It is crucial for the narrator to articulate his or her position in relation to the events narrated. Any methodological consideration of time for the practice of art history deserves to be situated in the context of conundrums and unfolding critiques of existing models of historical time in relation to the historian's subjectivity. The artwork's complex relation to time has always been central to the debates, though they took shape largely outside the discipline of art history. The topic of "anachronism" was discussed at length by historians of what came to be known as the French Annales School to express philosophical doubts about the practice of history as an exact science. Reconsiderations of the historian's "sin of sins," as Lucien Febvre referred to "anachronism" in 1942, were initially framed by Marc Bloch and Febvre, who worried about historians projecting their mental "equipment" (*outillage*) onto other eras.[26] The influential concepts of *mentalité* and *longue durée* emerged in response to the question of how, if ever, the past is objectively portrayed, given that historians necessarily approach the past from the present, anachronistically, "like a movie reel that is unwound in the opposite direction from which it is viewed."[27] In other parts of Europe, most famously in Frankfurt where another "School" was simultaneously forming, similar discussions of the contingency of historical truth developed on the same Marxist foundation.[28] The most sophisticated theoretical model of "anachronism" conceived as a term operating in opposition to "chronism" is undoubtedly Walter Benjamin's notion of the "dialectical image."

Not since Marx's shattering critique of the political economy in terms of the social relations involved in the production of commodities had European intellectuals been as politically engaged with the ongoing social crisis as they were during the years that World War II devastated Europe. The sudden loss of civil liberties, persecution, and genocide – the failed dream of the modern nation-state and its escalating nightmares – were the living conditions of the historians who first questioned the scientific historian's techniques of factual representation and linked them to explicitly political agendas.

Even though Bloch and Febvre understood the reductiveness of positivist historians' conception of historical time in this sense, the Annales School notion of the *longue durée* never called into question the ideological effects of chronological time itself. Benjamin on the other hand developed the Marxist understanding that art is a social practice into the argument that the revolutionary artist develops existing forces of artistic production to create new social relations between the artist and audience. Howard Caygill glosses Benjamin's concept of a dialectical cultural history as a concrete illustration of what it might mean to rub history against its grain in this manner. The decisive element in establishing new social relations through writing or other revolutionary ways of making art is not the restitution of past suffering by the present, which would be for the present to come into complete possession of the past, but rather the impossibility of ever possessing the past.[29] A dialectical cultural history would acknowledge that the past can unsettle and disrupt the present. A dialectical cultural history is possible if it adopts "the destructive element which authenticates both dialectical thought and the experience of the dialectical thinker."[30] The "destructive element" refers to the possibility that the reserve of the past will destroy aspects of the present and open it to the future. Ultimately, historical materialism fails to achieve this because its practitioners prescribe in advance the relationship between past and present, selecting what is relevant and why it is relevant and reducing the past to items in an inventory of the present.

The most fundamental problem at hand for conceptualizing disciplinary knowledge as an ethical practice at a planetary scale is the notion of identity itself. Emmanuel Lévinas has argued for a notion of truth that is at considerable odds with the dominant rationalist one: his framework relies upon the lived experience of the other. Against a notion of the truth as the instrument of a mastery being exercised by the knower over areas of the unknown as he or she brings them within the fold of the same, Levinas argues that there is a form of truth that is totally alien to me, that I do not discover within myself, but that calls on me from beyond me, and it requires me to leave the realms of the known and of the same in order to settle in a land that is under its rule. And this other is not a threat to be reduced, nor an object given to a knowing subject, but that which constitutes me as an ethical being. In this encounter I discover my responsibility for the existence of this other, a responsibility at the root of all my decisions: this is the ground of my response-ability, that is, my capacity to communicate with others and with myself in non-coercive ways.[31]

Connections between foundational critiques of disciplinarity as such and the concrete project of critiquing a given disciplinary practice are often obscure. It may be one thing to critically assess practices that conform to existing disciplinary expectations, but it is often quite another to question the configuration itself. Yet unless the subject position of the critic in the institution is brought into the equation, the past will always haunt the present, and the most significant epistemological and ethical issues remain unarticulated and unaddressed. The specter is invisible in the mirror, as Derrida put it, and this condition can either haunt us in the manner of the ghost of Hamlet's father reminding us that "time is out of joint," or we can remember our past, learn from it in the present, and use the lessons to devise a better future. History is founded on the rupture between a past that is its object, and a present that is the place of its practice. "History endlessly finds the present in its object and the past in its practice."[32] Yet "history" precisely cannot do this in case of worlds that are not part of history's past. It follows that history is not a fact of the world that is more or less accurately represented, but rather that it is but one way for a society to constitute the past and establish a relation with it. To live in history, and to wish to write it, is not a universal anthropological postulate, but is a certain way to conceive of and be in the world and it is a certain practice of subjectivity.

Writing history in terms of continuities and ruptures does not mandate reliance on the nineteenth-century concept of distinct historical periods identifiable by certain characteristic traits. In her study of anachronic interventions by artists since 1990 who challenge conventionalized chronological representations of history and art, Eva Kernbauer offers a thorough critical re-examination of European discourses on history in relation to art since 1800.[33] Kernbauer defines "anachronies" in the plural as "modes of connection" between events, ideas, and significations that, contrary to chronological time, "make meaning circulate in a way that escapes any contemporaneity, any identity of time with 'itself'" by paying attention to "repetitions, distensions, duplications, folds, bends," and, above all, the ability to "balance incompatible models of temporality."[34] Artworks that create new social spaces and subjects ("speculative collectives"), Kernbauer argues, raise everyone's awareness of their part in the co-constitution of our shared, yet multi-directional and hetero-temporal contemporaneity. The manner in which works of art exist "through" time requires vigorous shaking of our discipline's epistemological foundations. Is an analysis that begins in the nineteenth century sufficient if the goal is to provide an epistemic critic of the assumptions on which the discipline of art history was built in the nineteenth century? The first Fugue positions the sixteenth century as the critical opening for a future account of the planet's artifactual history with the aspiration of coming to terms with art history's Eurocentic past.

Notes

1 Robert Nelson, "The Map of Art History," *Art Bulletin* 79/1 (1997): 28–40.
2 Eva R. Hoffman, "Pathways of Portability: Islamic and Christian Interchange from the Tenth to the Twelfth Century," *Art History* 24/1 (February 2001): 17–50.
3 Dipesh Chakrabarty, "Universalism and Belonging in the Logic of Capital," *Public Culture* 12/3 (2000): 653–678, at 655; see also Chakrabarty, *Provincializing Europe: Postcolonial Thought and Historical Difference* (Princeton: Princeton University Press, 2000; with a new preface, 2008).
4 Pheng Cheah, *What Is a World? On Postcolonial Literature as World Literature* (Durham: Duke University Press, 2016), 28 and 44.
5 Homi K. Bhabha, "Spectral Sovereignty, Vernacular Cosmopolitans, and Cosmopolitan Memories," *Cosmopolitanisms*, ed. Paulo Lemos Horta, Kwame Anthony Appiah, and Bruce Robbins, Project Muse (New York: NYU Press, 2017), 141–152.
6 Hannah Arendt, *The Origins of Totalitarianism* (1951), rev. ed. (Orlando: Harcourt, 1968), 290–302.
7 Margaret Canovan, "Introduction," in Hannah Arendt, *The Human Condition*, 2nd ed. (1958), intro. Margaret Canovan (Chicago–London: University of Chicago Press, 1998), xviii–xix.
8 Teresa Brennan, "Why the Time Is Out of Joint: Marx's Political Economy without the Subject," in *Strategies for Theory from Marx to Madonna*, ed. R. L. Rutsky and Bradley J. Macdonald (Albany: State University of New York Press, 2003), 23–38.
9 Hayden White, "The Fictions of Factual Representation," *Tropics of Discourse* (Baltimore–London: Johns Hopkins University Press, 1978), 121–24.
10 Leopold von Ranke, "Preface: Histories of the Latin and Germanic Nations from 1494–1514," in *The Varieties of History: From Voltaire to the Present*, ed. Fritz Stern (New York: Vintage Books, 1972), 57.
11 Joan W. Scott, "Fantasy Echo: History and the Construction of Identity," *Critical Inquiry* 27/2 (Winter 2001): 284–304.
12 Michele De Certeau, "Psychoanalysis and its History," *Heterologies: Discourse on the Other*, trans. Brian Massumi, foreword Wlad Godzick (Minneapolis–London: University of Minnesota Press, 1986), 3–16.
13 Walter Benjamin, "Eduard Fuchs, Collector and Historian" (1937), *Selected Writings Volume 3, 1935–1938*, ed. Howard Eiland and Michael W. Jennings, trans. Edmund Jephcott et al. (4 vols., Cambridge, 2002), 268.
14 Walter Benjamin, *The Arcades Project*, trans. Howard Eiland and Kevin McLaughlin (Cambridge, MA: The Belknap Press of Harvard University Press, 1999), 462–463.
15 Gilles Deleuze, *Bergsonism*, trans. Hugh Tomlinson (New York: Zone Books, 1988), 59–63.
16 Jae Emerling, "To Render Time Sensible, Review of Keith Moxey, *Visual Time: The Image in History* (2013)," *Journal of Art Historiography* 13 (2015): 1–11, at 8.
17 Deleuze, *Bergsonism*, 118.
18 Emerling, Review of Moxey, 8.

19 Michel De Certeau, "Psychoanalysis and History," (1978) *Heterologies: Discourse on the Other*, trans. Brian Massumi, foreword Wlad Godzich (Minneapolis–London: University of Minneosta Press, 2000), 3–16.

20 The metaphor of the cone was first introduced in Henri Bergson, *Matière et Mémoire* (1896), *Matter and Memory*, trans. Nancy Margaret Paul and W. Scott Palmer (London: George Allen & Unwin, 1911), 152.

21 Helen Hills, "Conceptions and Determinations of Baroque and New Baroque in the Last Decade: A Discussion between Jens Baumgarten, Claire Farago, Stefano Jacoviello, Monika Kaup, and Gabriela Siracusano, moderated by Helen Hills," *Perspective* 1 (2015): 15–36, at 15.

22 Samuel Weber, *Institution and Interpretation* (1987), rev. ed. (Stanford: Stanford University Press, 2001), 28, citing Burton Bledstein's definition.

23 Sebastian Conrad, *What is Global History?* (Princeton–Oxford: Princeton University Press, 2016). See also Lynn Hunt, *History: Why It Matters* (Cambridge, UK: Polity Press, 2018).

24 Georges Didi-Huberman, *Devant le Temps: Histoire de l'Art et anachronisme des Images* (Paris: Les Éditions de Minuet, 2000), 28–49. Translated into English with a new preface as *Confronting Images: Questioning the Ends of a Certain History of Art*, trans. John Goodman (University Park, PA: Pennsylvania State University Press, 2005), 40–52.

25 Alexander Nagel and Christopher S. Wood, *Anachronic Renaissance* (New York: Zone Books, 2010), building on their earlier argument, "Interventions: Toward a New Model of Renaissance Anachronism," *The Art Bulletin* 87/3 (2005): 403–415, and "The Authors Reply," 433–457. I served as a discussant to that Intervention and draw on some of my arguments there, "Time out of Joint," 425–429.

26 Didi-Huberman, *Devant le Temps,* 30, citing here Febvre.

27 Marc Bloch, *Apologie pour l'histoire ou Métier d'historien* (*1941–1942)*, ed. E. Bloch (Paris: Armand Colin, 1993), 96–97.

28 David Held, *Introduction to Critical Theory: Horkheimer to Habermas* (Berkeley and Los Angeles: University of California Press, 1980).

29 Howard Caygill, "Walter Benjamin's Concept of Cultural History," in *The Cambridge Companion to Walter Benjamin*, ed. David S. Ferris (Cambridge: Cambridge University Press, 2004), 73–96.

30 Caygill, "Benjamin's Concept of Cultural History," 93, citing Benjamin, "Fuchs," *Selected Writings*, ed. Michael Jennings et al., 4 vols. (Cambridge, MA: Harvard University Press, 1996–2003), III, 268.

31 Emmanuel Levinas, *Otherwise than Being, or Beyond Essence*, trans. Alphonso Lingis (The Hague–Boston: M. Nijhoff; Hingham, MA: Kluwer Boston, 1981).

32 Sanjay Seth, "Reason or Reasoning? Clio or Siva?," *Postcolonial Traces*, ed. Brent Hayes Edwards, special issue of *Social Text* 78 (Spring 2004): 84–101.

33 Birgit Hopfener, "Art that Explores History: Reconceptualizing Contemporary Art's Historicity in the Global Framework," *Journal of Art Historiography* 22 (December 2022): 1–81, Review of Eva Kernbauer, *Art, History, and Anachronic Interventions Since 1990* (New York: Routledge, 2022).

34 Eva Kernbauer, *Art, History, and Anachronic Interventions Since 1990* (New York: Routledge, 2022), 7–14.

FUGUE 1

DEFINING AN ECOLOGICAL APPROACH

On the History of Human Exceptionalism

Eco-critics routinely point to the seventeenth-century European scientific and philosophical literature as the source of the Eurocentric binary of nature and culture, but is it really the case that human exceptionalism is a product of seventeenth-century secular philosophy? That question is the subject of this Fugue. Jason W. Moore, who studies the relationship between emerging global capitalism and environmental degradation in the sixteenth and seventeenth centuries, singles out "the binary of Humanity and Nature . . . inscribed in the intellectual DNA of the Anthropocene project" as deeply problematic because it omits consideration of these driving economic factors. He (and by now, many other eco-critics) emphasizes that capitalism is built on a specific form of human exceptionalism that excludes most humans from Humanity by regarding them as "part of Nature, along with trees and soils and rivers" and treating them accordingly.[1] Moore specifically points to René Descartes's separation of mind and body, and the broader scientific and philosophical movement that sought to master nature. However, as he recognized when he studied the flow of silver in the sixteenth century, the world capitalist system developed *before* the so-called secular age of the Enlightenment. There is an unacknowledged slippage in this historical account of human exceptionalism (humans versus nature) that deserves far more scrutiny if the goal is to transcend the binary thinking that sustains the present ecological and humanitarian crisis.

Drawing upon many different kinds of local and regional studies, Moore provides a synthetic narrative in which he argues that "historical capitalism has sustained itself on the basis of exploiting, and thereby undermining, a vast web of socio-ecological relations."[2] "The flipside of Potosí's extraordinary role in delivering a material basis for money capital-formation," he writes, "was the radical transformation of land and

DOI: 10.4324/9781351023429-3

labor in the service of world accumulation. This was a decisive moment in the world ecological revolution of the long seventeenth century, whose effects reached from Potosí to Southeast Asia to the Baltic."

Moore's knowledge of the global circulation of silver provides a good entry point for investigating how the philosophical justification for "excluding most humans from Humanity" developed during the early sixteenth century as part of the global economy emerging then in the Iberian world.[3] Moore examined the expansion of the global economy initially focused on Potosí, in the Viceroyalty of Peru (modern-day Bolivia), by far the largest producer of silver in the world in the sixteenth century. The place of American silver in the rise of capitalism had been well-studied before, but Moore is the first to articulate how the flow of silver was a world-ecological process. The sudden influx of silver to Europe beginning in 1545 quickly inaugurated successive fiscal crises leading to the imperial restructuring of Peru within a decade. As the quality of available silver ore declined, even the cheaper technology of smelting used to maximize profit could not prevent deforestation in the mountains which led to erosion. Meanwhile raising of livestock also necessary for large-scale mining multiplied out of proportion to resources and deeper mines increased respiratory diseases. Competition in the international market drove down wages and introduced round-the-clock shifts, which altogether resulted in more Amerindian miners dying from overwork and disease and the degraded environmental conditions I have just briefly described.

Moore defines capitalism broadly, not as a narrow set of economic or social relations – categories that he views as part of the impasse to addressing the climate crisis productively – but as a "world-ecology of capital, power, and re/production in the web of life" that can only be addressed through world history. His thesis is that capitalism is historically coherent from the sixteenth century on as a relentless, innovative quest to turn the work/energy of the biosphere into capital, understood as a dynamic process of creating value. The challenge is to account for the manner in which the work/energy of the web of life is incorporated into historical relations of power and re/production. The Dutch Republic was "the model capitalist nation of the seventeenth century" located at the epicenter of the "world-ecological revolution" that stretched from southeast Asia to the north Atlantic. Thus Descartes' concern with the "systematic rationality of the universe" is both symptomatic of the massive reorganization of power, capital, and nature, and contributed to it. The point of Descartes' philosophical concern with rational understanding of the universe was not only to interpret the world, but to control it: "to make ourselves as it were the masters and possessors of nature."[4] The question is *not* how humanity became separated from nature, *nor* how humans cause environmental degradation, but how humans put nature to work in accumulating wealth and power by working *through* nature. Moore's "web of life" approach treats nature itself as constantly renewing and evolving – above all, he insists that nature is historical.

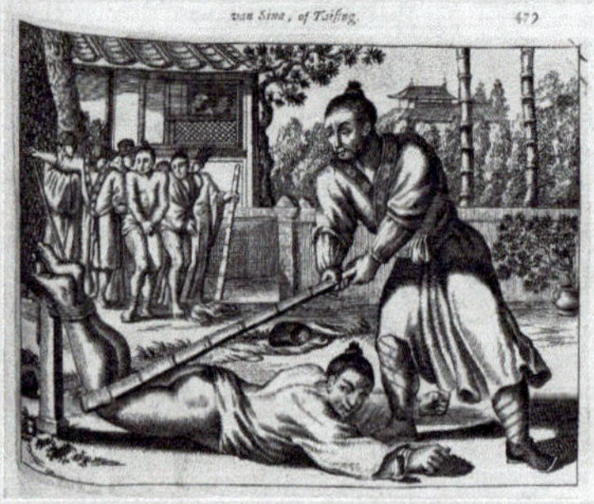
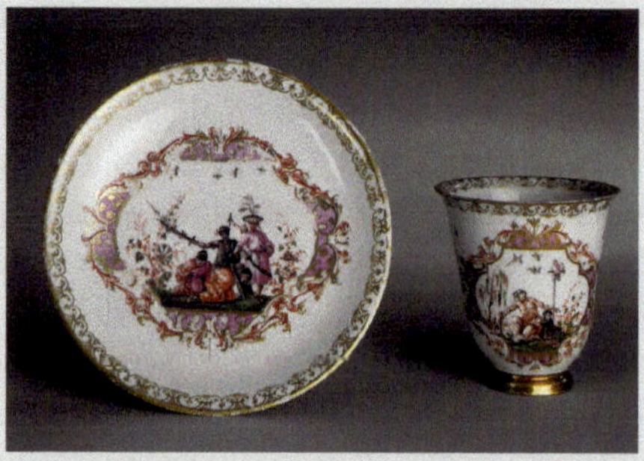

FIGURE 1.1 AND 1.2 (Left) Jacob van Meurs (atelier), Caning in courtyard (engraving), in *Olfert Dap-per, Gedenckwaerdig bedryf der Nederlandsche Oost-Indische Maetschappye, op de kuste en in het keizerrijk van Taising of Sina* (Amsterdam, 1670). (Right) Tea saucer and bowl, Meissen Manufactory (c. 1725); decorated by Lauche; hard-paste porcelain painted with enamel and gold. © The Trustees of the British Museum.

Decontextualized from their original contexts of use, or manufactured for export in the first place, a substantial body of foreign things, people, places, and practices, as well as images and descriptions of them, reached European consumers via Dutch shipping and workshops in the Netherlands. A wide range of unfamiliar material was reduced to a small body of conventional tropes: scenes of Chinese torture originating in Jesuit missionary accounts, for example, came to decorate pottery and provided repeating wallpaper patterns for stylish European interiors.

After Benjamin Schmidt. *Inventing Exoticism: Geography, Globalism, and Europe's Early Modern World* (Philadelphia: University of Pennsylvania Press, 2015).

How is nature historical? Most important of all to Moore's explanatory model is the role of raw materials and unpaid work in service to surplus value production. Thus, he argues, it is a mistake to see capitalism as Karl Marx analyzed it by considering wage-labor alone because *unpaid work outside the commodity system* supplied by enslaved and underpaid workers including women and children was necessary to create profit and this wealth (capital). Moore specifies labor-power, food, energy, and raw materials as the four categories of what he calls Cheap Nature. The development of global capitalism in the early modern era operated on "the logic of the commodity frontier":

> Ecological contradictions mobilized by the expansion of commodity production and exchange implied and indeed necessitated regional ecological crises. . . . Commodity production and exchange, a long-standing aspect of

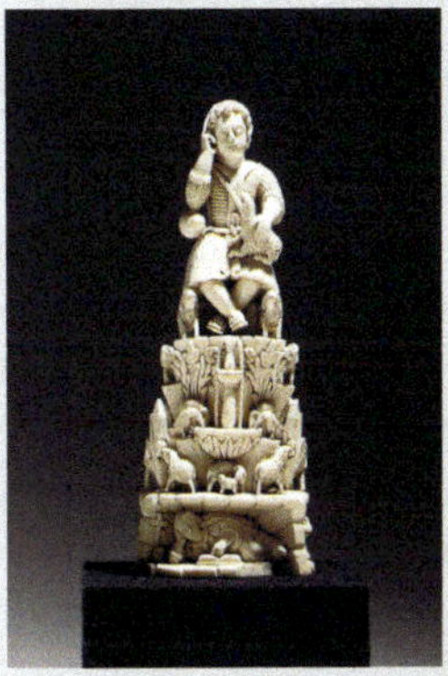

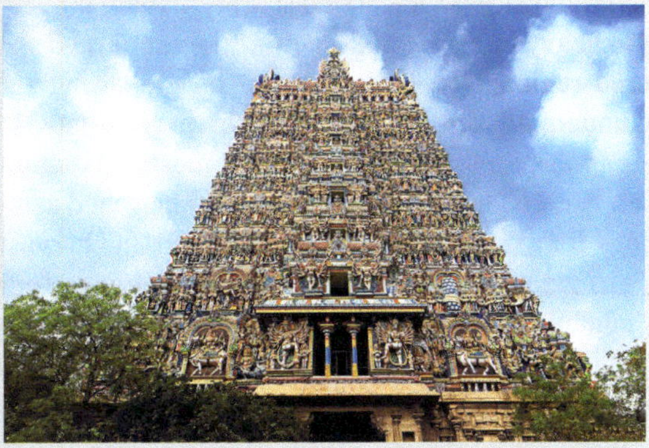

FIGURES 1.3 AND 1.4 (Left) Christ as the Good Shepherd, 17th century, ivory, 17.4 × 6.8 × 5 cm, Goa, India. Creative Commons License, Walters Art Museum, Acquired by Henry Walters with the Massarenti Collection, 1902, 71.324. (Right) Gopura, Meenakshi temple, Madurai. saiko3p/Deposit Photos.

Accounts beginning with Theophilus in 354 CE report a "Thomas Christian" community around his burial site in the state of Kerala. Ivory statuettes mass-produced in Goa by Indigenous artists after the Portuguese arrived in 1510 include enigmatic "rockeries" depicting Christ as the Good Shepherd circumscribed with animals, vegetation, and water on a mountain. They recall the layered appearance of Hindu temple architecture, a multisensory experience of the divine. Whether exported or placed in domestic shrines, rockeries document Christianity indigenous to India.

After Erin Benay, *Italy by Way of India: Translating Art and Devotion in the Early Modern World* (Turnhout: Harvey Miller, 2021).

> civilizational expansion, was fast becoming an end unto itself. *Commodity frontiers* increasingly supplanted resource frontiers. Global expansion rather than regional accretion became the first, best response to socio-ecological problems. . . . What took medieval Europe centuries – settler expansions, mining booms, forest clearance – early capitalism achieved in mere decades. Everything moved faster. The socio-ecological exhaustion of established production zones – in metallurgy, forestry, and sugar planting above all – was now overcome in rapid succession.[5]

The broad argument, sustained by empirical data that Moore collected and analyzed from an extensive range of groundwork studies, is that early modern capitalism was real capitalism in every major respect: labor productivity modification widened and deepened with no systemic reversals, ion accelerated sharply, capital moved into production from farm- ıdustry, and a new scale, scope, and speed of environment-making ıal ecologies across the global network.[6] Enslaved, conscripted, d forms of human work/energy ("labor") were often abused, treated like property no differently from domesticated animals and mechanical equipment. Both people and their animals functioned as instruments along with technology for extracting and purifying silver and harvesting other raw commodities such as wood for use in the mining industry and for export, depriving the rightful inhabitants of their land, resources, and lifeways. When the entire local or regional environment was wasted, or its profitmaking abilities too far diminished, early modern capitalists sought new extractive and uncommodified labor frontiers.

T. J. Demos, whose response to environmental catastrophe I cited in the Introduction, joins Moore to emphasize that Anthropocene's origins are important today because they are "inextricable from early modern globalization, practiced through resource extraction, military conquest, and culture-erasing colonialism."[7] Moore and Demos argue that it is crucial to date the emergence of the Anthropocene "specifically within capitalist, colonial history" because in the century following first contact, "some fifty million Indigenous peoples lost their lives owing to warfare, mass murder, communicable diseases, and forced labor, with colonization disrupting native agriculture and forest management."[8] Moore mentions, but only in passing, new artmaking and technological practices ranging from mapmaking to forms of surveying, schools of painting and music, accounting practices, botany, and techno-sciences such as shipbuilding. The current shift of interest among art historians to "transcultural" approaches in the form of case studies is expanding the field of study to many kinds of previously overlooked colonial objects, inventories, and other records of buying and collecting practices [Figure 1.1–1.4]. Moore's argument could be extended to the study of commercial luxury goods in relation to the emerging "global capitalist world-praxis." The following discussion is focused on the production of knowledge itself as constitutive of capitalist world-praxis.

Aristotle's *Politics* and Amerindian Society

The narrative that follows here is very different from conventional European accounts of art history that begin with Giorgio Vasari's biographies of artists (1550; rev. ed., 1568), J. J. Winckelmann's account of ancient sculpture (1764), or Jacob Burckhardt's praise of individualism and the Italian "spirit" as the hallmarks of modernity that began in the "Renaissance" (1860).[9] The history I am about to sketch in a few strokes has been told many times, but what merits attention in the context of the climate crisis is the role of the arts in defining the humanness of the Indigenous population – *techne* as Aristotle and his early modern interpreters understood it broadly to include all things created to adapt the environment to man's special needs. Theologians, jurists, and missionaries applied Aristotelian arguments to Amerindian peoples in various ways ranging from wholesale acceptance to wholesale rejection of their fully rational status, but whatever position individual authors took, the discourse developed within this frame of reference. Of course, European states are not the only ones that created colonizing empires, a practice known since ancient times all over the world, nor were Europeans ever exclusively responsible for the climate crisis. As argued by the novelist and cultural critic Amitav Ghosh in *The Great Derangement: Climate Change and the Unthinkable* (2016), industrialization dependent on oil also developed in southeast Asia where Cartesian dualism was not the underlying assumption. Nor is environmental degradation exclusively a modern phenomenon. Ghosh cites deforestation in medieval China during an economic revolution in the eleventh century that resulted in the use of coal.[10] Anthropologist Anna Lowenhaupt Tsing cites deforestation in eighth-century Japan to fuel iron forges and build temples as providing conditions for the mushroom delicacy, *Tricholoma matsutake*, to grow.[11] Many more historical examples of environmental degradation exist and deserve study.

If someday a global history of environmental degradation were written, it would certainly look very different from accounts limited to global capitalism, but that is not the point here. European colonial practices enabled global capitalism that caused an unprecedented scale and speed of environmental degradation. These events, I will argue in this Fugue, hold a unique place in the institutional history of the modern idea of art. The record shows that the modern discourse on art is inseparable from the discourse on human exceptionalism, and herein lies this history's untapped emancipatory potential.

The relationship between art and moral character is central to the entire European heritage of thinking about man's place in nature. According to Aristotle, who established the general terms of discussion, art is like virtue, but whereas the deliberations of art result in a product, virtue is the result of "a true and reasoned state or capacity to act with regard to things that are good or bad for men" (*Nicomachean Ethics* 1140b5–6). Practical wisdom, *phronesis* in Greek, *prudentia* in Latin, prudence in English ("mindfulness" is a modern English equivalent), as Aristotle described it, is a process of judging particular facts derived from experience about what should be done and avoided, what is right and wrong, what is good and bad.

The work of art has long been associated with individual judgment in both political theory and the philosophical literature on art and culture. In political theory, the Thomistic/Aristotelian notion of a "work of art" remained an undifferentiated analogy in which the difficulties of judging beauty point to the difficulties of individual judgment in general.[12] In the other strand of this genealogy, the tradition more familiar to art historians, as painting, sculpture, and architecture "rose" from their medieval classification as mechanical arts in Italy and elsewhere in Europe, they became associated with the seven liberal arts and other, newer branches of knowledge, such as optics and navigation, based on a combination of theoretical principles and empirically-based knowledge.

The terms of later discussions are substantially indebted to Aristotle's analogy in the *Physics* (199a12–21) that art is, like nature, an orderly sequence of intelligent actions carried out for the sake of an end product:

> intelligent action is for the sake of an end; therefore the nature of things also is so. Thus if a house, e.g., had been a thing made by nature, it would have been made in the same way as it is now by art [*τέχνη*] . . . If, therefore, artificial products are for the sake of an end, so clearly also are natural products. The relation of the later to the earlier terms of the series [of intelligent actions] is the same for both.

"Art" (Greek *τέχνη*, Latin *ars*) according to Aristotle does not deliberate: the agent with purpose deliberates when s/he makes something. Aristotle calls this agency in nature "the necessary in nature." Art made by humans on the other hand is "necessary on a hypothesis" (*Physics* 199a30–35). When the builder constructs a house, the house is made by the human agent not necessarily but purposefully "on a hypothesis." When mistakes are made, they produce monstrosities in both nature and art. Aristotle established the Western idea of human exceptionalism as the difference between human and animal intelligence, and also between human and animal art, which required the distinction between human rational fantasy, associated with reason and reminiscence, and the fixed imagination of animals, associated with a retentive memory. Aristotle questioned the intentionality of animal behavior, not necessarily the behavior itself. The actions of animals (excepting humans) are hardwired by nature: when the spider makes its web, the bee its hive, they act according to their inborn nature, whereas humans go beyond nature (*Metaphysics* 981a4 ff.).[13]

Aristotle's medieval commentators developed his discussions of the origin of art from individual experience and memory into further distinctions between humans and animals. His most famous thirteenth-century Scholastic commentator, Thomas Aquinas (1225–1274), commenting on Aristotle's argument for human exceptionality, claimed that humans are unique because "man can make for himself instruments of an infinite variety and for any number of purposes."[14]

Aquinas brought Aristotle's association between two processes of individual judgment – the operation of virtue and the production of art – into closer alignment. Debates in political philosophy concerned the relationship between "temporal" political authority and the "eternal Church." In the medieval period, the Latin Christian Church expanded its modes of governmentality through uniform practices, institutions, sacraments, codes, rituals, and doctrines, including colonization overseas through "the mass military incursions known as the Crusades in which the Church functioned as a state without borders," to cite Geraldine Heng's comprehensive study of racial thinking and practices in a variety of media before a recognizable vocabulary of race emerged in the West.[15]

The stakes were high when European presence in the Americas provided new occasions to apply longstanding arguments. Applications of ancient authority for classifying humans as exceptional developed alongside the extraction of raw materials and degradation of the environment in the Americas by European states. The Spanish Crown's principal claim to the Americas rested on the edict "*Inter caetera*" issued by Pope Alexander VI in 1493, which the Treaty of Tordesillas ratified the following year, granting rights to all lands westward of a line drawn through the Atlantic Ocean, while the Portuguese received lands eastward.[16] The authority of the Church granted by the Pope was limited to evangelization, not settlement. The question arose almost immediately as to whether Europeans could legitimately establish settlements if the Pope's authority was limited to the conversion of souls to Christianity. From the 1530s, debates focused on how to define the humanity of Indigenous peoples who were not mentioned in any ancient text. The issue was that if they were not fully human, they could not own property and they could themselves be treated as property in the same way as domestic animals and used to extract gold, silver, wood, and other material resources to benefit their conquerors.

Expanding applications of ancient authority for classifying humans as distinct from all other animals developed alongside the extraction of raw materials and degradation of the environment in the Americas. Crown policy in favor of peaceful conversion is clear in the early documents. Historian Lewis Hanke identifies the earliest royal instructions sent to the governor of Hispaniola, by Nicolas de Ovando in 1501, instructing the clergy to "inform them and admonish them with much love, and without using force, so that they may be converted as rapidly as possible." However, Crown policy in the early years of the Spanish Conquest/Invasion centered on economic expansion. In 1504, King Ferdinand II of Aragon created a commission of civil lawyers, theologians, and canon lawyers to provide moral and legal guidance to grant the king rights to the Amerindians.[17] In this context, longstanding accounts of human experience and cognition developed into new distinctions among humans. Were the Amerindians human or merely humanoid in appearance? Aristotle's *Politics*, a treatise on government based on the constitutions of ancient Mediterranean city-states (polities), provided the framework for discussion. The city-state for Aristotle, as interpreted by his sixteenth-century commentators, was a substitute for the entire human community and understood to be the necessary condition of civilized life.[18] Aristotle classified governments by their kind of rule and, in practice, he favored a constitutional democracy, a city-state or "polity" in which rich and poor respect each other's rights and the best qualified citizens rule by consent of all. Aristotle condemned profitmaking (as an improper use of money) but at the same time, he justified the enslavement of those who had committed some act for which the legal punishment was slavery because "slaves by law" provide a necessary labor force for every civil society.

In addition to such "civil slaves" defined by their legal status, in the *Politics* Aristotle also defined a second, hypothetical kind of slave "by nature" which refers not to an institutionalized practice but to a category of humans who are unable to govern themselves because they have failed to achieve proper mastery over their desires.[19] Such creatures have the power to deliberate, so they are capable of following instructions, but they are incapable of practical wisdom "which issues commands." In the ancient world, as in modern times, the defense of slavery in any form was intended as a justification to enslave members of another society. A number of discussions scattered elsewhere in the Aristotelian corpus have historically been associated with this key text in the *Politics*, which continues by discussing the threshold of the human, distinguishing between possessors of property (mental and physical) and slaves. Chief among related discussions is Aristotle's account of the mental capacity to recollect – that is, to draw a series of inferences, as he and a long history of commentators defined the distinction between the human faculty of memory and the retentive memory of all other animals.

In 1510, the Paris-educated, Scottish Dominican John Major (also spelled Mair; 1467–1550) applied the Aristotelian hypothesis of "natural slaves" to actual Amerindians. The principle of order in society, according to Aristotle, is the determination of what is just (*Politics* 1253a39). Since the state is made up of households, and households are in turn made up of property, the determination of justice inevitably turns on who has a right to own property. In Aristotle's *Politics*, property and justice are themes closely linked to the distinction between man, the political animal "who alone has any sense of good and evil, of just and unjust," and other animals, who are simply beasts (*Politics* 1253a16). When Major (who never saw the Americas) proposed that the Amerindians had no property rights because they were "slaves by nature," his argument potentially eliminated the Crown's need to justify war, that is, conversion by force, because he shifted the terms of discussion from the Crown's juridical rights granted by the Pope to the Amerindians' legal rights in a civil society as dependent on their fully rational status.

In 1511, the King of Spain appointed two jurists to rule on the question of Crown rights, which they addressed in terms of property rights in a civil society, the basis for all exchanges between truly civil men. In 1512, the Crown put the Laws of Burgos into effect, the first detailed regulations governing relations between Amerindians and Spaniards. It was also the first time that Major's argument about natural slavery was employed in Spain. The new Laws forbid enslavement of the Indigenous people although it was legal to organize them into *encomiendas* to grant tribute and provide labor. The colonists were ordered to build churches and instruct their Indigenous workers in Christian doctrine. Abuses and complaints continued against the mistreatment of Indigenous people. In 1532, the Council of the Indies established the first ecclesiastical administrative council (junta) which found that the natives were "rational beings capable of governing themselves" and carrying on "all mechanical and agricultural arts." Yet the next year the ruling was challenged by the Dominican Domingo de Betanzos before the Council.

Other ecclesiastics, including missionaries who worked closely with their Indigenous converts, continued to object to their mistreatment and miscategorization. A complex power struggle between Church and State lasted throughout the period described as "the long sixteenth century." The ability of Amerindians to be Christianized depended on their fully human (fully rational) status. The tension in the political and philosophical contradiction between Church and State runs throughout the early modern discourse on slavery and human rights. Among the most important events that focused discussions of the Amerindians on their mental capacities was a papal decree issued on 9 June 1537 by Pope Paul III against enslaving the Amerindians and seizing their property. The papal bull *Sublimus Deus* pronounced "Indians and all other people who may later be discovered by Christians" to be endowed with the "nature and faculties" necessary to receive the Christian faith solely by "preaching of the word of God and by the example of good and holy living."[20]

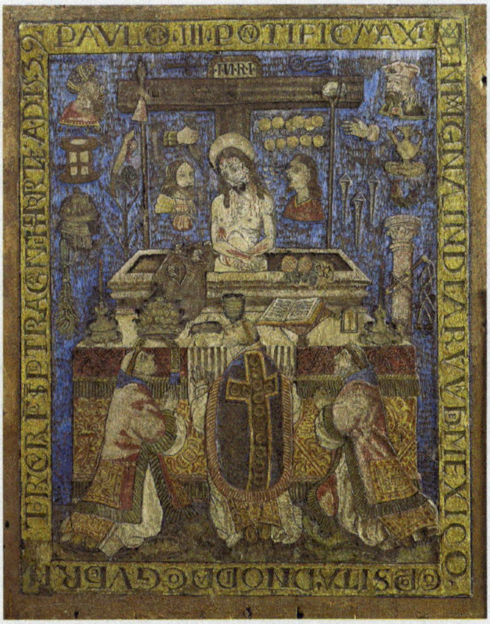

FIGURE 1.5 Nahua *amanteca* (feather artist), Convent School of Pedro de Gante, San José de los Naturales, Mexico City. *Mass of Pope Gregory*, 1539, feather mosaic on wood. Auch, France. Musée des Amériques – Auch, n° inv. 86.1.1. Photo: Musée des Amériques-Auch ©.

Pope Gregory I (c. 540–604 CE), known as Saint Gregory the Great, defended the use of images as the "Bible for the illiterate" because images can illustrate abstract religious concepts visually. According to a legend popular in the fifteenth century, as Gregory was celebrating Mass in the Basilica of Santa Croce in Rome, one of his assistants expressed doubt that Christ was actually present in the host. At that moment, Christ miraculously appeared rising from the altar, surrounded by the instruments of the Passion and displaying his five wounds. Meckenhem's *Mass of Saint Gregory* illustrates the central Christian doctrine of transubstantiation. Grouped around the Eucharistic image of Christ as the Man of Sorrows are rebus-like signs of the Passion known as the Arms of Christ. Each sign serves as an object of sustained contemplation just as a person reading Latin might ruminate over the many senses of Scripture.

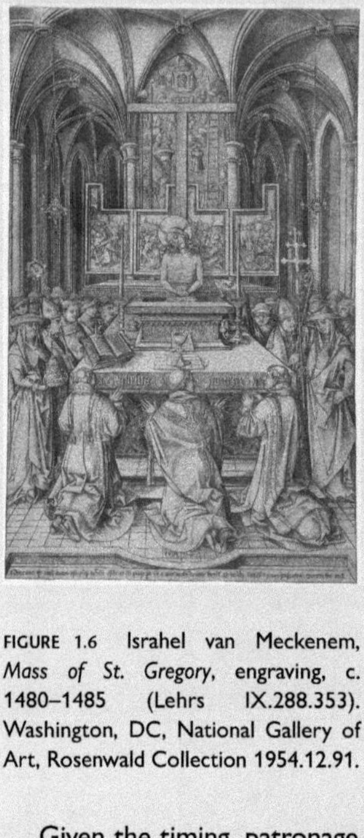

FIGURE 1.6 Israhel van Meckenem, *Mass of St. Gregory*, engraving, c. 1480–1485 (Lehrs IX.288.353). Washington, DC, National Gallery of Art, Rosenwald Collection 1954.12.91.

The *Mass of Saint Gregory* feather mosaic (*amantecayotl*) is the earliest dated work of art surviving from New Spain. Its imagery was directly derived from Meckenhem's engraving or a similar European print [Figure 1.6]. A Latin epigraph dated 1539 frames the image, stating that the featherwork was a gift made (*co[m]posita dono*) for Pope Paul III (designated in the dative case) under the supervision (*cura*) of the Minorite [Franciscan lay brother] Pedro de Gante in the great Indian city of Mexico (*in magna Indiaru[m] urbe Mexico*) directed by the governor (*didaco gubernatore*). Don Diego de Alvarado Huanitzin was the Aztec nobleman appointed governor of the Republic of Indians in 1538 by the first viceroy of New Spain, Antonio de Mendoza (served 1535–1550), at a time when the jurisdictions were still being sorted out. The Indigenous-occupied zone was referred to in the 1530s as "the great city of Tenochtitlan Mexico."

Given the timing, patronage, and choice of subject matter, the significance of this remarkable gift must be sought within a transcultural framework associated with Pope Paul III's bull *Sublimus Deus* issued in direct response to an escalating contest over human and material resources in the Americas. Paul III would have been well-disposed to understand what was implied by the choice of both the subject and the artistic medium, as would any beholder attuned to the ongoing debates over the fully rational status of the Amerindians. The subject and iconography of the Gregorian Mass including the Arms of Christ are also associated with the utopian concept of the universal Christian Church dear to the first

Archbishop of Mexico, the Franciscan Juan de Zumárraga, who was a chief source of the information about evangelization efforts in New Spain that led to Pope Paul III's famous 1537 bull declaring the Amerindians fully rational human beings who could be converted by peaceful means without the use of force.

The didactic message of the Gregorian Mass made it a frequent theme for murals depicted many times on convent walls and ceremonial Church objects during the early years of evangelization when language was an extreme barrier to communication. Pedro de Gante (1486–1572) is the Franciscan lay brother who established the famous mission school of San José de los Naturales (by 1524) where De Gante and other missionaries (including Valadés) used visual images extensively for teaching the catechism to neophytes to prepare them for baptism. This is known from numerous sources including De Gante's own illustrated catechism and the important pedagogical text written and illustrated by De Gante's pupil, Diego Valadés (1533–1579?), a Franciscan friar born and raised in Mexico and another Christianized, assimilated Aztec nobleman like Huanitzin.

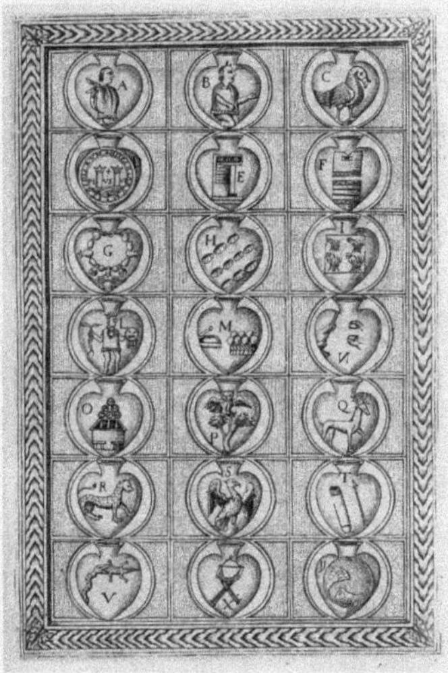

FIGURE 1.7 Diego Valadés, syllabary, *De Rhetorica Christiana* (Perugia, 1579), etching. Getty Research Institute, Call number 378237.

The Franciscans invented a visual/phonetic mnemonic system based on the belief that Amerindians would be more receptive to the Christian catechism communicated in pictures and symbols similar to Nahuatl pictorial writing. Valadés provided engraved illustrations of catechism classes being taught by De Gante in the open-air atrium of the Franciscan mother church at San José using these visual mnemonic signs to teach the Trinity and other basic Christian doctrines. Valadés also introduced a pictographic syllabary of his own involving signs in the shape of sacred hearts, a symbol with connotations on both sides of the cultural and linguistic divide [Figure 1.7]. Although their exact meaning has never been deciphered, the syllabary makes the important point that they are transcultural mnemonic signs with Nahuatl associations.

Valadés described and illustrated the process of cognition according to Scholastic faculty psychology. He focused on the role played by the art of memory in teaching Christian doctrine at San José de los Naturales, where images were also placed in strategic locations along liturgical procession routes. Mnemonic devices attest to the mental capacity of their users to "recollect," that is, to draw a series of inferences to retrieve a memory. Recollection is a distinctly human capacity according to Aristotle and his commentators. His most important Scholastic commentator Thomas Aquinas described memory as the faculty responsible for the conversion of images into abstractions or universals. Aquinas reserved the term recollection to describe a kind of human reasoning, a "quasi-syllogistic search" (*Summa Theologica* 1a, Q. 78, a. 4, response).

The Mass of Saint Gregory amantecayotl was a gift of fealty made at De Gante's school offered to the Pope from the highest government official in the Republic of the Indians. When news of the papal bull *Sublimus Deus* reached New Spain in 1538/39, large processions were held celebrating the Eucharist (*Corpus Domini*), the earliest documented case of Christian Indigenous festivals (described by Fray Toribio de Benevente Motolinia). Don Diego Huanitzin was an erudite, bicultural, multi-lingual nobleman directly related to Moctezuma II who used the language of the conqueror to attest to the fully human capacities of his people, who, in turn, exquisitely crafted his message in their most highly prized form of artistic production. It is perhaps not overstated to claim that by 1539, the terms on which the Amerindians' mental capacities were evaluated were part of an international, transcultural discourse in which the culturally dispossessed also participated. In one of history's unintended ironies, the gift never reached its intended audience. It was probably seized by pirates *en route*, its whereabouts unknown before it appeared on the art market for the first time in 1987.[21]

Pope Paul III addressed complicated issues in no uncertain terms: in the 1537 edict, he sided with the bishops of Tlaxcala and Mexico who corroborated the evaluation of missionaries with extensive firsthand experience. Bernardino de Minaya (c. 1485–c. 1565) went to Rome to meet with the Pope on this issue as did Bartolomé de las Casas (1484–1566), who evangelized widely in the Americas and wrote a treatise, *De unico vocationis modo* (*On the Only Way of Conversion*) on missionary principles he had used in Guatemala. This treatise, and debates between Franciscans and Dominicans on different methods of conversion that it addressed, helped convince the Pope that the Indigenous inhabitants of the Americas have the mental capacity to be converted without resorting to war. Las Casas, who initially supported importing Africans to spare Amerindians, later denounced that position and became the most famous European apologist for Indigenous peoples in the history of Spanish colonialism.[22] Las Casas' lobbying of the Crown also led to the passage of the New Laws of

Burgos in 1542, which legally abolished native slavery although the *encomendieros* were furious and the law was repealed in 1545.

The same arguments also spread by word of mouth and are documented in hundreds of legal cases involving Amerindians and Africans since the early sixteenth century, particularly in slave trading centers like Seville, Spain, and Cartegena de Indias, Colombia. Legal discourses regarding the illegitimacy of enslaving Africans also drew upon shared understandings of a just war, but in this case the arguments depended on establishing their preexisting Christian status in Africa on the understanding that Christians cannot justly enslave other Christians.[23] Legendary accounts that a Christian king, Prester John, had established a Christian nation in Ethiopia were known in Europe since c. 1250 and were fueled by increasing diplomatic ties between Europeans and Ethiopia since the early fifteenth century.[24] The legal precedent for the treatment of Africans was the concession granted by Pope Nicholas V (r. 1447–1455) to Alfonso, the king of Portugal, in 1455, to enslave all the pagans they encountered in the African territories who resisted as the "enemies of Christ." Africans who were forced to make the "Middle Passage" journey from the coast of West Africa to the West Indies and other American destinations in horrific conditions stripped of clothing and possessions, arrived as living "bio-energy," to adapt a term in keeping with Moore's analysis of work/energy. There is no indication discovered so far that cases involving Black Africans, who began arriving as human cargo on ships in the 1510s, were evaluated on the basis of their cultural achievements. Yet Africans arriving in bondage still brought cultural knowledge with them. Robert Farris Thompson began groundbreaking work on African diaspora culture in the early 1980s. Cécile Fromont has recently found Vodun articles preserved in Inquisition documents.[25] In the third Fugue, I devote a separate discussion to the assessment of Black Africans regarding the European discourse on slavery after the sixteenth century.

In the sixteenth century, Pope Paul III's decree was intended to strengthen Holy Roman Emperor Charles V's recent order against enslaving the Amerindians and looting their goods by adding the penalty of excommunication for those who violated imperial law.[26] This history of European events is relevant to the status of Indigenous people based on their *techne* and environmental degradation issuing from the Spanish colonizing mission in the Americas. As the Crown and Church continued their struggle to dominate one another in the Americas, the Pope also navigated complex political differences back home involving his request for aid from the Emperor to fight advances on Europe by the Ottoman Empire while also struggling to keep peace between Francis I of France and Charles V during increasing Protestant unrest in German lands. On 19 June 1538, the day after Charles and Francis signed a peace agreement negotiated by the Pope, Paul III rescinded the penalty of excommunication as the Emperor wished, thus compromising the ability of ecclesiastics to enforce the *Sublimus Deus*.

From the 1530s, HRE Charles V (who was also King Charles of Castile and Aragon, Spain) initiated further attempts to resolve the status and treatment of the Amerindians. The legitimacy of the Conquest became a regular subject for disputation in law and theology faculties of Iberian universities. The central issue was "property" or, in the language of Roman jurisprudence, *dominium rerum*. The Crown's advisors saw an opportunity to strengthen the Catholic Crown's claim that all rights were products of God's laws, not God's grace, as Protestant reformers argued that only the godly prince (Jesus Christ) can be a legitimate ruler. Theologians at the University of Salamanca who, unlike these advisors were not solicited by the Crown, discussed the nature and status of the Amerindians in terms of the law of nature (*ius naturae*). They read Aristotle through Thomas Aquinas on the inventive powers of the mind based in reason as a power peculiar to the rational soul.

Aristotle and Thomas Aquinas were central to the revival of Scholasticism known as the School of Salamanca founded by Francisco de Vitoria and more broadly referring to an intellectual movement by a group of theologians in Spain and Portugal in the sixteenth and seventeenth centuries who dealt with Spanish expansion in the Indies and the challenge of Protestantism to Catholic Christianity.[27] As Catholic theologians, they viewed the Spanish treatment of the Amerindians as a problem about the nature of relations between different groups of men within "the republic of the world" (*respublica totius orbis*). In university lectures and publications that became widely known in Europe, they deliberated the Crown's justification for European settlement (with direct implications for the use of native labor and extraction of material resources) in terms of the Indigenous peoples' ability to form a civil society (a polis).

The historical connections between capitalism, ecology, and the arts become clear from taking a closer look at these arguments and their consequences. Francisco de Vitoria (c. 1492–1546), a member of the Dominican order who held the prime chair in theology at the University of Salamanca from 1529 until his death, gave a series of lectures on the theory of natural law. The most famous was entitled *Relectio de Indis*, delivered 1539, on the nature of Amerindians and the possibility that the Spanish conquests were unjust, based on an Aristotelian and Thomist interpretation of the law of nature. Far from being a secular humanist as some contemporary cultural theorists have claimed, Vitoria was trained in Scholastic philosophy (and studied Logic in Paris with a student of John Major).[28] Both nature and humans have agency, "efficient cause" as defined by Aristotle and discussed by Aquinas as the first God-given law of nature. The question was, if all men are human and their values are grounded in the structure of reality as Aquinas insisted, was the "unnatural" behavior of the Amerindians who allegedly practiced cannibalism and idolatry fully human? All true humans (unlike animals) make moral decisions by distinguishing between good and evil and acting accordingly. On the basis of the account in the *Politics*, Vitoria introduced but then rejected the theory of natural slavery on the grounds that the Amerindians "had a certain rational order in their affairs" because they lived in cities, recognized a form of marriage, had magistrates, rulers, laws, religion, industry, and commerce, all of which require the use of reason.

Vitoria's account of Aristotle's requirements of *techne* for civil life was intended to prove that Amerindians were capable of exercising practical wisdom [*phronesis*] and free will, the requisite for accepting the Christian doctrine of salvation required for baptism. In true Scholastic fashion, he raised objections to his own argument to conclude that Indian communities possessed only the *minimum* requirements for social life – they had no knowledge of the liberal arts, no proper agriculture, no true artisans, and therefore no true *nobilitas*, so it would be impossible for them to live a life of true leisure (*otium*) without European oversight in the Aristotelian and Thomist sense required of a polis. Vitoria's solution, and that of his successors, was that all human cultural behavior was the outcome of "imprinting" or what Aristotle called *ethismos* or habituation (and we call behavioral social conditioning). By this he meant training of the speculative intellect, which requires education first in the liberal arts, then the sciences including knowledge of divine things that is reached after acquiring some understanding of the sensible world.

Over the next three decades, Vitoria's students and their students developed these arguments in their own lectures and publications, rejecting the Aristotelian theory of natural slavery while denigrating the cultural achievements of the Amerindians. If the Amerindians live "almost like beasts and wild animals," Vitoria argued, this is not because they are innately semi-rational, but because their poor education has made them incapable of exercising their rationality – they need the Crown of Castile to hold them and their lands in tutelage until they reach the age of reason, which could be considered an act of charity and might take generations.[29]

The most famous debates on the status of Amerindians as rational creatures were held in Valladolid, Spain, in 1550–1551, between Emperor Charles V's chronicler, Juan Ginés de Sepúlveda, author of a highly respected translation of Aristotle's *Politics* dedicated to Charles V's son, Prince Philip of Spain, and Las Casas.[30] Las Casas is best known today for his polemical account of Spanish atrocities in the Indies, *Brevisima relacíon de la destrucción de las Indias (A Short Account of the Destruction of the Indies)*, first published in 1552. Reprinted many times, published in 1593 with sensationalizing illustrations by the Protestant publisher Theodor de Bry, it fueled resistance to Spanish domination and familiarized readers across Europe with the main features of Las Casas' arguments concerning the mistreatment of Amerindians [Figure 1.8].[31]

Las Casas interpreted the 1493 papal bull of Donation as a charter for evangelization only and Charles V's only legitimate claim to dominium would be if the Amerindians were willing vassals of the Crown. In the debates, Las Casas

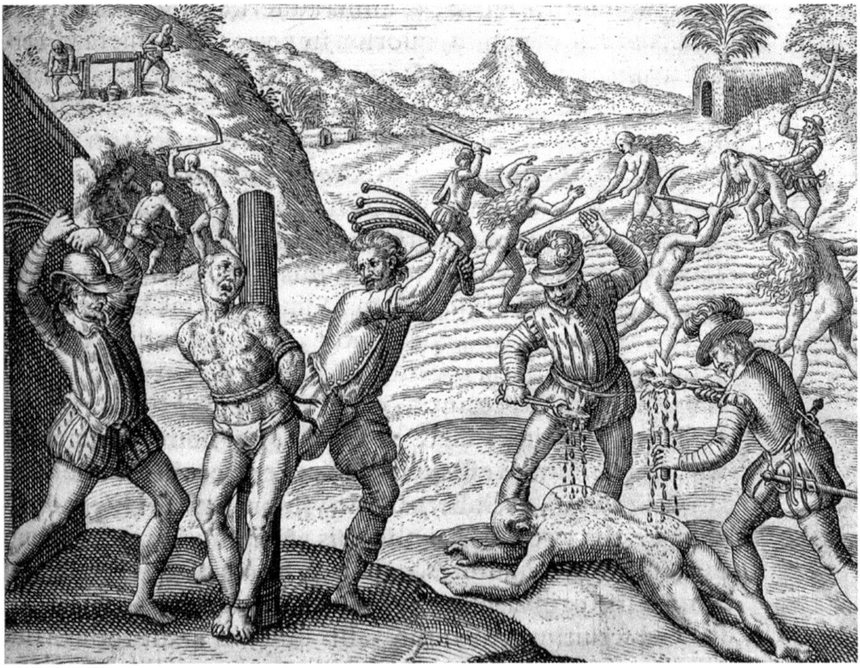

FIGURE 1.8 Bartolomé de las Casas, *Brevisima relacíon de la destrucción de las Indias (A Short Account of the Destruction of the Indies)*, first published in 1552. Reprinted many times, published in 1593 with this sensationalizing illustration by the Protestant publisher Theodor de Bry. Wiki.

was infuriated by the arguments Sepúlveda advanced upholding the Aristotelian theory of natural slavery (for which he had been condemned at the University of Salamanca in 1548). Sepúlveda's views circulated in manuscript before the debate. Immediately after the debate, Las Casas published a summary of both arguments prepared by Vitoria's colleague Domingo de Soto on whether it was lawful for the King of Spain to wage war on the Americans before preaching faith to them.[32]

Vitoria's lecture, *Relectio de Indis,* published in 1557, offered an unprecedented argument for cosmopolitanism based on the time-honored criteria of hospitality and exchange (he cites Saint Augustine): according to the natural right that survived the division of property, Spaniards "have the right to travel or dwell in those countries" and exchange in commerce.[33] Some jurists consider Pope Paul III's unprecedented position on human rights to be the foundation of international law, issued in direct response to an escalating contest over human and material resources in the Americas. Europeanist historians also hail Vitoria's text as a foundational argument for universal human rights based on natural law. In the words of Anthony Pagden, the modern editor of Vitoria's writings, the new movement in theology, logic, and law whose creators were known informally as the "School of Salamanca" restructured theological thinking throughout Catholic Europe by explaining the natural world and man's place within it without recourse to arguments from Christian revelation.

Yet Vitoria's understanding of human rights was flawed from the beginning because it excluded most of humanity from civilized status. At the same time that he claimed fully human rationality for Indigenous people (the necessary condition for their conversion to Christianity), Vitoria also denigrated and misrepresented their cultural achievements. If the Indigenous population did not cooperate, their actions justified war. This was the lead-up to his argument justifying the Crown's claims to entitlement: since the Amerindians are capable of exercising practical wisdom [*phronesis*] and free will, they are capable of becoming Christians and owning their native lands. In this case, the Crown has only one basis for entitlement, the natural law guaranteeing hospitality and commerce that was not taken away by the division of property (*divisio rerum*) by nations accompanying the creation of civil society. Therefore, Vitoria continues:

> the Spaniards may lawfully trade among the barbarians, so long as they do no harm to their homeland. In other words they may import the commodities which they lack, and *export the gold, silver, and other things which they have in abundance*."[34] [emphasis added]

Vitoria justified war if the Indigenous population resisted the Spaniards' natural rights to travel and trade. The novelty of his argument was to introduce the ancient (and subsequently Christian) cosmopolitan principles of hospitality and commerce binding all humans to justify Spanish presence in the Americas, including the use of force if the Indigenous inhabitants refused to cooperate.

Rather than being a defense of human rights across colonial difference, as Walter Mignolo has argued, the claim that hospitality and commerce bind the universal "republic of men" into a single polity was an important initiating argument with vast institutional consequences that *denied* Indigenous people civilized status and justified the extraction of their material resources.[35] Readers of Vitoria's text also learned that he subordinated Indigenous people to their Christian conquerors and characterized them as inferior because they lack *techne*, that is, the arts as defined in the broadest terms by Vitoria's source in Aristotle's *Politics*. Pagden also traced the subsequent history of Vitoria's argument that the natural right of communication and sociability survived the division of lands into property. The *Relectio de Indis* circulated widely in Europe to become one of the earliest and "probably the most consistently influential text on the question of the legitimacy of European imperialism."[36]

Another, less charitable way to put Pagden's account of Vitoria's argument, the natural right to peaceful exchange between states was used to justify war and the extraction of raw materials with its attendant deep damage to the environment and abuse of laborers, which Moore and others discuss as essential conditions of global capitalism in its formative stages. Profits from the silver industry, for example, depended on continuing to identify sources of cheap labor and raw materials, with devastating results to Indigenous peoples and the environment worldwide.

Of course, this is not the view expressed by the distinguished professor of international law, Dr. James Brown Scott, when he honored Vitoria at the University of Salamanca in 1927.[37] Brown Scott stressed Vitoria's belief that "the whole world is in a certain sense a single community [with] the right to prescribe equitable and appropriate laws for its members." European political theorists beginning with the Dutch scholar Hugo Grotius (1583–1645), redeployed Vitoria's arguments to imagine a possible world order based on trade and exchange rather than conquest and occupation. From this came a new historical account of origin and growth of human societies, most fully developed in Adam Smith's "four stages theory" to explain origins of market society but it could be mapped onto others whose differences in cultural behavior was used to account for different stages of historical growth.[38]

The understanding of universal human rights established by Enlightenment thinkers and their sixteenth-century predecessors has recently become the subject of decolonial critique as parochial ideas masquerading as universal concepts.[39] I will return to art and the discourse on cosmopolitanism after Vitoria in the third Fugue, but first more groundwork is necessary to identify the epistemological structures and ontological premises on which Europeans initially made claims for the universality of art as an exclusively human trait in the sixteenth century, in the process denying the civility of those who did not fit their criteria.

Las Casas in Defense of Amerindian Civility

Las Casas wrote an extensive refutation of the natural slavery argument, entitled *Apologética sumaria historia*, which remained unpublished until the twentieth century.[40] He agreed with Vitoria in rejecting claims that the Amerindians were slaves by nature and the only right of the Spanish was the right to preach, but he departed sharply from his fellow Dominican's negative assessment of their civility. Las Casas discussed Amerindian artisans and their craft in the *Apologética* in terms that have been recently described as "a bold statement" in relation to the American populations and "to the art theory that was being written in Europe at the time."[41]

However, the significance of Las Casas' text, viewed transculturally and historically, is actually far less reassuring when compared with the contemporaneous efforts of European writers who argued that artistic practices based on theoretical knowledge should be recognized as "liberal arts." By contrast, Las Casas understood Indigenous artmaking practices as belonging to the lower "mechanical arts."

Reading Aristotle's *Politics* through Aquinas's commentary, Las Casas organized his *Apologética* according to Aristotle's requirement for civil society, defined as a polis composed of social classes, which he divided by geographical region into six: workmen, artisans, warriors, rich men, priests, judges, and a ruler. Las Casas thoroughly rejected claims by Sepúlveda also derived from Aristotle and Aquinas that the Amerindians' mental faculties are limited to learning through imitation and incapable of rising above the achievements of bees and spiders.[42] Las Casas' treatise is dedicated to proving that all Amerindian communities are organized in this way and thus possess civility, despite not being Christian or having a written system of knowledge.

However high his regard was for their artistic achievements, Las Casas forced Indigenous arts and society into a Eurocentric frame of reference. He constructed an image of Amerindian societies as independent collectives each organized in a hierarchy of occupations that depend on *techne*, which he identified as the "mechanical arts" whose purpose is to adapt the environment to meet humans' special needs. The more gifted and hard-working, the more splendid a community's material culture (*Politics* 1256a30 ff.). Thus, Indigenous communities could practice civil virtues, achieve a state of active happiness, and acquire knowledge of moral philosophy, thus meeting all the requirements for a true polis. It was in this context that Las Casas made his extraordinary claim that cannibalism and human sacrifice did not disqualify Amerindians from fully rational status as humans. The argument had already been made by Vitoria based on the unity of the whole species guaranteed by divine revelation. Their religion was part of the world of invention: they might be "satanic in inspiration and foul in practice," but the Mexica and Inca had all the things Christians understood by the word "church," cult, places of worship, and a priesthood, in compliance with Aristotelian requirements for civility (*Politics* 1328a13ff). Sepúlveda challenged this view with the argument that all property relations are the product of civil society. Since the behavior of an entire group consistently violated the laws of nature, Amerindians are not civil beings, providing grounds for a just war and depriving Amerindians of all rights, including their liberty (*dominium corporis suis*), setting up many later arguments for a just war. Furthermore, the Amerindians abused their property and had used their gold and silver only for idolatrous ends.

There is no doubt that Las Casas, like many other missionaries with firsthand knowledge, held the artistic achievements of the Amerindians in high regard. Las Casas, to cite just one brief example from his writings, described the skill of the *amanteca* who placed the feathers in a Mexican featherwork bishop's miter literally in glowing terms [see Figure 1.9]. Directly refuting Sepúlveda, who dismissed the Amerindians' knowledge of "mechanical arts," Las Casas writes in the *Apologética* that the Indigenous peoples possessed skill in the mechanical arts which were a function of the rational soul ("habitus est intellectus operativus'").[43] He

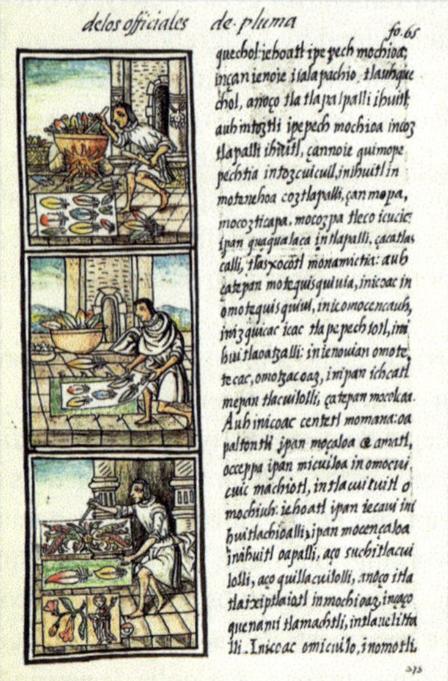

"Looked at from one angle, it will seem golden while lacking gold; from another angle, it will have a green sheen without being green; looked at crosswise, it will display another lovely color; and the same from many other angles, all shimmering marvelously."

Bartolomé de las Casas, *Historia general de las cosas de la Nueva España*, ed. Edmundo O'Gorman and Jorge Alberto Manrique (Mexico City: Porrüa, 1966), 25.

FIGURE 1.9 Bernardino da Sahagún and Nahuatl collaborators. The Florentine Codex, Florence, Laurentian Library, 1577. Artist K, The art of featherworking, Book 9, folio 65r. Top to bottom: Dyeing feathers, affixing feathers, final affixing of feathers. Florence, Laurentian Library. Library of Congress, https://hdl.loc.gov/loc.wdl/wdl.10620

praised their ability in grammar, logic, music, painting, featherwork, and other endeavors, so how did he help to construct an inferior collective identity for the Indigenous peoples of the Americas relative to Europeans?

In the contemporaneous Italian literature on art, by contrast, the new status claimed for painting, sculpture, and architecture as *more* than mechanical arts – sometimes claimed as "liberal arts" – was based on their association with optics, anatomy, poetry, and other branches of natural and moral philosophy requiring theoretical knowledge, that is, knowledge of the principles guiding practice. Benedetto Varchi and Vincenzo Borghini, two humanists closely associated with artists of the first art academy founded in 1563 in Florence under Duke Cosimo de' Medici (1519–1574), defended the eminence of both painting and sculpture by showing how they served the state. They argued that painters and sculptors are by nature *imitatrici*, not *fattrici*, or laborers, because their counterfeiting of a "quality of body or mind" requires an intellectual capacity and can, like oratory, be judged by a universal audience. Varchi divided the arts into Aristotelian categories, distinguishing the liberal from the mechanical arts according to their relative expenditures of *ingegno* and *fatica*, or mental and physical effort (paired qualities that already appear in fourteenth-century vernacular texts on art). Both writers argued that painting and sculpture are higher than the mechanical arts and yet not as high as the intellectual virtues. Las Casas, by contrast, was arguing for the rationality of Amerindians based on a much broader definition of *techne* that covers all occupations that adapt the environment to meet human needs. The next Fugue takes a closer look at the discourse on art that developed in Europe, specifically in Italy during the sixteenth century.

One of the main challenges confronting any attempt to rethink the history of art and material culture on a planetary scale is whether such a history inevitably follows the logic of economic globalization, or whether it can offer an alternative vision that equally respects the multiple subjectivities of the actors involved. The discussion in this first Fugue provides a foundation in the logic and the history of economic globalization framed in terms of dehumanization and environmental degradation. The discourse on art that both denigrated and praised Indigenous *techne,* even though the latter recasts Indigenous societies in a Eurocentric set of values and criteria, confirms but also complicates the narrative history of capitalism as told by Moore and others. In the remaining chapters, I will return to the implications of locating the emergence of modern dehumanizing arguments about art and the origins of society in the initial period of global capitalism. By viewing the events transculturally over several centuries, rather than limiting the frame of reference to secular arguments developed in Europe during the Enlightenment, the narrative throughout focuses on the emancipatory potential of art to imagine a sustainable future out of the existential ecological crisis facing the planet.

Notes

1 Jason W. Moore, "The Rise of Cheap Nature," in *Anthropocene or Capitolocene: Nature, History, and the Crisis of Capitalism*, ed. Jason W. Moore (Oakland, CA: PM Press, 2016), 79.
2 Jason W. Moore, "'This lofty mountain of silver could conquer the whole world': Potosí and the political ecology of underdevelopment, 1545–1800," *The Journal of Philosophical Economics* 4/1 (2010): 58–103.
3 Moore, "'This lofty mountain of silver.'"
4 Jason W. Moore, *Capitalism in the Web of Life: Ecology and the Accumulation of Capital* (London–New York: Verso, 2015), 20, citing Descartes, *A Discourse on the Method of Correctly Conducting One's Reason and Seeking Truth in the Sciences* (1637).
5 Jason W. Moore, "Amsterdam is Standing on Norway, Part I," *Journal of Agrarian Change* 10/1 (Jan 2010): 33–68.
6 Moore, *Capitalism*, 92.
7 T. J. Demos, *Beyond the World's End: Arts of Living at the Crossing* (Durham: Duke University Press, 2020).
8 Demos, *Beyond the World's End*, 9.
9 Jacob Burckhardt, *Die Kultur der Renaissance in Italian* (1860).
10 Amitav Ghosh, *The Great Derangement: Climate Change and the Unthinkable* (Chicago: Chicago University Press, 2016), 96.

11 Anna Lowenhaupt Tsing, *The Mushroom at the End of the World* (Princeton: Princeton University Press, 2015), 6.
12 Howard Caygill, *Art of Judgement* (Oxford: Blackwell, 1989), 11–18.
13 Roger Bacon, *Opus Maius* 2.9 and 2.128.
14 Thomas Aquinas, *De virtutibus in communi*, q. 1, a. 6.
15 Geraldine Heng, *The Invention of Race in the European Middle Ages* (Cambridge–New York: Cambridge University Press, 2018), 31–32.
16 Modified by the Treaty of Tordesillas, ratified in 1494. Tatiana Waisberg, "The Treaty of Tordesillas and the (Re)Invention of International Law in the Age of Discovery," *Journal of Global Studies* 47 (12 May 2017), https://ssrn.com/abstract=2967633.
17 Unless otherwise noted, the following summary is drawn from the publications of Lewis Hanke and Anthony Pagden, with full documentation: Lewis Hanke, *All Mankind Is One: A Study of the Disputation between Las Casas and Sepulveda. . .* (Dekalb: Northern Illinois UP, 1974); Hanke, *The Spanish Struggle for Justice in the Conquest of the Americas* (Dallas: Southern Methodist University Press, 2002); Hanke, "Pope Paul III and the American Indians," *The Harvard Theological Review*, 30/2 (April 1937): 65–102; Hanke, *Aristotle and the American Indians: A Study in Race Prejudice in the Modern World* [1959] (Chicago: University of Chicago Press, 1970). Anthony Pagden, *The Fall of Natural Man: The American Indian and the Origins of Comparative Ethnology* (Cambridge–New York: Cambridge University Press, 1982); Pagden, *Spanish Imperialism and the Political Imagination: Studies in European and Spanish-American Social and Political Theory, 1513–1830* (New Haven–London: Yale University Press, 1990).
18 Anthony J.P. Kennedy, "Political Theory of Aristotle" (May 27, 1999, revised March 2, 2021), *Encyclopedia Britannica*, www.britannica.com/biography/Aristotle/Political-theory, accessed June 8, 2022.
19 Aristotle, *Politics* Book 1, chapter 5–7, especially 1254b16, 1259b27–8, 1260a12.
20 Hanke, "Pope Paul III," is the best source for this documentation.
21 For the documentation of the *Mass of Saint Gregory*, I have drawn on Elena Isabel E. de Gerlero, Donna Pierce, and Claire Farago, "The Mass of St. Gregory," in *Painting a New World*, exh. cat., ed. Donna Pierce, Rogelio Ruiz Gomar, and Clara Bargellini, intro. Jonathan Brown (Denver: Denver Art Museum, distributed by University of Texas Press, 2004), Cat. n. 1, 94–102; Gerhard Wolf, "Incarnations of Light: Picturing Feather in Europe/Mexico, c. 1400–1600," *Images Take Flight: Feather Art in Mexico and Europe 1400–1700*, ed. in Alessandra Russo, Gerhard Wolf, and Diana Fane (Florence: Kunsthistorisches Institut in Florenz and Munich: Max-Plank Institut: Hirmer Verlag GmbH, 2015), 77–90; and Barbara E. Mundy, *The Death of Aztec Tenochtitlan and the Life of Mexico City* (Austin: University of Texas Press, 2015), 99–107.
22 In 1511, Las Casas advised the king to import African slave labor to spare Amerindians, which he was said to have regretted by 1561 after reading Gomez Eanes de Zurara (1410–1474), *Crónica dos feitos da Guiné/The Chronicle of Discovery and Conquest of Guinea*, first published in the nineteenth century. In a widely cited study, Sylvia Wynter, "Unsettling the Coloniality of Being/Power/Truth/Freedom: Towards the Human, After Man, Its Overrepresentation—An Argument," *The New Centennial Review* 3/3 (fall 2003): 257–337, condemned Las Casas' opinions of Africans, but she did not cite this complex history.
23 Chloe L. Ireton, "Black Africans' Freedom Litigation Suits to Define Just War and Just Slavery in the Early Spanish Empire," *Renaissance Quarterly* 72 (2020): 1277–1319, with further bibliography.
24 John K. Thornton, *A Cultural History of the Atlantic World, 1250–1820* (Cambridge: Cambridge University Press, 2012), 16–17.

25 Cécile Fromont, "Paper, Ink, Vodun, and the Inquisition: Tracing Power, Slavery, and Witchcraft in the Early Modern Portuguese Atlantic," *Journal of the American Academy of Religion* 88/2 (2020): 460–504.
26 Hanke, *Theological Review*, 72–73, probably the order dated 2 August 1530.
27 Thomas Izbicki and Matthias Kaufmann, "School of Salamanca," *The Stanford Encyclopedia of Philosophy* (Fall 2023 Edition), ed. Edward N. Zalta and Uri Nodelman. https://plato.stanford.edu/archives/fall2023/entries/school-salamanca/.
28 Pagden, *Fall of Natural Man*, 60–61.
29 Francisco de Vitoria, *Obras de Francisco de Vitoria, Relecciones teológicas* (1527–41), ed. Téofilo Urdanoz (Madrid, 1960), 104.
30 See now, David M. Lantigua, *Infidels and Empires in a New World Order: Early Modern Spanish Contributions to International Legal Thought* (Cambridge: Cambridge University Press, 2020), especially Chapter 4.
31 Catholic Spain's Protestant rivals published his devastating *Account of Destruction of the Indies* in Dutch, French, English, German, 1578–1599. Reprinted along with shorter tracts in many other editions and translations, Las Casas' *Brevisima relacíon* was re-published with illustrations by the Protestant publisher Theodor de Bry in 1598. Surekha Davies, *Renaissance Humanism and the Invention of the Human: New Worlds, Maps, and Monsters* (Cambridge: Cambridge University Press, 2016), 176–178, 219–227.
32 Sepulveda's basic thoughts on just war were published in Rome, but in October 1550 the Council of the Indies ordered that the book, printed without a license, not be allowed to be sent to the Americas.
33 Francisco de Vitoria, *Relectio de Indis* (1539), ed. L. Pereña and J. M Pérez Prendes (Madrid, 1967), 97, translation cited from Pagden, *Fall of Natural Man*, 90. Francisco de Vitoria, *Political Writings*, ed. Anthony Pagden and Jeremy Lawrance (Cambridge [UK]: Cambridge University Press, 1991), Question 3, article 8, § 18, p. 290. The list of arts required for a civil society is based on Aristotelian criteria for distinguishing civil from barbarian societies. Pagden, in Vitoria, *Political Writings*, 290, n. 88.
34 Vitoria, *Political Writings*, 279. Question 3, Article 1.
35 Walter Mignolo, "The Many Faces of Cosmo-polis: Border Thinking and Critical Cosmopolitanism," in *Cosmopolitanism*, ed. Carol A Breckenridge, Sheldon Pollock, Homi K. Bhabha, and Dipesh Chakrabarty (Durham–London: Duke University Press, 2002),157–189, at 166–167, 174.
36 Anthony Pagden, "Stoicism, Cosmopolitanism, and the Legacy of European Imperialism," *Constellations* 7/1 (2000): 3–22, at 7.
37 James Brown Scott, *The Spanish Origin of International Law: Francisco de Vitoria and his Law of Nations* (Oxford: Clarendon Press, 1934).
38 Pagden, *Fall of Natural Man*, 1.
39 See Fugue 5.
40 Bartolomé de Las Casas, *Apologética historia sumaria (1551–)*, ed. Edmundo O'Gorman (Mexico City, 1967) 2 vols. The date of Las Casas' *Apologética* is disputed: Pagden, *Fall of Man*, 119.
41 Alessandra Russo, "An Artistic Humanity: New Positions on Art and Freedom in the Context of Iberian Expansion, 1500–1600," *RES* 65/66 (2014/2015): 353–363, at 361; Russo, *A New Antiquity: Art and Humanity as Universals, 1400–1600* ((University Park, PA: Pennsylvania State University Press, 2024). Russo relies partly on George Kubler's misleading claim in *Aesthetic Recognition* of *Ancient Amerindian Art* (1991) that Las Casas' Aristotelian account was a rudimentary history of art and partly on secondary sources by Robert Williams and Larry Shiner that do not mention ecclesiastic writers associated with Church reform, the subject of the next Fugue. See Russo, *A*

New Antiquity, 106–127, on Las Casas' career and his extensive praise of *artificers* (art makers) in the *Apologética* in terms of his universalism, which she does not situate in the intellectual context of Aristotle's *Politics* or the historical debates on the humanity of Amerindians discussed in this Fugue.

42 The artwork of bees and spiders was noted by Roger Bacon and interest in animal architecture was revived at the end of the nineteenth century. See Fugue 4.

43 Las Casas, *Apologética historia*, chapters 61–65.

FUGUE 2

HOW THE EUROPEAN DISCOURSE ON ART SHAPED ACCOUNTS OF HUMAN EXCEPTIONALISM

Concepts of art, of being human, of who is considered human, and how to relate to each other as humans mutually defined one another over several centuries. This Fugue focuses on the construction of new categories in the sixteenth-century European literature on art. Using a transcultural approach, it reflects on ways that studying the historical idea of human exceptionalism as it is interwoven with the emerging discourse on art can advance our interconnectedness with the planetary life-support system that so urgently needs to be restored. The first Fugue introduced two separate historical trajectories for understanding art as the product of human reasoning, both indebted to Aristotle and brought into closer alignment by Thomas Aquinas in the thirteenth century. In political theory, the Thomistic notion of a "work of art" remained an undifferentiated analogy in which the determination of beauty served as the test case for individual judgment. In the case of judging artistic images, highly nuanced arguments involving the justification of images in Christian worship were debated in the latter half of the sixteenth century. What John O'Malley, a leading specialist in the religious culture of early modern Europe, calls a "wave of moralizing reform" spread over parts of Europe, notably wherever Calvinist Protestantism and to some degree Catholic influence were strong.[1] The Church of Rome tried to defend and clarify Catholic doctrine after decades of Protestant attacks, including the violent destruction of images and church furnishings, by establishing the Inquisition (1542), the Council of Trent (1545), and the Congregation of the Index (1571) which issued lists of prohibited books (and had unrealized plans to do the same for music and the visual arts), all mechanisms of censorship and institutional control.[2]

The time-honored role traditionally granted to artists to interpret sacred subject matter was definitively rejected by the Church of Rome at the ecumenical

DOI: 10.4324/9781351023429-4

Council of Trent (meeting intermittently from 1545–1563) at its final session on December 3–4, 1563. Its Decree on Images reads in part:

> [in] the sacred use of images, every superstition shall be removed; all aiming at base profit must be eliminated; finally, all sensualness (*lascivus*) must be avoided so that figures shall not be painted or adorned with a beauty exciting to lust . . . And lastly, bishops should give very great care and attention to ensure that in this matter nothing be placed on view that is disorderly or arranged in an exaggerated or riotous manner, nothing profane and nothing unseemly, since holiness befits the house of God.[3]

Responding to Protestant charges of idolatry, the Council's decree upheld the necessity of images in worship but rejected the explicit display of artifice for its own sake. It attempted to control interpretation by imposing an improved and proper "fit" between the subject of representation, the way in which it is presented, and the audience for whom the representation is intended – time-honored issues of decorum (to use the rhetorical term). The appearance of the work of art, that is, its artifice, was considered an optimal instrument for enlivening the beholder by appealing to his emotions and imagination through his senses. Today, scholars agree that there is no such thing as a "Tridentine style" in the modern sense of style, but Trent had an impact on artists, patrons, and others with vested interests "to the point that it is legitimate though perilous to speak of Tridentine art," O'Malley writes.[4]

Trent's decree on sacred images was brief and general. Sacred images were not even an issue at Trent until the final month of its final session. However, the image debates in the fifteen years prior to 1563 were far more important than the Council records indicate, and many new sources became available after the unsealing of the Vatican Secret Archive in 1998. An important contributing factor to the Council's decision in 1563 were debates during the middle decades of the sixteenth century on the veneration of images among Catholic theologians, part of the revival of Scholasticism in Rome, Paris, and Salamanca. These debates applied the arguments from the Byzantine image controversies to practical problems such as evangelization and the legality of slavery.[5] As far as the argument of this book is concerned, it is significant that Vitoria's students were centrally involved in these debates and also participated in the Council of Trent (1545–1563). Justifying the use of images by accounting for the cognitive process of veneration on Aristotelian and Thomistic terms, Catholic writers including the "School of Salamanca" discussed in the first Fugue also selectively drew upon recently rediscovered records of the Byzantine image controversies, notably the records of the only other occasion on which the Catholic church as an institution made a universally binding, official declaration on the use of artistic images, the Seventh Ecumenical Council, known as the Second Council of Nicaea (787). Published in a new Latin edition in 1540, the canons from Nicaea emphasized the indispensable role of images in aiding human memory to stimulate devotion, terms that augmented the Scholastic defense and contributed behind the scenes to the final Decree in 1563.[6]

The justification of images was based on the claim that the honor paid to the image passes over to its prototype, that is, to the holy person depicted. The key question was the problem of its materiality, which raised seminal questions about the psychology of visual perception. Thomas Aquinas used Aristotle's theory that cognition begins from the senses to explain that images are observed in a twofold "movement of the soul" (*motus animi*) fundamentally different from one another. One movement observes the image as image, the other observes the thing it represents, its "prototype" to use the theological term. Limiting the worshiper's engagement to the referential function of the image, Aquinas denied any ontological connection between the image and its prototype. This semiotic argument avoids the central concern regarding idolatry, namely the question of divine presence in the material image, by treating the image exclusively as an immaterial sign.[7]

In the late 1540s, there were significant disagreements regarding religious images among established Catholic theologians around the key problem of materiality in which Aquinas's analytical framework provided the terms of discussion. Debates while the Council of Trent was in session (1551–1552) were centered in Rome around the papal court, led by Dominican theologians such as Cardinal Marcello Cervini, a sophisticated humanist scholar involved in the rediscovery of the Second Council of Nicaea documents.[8] To cite one example significant for its similarity to post-Tridentine art treatises that endorse pictorial artifice beyond the semiotic function of images, the Dominican French inquisitor, Matthieu Ory (1492–1557), wrote two unpublished treatises, both dated 1552, dedicated to Cervini, as recently studied by Wietse de Boer. Defending the Thomist argument that the image *as image* is restricted to its semiotic function, Ory also argued that the notion of the image *as a thing* includes features like color, artistic quality, correspondence with the prototype, and setting or location. Ory maintained the notion that images could be adored as signs and he acknowledged the importance of rhetoric as the art of persuasion necessary to instruct the illiterate masses.[9]

Aquinas's analytical framework focused on the distinction between the image as a sign and a thing also informed heated discussions at Trent, but fear of controversy at its final council was enough "to muffle" the acknowledgment of different interpretations in the Tridentine decree.[10] The greatest challenge that reform-minded ecclesiastics who fleshed out the Decree on Images faced in the following years was in defining the *proper limits* of artistic license, given that the justification of images in worship had focused on the semiotics of veneration solely as a cognitive process. The disagreements surrounding sacred images concerned ontological issues, but as the text cited above from the Tridentine Decree shows, discussions were conducted in terms of rules derived from literary theory governing artifice. Unsurprisingly, no one could agree on the rules, much less on how to enforce them. A complex set of intersecting historical issues confronted any late sixteenth-century European writer who wished to redirect the discourse on art toward objective truth. There is a consensus that, after Trent, praise of the artist's unlimited license to invent images out of his imagination quickly dropped out of the literature.[11] Roman Catholic writers directed the discussion of artistic license and imagination to emphasize the role of God in the artist's creative process and the acquisition of adequate representational skills for making sacred images that conform both to Scripture and nature.

In its Christian formulation, the "truth" of the artistic representation was crucial for it justified the use of images in religious worship altogether. On the opposite side of the sixteenth-century image theory controversies, Protestant Reformation writers developed sophisticated theological arguments on the dangers of idolatry that protested the accumulation of material things as an issue of social justice.[12] One of the most significant theological contributions to the sixteenth-century discussion of idolatry was Ulrich Zwingli's analysis of the psychological roots of false worship couched, like Francis Bacon's discussion a century later, in terms of "inner" and "outer" idols.[13] In 1525, Zwingli defined the idol as a "portrait of a strange god" that is established in man's heart before it is expressed externally in a work of art.[14] The inner idol, or "Abgott," is anything that displaces God, be it money, glory, or another deity: as man becomes reliant on these "strange gods" within, Zwingli argued (in terms that Marx would later develop into a critical theory of the political economy), they inevitably lead to some specific external form because of the human need to comprehend reality through material means.[15] What the mind of man grasps is always made into an image: externalization of the inner gods inevitably finds expression in a physical idol. For Calvin, too, the root of idolatry is located in man's efforts to domesticate God: man transferred the honor due to God to material objects. One of Calvin's most popular published works against idolatry, *The Inventory of Relics (*1543), compares idolators to unreasoning beasts and considers idolatry an ever-present danger because men are by nature "metaphysically deranged."

The discourse on the grotesque and monstrous developed first in Protestant Reformation writings. Zwingli's condemnation of idolatry as first an inner monstrosity leading to outward manifestations is one extreme position in the critical spectrum. Other, mostly Italian, writers discussed the artist's inventive powers in positive terms using the same metaphors connoting the difference between the rational intellect and the sub-rational powers of the imagination. What is at stake in all these arguments is the ontological distinction between a lifeless commodity and the living, divine presence in human form. Idols may delight or inspire fear, but in either case they are deceptive because they disguise their true ontological status. While Protestant Reformation theologians denounced lavish religious displays and material aids as idolatrous, Catholic missionaries and theologians levied charges of idolatry against their converts, the newly colonized subjects of European monarchies.[16] Relationships of power materialized in such complex exchanges simultaneously taking place at close range and over long distances. It is important to bear in mind that the same Aristotelian theory of human cognition arising from sense experience underlies all the arguments.

Framing a Transcultural Approach to Catholic Reformation Art Theory

To pursue the question of how the discourse on art shaped accounts of human exceptionalism in the sixteenth century, one of the main challenges is to think otherwise about the "thought structures" that define the parameters of research. Art defined as the object of individual aesthetic contemplation is a relatively recent construct that developed between the sixteenth and nineteenth centuries. In the following analysis of sixteenth-century texts, I intentionally avoid anachronistic stylistic terms that are still widely used because they project categories, ideas, and biases that hinder our capacity to think otherwise about the primary sources. The most problematic term as far as the following discussion is concerned is "mannerism" which was first applied to the sixteenth century by seventeenth-century art theorists, notably the Bolognese-born ecclesiastic, a Papal diplomat and art theorist, Giovanni Battista Agucchi (1615); the Roman writer Giovan Pietro Bellori (1672); and the Bolognese writer Cesare Malvasia (1678).[17] They used the word *maniera* ("manner" or "mode") as a pejorative term to describe the art of the later sixteenth century that departs from natural appearances.[18] Their negative views were widely adopted by nineteenth-century art historians who applied the term "mannerism" to define more general trends. The Italian historian and archaeologist Luigi Lanzi who wrote a history of Italian painting (1792) organized by regional "schools," is widely recognized today as the first to adopt investigative research methods that do not depend entirely on individual biography. For Lanzi and many others, the term "Mannerism" defined a decline that began in Florence and Rome after 1530–1540 when artists allegedly based themselves solely on their imaginations and adopted quick ways of working rather than studying nature and ancient sculpture directly.[19] Lanzi and many other nineteenth-century historians understood Mannerism, much as their seventeenth-century predecessors had understood personal *maniera*, as the portrayal of the human figure and virtual space in ways that depart from the harmonious classicism and idealized naturalism they associated with "Renaissance art" in the first two decades of the sixteenth century.

In 1925, Walter Friedländer inverted these long-established critical values when he presented his theory of a new experimental style born in Florence around 1520, which he also called Mannerism.[20] There are actually two different mannerist eras under discussion: the initial departure from High Renaissance ideals that began in Florence c. 1520; and the development of Mannerism as a broadly practiced set of conventions popular around the mid-sixteenth century. Vasari's "bella maniera" refers to the latter in which Vasari also participated. In Friedländer's view, a younger generation of artists following the death of Raphael (1483–1520) disregarded nature for expressive purposes, replacing the balanced naturalism of the previous generation with unreal spatial formations, anatomical distortions, and subjective rhythmic structures that he considered anti-classical.

Friedländer wrote a second essay, less frequently cited, originally published in 1929, on why certain artistic practices abruptly came to an end around 1580–1590. Various artists from different Italian centers, all sharply opposed to the basic premises of Mannerism, Friedländer argued, reveal a coherent, new artistic spirit in their treatment of religious subjects. This group of painters who had no direct relationship with one another, "appear united in a general trend toward greater pictorial immediacy and directness in dramatic presentation" which Friedländer connected to the new religious spirit that orders like the Franciscans and reformers such as Carlo Borromeo were promoting at the time, as distinct from but connected to the seventeenth-century "age of the Baroque."[21] The complex issue of what and how post-Tridentine or Counter-Reformation artistic practices have been defined historically in art criticism is the subject of an extensive body of scholarship that remains tightly focused on these sources.[22] Today, the emphasis is on the new reformed orders such as the Jesuits, the Barnabites, and the Theatines, but the embrace of a literal, idealized representation of nature in the late sixteenth century continues to be associated with the "reform" of painting intended to appeal both to learned connoisseurs and the common people (*popolani*).

When the term "mannerism" was reconsidered again in the 1960s, the scholarship accepted Friedländer's descriptions but attached entirely different meanings to the formal features of Mannerism. Art historians turned their attention to visual structures such as antithesis, which they understood with reference to contemporaneous literary theory based on classical rhetoric and associated with the revival and imitation of antiquity. This generation of scholars considered "mannerist" traits more in terms of stylistic modes rather than the practice of a Mannerist style, but the reason for their inquiry was still to examine how the term *maniera* was used historically so that "we may compare our modern concepts of Mannerism" derived from studying the formal features of the art. However, they never questioned the value of defining period styles based on formal features, that is, on the appearance of works of art.

The term "mannerism" and its main cognate *maniera* took on broader significance for the field of art history at this critical moment of self-reflection because it shifted the discussion from *what* something means to questions of *how* the work of art bears meaning in a relational way, in a particular time and place, for a particular audience. The idea that style could be defined historically in rhetorical terms was groundbreaking because it considered how the work of art formally, visually conveys culturally specific content to an informed audience. Nonetheless, these art historians considered only a narrow cluster of terms, ideas, and texts without much historical context because they understood the history of art to be concerned with a succession of formal styles. This project was long over by the 1980s, but the construction of classicism versus mannerism as successive or contrasting period styles is still widely used.[23]

In the following discussion, my first point is that these *new* formalist concerns (with their significance to their audiences defined historically) open up many other questions: what happens when values, beliefs, and information are *not* held in common? What happens in such a case if we focus on the heterogeneity of the audience, or of the artwork itself? How have different styles and even entirely different systems of signification come into contact and transformed into something unprecedented? Chief contributors to the debates regarding mannerism since the 1960s such as Craig Hugh Smyth recognized an important difference between sixteenth- and seventeenth-century discussions of *maniera* but they did not explain *why* the meaning of the term and its critique changed abruptly to condemn fantasy and capriciousness. Vasari, for example, praised artistic license within the rules and associated "*la bella maniera*" with the idealized imitation of nature (1550), and even Ludovico Dolce (1557), singled out as a direct antecedent to Bellori for his negative views on *maniera* as monotonous and lifeless, did not blame these deficiencies on the capricious imagination of artists as writers in the seventeenth century uniformly did.

My second point is that "Mannerism" and other modern stylistic and period labels invented by nineteenth-century art historians impose anachronistic categories on the historical evidence that also played a significant role in excluding or demoting many other kinds of cultural artifacts. To take a more contemporary example, Hans Belting's widely cited formula (1990) that medieval cult images were replaced in the Renaissance by a "cult of images" remains largely unquestioned.[24] Belting claimed that the cult image was transformed from something that formerly had been assigned a special reality and taken literally as a visible manifestation of the sacred person into the modern, secular notion of art as the product of the artist's imagination, now granted the same agency as the Divine. Belting imposes a linear model of progressive change and entrenched binaries on what is actually a much more complex history: according to his reductive scheme, first there were religious images, then there was secular art. Belting never mentioned the intense sixteenth-century debates over religious images and the redirection of the artist's imagination by writers sympathetic to the Council of Trent's evolving position that is the subject of this Fugue.

To follow the consequences of such reductionism a step further in preparation for the following discussion, Belting's *Florence & Baghdad: Renaissance Art and Arab Science* (2011) addresses intersections between signifying practices associated with different cultural systems and worldviews to develop a model of exchange that does not suffer from Eurocentric assumptions.[25] There is both urgency and justification for taking up the subject at the heart of Belting's study of Arab science and Renaissance art, which unfolds from his insight that the same theory of optics, that is, the same explanation for the action of light and the process of vision leading to cognition, hence understanding of the world, had two very different historical outcomes in their Islamic and European Renaissance contexts, respectively (his terms, not mine). Yet Belting fails to realize these goals due to the same unexamined assumptions that history is linear and art "represents" social identity. He argues that the contribution of Ibn al-Haytham to Western ideas of pictorial perspective has been overlooked by art historians and was delayed until art based on science was "liberated from every kind of theological baggage" because the artist was considered the author of the work.[26]

Belting's key assumption is contradicted by the Christian context which continued to inflect the role of the artist in specific ways. The material side of religion, of course, is art – broadly defined, both include many different types of cultural production, textual, material, visual, oral, ritual, time-based, static, and so on. In fact, religion itself should also be a contested term – it would be less of a specific historical and cultural imposition to say "belief system," defining "belief" and "system" just as broadly as "art." We don't usually think of Western styles of representation as ideologically freighted by the ontological concerns of Christianity, but it was precisely on this basis that naturalism informed by the science of optics was deemed to conform to human ways of knowing based on sense experience. The very palpable *danger* of art, and especially art that imitates the way nature appears to the sense of sight, as documented from Plato to Early Modern writers engaged in Church reform, lay in its tendency to *jeopardize the stability of institutionally imposed values*, thus endangering the health of society. What is important to stress here is the understanding of *artifice as a form of truth*, as writers engaged in Church reform emphasized.

Belting missed the opportunity to investigate the complex processes of transculturation in his study of optical theory in the Mediterranean. He uses terms such as "East" and "West" as if they were ever-present natural entities; and he collapses "Islam," "Arab," and "Arabic" into one interchangeable category on the basis of a brief caveat at the beginning of the book to the effect that the Arabic language was the *lingua franca* of Islam (the language of the Qur'n, which could not be translated). Arabic language and Arab as an ethnic term are used interchangeably, with the unfortunate result that Constantinople during the period it was ruled by the Ottoman Turks is discussed as being just as "Arab" as the rest of Islam, even though the Turks were neither Arabs nor Arab-speaking and Constantinople, by the direct order of Sultan Mehmed II at the point of conquest in 1453, ordered a diversity of populations – Christian, Jew, Moslem – to be relocated from all parts of the empire so that its new capital could become a microcosm of the empire as a whole. This was a very different model of social identity from the homogenous model of the modern nation-state. Islamic understanding of a healthy society was one that thrived on heterogeneity, a topic that never came up in Belting's book. It would have played havoc with his reductive thesis that the tenth-century philosopher Ibn al-Haytham never saw pictorial images and therefore drew no connections between internal images and external pictorial representations in his treatise on optics.

To state the case for the agency of the artist in Christian sacred art systemically, in structural terms, the Eucharist and the bodily relic are the most sacred kind of Christian objects (or matter) in a hierarchy ordered according to proximity to the Divine. Throughout the Middle Ages, the Eucharist was treated like a bodily relic, though its actual physical presence was slight compared to the presence of the Divine located in it. Even for those, like Thomas Aquinas, who raised doubts about the presence of the divine in [some] bodily relics, the Eucharist occupied the top of the semiotic hierarchy that secured the entire system of belief because it remained the one case in which the sign and its referent are identical – that is, the consecrated bread and wine *are* Christ not just signs *of* him. Locating the presence of the Divine in a material object establishes the truth of the central Christine doctrine of salvation in a form accessible to humans. In the economy of the Christian motivational system, the efficacy of a contact relic, like the Shroud of Turin, likewise depends on the presence of the Divine in the material object. In this case, the sacred image is made when the shroud comes into direct contact with the Divine. From within the belief system, this constitutes actual contiguity: an indexical claim about direct physical contact with the Divine is made for any image miraculously made without human hands [*achiropoïetes*]. The efficacy of a particular relic might be contested or denied outright, and in actual practice different categories of relics were often conflated in a single object, but the logic of direct contact (construed in a wide variety of ways) between the divine and created matter remains the basis for making as well as denying claims about sacred Christian objects to this day. With the questioning of the academic system of institutionalized instruction beginning in the later eighteenth century and associated with the label "Romanticism," appreciation for the artist's unlimited creative powers established the idea of artistic genius as independent giftedness – grace endowed by a higher power, perhaps, but not subservient to the institutional controls of religion or the state. To apply this understanding of artistic genius to the sixteenth century is anachronistic.

The semantic mutability of the concept of style, as Philip Sohm proposes, can be productively understood as a receptive ground onto which writers project their personal views.[27] A key finding in the following discussion is that the different ways in which the word "*maniera*" and its cognates were used in the later sixteenth-century Italian literature on art that Friedländer associated with a new religious spirit yields important information about the construction of theories of human exceptionalism. What sociologist Pierre Bourdieu, borrowing the concept of field from the physical sciences, calls a "field of cultural production" situates works of art within the social conditions of their production, circulation, appropriation, and consumption where goods, services, knowledge, status, and competitive positions are held by actors with different kinds of resources to power (capital). According to Bourdieu's concept, a field brings separate units such as institutions, organizations, markets, individuals, and groups into a broader framework that stresses their relational properties rather than their intrinsic features.[28] A relational approach grounds the agent's actions in objective social relations and brings to the fore the multiple forces shaping behavior.[29]

My analysis takes a relational, transcultural approach to the period texts that builds upon Bourdieu's concept that a field is broader than a community in which interests that individuals do not share may still link their actions in a socio-cultural-political network that produces concrete effects. This framework is similar to Foucault's concept of a discursive formation, but it places more emphasis on individual agency. When ecclesiastical writers such as Giovanni Andrea Gilio da Fabriano, Johannus Molanus, Gabriele Paleotti, and Carlo Borromeo began to flesh out the Church's increasingly absolute position on the kinds of artistic images suitable for use in religious devotion, they supported a return to naturalistic observation. The scientifically-based "naturalism" that dominated trends toward the end of the sixteenth/beginning of the seventeenth century was interpreted at the time as being "*devoid* of seductive artifice," despite the fact that artists had to have a great command of proportion theory, perspective, anatomy, drawing skills based on the direct observation of nature, and the ability to combine individual elements into a coherent, idealized representation defined according to certain rules to engage the viewer's senses. The understanding of the idealized imitation of natural appearances as a form of sensuous attraction that is *not* seductive was aligned with Tridentine reforms.[30] What they did *not* embrace is the subject of the following analysis.

Rethinking Binary Approaches to Art History

The legibility of an idealized imitation of nature (assumed to be universally accessible to all viewers, though its colonial applications certainly proved otherwise) and the teachability of artifice rendered on these terms, made Western styles of representation an ideal vehicle to express other forms of institutional authority. We currently identify a framework of modern ideas about art with a secular process that began during the eighteenth century when European writers interested in establishing the origins of culture constructed the idea of "primitive" art and distinguished it from art of the classical tradition. Art historian Frances Connelly aptly describes this dynamic antimony operating in Enlightenment texts, collecting practices, and many other forms of material culture as the "classical norm cast[ing] the 'primitive' as a dark mirror image of itself."[31] She consulted philosophical treatises in natural philosophy, travel accounts, ethnographic studies, art criticism, popular literature, and a wide variety of material evidence to find that this thought structure remained unchanged at the end of the nineteenth century. Classicism, with its rational principles of composition and design, provided the standard or norm for assessing the (anti-rational) culture of "primitive people," emblematized in the "arabesque" or the "grotesque ornament." The anti-rational "grotesque" provided a *systemically necessary periphery* to the classical. In some cases, the Romantic fascination with the grotesque and the monstrous, Connelly writes, led European artists to study and directly incorporate elements of non-Western design directly into their work.

Connelly locates the first crucial definition of "primitive" art in Giambattista Vico's *La scienza nuova* of 1725, and her groundbreaking account ends with what was previously understood to be the beginning of primitivism, Pablo Picasso's *Demoiselles d'Avignon* of 1907. Vico and many others who made the same distinctions assumed that early peoples lacked the power of reasoning (ratiocination) but possessed a robust and vigorous imagination. On these grounds, "primitive" humans, in contrast to Europeans, were thought to be deeply immersed in their immediate sensory experiences without the mediation of abstract reasoning. Some writers, like Jean-Jacques Rousseau (1712–1778), ennobled early peoples precisely because they were thought to live in *harmony* with nature, but for most writers working with European ideas, these "Others" were assumed to possess minimal cultural traditions and to live with little awareness of the past or future. Their inability to abstract from experience was thought to explain the "absence" of European artistic styles of representation based on the techniques of chiaroscuro and linear perspective associated with academic artistic instruction. Basically, the same assumptions about human character expressed in their cultural practices animated Kant's writings on anthropology at the end of the eighteenth century, as I will discuss in the next Fugue.

In approaching the primitive as a framework of ideas, Connelly found that a surprisingly small set of terms and a common set of expectations provided the conduit through which the notion of "primitive art" was codified over several centuries, appropriated by European artists, and translated into European experience. She identifies a cluster of terms and ideas that my own study shows already appear in the sixteenth-century literature on art: grotesque, ornament, caricature, hieroglyph, and idol established the categories associated with "primitive art" that Europeans used to articulate the issues and justify their domination of "primitive" societies. At the end of the eighteenth century, these terms were used interchangeably to describe the astonishing creativity found in many "primitive" arts. *Ingegno*, ingenuity, inventiveness, all connoted native wit or natural ability with various shadings but, as Connelly documents, in the absence of the classicizing representational skills taught in academies of art, ingenious "ornament" and "decoration" were often presumed to be due to a lack of reason as well as the skill that separated them from the "civilized" peoples of Europe. Connelly presents extensive citational evidence regarding double-edged praise for concrete works of art ranging from Maori carvings to the Aztec (Mexican) codices collected by kings, attitudes that are confirmed in numerous accounts of racialized climate theory in a variety of genres.

Connelly argued further that the presumption of reason as the governing artistic faculty taught in art academies all over Europe framed the key characteristic of "uncivilized" imagery as unreason. All manner of art was excluded from the European category of fine art established in the eighteenth century, lumped together as "ingenious" and "full of invention," but excluded from the category "fine art" if not accompanied by reason, defined in terms of the rationalized program of study offered at art academies.

Reframing the Enlightenment

Is it sufficient to look only as far back as the eighteenth century to understand the binary of the classical norm versus the grotesque as its necessary supplement? By the time Picasso incorporated references to African masks in his paintings, setting off a (newer) modernist romance with "primitive art," the dyad of grotesque versus classical beauty had been underpinning the Western discourse on art for more than three centuries. Two centuries before art acquired its secular aura in the eighteenth century, Catholic Reformation defenses of images distinguished between classically inspired naturalism and its opposite, the grotesque, as two alternative practices of artistic representation issuing from two different kinds or uses of the imagination. Distinctions between two kinds of imagination echoed charges of idolatry by Protestant reformers that the authors rarely mention directly and in fact agree with on the fundamental principle that outward visual signs mirror inward states of mind.

The following argues that Connelly's thesis needs to be amended in one important respect. Her account misses the transcultural religious, political, and economic framework in which these same distinctions arose two centuries earlier during the initial period of European colonial expansion when extractive capitalism was first practiced on a global scale. The remainder of this Fugue examines some reframings of Indigenous material culture from the colonizer's point of view that took place *prior* to the eighteenth century. The secular distinction between civilized and primitive art initially emerged in Catholic Reformation writings that were disseminated around the world throughout the colonial period. What are the implications of pushing back the emergence of the modern concepts of art and interest in the origins of society from the eighteenth century to this initial period of global capitalism driven by European initiatives? Only then does it become apparent that arguments advanced by European philosophers in the eighteenth century are an effect of the "coloniality" of power and knowledge operating since the early sixteenth century. The definition of humanity that excludes most humans from fully civilized status defined in terms of their *techne* including their forms of social organization was driven by extractive capitalism since the beginning.[32] In fact, Indigenous colonial subjects were accused of lacking the *techne* necessary to make them fully civilized at the same time that they were performing highly skilled labor in the mines and forests for their colonial oppressors.[33]

As I have already mentioned, today scholars agree that there is no such thing as a "Tridentine style." There is nonetheless a broad scholarly consensus that a major shift in the discourse on art took place in the second half of the sixteenth century, keyed to Church reforms leading up to and articulated at the final session of the Council of Trent. There are many indications that the "reform" of painting associated with the Council of Trent, its lead-up and its aftermath, provided conditions for scientific literature on art to flourish – at least of a certain kind. The accelerated publication of treatises written by and for artists, both illustrated and unillustrated, printed editions and circulating manuscripts, is a notable development during this period. Church and state were both involved in the redirection of artistic knowledge that set new limits on artistic freedom. The first official art academy, the Florentine *Accademia del Disegno*, dedicated to the [holy] "trinity" of the arts of painting, sculpture, and *disegno* (a term that designates both drawing and design), was established in 1563 under the patronage of Duke Cosimo de' Medici, in the same year that the Council of Trent issued its Decree on Images at its final session. The Roman *Accademia di San Luca*, established by artists in 1577, was authorized in 1588 by Pope Sixtus V (in office 1585–1590) and finally realized in 1593 under the protection of Pope Clement VIII (in office, 1592–1605), two pontiffs active in establishing post-Tridentine policies governing intellectual activity.[34]

In some arenas, writers with institutional authority succeeded in redirecting the discourse on art, partly through their own treatises and institutional reforms and, significantly, through a widely distributed text prepared by an unidentified editor (or editors) around 1570 that has not been previously considered as a contributing factor. Leonardo da Vinci's (1452–1519) *Libro di Pittura* (Book on Painting), compiled by his student Francesco Melzi (1491/3–1567) from autograph notes, was aggressively edited to conform closely with the Church of Rome's decree on images issued a few years earlier. Melzi's original manuscript never circulated and was rediscovered in the Vatican Library at the end of the eighteenth century. The abridged and expurgated version began circulating in manuscript copies soon after Archbishop Carlo Borromeo undertook his intensive measures for reforming the arts in Milan. The young Borromeo arrived in Milan in 1565, appointed by his uncle Pope Pius IV, on whose orders he had helped to pass the famous decree on images adopted at the Council of Trent's last session in 1563 and ratified the next year. Borromeo was widely regarded as a model post-Tridentine reformer, throughout his life a selfless minister to the poor and sick. In addition to his own treatise on reforming the arts, a manual on church building and decoration entitled *Instructiones fabricae et supellectilis ecclesiasticae*, published in 1577 (among the earliest responses to the Tridentine decree on images), Borromeo actively managed the reform of ecclesiastical architecture, the theater, religious drama and liturgy, the educational system, and commissions of sacred images in his vast Milanese diocese.[35]

For more than four centuries, no one suspected that Melzi's compilation had been bowdlerized by a Catholic Reformation ideologue. Today, there is still resistance to the idea that Leonardo's writings were edited to conform with Tridentine views, and many questions remain that only the discovery of new archival evidence could answer, but the evidence internal to the manuscripts is indisputable. As far as can be determined, the full-length version never circulated. It survives in a unique manuscript rediscovered in the Vatican Library in 1797, and first published in 1817.[36] It has only recently been established that this version of Leonardo's writings on painting, long ignored by scholars since Nikolaus Pevsner's foundational text on the history of art academies (1940), is actually a key text in the institutionalization of Western representation [Figure 2.1].[37]

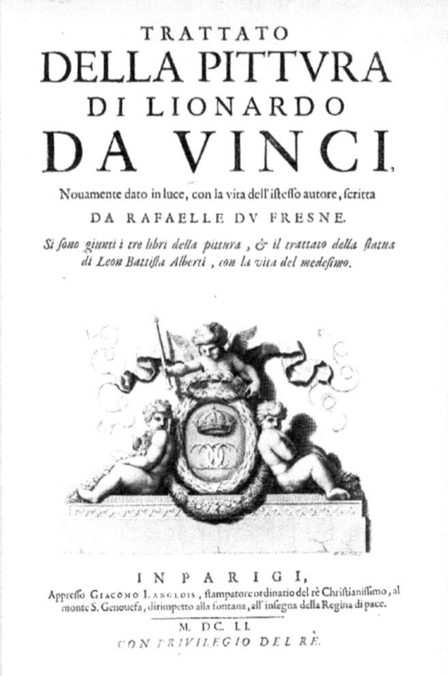
TRATTATO
DELLA PITTVRA
DI LIONARDO
DA VINCI,
Nouamente dato in luce, con la vita dell'istesso autore, scritta
DA RAFAELLE DV FRESNE.
Si sono giunti i tre libri della pittura, & il trattato della statua di Leon Battista Alberti, con la vita del medesimo.
IN PARIGI,
Appresso Giacomo Langlois, stampatore ordinario del rè Christianissimo, al monte S. Genouefa, dirimpetto alla fontana, all'insegna della Regina di pace.
M. DC. LI.
CON PRIVILEGIO DEL RÈ.

FIGURE 2.1 Title page, Leonardo da Vinci, *Trattato della pittura di Lionardo da Vinci, novamente dato in luce, con la vita dell'istesso autore . . .*, ed. R. Trichet du Fresne (Paris: Jacques Langlois, 1651). Washington, DC, Folger Shakespeare Library ND1130.L29 1651.

The *Trattato* is a complete compendium for instructing painters. It includes sections on the posing and expression of the figures, the composition of the narrative, the treatment of light, shadow, and color, and many other topics. Cassiano dal Pozzo prepared a publication of the abridged text in the 1630s under the patronage of Cardinal Francesco Barberini, nephew of Pope Urban VIII. In 1640, the project was transferred to the French editorial team who published a deluxe edition dedicated to Queen Christina of Sweden with many paratexts, new illustrations, and a separate French translation.[38]

Published in 1651 in the original Italian and a French translation identifying Leonardo as the sole author despite extensive editorial interventions, the Treatise on Painting was closely associated with the foundation of the French *Académie royale de peinture et de sculpture* in 1648. Translated into all the major Western European languages by the end of the eighteenth century, this text and others based on its ideas formed the core of academic methods of artistic instruction and it was widely read by a diverse network of professionals. The Intermezzo following this Fugue discusses the contribution of this widely known version of Leonardo's treatise on the formation of national style.

The only version of Leonardo's *Trattato della Pittura* that was available until the nineteenth century still contains a great deal of valuable information on color, light, and atmosphere, and the mechanics of human movement and expression, unavailable elsewhere and highly sought by artists. There is a consensus among specialists that this text was intended for teaching purposes. However, it does not explain why the editor eliminated Leonardo's discussions about inventing new compositions out of one's imagination as well as the entire second half of Melzi's compilation containing many detailed, advanced observations of the behavior of light, color, shadow, and air in open-air settings at different times of day and under various atmospheric conditions. These nuanced descriptions and advice would have been of great interest to practicing artists who had no comparable resources at their disposal. Why were they eliminated? To address this question, the next section introduces issues animating debates over the value of artifice (style, embellishment) and the religious decorum of images.

Two Senses of *Ingegno*

For Christian writers, the reliability of images had always been a key requirement. The standard defense of sacred images since the sixth century CE was that the illiterate rely on images to understand Christian doctrine because humans learn through sense experience. Images were deemed necessary, but the significance that any individual worshiper attached to images was difficult to control. The crux of the problem is that images can have multiple meanings and are therefore always tied to interpretation. Ecclesiastics tried to steer the interpretation of sacred works of art by making them subject to religious decorum. According to the ancient arguments beloved by humanists, works of art are subject to decorum, that is, there must be an appropriate fit between the subject matter, the work of art, and the audience. Writers had at their disposal to support these arguments two surviving Roman treatises on art from the first century BCE, which held that artistic images should conform to what is possible in nature, Horace's *Art of Poetry* and Vitruvius's treatise on architecture. Sixteenth-century grotesque ornaments composed of hybrid plant and animal forms were part of a continuous tradition from Early Christian art across all media from vaults with mosaics to illuminated books and architectural elements such as capitals and other sculptural ornaments. By the middle decades of the sixteenth century, even though they were not objecting to anything having to do with Christian sacred images, Horace and Vitruvius were frequently cited by ecclesiastic critics of *grottesche, capricci, bizarrie* and other figments of the imagination that came to epitomize the artists' unrestrained powers of invention. The rediscovery around 1480 of ancient wall paintings in Rome led to a widespread fashion beginning with Pope Julius II (in office 1503–1513) for the style of decorative wall painting known as *grottesche. Grottesche* originally referred to the underground rooms or "grottos" in which Nero's buried palace complex was rediscovered. In imitation of the Domus Aurea, the ostentatious villa complex built by Emperor Nero in the heart of Rome that was destroyed by fire in 64 CE and built over within a century, the new fashion for decorative wall paintings involved elements that Vitruvius had specifically condemned for defying the laws of actual built environments [Figure 2.2]. Horace had similarly objected to fabulous hybrid inventions for marrying parts that don't belong

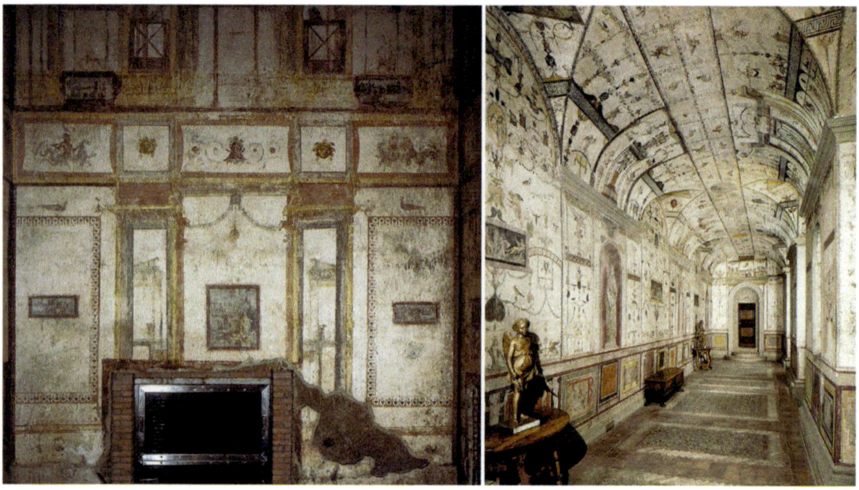

FIGURE 2.2 AND 2.3 (Left) Rome, Domus Aurea, Sala di Ettore e Andromaca, c. 64–68 AD, Rome. Photo Alessandro Vasari; (Right) Giovanni da Udine (Raphael's Workshop), Loggetta of Cardinal Bibbiena, c. 1517, Vatican Palace. Photo Scala, Florence.

together, such as a figure that is a woman above and a fish below which is nothing but "a sick man's dreams."

In open disregard of any restrictions on artistic license, the visual splendor and playfulness of sixteenth-century *grottesche* painting can still be appreciated today because many examples survive.[39] As evidence of the artist's imagination and powers of invention, this imagery was associated with endless improvisation and wit in the new literature on art. By mid-century, this literature comprised a considerable corpus of texts that praised grotesque imagery in defense of artistic freedom, aligned with similar defenses of the poet's freedom to feign impossible things, a direct inversion of Horace's dictum that poets and painters are limited to what is possible in nature. Prominent examples include a fictive dialogue featuring Michelangelo by the Portuguese artist Francisco de Hollanda, who lived in Rome from 1538–1545; and Giorgio Vasari's praise of Giovanni da Udine's mix of *naturalia* and monstrosity painted in a highly realistic manner is illustrated here in Raphael's Loggetta [Figure 2.3]. Vasari specifies that Giovanni da Udine's grotesques include lifelike and natural birds of many varieties, all kinds of vegetables, fish, sea monsters, fruits and flowers from all seasons and all parts of the world, and musical instruments, which are likewise painted in a highly realistic manner. In Anton Francesco Doni's dialogue, *Disegno* (Venice, 1549), his interlocutors discuss *grottesche* in positive terms as "a new invention discovered by Sculpture and Painting" that is not limited to imitating nature, "but has created forms in a disproportionate manner beyond measure" to depict fantasms and dreams.[40] Defense of *grottesche* as representative of a kind of invention recurs in the literature immediately surrounding

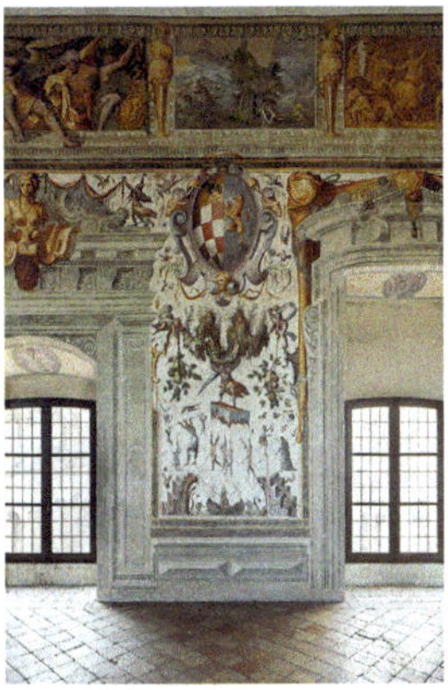

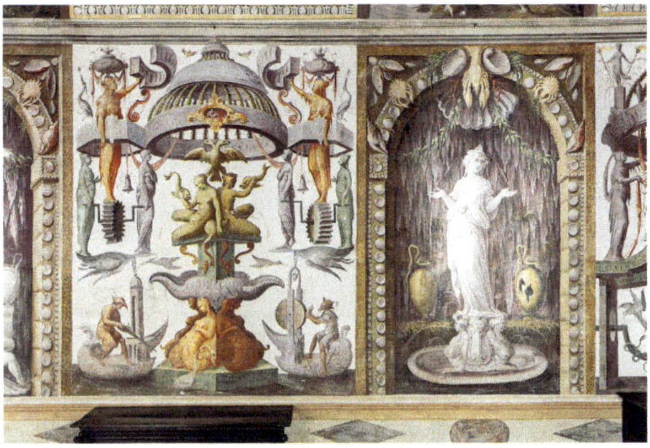

FIGURE 2.4 AND 2.5 (Left) Cesare Baglione and Giovanni Antonio Paganino, Sala dei Giocolieri, Castello di Torrechiara, c. 1583, wall elevation. Photo Pernille Klemp. (Right) Cesare Baglione, fountain and grotto, Sala at Rocca di Meli Lupi, Soragna, c. 1588, wall elevation. Photo Pernille Klemp.

Michelangelo. Michelangelo's follower Vincenzo Danti used the metaphor of *grottesco* to describe the process of architectural invention, where the parts are composed in a way not found in nature (1567).[41]

However, the painter/poet who composed such drolleries out of his imagination was a far cry from the representational model favored by sober Christian writers who associated the painter's inspiration with divine revelation. In a church setting, ornament *all'antica* bursting with life of the most improbable kind distracted from the sacred message in numerous ways. Yet wealthy humanist patrons, many of them ecclesiastics – including the Milanese Pope Pius IV – also appreciated the sumptuous displays of artistry which continued to be a mainstay in villa settings [Figures 2.4 and 2.5]. While the Pope's nephew Carlo Borromeo redirected sacred images toward the idealized but literal imitation of nature, the burgeoning decorative arts business centered in Milan supplied the affluent lifestyles of the upper class and courts throughout Europe with *grottesche*, *fantasie*, and *capriccie* fashioned into theatre costumes and sets, festival ephemera, and wall paintings, as well as vases, cups, bowls, cameos, and other objects in rock crystal, metal, ceramics, precious stones, and other materials [Figure 2.6].[42]

The historical record suggests *both* resistance and creative accommodation to the new standards of religious decorum emerging in the mid-sixteenth century, during and after the years that the Council of Trent met three times between 1545 and 1563. Optical naturalism, to use a modern descriptive term intentionally broader than any specific representational practice, offered the most viable option for ecclesiastics because it was in accordance with the way *the eye sees nature directly* and so it was not thought to distract worshipers from the religious purpose of art to guide souls toward a state of grace. By contrast, the

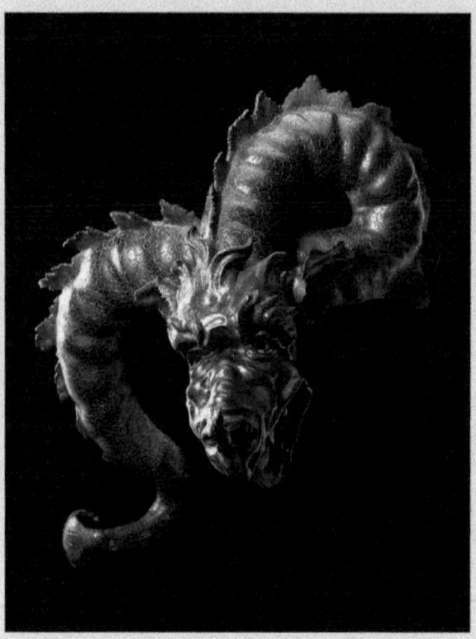

FIGURE 2.6 Annibale Fontana, ceramic dragon, 1582, Milan. © Sotheby's/Bridgeman Images.

Leonardo da Vinci is well known today for encouraging the free play of imagination – his drawings of dragons, of cats turning into dragons, or lions into fierce horses, are among the most iconic. These ideas and images left a rich legacy in Milan, where most of Leonardo's papers were kept after his death. Annibale Fontana (1540–1587) was a leading Milanese sculptor and a member of his friend Lomazzo's *Accademia della Val di Blenio*. As the head of a leading decorative arts workshop, Fontana supplied luxury goods for an international market before, during, and after Carlo Borromeo's tenure as Archbishop. He engraved cameos and objects in crystal, ebony, marble, and precious stones. He was known internationally for his experimental use of materials and his designs of fantastic zoomorphic creatures. Fontana, like Lomazzo, studied Leonardo's unpublished notes and is said to have acquired machines that Leonardo designed for cutting and polishing crystal, iron, and precious stones.

playful wit and artistry displayed in *grottesche* ornamentation invoked ecclesiastic fears that viewers would absorb such outrageous aberrations of nature and become spiritually deformed themselves.[43] The underlying assumption in Archbishop of Bologna Gabriele Paleotti's extensive discussions of *grottesche*, discussed further below, and similar considerations of the time by Giovanni Andrea Gilio, Carlo Borromeo, Gian Paolo Lomazzo, Pirro Ligorio, and other writers, regardless of their critical stance, was the Scholastic distinction between the "delusions" of a dissolute person and the "true visions" of a prophet. The same distinction is the pivotal point in a wide variety of sixteenth-century discussions of art and idolatry by Protestants and by Catholic missionaries. In the thirteenth century, Thomas Aquinas articulated the range of logical possibilities in his differentiation between the eternal *substance* of an object and its accidental, external *appearance*. Mutations in appearance were *external* to the visionary's eyes, but the imagination of the "dissolute person" caused him to mistake the image for the thing itself, and he was thereby captivated by demonic illusions (*Summa*

Theologica 3.76.8). The same logic, based on the same widely held beliefs, is at work in pictures of redemption held against the face of criminals led to execution [Figure 2.7]. These little tablets, *tavolette*, or *tavoluccie* [dazzling tablets] as they were sometimes called in the sixteenth century, were used to comfort condemned criminals with the promise that if the victim accepted his physical torture as penance on earth, his soul might win eternal redemption in heaven.[44]

Explicit condemnation of artists' free use of their imaginations was part of the Catholic Reformation strategy in Milan and elsewhere and arguably one of the main reasons that praise for *grottesche* went out of fashion toward the end of the century. As already mentioned, there is broad scholarly consensus on this sudden shift, but different reasons have been proposed for what is a complex combination of factors. The concept of expurgating parts to save the whole had very recently been introduced in the revised and more moderate Index of Prohibited Books published in 1559. Leonardo's abridged text tones down and, in several cases, deletes entirely, passages on the freedom of the artist to invent new compositions and pursue painting as an investigative science. Leonardo praised the painter's

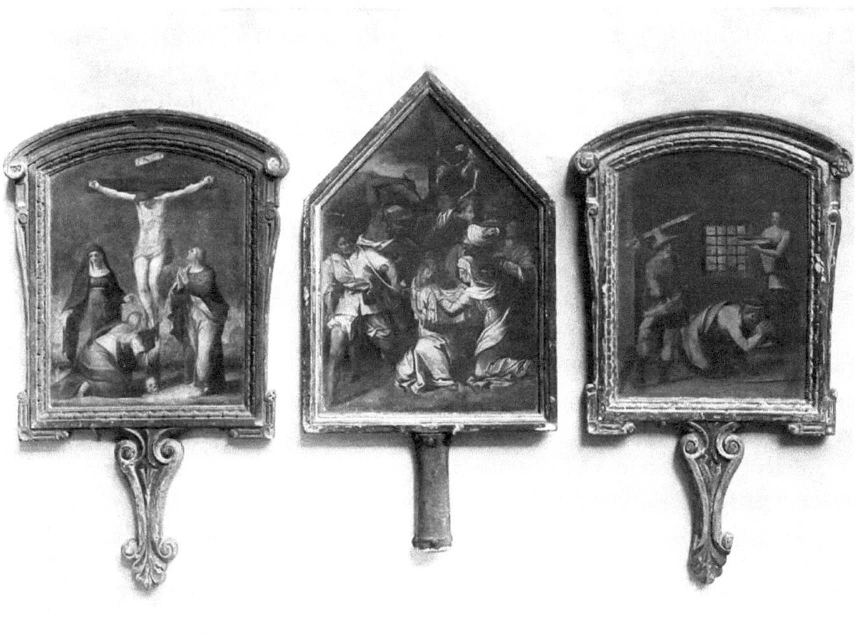

FIGURE 2.7 Three tavolettas: Crucifixion, Mocking of Christ, and the Beheading of St. John the Baptist by anonymous artists. 16th century, oil on panel. Rome, Camera Storica San Giovanni Decollato. Photo: Guido Laudani, courtesy of the Archconfraterinty of San Giovanni Decollato, Rome. Photo Alessandro Vasari.

independence extensively, while the editor responsible for the expurgated version downplayed these statements considerably.[45]

There are actually two different kinds of *ingegno* operating in Leonardo's text, one of which the editor systematically retained, the other of which he systematically eliminated. A systematic comparison of Melzi's text with the abridged version in its earliest known form shows that the editor eliminated most discussions of the artist's *ingegno*, roughly translatable as his inventive powers or active imagination, while retaining references to the artist's diligence and observations of natural phenomena. Ironically, turning these observations into artistic representations also requires *ingegno*, according to Leonardo's praise of painting in the first section deleted entirely by the editor.

The question is why one understanding of *ingegno* but not the other was retained. The Italian word "*ingegno*," often translated as "inborn talent," is a category historically associated with the individual. The term, its synonyms, and alternatives first appear in the Italian literature on the visual and spatial arts around 1400. Aristotle and Cicero provide two anchor points for these discussions. In a text that became widely available in the sixteenth century, Aristotle wrote about the faculty of "quick wittedness" (*Poetics* 1459a), that is, the "faculty of hitting upon the middle term instantaneously" (*Posterior Analytics* 89b34), a principle of inherited individual difference that achieves its highest form in the *phantasia* of the prophet. Aristotle's influential eleventh-century Arabic commentator Avicenna (who was translated into Latin and served as an important source of Aristotelian ideas for Thomas Aquinas and other Scholastic writers) associated *ingenium* with perceiving what is right immediately by a kind of illumination.[46] Cicero wrote about innate capacity (*ingenium*) as distinct from learned skill (*ars*) and, in doing so, brought them into close alignment. With the pairing of *ingegno* and *mano* (hand), to use the terms often encountered in the vernacular literature, the ear and the eye become the final arbiters of quality. According to Cicero, these are exceptionally skillful human organs of discrimination (*iudicium*) for judging differences of tone, pitch, and key, for example, in music and rhetoric.[47]

Ancient discussions of *ingenium* are concerned with sensate judgment, what we still call "discrimination" in the strictly quantifiable sense of the word. David Summers, who has studied the history of aesthetic judgment in medieval and early modern European texts and their ancient sources, argues that imagining *ingenium* or "quick wittedness" on a sliding scale running from mere cleverness to prophetic vision also explains why some writers thought that it could be taught.[48] If it is possible to teach quick-wittedness, Summers observes, then human nature can be corrected by art. Based on this philosophical heritage, it follows that the Christian justification for using images to acquire religious understanding – that is, its core defense against charges of idolatry since St. Augustine (354–430 CE) and Pope Gregory the Great (c. 540–604 CE) – has been expressed as the need to address human modes of cognition proceeding from sense experience.

A second account of *ingegno* operating in Leonardo's argument derives from the classical idea of divine inspiration associated with the philosophy of Plato. It was a commonplace of the Platonic tradition that *furor poeticus* refers to the inspiration of the poet as it took form in the language of poetry. The Platonic tradition of artistic inspiration is combined with the Aristotelian one of inferential analysis.[49] The Platonic idea of *furor* was widely disseminated in Christian and secular sources. The effort to synthesize divine inspiration with scientific analysis provides the framework for one of the most productive debates in sixteenth-century artistic literature. Applied to the visual register, *furor* refers to the spontaneous quality of works of art resulting from the excited state of the artist. Sixteenth-century writers such as Vasari, Vincenzo Danti, and others close to Michelangelo understood *furor* as a hallmark of divine inspiration linked closely both to the artist's initial idea, or *concetto*, and his inspired execution. The presence of so many similar accounts of the creative process in so many sources indicates the existence of a shared oral tradition of workshop practice with a theoretical component – artisanal knowledge orally transmitted through the workshop found its way into the new sub-philosophical literature on art, some of which was also circulating in workshops.[50] The sources point to a complex interplay between written and oral transmission of artisanal knowledge.

Ingegno also appears in contexts associated with engineering, another word that derives from the same Latin root *ignis* (fire).[51] Some historians of art, science, and technology are pursuing connections in a wide range of sources among new forms of artisanal and industrial knowledge production requiring mechanical knowledge.[52] Ancient sources shared by early modern practitioners in these fields include Vitruvius and Lucretius, who assigned prominent roles to *ingenium* in the development of technology.[53] Vitruvius devoted extensive discussions to engineering practices based on knowledge of geometry and mechanics, reflected for example in Roberto Valturio's fifteenth-century treatise on the military arts that Leonardo and his associates studied extensively.[54] Globalization, industrialization, and capitalism encouraged innovation put to practical purposes. Artists like Leonardo who practiced as engineers and technical consultants are evidence of the increasing stature awarded to the emerging technology requiring theoretical knowledge. The next two Fugues offer further reflections on the complex history of the concept "ingenuity" after the sixteenth century.

To return here to Leonardo's *Libro* with this brief introduction to the historical concept of *ingegno* in mind, the editor who eliminated nearly 60% of the original compilation filtered out things that did not conform to Tridentine attempts to redirect artistic license toward preserving religious decorum. Leonardo's lofty arguments for painting as an investigative science and for the painter as someone with great imagination and analytical ability were reduced to

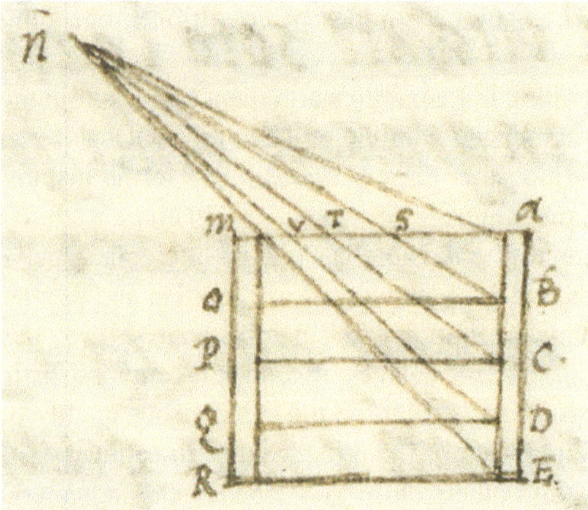

FIGURE 2.8 Leonardo da Vinci, *Libro di Pittura,* f. 143v, transcribed by Francesco Melzi. On cities and other things seen through thick air, original lost, c. 1510–1515. Detail: diagram for training the eye to judge color and acuity. The diagram shows how the thing seen (city building, a tower) will take on the color of the air by degrees depending on two variables, its distance from the eye and its height above the ground. Leonardo da Vinci, *Libro di Pittura. Codice Urbinate lat. 1270.* Biblioteca Apostolica, Vatican.

almost nothing while his practical advice on painting and representation was retained. Leonardo gave concrete advice and offered diagrams to train the eye to discern differences in appearances due to factors of distance, position, atmospheric conditions, lighting, and so on, derived from the literature on geometric optics and vision. He literally taught artists how to use their powers of *ingegno* to rationalize sight [Figure 2.8].

In the hands of Leonardo's anonymous editor/s, painting became a transparent imitation of natural appearances reproduced according to certain rules for engaging the senses of worshipers. This editorial campaign left only the bare bones of Leonardo's richly conceived account of *ingegno*, just enough to acknowledge its necessity in the design process. The editor/s selectively excised Leonardo's account of the painter's active imagination. The likely reason follows directly from the Council of Trent's decree on images, which specified that nothing extraneous to the biblical narrative should be included in a sacred work of art. In 1576, Borromeo issued a new rule that reinforced the proscription against the kind of artistic embellishment long associated with *grottesche* and *capricci*.[55] In his interpretation of the Tridentine decree published the following year (1577), Borromeo elaborated on its terms, specifying that the prohibition includes the borders of images, which cannot portray

> grotesque human heads, such as are commonly called *mascaroni*, nor small birds, nor the sea, or green pastures, nor other things of this kind which are designed for pleasure's sake, for delightful views and decoration – only if they agree with the sacred story that is represented.[56]

Borromeo did not think such elements belonged in sacred paintings because they distract the viewer from engaging emotionally with the scriptural content of the image.

Setting limits to the signifying process occupied many ecclesiastics engaged with the redirection of artistic license to the forms of artifice that Leonardo's treatise promotes. In its abridged form, Leonardo's text avoided contradicting Tridentine views that pictorial embellishment is at the service of the sacred subject matter rather than an opportunity for the artist to distract viewers by drawing attention to his skill and ingenuity. Toward the end of the sixteenth century, transparency became the new function of representation. This is not to imply that post-Tridentine art theory was monolithic or that writers directly dictated pictorial practices, but the commonalities are significant. Evidence also survives to shed light on Carlo Borromeo's personal use of sacred images as affective instruments of devotion. His own art collection included a copy of Leonardo's *Virgin and Child with St. Anne*, the original of which is now in the Louvre Museum, Paris. Borromeo's biographer Carlo Bascapè gives a concrete sense of how Borromeo personally and intimately interpreted the Council of Trent's mandate to set salutary examples "before the eyes of the faithful" so that they might be "excited to adore and love God, and to cultivate piety."[57] Borromeo also developed a network of *Sacro Monte* pilgrimage sites in Lombardy featuring simulated biblical scenes that share many features with paintings, including Leonardo's, such as the heightened treatment of light, dark, and color, that had both symbolic value and a perceptual function. These elements move the worshipper through contemplation of the external image to internal "imaginative vision" to persuade them to practice piety and to direct them to God. The viewer's individual experience is never saturated, because new visual discoveries and associations are always possible. In fact, the openness of the signifying process keeps the beholder engaged.

Archbishop Gabriele Paleotti (1522–1597) was the author of a widely influential treatise on sacred and profane images that he shared with his close friend Borromeo before publication. Borromeo had far greater institutional authority, thanks to his uncle Pope Pius IV, and their personalities differed greatly, yet their collaboration and shared aspirations continued until Borromeo's death in 1584. Borromeo and Paleotti's efforts to institute practical pastoral reforms in their respective dioceses of Milan and Bologna were closely aligned.[58] Both were also closely associated with the Roman Oratory of Filippo Neri, of which Paleotti established a branch in Bologna. Paleotti understood the viewing process as an ascent to knowledge comparable to looking at a starry sky at night. Each level of cognition has its own level of delight accompanied by an increasing level of rational knowledge until attaining spiritual cognition [*cognizione spirituale*] under divine inspiration. In essence, the three levels of Paleotti's hierarchal cognitive process can be associated with the three traditional aims of rhetoric differentiated by their manner of embellishment: plain, unadorned text to instruct; natural sounding speech (Cicero's Attic or middle style) to move; and text embellished with highly wrought artifice to delight (epideictic rhetoric and artifice associated by ancient writers with the suave Asiatic style).[59] Citing Aristotle's *Poetics* that man alone among all the other animals was born to imitate by "the virtue of reason," Paleotti also applied his account of the cognitive process to the act of viewing paintings. He described viewing in rationalized terms very similar to Leonardo: the viewer receives "pleasure and recreation" from "the variety of colors, shadows, figures, and ornament, and the diverse things represented in them – such as mountains, rivers, gardens, cities, landscapes, and other things."[60]

To understand why Leonardo and many other artists engaged in unprecedented efforts to imitate the play of actual light, shadow, and color as a resource for making material images of sacred subjects that seem to resonate with life, imitating and exaggerating natural appearances with great rhetorical force, requires viewing concrete events at a scale broad enough to consider artistry in the general terms I have just sketched. These artificial images (that is, images crafted by humans, as opposed to images found in nature) conformed to the longstanding ontological requirement that sacred Christian images be reliable and true, as artless or "perfect" as possible, to recall the Dominican friar Gerolamo Savonarola's (1452–1498) understanding of poetry's moral efficacy. Like his mid-fifteenth-century predecessor Cardinal Giovanni Dominici, Savonarola asserted that only scripture has true allegorical meaning and only natural things not created by art are perfect.[61] From Thomas Aquinas to Carlo Borromeo to Federico Zuccaro, first director of the Roman art academy, *Accademia di San Luca* founded in 1593, the assumption was that the mind of the artist is in contact with the Divine when he receives his exemplum and works out his mental image or *concetto*. The same logic guarantees the truth of a miraculous painting, a contact relic like the Shroud of Turin, or any other *acheiropoietos*, a sacred image made in direct contact with the divine without human intervention.

A great deal of tension in Early Modern Italian writings about art revolves around the double-sided issue of the artist's share, his freedom to interpret Scripture versus the limits of his human understanding, which is the substantive issue driving humanist and Scholastic disagreements since the fourteenth century over the value of poetic figured language. Were poets divinely inspired as humanists claimed or was poetry the lowest form of "scientific knowledge" in a hierarchical Scholastic scheme of classification because it cannot achieve a form of truth higher than opinion? The next section takes a closer look at key issues that excluded and demonized artistic practices that did not conform to the criteria articulated by writers associated with Church reform.

The Signifying Grotesque

Today, the important point is to understand the *tensions* that run through a vast variety of texts on art because they shaped European accounts of human exceptionalism for centuries thereafter that are still operating today. Paradoxically, the pressure on practicing artists to acquire knowledge of geometry, optics, anatomy, human movement, impetus mechanics, natural philosophy, and other subjects requiring theoretical understanding imperative to the Catholic Reformation's redirection of the visual arts, was initially formed within craft traditions. The complex entanglement of art, nature, and technology during this formative period before art was defined in modern secular terms suggests that many factors were involved. In the age-old European contrast between the fictions of the human imagination and the mysteries of divine revelation, old categories were stretched to fit new situations. The discussion of *grottesche* and other *capricii* in Italy further suggests how unclassicizing images, regardless of their origin or significance for the cultures that produced them, became emblematic of the opposition built into the Western definition of image as likeness. The following discussion focuses on the writings of Gabriele Paleotti, Archbishop of Bologna and a key player in articulating Tridentine rules of decorum limiting artistic images of sacred subjects to what is verisimilar in nature and close to God, modeled closely on thirteenth-century Scholastic thought, which was itself modeled on the Pauline doctrine that Christ is made in the image (*eikon*) of God. The more closely the artist's inborn talent can be aligned with its "divine source," the more the *truth* of the sacred image is guaranteed, and the more *reliable* that image is. For the same reasons, Paleotti also abandoned the longstanding Christian practice of meditating on difficult figures and allegories, as I will discuss in the next section. He also restricted to educated viewers delight in certain kinds of artifice, such as the beautiful painted landscapes Leonardo described verbally and visually.

Paleotti offered the most extensive considerations of the grotesque in the literature, although there are other prominent writers from the second half of the century who held similar views, including Giovanni Andrea Gilio (1564), Daniele Barbaro (1556), Carlo Borromeo (1577), and Pellegrino de' Pellegrini (Tibaldi; 1587, unpublished). There were still others like Lomazzo, Armenini, and Federigo Zuccaro, who either changed their minds as the oppressive religious climate intensified or else tried to accommodate apparently contradictory views about how to interpret nature. Educated in the humanistic environment of Bologna, Paleotti sought advice on the grotesque when he was developing his treatise on sacred painting from his friend since childhood, Ulisse Aldrovandi, the great Bolognese collector of Americana artifacts and natural specimens, a professor at the University of Bologna. Although the scholarship has focused exclusively on the connections to the ancient Greek and Roman sources cited throughout his text, Paleotti occasionally offered opinions on Americana as examples of the grotesque.[62] His *Discourse on Sacred and Profane Images* (*Discorso intorno alle imagini sacre e profane*) begins with a statement that could have been lifted directly from Vitoria's published lecture (1557) on the Amerindians' complete lack of cultural refinement:

> There are no people so untamed or so savage that they do not believe in God, though they may have no capacity to know him correctly. And those who have described the recent voyages of discovery relate that in many countries, albeit physically remote from one another and absolutely uncultivated, there are to be

found peoples without letters, arts, laws, or magistrates – but not without some sort of religion.[63]

Religion was last on Vitoria's list as part of the world of invention, the highest possible manifestation of man's creative reason. Like many others, he considered the alleged practice of idolatry, human sacrifice, and cannibalism to be crimes against nature. To avoid the Lutheran error of supposing that dominium is conferred by God's grace, not God's law, Vitoria argued, in terms that are implied in Paleotti's statement, that they are offenses against God, not man. Their religion might be "satanic in inspiration and foul in practice," but the Mexica and Inka had all the things Christians understood by the word "church": cult, places of worship, priesthood. The stated purpose of Paleotti's treatise was to "reform the Catholic, not to oppugn the pagan or heretic directly – except where we judge it expedient, to clarify the point we wish to make." In later chapters on the grotesque, Paleotti clarifies many points on what to include and why. He defines monstrous painting (*la pittura mostruosa*) broadly *and* in exhaustive detail as "natural or imagined or both or neither" (Book 2, Chapter 36). Sometimes his descriptions recall images from world maps, travel accounts, and cultural geographies, or suggest material in Aldrovandi's collection. Paleotti also referred to "infernal rites and demonic gods," descriptions that repeat tropes available in the ancient sources (such as Cicero) that also figured prominently in sensationalized accounts of indigenous customs by Vitoria, Sepúlveda, and other ecclesiastics who dwelled on idol worship, human sacrifice, and cannibalism.[64]

Contemporary historians think of the Counter Reformation as promoting various "reformed" approaches to naturalistic representation. In line with these values, Paleotti's text attests to his belief that painting, because it represents the similitudes of things just as the eye experiences nature in direct vision, is a universal language. However, Paleotti formulated an equally universalist theory of the grotesque, which has not received much attention as an aspect of Counter Reformation art theory, in which he condemned (with one exception, discussed below), regardless of the source if the representation does not correspond to a counterpart existing in nature. The focus of the following discussion is on Paleotti's understanding of the grotesque given his position on native religion. It unpacks the associations he made between *techne* and civility, to use the sixteenth-century Aristotelian terms for evaluating a people defined by their social organization, religion, and material artifacts.

Paleotti divided the world into "pagans, also called gentiles," who adore idols, "Mohammedans," Jews, and "other Christians called heretics or schismatics" who reject the doctrines, customs, and institutions of the Church and "the majority of which reject images and are waging open war against them" (Book 1, chapter 1). The central problem on his mind was individual salvation, or what theologians call the problem of grace: who mediates between the human and the divine. As stated in the first chapter of his treatise, Paleotti's curb of the grotesque was based on principles of rationality derived from ancient sources that he addressed to Protestants, those modern "heretics and schismatics" who "reject images and are waging open war against them," and he also addressed his concerns to all of humanity that needs to reform. He distinguished sharply between "all the arts that form images" that "are derived from another form" and the rest: pagans who adore idols and heretics [Protestants] who get rid of images altogether (Book 1, chapter 2). Paleotti connected but also distinguished sharply between "vestiges" which are "irrational and imperfect" traces like a footprint, and images produced by the art of "*disegno*." Painters were now meant to rely upon the "natural light" of reason and on piety to express inner feelings and concepts, a gift that allows man to share in the divine creative capacity. He followed St. Augustine, who conceived of a continuum of images produced by art and nature (like reflections in mirrors or clear water) as being on the same order as the resemblance between father and son. For both Augustine and Paleotti, the source of the material imprint is crucial: footprints and smoke are limited in their usefulness, while the abstract and incorporeal images used by theologians or the *fantasmi* and *concetti* that give painters the ability to paint, are a "gift of God and a sign of the loftiness of human nature."

Paleotti clearly understood that the value of an image made by human art – whether the figure was described in words by a theologian or the figure fabricated by a painter – is due to its divine origin. The rationality of the artistic image is due to God, while its semiotic opposite, the irrational artistic image, is due to its alleged lack of divine origin. The eighteenth-century distinction between the fine arts and the fetish is a manifestation of the same systemic antimony operating in the late sixteenth century. In other words, the pairing of rational and "irrational" artifice did not emerge from eighteenth-century secular philosophy: it was initially established in the late sixteenth century as part of a Christian discourse for evaluating extra-European people by judging their artistry.

Categories of rational and irrational art together established the contours of a collectivity, what Rancière calls a "partage du sensible" (distribution or partition of the sensible) that simultaneously distinguishes between and binds the partitions of its own making. This is also what Connelly identified as the classical norm and its necessary supplement, the grotesque. In contrasting the rational imagination to capricious, unbridled fantasy, Paleotti introduced new qualifications to define the kinds of ornament that interfered with religious decorum. In the first of six chapters devoted to the subject, he defined the grotesque in the following terms:

> By grotesques we mean exclusively those forms of men or animals or other things that never did or could exist in the manner in which they are represented and are the mere caprices of painters, vain phantasms, irrational imaginings on their part . . . this imagery is everywhere, widespread in public and private

> buildings, even in venerable buildings, conjoined to altars and sacred vessels and vestments.[65]

In the same passage, Paleotti praised representations of "leaves, branches, and festoons" as harmless while he condemned the representations of monstrous races, infernal rites, demonic gods, idol worship, and human sacrifice. He traced the origins of *grottesche* to paintings in caves, Egyptian hieroglyphs, and many other sources (Book 2, Chapters 37–42).

The additions to the standard authorities that Paleotti summoned to define inappropriate ornament – Plato, Horace, St. Bernard of Clairvaux – point to a crisis in representation, but the situation was complex. As their correspondence documents, Paleotti took Aldrovandi's advice when he wrote that painters should be allowed to represent novel things that seem to lie outside the order of nature (*se bene fuori dell'ordine suo*) as long as they actually do exist. These include "monsters of the sea and other places" (Book 2, Chapter 37).[66] The difference is that ornaments that have counterparts in nature are "proportioned to reason" while "*grottesche*" refer to fantasms, things "that have never been, that could not exist in the manner in which they are presented." These mannered depictions are the *capricci* of painters, products of their irrational imaginations (*irragionevoli imaginazioni*).

The Thomistic distinction between two kinds of figured language, divine truths and the fictions feigned by poets, gained an unprecedented number of auxiliary qualifications in Paleotti's discussion.[67] In his correspondence with Paleotti, Aldrovandi had defended the utility of painting as an instrument of truth. Following his advice, Paleotti supported the painter who out of necessity records strange new objects, sometimes even employing vivid colors and other forms of conspicuous artifice that the Council of Trent might have rejected as "sensuous charms" which lead the worshiper astray. Citing Saint Jerome's Life of Saint Anthony, a saint with horns on his forehead who is documented in Alexandria during the reign of Constantine, Paleotti writes in the conviction that actual human monsters exist elsewhere, in Africa for example:

> Hence anyone portraying things from Africa or the newly discovered lands may paint, without blame, the various monsters both human and animal described by the authentic writers about those places. . . . Imagined monsters as a category may be taken in two modes: either they are falsely feigned by our pure imagination or they are formed by our imagination, but the latter is moved by superior causes and divine revelation.[68]

The medieval idea that the artist is one with the divine mind in the act of creating an image, preserved in Leonardo's approach to nature, had become an enormous problem for ecclesiastics attempting to control and guide worshipers in the latter part of the sixteenth century. The medieval Greek texts dealing with the resolution of the Iconoclastic controversy that are so important to the subsequent history of the Western idea of art do not even mention the artist. They are concerned with the relationship between God and the worshiper. The main thrust of these arguments is to justify the use of images. Long before Thomas Aquinas made the same argument, the Patriarch Photios writing in 867, building upon the arguments developed a century earlier by his predecessor the Emperor Nikephoros I (760–811), justified the use of artistic images as merely mnemonic devices.[69] Explaining the proper use of images in optical terms, when he commemorated their restoration in Hagia Sophia, Photios stressed the absence of real presence in artificial images and argued that images are necessary to religious devotion because the senses, and sight above all others, are our natural human way of learning. When these arguments concerning cognition beginning with sense experience came to the fore in sixteenth-century Italy under pressure from Protestant reformers, ecclesiastical writers like Paleotti attempted to redirect artistic invention to conform to sense experience. A certain heightened form of optical naturalism (the kind of painting that Leonardo advocated) was intended to keep the worshiper focused on the Scriptural story or holy figure, rather than being distracted or "seduced" by the artist's virtuosity.

Paleotti repeated Thomas Aquinas's argument about the twofold "movement of the mind towards an image" that Catholic theologians used in the mid-sixteenth century to defend the use of images against the charge of idolatry, but he added a third mental movement concerned with artifice in the material image.[70] Paleotti's larger concern is that images can lead worshipers astray without proper guidance, for how is one to distinguish between inappropriate fantastic *grottesche* and virtuous naturalistic representations, visually or ontologically? How does one distinguish between the true images of a prophet revealed by God, the false illusions implanted by demons, and the strange but actually existing things from "newly discovered lands"? For the beholder, it is important to be guaranteed that the worshiper worships the *holy figure represented* in the image, rather than the material image itself, whose artifice is due to human hands. Paleotti writes pointedly that *grottesche* are found below [as in Nero's palace] *and* above ground, and are perhaps acceptable in private contexts, but not in churches. Paleotti also condemned the artistic practice of incorporating foreign elements generally, comparing painters to poets who cite verses without knowing their significance, because they fantasize without fruit: such artists portray the places of their fictions and dreams without examining what they have at hand (*per le mani*; Book 2, Chapter 37). The threat of *grottesche* that Paleotti perceived also made him sensitive to the problem of exoticism. He recognized a fundamental problem with the signifying power of images if artists and worshipers are unchecked:

> same image can produce differences as many as the various concepts that spectators taken from [these images] . . . Therefore we see the case of the nectar that is found in flowers in the countryside, that bees can make of it sweet honey and spiders can made deadly venom.[71]

Paleotti's awareness of the ambivalence of images is linked to his most insistent objections: "monstrous" transformations of the human figure that would confuse common people because such distortions conflict with external reality defined in geometric terms of proportion, symmetry, and decorum: "if art imitates nature, then grotesques fall outside the bounds of art" (Book 2, Chapter 41). It is followed by the important discussion in Chapter 42 of verisimilar images as appropriate for moral instruction, as opposed to recondite and abstruse allegories and grotesques, the latter ordinarily having no hidden, beneficial meaning. His main concern is with safeguarding the Christian practice of using images in keeping with human modes of cognition. His solution, recalling Matthieu Ory's embrace of visual artifice to instruct the illiterate masses, is that Christian paintings have the power to guide the public who need to be convinced to adhere to a certain aspect of religion, thus pictures potentially have the same function for the public as Scripture. Paleotti's emphasis on how images replicate the written word in an instant, for a universal audience, is an incredible suggestion because the manifold meaning traditionally believed accessible only through contemplation was now granted to sacred painting, instantaneously without requiring interpretation (Book 1, Chapter 23).[72]

The ideas that Paleotti and Aldrovandi exchanged about the nature of representation, while exceptional in providing historians with direct connections between American artifacts and theoretical discussions of art in Italy, were certainly not unique. Although Leonardo's full description was not available in the abridged version of the treatise on painting that enjoyed vast institutional authority for more than two centuries, he was by no means the sole source of the idea that the excited *ingegno* is the motivating force for the rapid-fire sketch of the initial compositional idea. It occurs elsewhere independently in the sixteenth-century literature of art, particularly in association with *disegno*. It is even possible that Paleotti had direct access to Leonardo's full-length *Libro di pittura*, but the main arguments extolling painting that Leonardo invented were well-known in and beyond Italy through other sources, notably Baldassare Castiglione's *Libro del Cortegiano (Book of the Courtier)*, first published in 1528 and frequently reprinted. With this background, the following discussion looks more closely at the historical role of artistic judgment in defining human nature.

On the Artist's Judgment

Writings in praise of *grottesche* and the artist's personal *maniera* quickly fell out of favor in the final decades of the sixteenth century after they became the object of criticism by Catholic Reformation writers.[73] Optical naturalism that idealized nature on classical principles of proportion led to the institutionalized understanding of the fine arts of painting and sculpture as founded on rational principles, which became the hallmark of Western representation. Writings that extolled products of the artist's imagination associated with license and wit, ranging from *grottesche*-style wall decoration to the strange and wonder-inducing objects prized by collectors for their *wunderkammers* and curiosity cabinets, flourished elsewhere but were absent from the same institutionally supported discourse. This included artistic instruction in the new academies and art schools that emerged all over Europe and around the globe wherever evangelization and trade established a European presence. *Grottesche* and other images deemed unacceptable by Catholic Reformation writers and others sympathetic to them were often associated with those who produce idols, the grotesque, "hieroglyphs," allegories, distorted human and animal figures, and all kinds of images held to be lacking in the rational principles governing the fabrication of images made according to the laws of geometric proportions. These "rational" features included pictorial perspective, modeling or the science of *chiaro e scuro* and the naturalistic use of color, knowledge of anatomy and the mechanics of the human body, including the use of gesture and expression. Enlightenment thinkers assertively favored rational principles on the basis of the same neo-Aristotelian theory of cognition.

The same neo-Aristotelian theory of human cognition that justified certain forms of artifice also justified their condemnation. The artifice of any work of art was most often evaluated as part of a "contest" between nature and art but, whatever the narrative framework, the artist's invention was always conceptually conjoined with the needs of *both* the subject *and* the particular viewing audience. In the three-way relationship among subject, artist, and audience, the intentions of the artificer were considered *embodied and manifest in the work of art*. In this manner, artifacts of non-European origin became part of a larger European category of objects of lesser or greater value depending on the author's critical stance.

Therein lies the emancipatory potential of early modern writings and other practices associated with the grotesque. The differences lay in how value was to be attributed to the relative positions of agent, object, and function. A complex discursive field about artistic invention encouraged certain generalizations. The perennial challenge for writers sympathetic to Catholic Reformation views was to establish the ontological status of the artistic representation in relation to divine truth. The danger of artifice lay in its tendency to jeopardize the stability of institutionally imposed values, thus endangering the health of society. Paleotti understood the truth of sacred images in just these terms when he praised the abstract and incorporeal images used by theologians, like the *fantasmi* and *concetti* conceived by painters, as a "gift of God and a sign of the loftiness of human nature." At the same time, he restricted the longstanding practice of meditating on visual allegories, identified with *grottesche* by his contemporaries (including the humanist architect Pirro Ligorio, an authority on *grottesche* whom he consulted). Paleotti grudgingly allowed such visual allegories (his single exception) but only if they were clearly labeled, which defeats their entire purpose to exercise human cogitation as a path to religious understanding (Book 2, Chapters 36 and 45). If *grottesche* are understood as antithetical figures or contrappostos, suggests art historian Maria Fabricius

Hansen, they may be interpreted as a kind of *antiphrasis* or irony, which ancient authorities on rhetoric equated with illusion or *dissimulatio*.[74] The truth is not found by taking the image at face value but is instead contained in the very ambiguity and paradox that are acknowledged as the basic conditions of the world. There is also a rapport between *grottesche* and dreams: they are intentionally difficult, non-transparent, simultaneously literary and figurative, concealing profound and sacred meaning under a fantastic form. According to the Milanese painter Gian Paolo Lomazzo (1538–1592), whose views on artistic inspiration will be discussed further below, "they are not made by chance, but by study, to make that effect that they make."[75]

Writers were caught between allegiances to the artist, emphasized in humanist discourse relying on classical sources, and the truth of sacred artistic representations when the Church of Rome redirected artistic license away from *grottesche*, *capriccie*, and other fantastic forms emblematic of the artist's powers of invention. Lomazzo, a Milanese artist/theorist who was familiar with Leonardo's unpublished writings and drawings, echoed his views.[76] He embraced both the scientific and the fantastic dimensions of artistic license that he found in these sources. In his treatise on painting published the year Borromeo died (1584), Lomazzo describes how the artist's greatest challenge is to impart graceful life and movement to his figures. He is credited with being among the first theoreticians to understand *grottesche* as both a decorative form and also an impetus to artistic invention. Imparting *grazia* to one's figures, Lomazzo writes, depends on being personally endowed with *furor*, the quality that artists share with poets, a divine gift that appears to be *almost* human in origin (in other words, not quite):

> knowledge of this movement (*moto*) . . . is considered to be the most difficult and is esteemed a divine gift . . . which the ancients called the *furor* of Apollo and the Muses: so it is also necessary for the painter, together with the other things required of him, to have knowledge and force and to express the principal movements *almost* as if generated out of himself and raised by him from a babe.[77] [emphasis added]

He continues, speaking of *grottesche* in nearly the same terms, that "in the invention of *grottesche* more than in anything else there runs a certain furor and a natural *bizarria*, and being without it, [artists] are unable to make anything, for all their art." Only artists in the mental state of excitement long associated with poets (*furor*) are capable of either grace or this kind of invention, which Lomazzo describes as an enigma or hieroglyph, deliberately constructed to conceal precious truths. Grotesques for Lomazzo were essentially figurations of the artist's ability to surpass nature and express himself through a personal style, terms in which he identified Michelangelo as the inventor of the *figura serpentinata*, the most attractive figural movement of all, like the spiraling dynamic of a flame, a metaphor that alludes to the artist's *furor* as his burning imagination.

In Milan, Lomazzo founded an art academy in 1560, the *Accademia della Val di Blenio*, whose members embraced the category grotesque.[78] The academy derived its name from a valley cutting through the Alps from Lombardy to Switzerland, a region then belonging to Milan that was widely known for its Protestant sympathies and religious unrest. Lomazzo and his fellow academicians gave themselves nicknames in mock identification with porters who carried heavy goods (wine in particular) from the region of unrest, and they published satirical images and verse in their own version of the Swiss dialect spoken there, placing themselves under the protection of Bacchus.

None of this arcane frivolity was even slightly amusing to the Milanese ecclesiastical authorities.[79] Lomazzo and his associates at their academy had no institutional authority even remotely comparable to that of Catholic Reformation writers like Paleotti and Borromeo or Leonardo's treatise on painting. Everything Lomazzo wrote about *grottesche* is exactly the opposite of what Paleotti (and Borromeo and many other reformers) wanted an image made by art to be: free of ambiguity, stable, not constantly transforming, not emblematic of poet's rapturous *furor* and independent *ingegno*. According to Paleotti:

> If art imitates nature, then grotesques fall outside the bounds of art. If pictures are meant to serve as books for the illiterate what else will they learn from grotesques than fibs, lies, deceits, and things that do not exist? If the soul of a picture is to be beneficial, and if it is like a dead body without this end, what shall we say about grotesque pictures, which will not only offer no benefit but can draw the minds of simple folk into a thousand errors? . . . What else can one call such pictures but lying, inept, vain, imperfect, nonverisimilar, disproportionate, obscure, and extravagant? . . . now they penetrate in the sacred places of God . . . seeing pictures of frivolities, dream apparitions, lunatic masks, chimeras of vanity, and childish games all around one corresponds to the majesty of what is after all a temple, or the gravity of the mysteries that are celebrated there.[80]

These varied concerns with the judgment of the artist and his imagination may initially seem distant from the contemporaneous Spanish literature on natural slavery, but it is important to bear in mind that the province of Milan was under the direct control of the Spanish Hapsburgs (1536–1746). It is more than likely that ecclesiastics in Milan, Bologna, and elsewhere in Italy were familiar with events and publications associated with the Thomistic–Aristotelian debates over natural slavery that led to Valladolid in 1550 *and* the justification of images by the same writers such as Domingo de Soto who were associated with Vitoria at the University of Salamanca during the same decades. Many of the same ecclesiastics, including De Soto, participated in the Council of Trent. Lomazzo's 1584 treatise on painting was widely disseminated after it was translated into English in 1598 as R. Haydocke, *A Tracte Containing the Arts of Curious Paintinge*, printed at Oxford by Ioseph Barnes for R. H. The taste for the *bizzarrie* sometimes involved exchanges between Northern and Central Italian traditions. Lomazzo became a major European phenomenon in Germany, France, Bohemia, Austria, Slovakia, Hungary, Slovenia, Croatia, and beyond. Central Europe and Habsburg Spain were especially receptive to the trends that Lomazzo had promoted.[81] In his later treatise *Idea del tempio della pittura*, 1590, Lomazzo conformed with the naturalism that the Church authorities demanded, that was also part of Leonardo's legacy when he stated that "[o]ne must be sufficiently practiced so as to fabricate clay or wax models where the proper placement of shadows and lights on the bodies can be more easily recognized, as the most excellent artists in this have done."[82]

Embedding the Sacred in the Natural

The assumed legibility of naturalism based on optical principles and the teachability of artifice rendered on these terms, made European styles of naturalism an ideal vehicle to express other forms of institutional authority. The idealized imitation of nature was deemed to conform to human ways of learning from sense experience. We do not usually think of Western styles of "naturalism" as ideologically freighted by the ontological concerns of Christianity, but it was precisely on this basis that academic instruction developed the teaching methods that came to be in common use throughout Europe and far beyond. Discussions of painting in wide-ranging locations following the Council of Trent increasingly advocated a style of optical naturalism close to Leonardo's own conception of painting – though turned to very different purposes in this religious climate. In seventeenth-century Rome, the painter Guido Reni (1575–1642) was considered "divino" by his contemporaries. The Christian context for discussing the artist's source of inspiration is even more overt in his biography. Writing in 1672, Giovanni Pietro Bellori described the relationship between the artist's acquired skills (his *arte*) and his God-given talent (his *genio*) in the following terms: Guido's noble genius gave him a mind uplifted to beauty and, through the study of the most beautiful forms, he amplified his *genio* to the highest degree.[83] What is perhaps most striking about this well-documented case is the manner in which artists' biographies articulate connections between theological grace and the visual grace of Guido's painterly style by using the same descriptive language that appears in prayers and devotional literature dedicated to the artist's sacred paintings.[84]

In her study of post-Tridentine texts on art, art historian Pamela Jones cites seventeenth-century testimony by Francesco Scannelli, 1657; Carlo Cesare

Malvasa, 1678; Luigi Pellegrino Scaramuccia, 1674; and Giovanni Battista Passeri, the poet and painter, ordained a priest in 1672, who often cited theological sources. She compares their language with numerous seventeenth-century prayers and poems in which the same terms are used to draw connections between the theological and visual connotations of grace, long associated with the artist's elevated *ingegno*. In Antonio Glielmo's *Le Grandezze della Santissma Trinita* (Venice, 1658), for example, the artist was credited with the ability to evoke in paint on canvas the beautiful, bright, loving, charming, majestic, grand, and eternal God filled with grace, as if seen in a vision (*bellissima, vaga, gioconda, svelata, chiara, amorosa, goiosa, gaudio, felicita, lume superno; lume puro; fiamma gioconda; gioia immense; amore felice; belo vis*).[85]

The seventeenth-century discourse put increasing emphasis on the artist's powers of invention, while at the same time amplifying the underlying Christian ontology of images by emphasizing that the artist's powers, his *ingegno*, imagination, inspiration – the language and terminology varied and gained in richness over time – were gifts bestowed upon the artist that he (or, rarely, she) developed through diligent study. "Art" in this sense referred to a body of skills that could be learned, while "ingegno" (from the Latin *ingenium*) referred to the artist's inborn powers, a divine gift.

To give an extended example, the Florentine-born Spanish artist Vicente Carducho (1570–1638) published a treatise, *Dialogos de la Pintura* (Madrid,1633), that expresses the same post-Tridentine understanding of the artist's *ingegno* bestowed by God and is one of the earliest printed texts to incorporate passages from Leonardo's abridged (expurgated) *Libro di Pittura*, appearing two decades before the first printed edition (1651).[86] Eight short dialogues between a master painter and his student argue that painting is a liberal art, each illustrated with a full-page engraving designed by Carducho that is allegorically related to the text and accompanied by a poem he commissioned from his literary friends.[87] The implied narrative follows the painter's progress: the first three dialogues stress industriousness and diligence in the education of the young painter, the next two dialogues focus on the more advanced topic of imitation and judgment stressing the relationship of painting to poetry in portraying nature; followed by two dialogues on the relationship of painting, nature, and God; and a final dialogue that describes painting as the supreme art to which all the others belong.[88] The seventh dialogue, on the decorum required in sacred painting, is accompanied by a poem that scolds painters who propose new and base themes, praising Carducho for using his divine gifts reverently and avoiding profane subjects. The eighth dialogue is the most original, offering a glossary of terms, descriptions of artistic materials and techniques, and references to outstanding collections in Madrid. Carducho also names a group of courtiers at the Spanish court to enlist their aid in gaining recognition for painters as liberal artists.

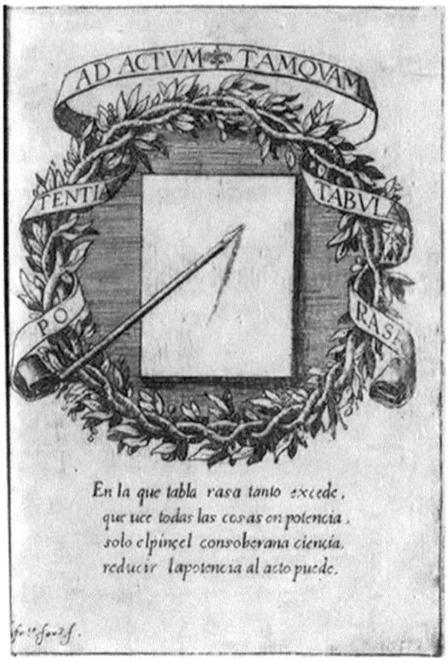

FIGURE 2.9 Vicente Carducho, *Dialogos de la Pintura* (Madrid, 1633). The final, ninth engraving does not accompany a dialogue. Getty Research Institute, Call number 11926.

The final, ninth engraving does not accompany a dialogue [Figure 2.9].[89] Instead it is placed at the very end of the treatise and depicts Aristotle's famous concept of the mind as a blank slate (*tabula rasa*), like the cleaned surface of an ancient wax writing tablet, on which anything thinkable can be inscribed.[90] A banner in the image is labeled in Latin with clear reference to Aristotle, "to act as a potential blank slate" (*ad actum tamquam potentia tabula rasa*). The engraving is accompanied by a poem which closes with a Spanish play on words that unites the two central themes of the *Dialogos* with reference to light, natural and divine: God is the source of the painter's divine gift to depict nature because "only God can give birth (*dar luz*) to such an excellent light (*luz*) as Vincenzo Carducho who is my Apollo because it takes God to make a painting and an Apollo to publish it to the world."[91]

In the institutional context of the teaching academies maintained to produce artists in service to Church and state, the structure of artistic instruction developed in the later sixteenth, seventeenth, and eighteenth centuries where artistic invention was taught as something transmissible and attainable through the acquisition of a specific skill set. That, in fact, is how Leonardo's treatise had been organized by his student Melzi: as a recursive set of exercises of increasing complexity to build a skill set. The orderly, progressive acquisition of skills and knowledge drew on longstanding workshop practices as well as a written tradition infused with Christian humanist ideas and values. For example, the ubiquitous *ut pictura poesis* comparison associated with Horace that reverberates throughout Carducho's *Dialogos*.

This history is not innocent. The persuasive visual rhetoric that was manufactured by Church and state-run institutions of artistic instruction throughout Europe and far beyond was an effective tool of empire capable of generating enormous economic profit as well as culturally specific attitudes about art posing as universal attributes of humanity.[92] Seventeenth- and eighteenth-century artists and theorists endorsed longstanding Christian ideas about the truth of artistic representation to promote the nobility of their own professions and to negotiate the ontologically slippery terrain between independent artistic invention and the truthfulness of sacred images. The science of optics continued to play a leading role in offering a type of artistic invention that conforms to the truth of natural appearances. Nature, in other words, regulates the decorum observed by artists. For example, in *Dialogos de la pintura*, Carducho defined *disegno* (*dibujo*, to use the Spanish term) as a method of understanding and revealing what is real and true in nature.[93] Carducho stressed that painters had the special ability to render visible the otherwise invisible nature of their subjects. The Spanish artist and intellectual, Francisco Pacheco (1564–1654), who assumed leadership of Seville's prestigious humanist academy in 1599 and also served as an Inquisition censor, confirms this understanding in his *Arte de la pintura* (1649), which incorporates twenty-seven passages from Leonardo's as-yet unpublished treatise. Pacheco writes that decorum is inseparable from invention, "because all of the good parts of drawing are derived from it."[94] The orthodoxy of image production is one of Pacheco's primary concerns and, like Carducho, he admonished all artists to temper their inventive license with a deep sense of decorum and conformity to acceptable methods of representation. Carducho and Pacheco disagreed with one another over what constitutes an ideal artistic rendering of nature, but they both read and incorporated elements from Leonardo's treatise on painting before the first printed edition even appeared. They both infused their definitions of *disegno* with theology *and* a scientific grounding in symmetry, proportion, anatomy and perspective, which they identify as *disegno*'s constituent elements.[95]

Paleotti's core understanding that images are the common language of all people and all social classes, with the artist serving as a "silent theologian," was exported and actively received worldwide (with unanticipated results). Pacheco's *Arte de la pintura* with its moralizing account of the artist adapted straight from Paleotti and Federico Zuccaro, became a foundational text at the Colegio de San Andrés in Quito, now in Ecuador, for example.[96] Accelerating the process of global connectedness beginning in the sixteenth century, printed images and texts alongside manuscript sources and other mobile objects made a multi-forked trek across Europe and the Mediterranean, the Americas, Asia, and the entire planet.[97] Archbishop Gabriele Paleotti of Bologna and his contemporaries who further articulated the recommendations of the Council of Trent might also have been informed by the new, widely distributed illustrated genres of printed cultural geographies, travel literature, and maps made for armchair traveling [Figure 2.10].

As I will discuss further in the next Fugue, lavishly illustrated, large-format cultural geographies as well as more portable formats attracted a considerable audience by the late sixteenth century, and sales were booming in the 1600s. Even if the majority of Europeans were not literate by modern standards, these vernacular texts with extensive illustrations made information about peoples newly discovered by Europeans widely accessible. Surekha Davies calls attention to the importance of cities in this literature for readers familiar with Aristotle's *Politics*.[98] For other readers as well, visual ethnographies organized by city or state invited comparative judgments on different peoples' levels of civility according to categories derived from ancient writers such as Pliny, Solinus, Herodotus, and above all, Aristotle because he wrote about the origins of society in similar terms.

The early modern explosion of print culture is comparable to our own information age. This illustrated literature was the successor to centuries of mapmaking and travel writing about other worlds where eyewitnesses encountered all kinds of

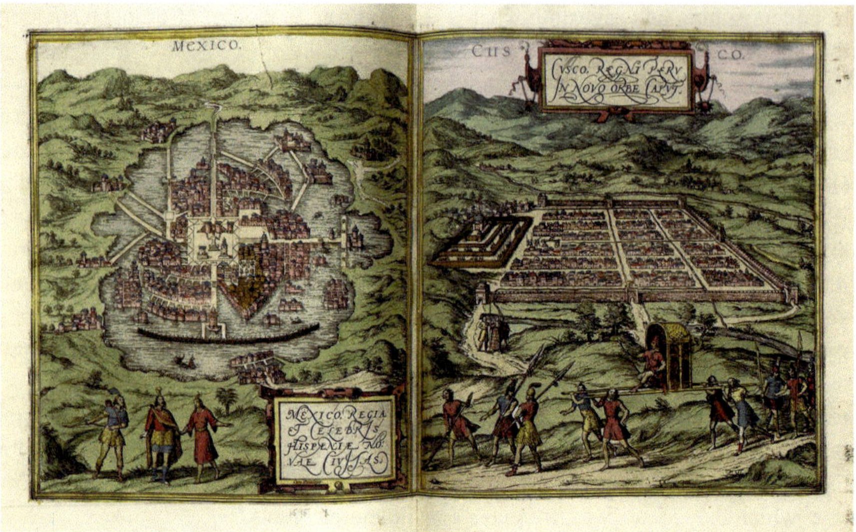

FIGURE 2.10 Georg Braun and Franz Hogenberg, *Mexico and Cuzco. Civitates Orbis Terrarum* (*Cites of the World*), hand-colored etching, first edition 1572, 6 vols. (Cologne: Peter von Brachel, 1572–1617port). Retrieved from Washington, DC, Library of Congress.

monstrous humanoid creatures. Christian doctrine held that no creature capable of existence had been omitted from the divine plan. According to a myth widespread in medieval literature and art, "wildmen" were creatures on the borderline between man and beast due to degeneration (not evolution). Like present-day mass media, the popular and profitable printed publications varied widely in accuracy partly because such older confabulated ideas remained in play and partly because the new illustrated literature typically involved many agents under the direction of publishers who bought accounts of various kinds and commissioned artists (who by and large had not themselves seen the various lands) to illustrate them. Sometimes the narrative source painted a rosy picture because it was written to encourage investment in land and resources.[99] These accounts were persuasive because of the way they were presented visually and verbally. Literary credibility is what Mary Baine Campbell, a leading expert in the medieval literature, calls a sort of "intertextual verisimilitude" that sounds like truth because it is structured as an eyewitness account filled with details of the phenomenal world.[100]

One of the most difficult lessons to *unlearn* has been the logic of representational knowledge. Often the "global turn" in contemporary art reinforces Eurocentric hierarchies by showing work that favors artists trained in Euro-American art schools, as in the case of many international biennales and similar exhibitions today, unless they address representation itself and the framework of national culture critically, sensitive to the context of display. Contemporary attempts to democratize international exhibitions in terms of identity politics and representation, like past iterations of *documenta*, the exhibition program founded in Kassel, Germany in 1955 that coincided with decolonial liberation movements, have focused on taxonomic questions of representation such as quota, proportion, and access. Attempts to politicize exhibitions in the name of an ethics of representation reinforce essentializing notions of cultural identity if they do not consider the *processes* of concept formation, appropriation, and re-signification as concepts migrate to new settings. Even ambitious, revisionist, de-centered international exhibitions such as the recent *documenta* 15 (2022), co-curated by multiple collectives led by the Indonesian collective *ruangrupa*, raise controversy when "representation" is imagined as being unproblematic.[101]

For *documenta 15* curatorial responsibility was handed over to a large group of art collectives in the Global South that functioned without a review process to support dialogue without censorship or hierarchy, but it backfired badly. The Indonesian art collective Taring Padi's towering installation depicted various historical events in Indonesia since the 1960s. Political caricatures in the form of large cardboard puppets in the *wayang* tradition of portraying antagonistic figures as dehumanized demons drew on Jewish stereotypes plucked from the media to show solidarity with victims of violence. Its German context of display in 2022 was very different from the original venue at the 2002 South Australian Art Festival devoted to empowering the creativity of groups marginalized by hierarchical concepts of art (the "global white cube"). In Germany, the antisemitic portrayals caused a political scandal and furious calls for greater government control. The director of *Documenta* resigned, the mural was first draped in funereal black and then removed, but dialogue became impossible. Taring Padi, a collective of art students and activists founded in 1998 in response to the authoritarian state in Indonesia that the West supported, had intended to denounce fascist ideologies and promote friendship and interconnectedness beyond identity by showing solidarity with victims of violence in Myanmar and Palestine. Apologizing for their "sloppy mistake," they also wanted to own their own blind spot as a starting point for discussion [Figures 2.11 and 2.12]. Charges of antisemitism continue to roil *Documenta*, which has just announced a new Finding Committee for the next exhibition after the previous committee resigned in protest.[102]

As argued here, the entangled processes of globalization, capitalism, and colonialism are not unique attributes of nineteenth-century modernity, or even eighteenth- or seventeenth-century modernity. Inclusion invariably entails exclusions, and claims of diversity in the name of democracy replay the entanglements of the modern nation-state with colonialism and capitalism that shaped art history's nineteenth-century universalist claims and masked hierarchies in a complex network of agencies. The material texts, images, objects, and human agents that established the authority of Western representation and technology for hundreds of years are a magnificent but also a troubling and contested legacy entangled with European imperialism. Framing historical inquiry transculturally asks about these various connections among things, peoples, ideas, and the environment. Geographical and period designations need to remain porous to avoid the very trap of Eurocentrism that a global context is intended to mitigate.

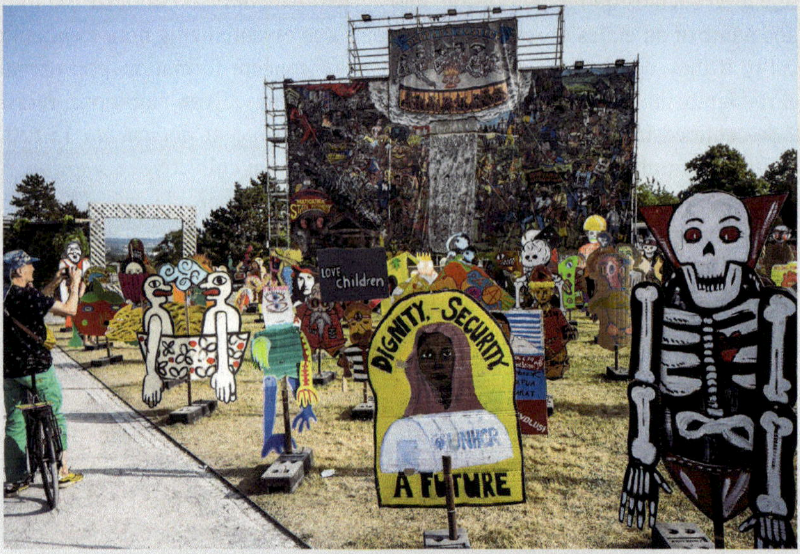

FIGURE 2.11 Taring Padi, *People's Justice*, 2002, Installation view of "The Flame of Solidarity" at *Documenta 15*, Friedrichsplatz, Kassel, Germany, 2022. Photo Thomas Lohnes/Getty Images.

While *Documenta* exhibitions have tried to democratize the curatorial process, these efforts have been hobbled by the gap between theory and praxis. Even when the aim was to investigate the postcolonial condition of globalized capitalism, the underlying problem has been repression of the *impossibility* of representation. Non-hierarchical conceptions of cultural difference do not disturb the hegemony of the norms that marginalize marginal groups. It has proven impossible for *Documenta* to avoid the blind spots that come with curatorial power limited by institutional structures, socio-economic conditions, and political contexts.

Nanne Buurman, "d is for . . .? *Documenta* and the Politics of (Re)presentation," *Field: A Journal of Socially-engaged Art Criticism* 18/19 (Spring 2021): 1–18.

How these histories became connected is always linked to economic, political, and religious agendas. Faced with linguistic barriers, early missionaries learned indigenous languages and created a copious literature including dictionaries, grammars, catechisms, collections of sermons, and confessionaries, writes art historian Daniela Bleichmar, and they worked in close collaboration with and depended on Indigenous experts. Indigenous, *mestizo*, and *criollo* artists, writers, and scholars produced numerous collaborative works. Books, such as the Mexican colonial manuscript known as the Codex Mendoza,

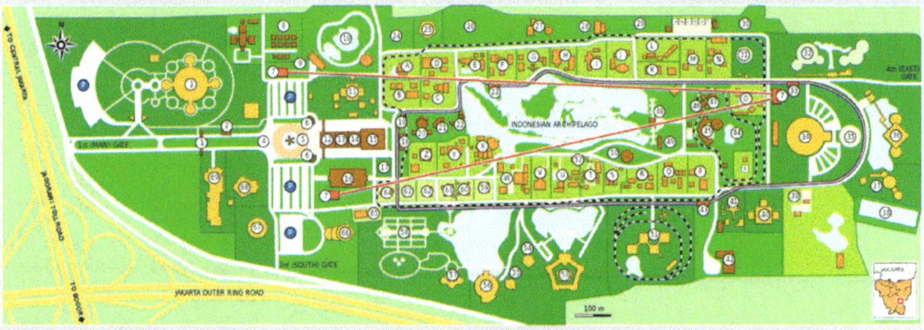

FIGURE 2.12 Plan of Taman Mini theme park, southeastern Jakarta, Indonesia. Photo Gunkarta Gunawan Kartapranata, 2010. Wiki/Gunawan Kartapranata.

In Indonesia, visual symbols (such as parks configured as maps of the nation-state) appear to give equal time to different ethnic groups while simultaneously preserving the centrality of the ruling elite. The state-sponsored national theme park of Taman Mini "is a fantasized community which is not a community at all, since no one lives there, but the fantasized image of a fantasy polity, an imaginary Indonesia mapped as a conflict-free, cleaned up version of the nation state."

Shelley Errington, *The Death of Authentic Primitive Art and Other Tales of Progress,* 1998, 222.

c. 1542, and many other portable objects operated like ships: they were neither static nor stable signifiers, but textual, visual, and material mediators [Figures 2.13 and 2.14].[103]

Today, the objects and documentary evidence assembled by early collectors provide valuable resources for studying processes of cultural mediation and the circulation of cross-cultural knowledge in the early modern world. Travel literature, topographical writings, catalogues of rare and marvelous places, buildings and things, as well as collections of the rare, the beautiful and the strange, have in recent years led to many new, creative strategies for studying the fluctuating early modern senses of "art." This history in the making is one of the most promising ways in which old Eurocentric narratives are being reconceptualized in the present while also recognizing the coloniality of power.

One of the advantages of identifying such a broad range of interpretative strategies by the single term "transcultural" is that it names a relational approach that is not delimited by categories that date from the nineteenth century. It expands the range of cultural activities to a wider field than the category "work of art" usually implies. Often, the standard categories of analysis based on a modern European understanding of art do not account for the history of complex "transcultural"

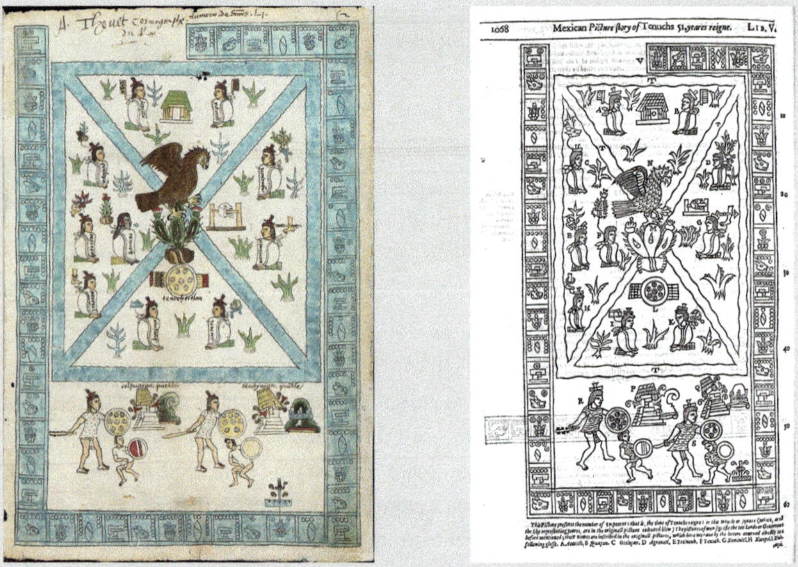

FIGURE 2.13 AND 2.14 (Left) Codex Mendoza, Mexico City, c. 1542, fol. 2r. Oxford, the Bodleian Library, University of Oxford (MS. Arch. Selden A.I.) CalimaX/Alamy Stock Photo; (Right) Samuel Purchas, *Hakluytus Postumus: Or, Purchas His Pilgrimes: Contayning a history of the world, in sea voyages, & lande-trauells, by Englishmen and others . . .*, 5 vols. (London: William Stansby for Henrie Fetherstone, 1625–1626), vol. 3, p. 1068. San Image courtesy YCBA.

The Codex Mendoza is the only known codex that offers a translation of both Nahua pictorial writing and Mexica (Aztec) history, economics, and social life in Spanish, with an alphabetic gloss accompanying each painted pictograph. Amerindian aspects include the pictographic writing and oral account, the artists and interpreter, some of the pigments, and the information. European aspects include paper, ink, some pigments, the book format, and adherence to pages as the narrative unit. European and Nahua elements carefully relate image and text, but the elements remain distinct, negotiated translations of differences between languages, writing systems, and cultures. The last page of text indicates that the project came directly out of the court system, where Indigenous litigants routinely presented pictorial statements as legal evidence. The Codex Mendoza's enormous impact in Europe began with Samuel Purchas, who acquired the manuscript c. 1616 and reproduced it almost in its entirety with black and white woodcuts, translating the Spanish into English while separating the text from the images. There were no fewer than six other reinterpretations over the next two centuries.

Daniella Bleichmar, "Translation, Mobility, and Mediation: The Case of the *Codex Mendoza*," 2016.

processes in any meaningful way. Periodization and geography, while they may continue to define the training and expertise of art historians, obstruct long enduring connections among agents, including the artisans, patrons, collectors, historians, the material objects themselves, and the materials and technologies involved in their fabrication and circulation.

"Philosophy, Not Facts"

Western critical language for evaluating pictorial embellishment has been framed in *optical* metaphors since antiquity. Terms of praise and blame such as "brilliant," "vivid," and "obscure," were never a transparent code; rather they refer to a complex system of figuration based on the assumption that abstract content can be communicated in images presented to the senses. The possibility of understanding the product of the artist's *labor* as well as his mental conception as an *index* of his character – his ingenuity, his devoutness, his *grazia*, *terribilità*, and, even more fundamentally, his *humanness* – is at the root of the modern European idea of art. The artist's powers of conceptualization embodied in his "scientific" process of fabrication from initial sketches to completed work of art became a way of assessing the epistemological status of the work *as well as* the moral character of its maker. The sixteenth-century debates over the nature of Amerindian intelligence and ingenuity developed two centuries before Vico's *New Science*, published in 1725, identified by Frances Connelly as the first systematic analysis of the origin of culture and the founding text for the modern discourse on primitivism. Another widely recognized foundational text is the rebuttal to Thomas Hobbes's *Leviathan* (1651) by Jean-Jacques Rousseau, in his *Discourse on the Origins and the Foundation of Inequality Among Mankind*, published in 1755. Rousseau argues that hunter-gatherers were "noble savages" living in small bands in a prolonged state of childlike innocence, who were egalitarian and happy before the rise of agriculture, cities, written language, science, philosophy, but also all the miseries of modern human life.[104]

Connelly's narrative relies on long established European conventions for dividing time into historical periods, with Enlightenment thought serving as the foundation of modernity. It is worth dwelling on the actual recursive nature of this timeline, conventionally characterized as a linear progression, in a transcultural framework. A century and a half before the publication of Vico's *New Science*, Michel de Montaigne (1533–1592) established the noble savage as a utopian theme in European thought with his famous critique of European society, *Des Cannibales* (1580).[105] Montaigne's main source of information was Jean de Léry's *Histoire d'un voyage faict en la terre du Brésil (History of a Voyage to the Land of Brazil)*, an instant success when it was first published in 1578 and acknowledged as a foundational text for the discipline of anthropology.[106] In his own landmark publication of 1955, *Tristes Tropiques*, the anthropologist Claude Lévi-Strauss (1908–2009) remarked that he carried a copy of "that masterpiece of anthropological literature" when he arrived in Rio de Janeiro in 1943.[107] *Tristes Tropiques* is one of the first studies to call attention to the expository conventions of anthropological discourse. By 1988, when it was commonplace in- and outside the field of anthropology to study the relationship between systems of interpretation and their historical contexts (the history of the text as text), Michel de Certeau (1925–1986), a widely esteemed multidisciplinary scholar, referred to the lasting effect of *Histoire d'un voyage* in ambivalent terms.[108] He argued that the Calvinist missionary Jean de Léry's firsthand study of the Tupinamba people both preserved and mastered their alterity, making them appear fascinating to a European audience while suppressing the natives' uncanniness.

Despite its recognized historical importance within the discipline of anthropology, and widespread critical interest in the history of vision in a number of fields, de Léry's scientific expository style with its innovative illustrations was largely ignored by art historians until the 1990s. Art historians stayed away from *Histoire d'un voyage du Brésil*, an exemplary product of material culture in another field.[109] This oversight indicates how the canonical hierarchy of European (Western) art and its attendant distinctions between art and artifact continued to be maintained and reproduced in the scholarship until the interest in transcultural studies broadened the field of inquiry. De Léry, it appears from an integrated study of rhetorical conventions operating across word and image in his text, adapted categories from sixteenth-century cosmographers like Johann Boemus (fl. 1520) and Jean Bodin (1530–1596), whose writings are discussed further in the next Fugue. In De Léry's narrative, discussion of customs unfamiliar to Europeans predominate. He ennobled a people who were known in Europe for their practice of idolatry and their sensational habit of cannibalism. De Léry confronted the problem of cultural difference and his open-mindedness toward his subject earned him a position at the foundation of modern ethnographic study. Yet he was working with categories derived from Herodotus, Solinas, Pliny, and other ancient Greek and Roman ethnographic sources such as "family," "religious rites," "marriage customs," "food habits," and "burial practices" that recontextualized the worldviews and practices of his subjects within a European framework. De Léry admired the vibrant colors and skillful construction of Tupi featherwork. As a visual complement to the text, the Tupi dancers illustrated here are compared with each other through contrasts of pose and attire and two animals known to Europeans for their ability to mimic humans [Figures 2.15 and 2.16]. Those with sufficient knowledge of Aristotle would have recognized his deliberate juxtaposition of subordinate features as a comparison between the products of nature and man, visual comparisons that can be "read out" of the image as a conceptual contrast.

The distinction between the classic norm and its antithesis – the grotesque, the monstrous, the mannered distortions of that norm – emerged in Protestant and Catholic Reformation writings that were disseminated around the world throughout the colonial period. What are the implications of pushing back the emergence of modern European concepts of art and the origins of society from the eighteenth century to the initial period of global capitalism driven by European initiatives? First, it becomes clear that secular Eurocentric arguments advanced by philosophers in the eighteenth century are an effect of the "coloniality" of power and knowledge operating since the early sixteenth century in

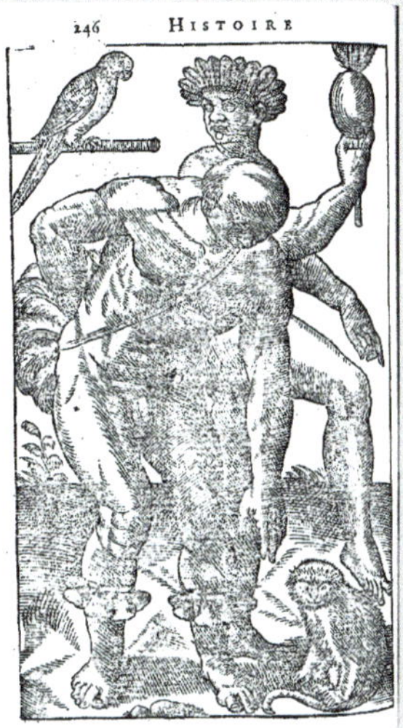

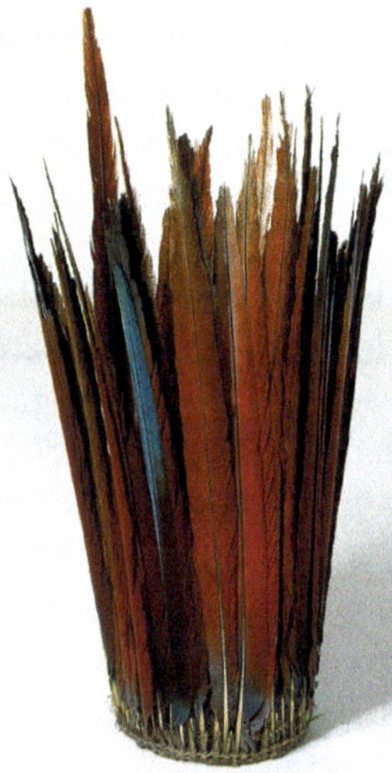

FIGURE 2.15 AND 2.16 (Left) Jean de Léry, *Histoire d'un voyage faict en la terre du Brésil* (Geneva/La Rochelle, 1578), dancers wearing featherwork ceremonial attire. © John Carter Brown Library, Providence, RI; (Right) Feathered headdress, Tupinambá, Brazil, before 1689. Ara (macaw) tail feathers and fibers. Copenhagen, National Museum of Denmark, Ethnographic Collection, Hc.56. Photo Lennart Larsen for Nationalmuseet, licence CC-BY-SA, http://samlinger.natmus. dk/ES/asset/25893

The Tupi were semi-nomads inhabiting Brazil's eastern coastal forests whose practices centered on ceremonial traditions involving dance, sound, movement, and adornment documented in the material evidence and colonial European sources. They practiced *tapirage*, a technique for altering and intensifying the color of feathers highly valued by European collectors. The Tupi connected many birdsongs to spirits, described by de Léry as a "fantasy imprinted in their brains that . . . when they die their souls will rejoin their ancestors behind the mountains and dance with them." The Jesuits, who procured featherworks for the market and dominated the Brazilian missionary enterprise, incorporated aspects of Indigenous culture into multisensory performances of Christian sacraments, including the use of Tupi feathered capes in baptismal rituals. These capes probably functioned as supernatural skins, transferring the vital force from one living organism to another, transforming the performer into a bird or divine entity in avian form. This book was already in press when the Denmark National Museum announced that it has reunited a 300-year-old feathered cloak made of thousands of scarlet ibis feathers with the Tupinambá de Olivença, who regard their capes as sacred, living forces and evidence for land rights and other legal matters. About 200 Tupinambá made the 775-mile journey from their land in Bahia to Rio de Janeiro to celebrate its return on the grounds of the national museum that is being rebuilt after a fire destroyed about 85% of its collection in 2018.[110]

Christian texts that linked art to humanity. The definition of art linked to humanity, as documented in Paleotti's lengthy discussion of the grotesque as a universal category, excluded many other humans in terms of their *techne* and forms of social organization. Second, when these dehumanizing exclusions were applied to actual Indigenous peoples and other colonized subjects, they effectively justified extractive capitalism linked to environmental devastation since the early sixteenth century.[111]

Third, there is not a shred of evidence to uphold the "big picture" of social evolution. The idea that human societies can be arranged according to stages of development leading from hunter–gatherers to agriculture to the formation of cities, each with their own characteristic technologies and forms of organization, have their roots in philosophy, not facts, write the co-authors of a monumental (though controversial) study published in 2021, *The Dawn of Everything: A New History of Humanity*, based primarily on empirical, archaeological evidence.[112] In a slim volume published in 1967 on ancient Greek theories of cultural origins, philologist Thomas Cole meticulously documented a rich, heterogeneous tradition of writings dealing with the early history of technology and the social progress of humanity through technological advances.[113] Whether ancient theories of cultural evolution derive from a single source as Cole argued or from widely diffused common ideas as some of his critics maintain, it is important to bear in mind that all ancient accounts in the Western tradition portray a history of progress leading from savagery to civilization, a culturally specific (certainly not universal) narrative that remains in play even now. Ancient Mediterranean authors, like their modern successors, glorified their own era or profession and portrayed themselves as belonging to the final and culminating phase of civilization.[114] For sixteenth-century authors such as Las Casas, Vitoria, and Sepúlveda, writes Pagden, culture was the medium through which men learned to explore the God-given potential of nature: men acquire true *scientia* through conversion to Christianity. Las Casas's *Apologética historia* was the first large-scale attempt to apply the categories of sixteenth-century Aristotelian anthropology to a substantial body of data.[115]

Assumptions regarding cultural evolution were developed in the sixteenth century on the basis of ancient sources, Aristotle's *Politics* chief among them, that put to new uses a text written in the fourth century BCE by a Greek philosopher about Mediterranean city-states that practiced slavery. Herein lies the problem: "universalism" is the heritage of Enlightenment metaphysics rooted in ancient Graeco-Roman thought and modern colonialism. Decolonial writers and art practitioners demand scrutiny and reconceptualization of colonialist assumptions while others who likewise wish to integrate past and present in accounts of global art, find the values associated with the same categories and goals to be self-evidently "universal." What would make contemporary practices "global" without reinstalling the same values in displaced form? Beyond the public act of restitution acknowledging the consequences of the past, there is still the pressing need to contextualize how formerly colonized objects functioned in their societies of origin, circulated in trading networks, and reached their current destinations. Framing historical inquiry transculturally asks about these various connections among things, peoples, ideas, and the environment.

Museums as Cultural Mediators

Transcultural approaches also consider how gaps and discontinuities of historical understanding are to be negotiated. The epistemic trauma that separated ethnography from "art" in Eurocentric disciplinary practices, glimpsed in the differentiated treatment of De Léry's text by anthropologists and art historians, haunts the present in many ways even when the categories themselves are avoided. An extended concrete example can demonstrate the continuing effect of colonialist assumptions about the "artifacts of the primitive" versus the "art of the civilized," but also the ability of artists, art historians, curators, critics, and government officials working together to change Eurocentric perceptions by redressing colonial injustices. A widely discussed effort to reclaim cultural patrimony illicitly acquired by colonial powers, ongoing since 1960, concerns a group of several thousand metal plaques and sculptures that once decorated the palace of the Oba (ruler) in the kingdom of Benin, now Edo State, Nigeria, known as the Benin Bronzes. I begin *in medias res* with an essay from the 24 July 2004 issue of the British newspaper, *The Guardian*, by Neil MacGregor, then director of the British Museum, entitled (surely unselfconsciously) "The whole world in our hands." MacGregor discussed the Museum's Benin bronze collection, one of the largest in the world:

> A British legation, travelling to Benin at a sacred season of the year when such visits were forbidden, was killed. . . . In retaliation, the British mounted a punitive expedition against Benin. Civil order collapsed (Baghdad comes to mind), the plaques and other objects were seized and sold, ultimately winding up in the museums of London, Berlin, Paris and New York. There they caused a sensation. It was a revelation to western artists and scholars, and above all to the public, that metal work of this refinement had been made in 16th-century Africa. . . . I don't know where else a visitor can apprehend Africa in so many contexts. A collection that embraces the whole world allows you to consider the whole world. That is what an institution such as the British Museum is for.[116]

Twenty years ago, MacGregor defended his institution's refusal to return its plundered treasures by repeatedly citing its obligation to preserve large portions of the world's artistic heritage which have somehow "wound up" in his museum when Benin "civil order collapsed." In the case of MacGregor's vision of the British Museum, these new relationships are determined by the collector/conqueror: after

British troops killed Benin civilians in a punitive action stemming from British disrespect for Benin sacred customs and laws, the world gained appreciation of the African art it acquired as a result. Here are the facts: in February 1897 about 1,200 British soldiers ransacked and burned the Benin Royal Palace and neighboring wealthy residences located in Benin City. Thousands of people were killed in the raid, which is known in Nigeria as the Benin Massacre. The soldiers who participated in the Punitive Expedition looted up to 10,000 royal and sacred bronzes, ivories, and other objects, while administrators took photographs. About three hundred brass plaques and other objects were taken to the British Museum in July 1897 and put on display within six months. Two hundred were selected for retention, the rest turned to the Foreign Office. Afterwards, dealers and shippers sold the artifacts to Western European and North American museums – 165 institutions have been identified, with the largest holdings in Berlin and London, and many others in regional and university museums. Today, there are still extensive holdings in private collections because, in addition to the 900–1,000 brass plaques that became the official booty of the Punitive Expedition, soldiers and officers took the loot for themselves or gave it away as gifts. These included the Acting Consul General Ralph Moor who ordered the Expedition taking over several weeks and covering 5,000 square kilometers. Many of the looted items were later bequeathed or sold to museums. The knowledge that lies with Euro-American museum curators needs to be shared, writes Pitt-Rivers Museum Curator Dan Hicks in the most comprehensive account yet to establish what he calls the "necrography" of the looted items.[117] These colonial actions followed three centuries of British colonial extractive capitalism in the Niger Delta, Hicks emphasizes, built on the desire for slaves linked with the "drug foods" of sugar, tobacco, and coffee that led to "militarist colonialism" after restrictions on the slave trade and firearms were imposed by the Brussels Anti-Slavery Conference in 1889/90: "The twin concerns of sovereignty and profit run through this process from start to finish."[118]

The power of the director of the British Museum to enable the institution to evoke, elicit, and stage our desires depends on maintaining the fiction that it is better for the Benin Bronzes to remain in London rather than in Africa. To remain in London is better than being "orphaned," MacGregor writes in the same article, because "the British Museum must now reaffirm its worldwide civic purpose. That must be the goal that shapes our future plans. Where else can the world see so clearly that it is one?" Unsurprisingly, MacGregor was a signatory to the controversial Declaration of the Value of Universal Museums signed by an international consortium of museum directors in 2002.[119] The underlying argument is that art is that which makes us one. But at what cost? And whose version of art? Most Benin Bronzes entered European ethnological collections such as the British Museum, not art museums. Indeed, their extraordinary artistic quality was a revelation to ethnologists such as Adolf Bastian (1826–1905), a founding director of the Berliner Museum für Völkerkunde, established in 1873. Bastian, who traveled the world collecting material culture, conceived of his vast collection as a scientific project for comparing the worldviews (*Weltenschauungen*) of their makers, a "reading room for the inductive study of the science of man."[120] His successor Felix von Luschan saw himself as an enlightened progressive when he wrote about deploying looted bronzes and ivories to "annihilate the thesis of race inferiority."[121]

Cultural historian H. Glenn Penny and other contemporary advocates of the universal ethnology museum envision an updated version of the Enlightenment project that works with willing Indigenous groups to produce "joint knowledge." The question is, what would make Indigenous people willing to participate in a project that does not consider the possibility of reclaiming their alienated heritage on their own turf, speaking both literally and figuratively? Art historian Matthew Vollgraff, responding to the most extreme denials of Germany's colonialist past by contemporary museum professionals, notes that Berlin's ethnographic museum collections were embedded in a densely networked transnational colonial context that existed well before Bismarck convened the Berlin Conference [1884–1885], otherwise known as the Scramble for Africa that formalized German claims to territory on the continent. Bismarck intervened in the rivalry between Great Britain and France. Consequently, the peoples of Africa had no say in the partitioning of their homelands then or later: by 1900, European states had claimed nearly 90% of African territory.[122]

After MacGregor retired from his post as Director of the British Museum in 2015, he became a founding director of the Berlin museum called the Humboldt Forum, the rebranding and relocation of Bastian's ethnology museum which implicitly still preserves the longstanding Eurocentric hierarchy of art versus artifact in housing everything that is "non-European art." The Humboldt Forum has experienced considerable birthing problems in trying to remain wedded to a colonialist philosophy of art.[123] Decolonial writers and art practitioners demand scrutiny and reconceptualization of colonialist assumptions while MacGregor and others who likewise wish to integrate past and present in their accounts of global art, find the values associated with the same categories and goals to be self-evidently "universal." The immediate origins of these categories about individual and collective cultural identity are in nineteenth-century European theories of national, biological, and social development.[124]

A closely related problem is the binary model of center and periphery that grants privilege to European civilization, a position to which MacGregor's editorial about the value of universal art museums in certain urban centers but not others testifies. Even in the act of admitting "looting" and "facing the consequences of the past," as the current website of the Humboldt Forum does, this anodyne version of a decolonial narrative does not acknowledge the uneven economic, social, and political conditions that affect the circulation, reception, and use of different cultural traditions, signifying systems, worldviews, and contexts of use to this day. Not to mention that the extraction of cultural patrimony is directly aligned with economic globalization, its extraction of raw materials, and destruction of the environment

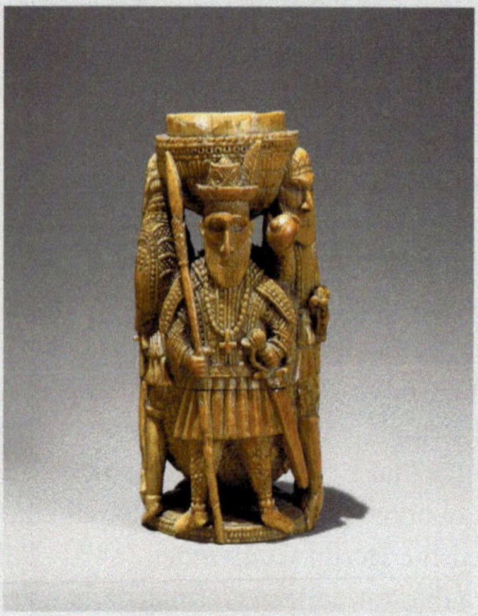

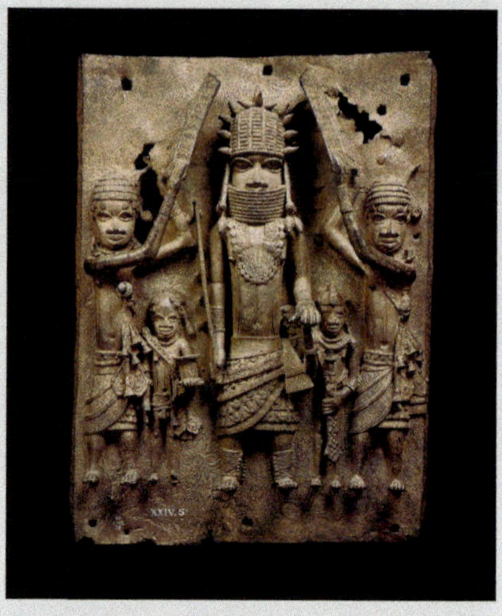

FIGURE 2.17 AND 2.18 (Left) Master of the Heraldic Ship (Court of Owo or Benin, Nigeria), Saltcellar with Portuguese figures, ivory, c. 1525–1600. New York, Metropolitan Museum of Art, Louis V. Bell and Rogers Funds, 1972.63a, b. One of four nearly identical works that originally included a lid with a carved ship on top; (Right) Benin City (formerly Edo), Nigeria, Relief plaque depicting ritual court life with figure of Oba (possibly Esigie) flanked by two standing warrior attendants holding shields in a formal protective stance, with two smaller scale attendants. Lost wax cast in brass, 16th/17th century. London, British Museum, Af1898,0115.38, part of a pair with Af1898,0115.39. © The Trustees of the British Museum.

The brass plaque and the ivory container were both made in Benin's royal workshops and estimated to date from the sixteenth century. They share formal characteristics such as the rigid frontal stance of the figures and elaborate surface decoration. The ivory depicts fashionably dressed, high-ranking European officials wearing the cross of the Military Order of Christ, while the brass plaque depicts the Oba with attendants, using casting methods developed as early as the 900s, made to be displayed in a ritual context in the royal palace. Both are connected with the colonial slave trade, but their paths out of Africa were very different: carved ivories were made as commodities while the plaques were sacred ancestral images looted in a violent act of cultural destruction. The earliest ivories brought back to Europe were given as gifts to the Portuguese monarch by the ruler of the Kongo in 1482. Later ivories, praised by Europeans for their ingenuity and skill, were made for the market. They were acquired primarily in what is now Sierra Leone and, beginning in the 1520s, in Benin. These three areas share complementary beliefs that the dead travel across a great body of water to reach the place of the ancestors. When the first Portuguese slave traders arrived by sea, they exhibited characteristics of the dead: they were white, spoke an unintelligible language, possessed superior technology, and dropped anchor in the port of Ughoton from where the Bini dead were believed to depart. The ivory pictured here includes references to the watery world of Olokun, Benin's ruler of the seas believed to have been subdued by the Oba who controlled all the trade routes.

The Oba purchased slaves from surrounding countries with uncarved ivory and traded slaves for the metal needed to make ritual objects. Later merchants living along what became known as the Slave Coast were a mix of African, Jewish, and other Europeans without a single fixed identity who called themselves Portuguese and served as intermediaries in the coastal trade.

and lifeways of Indigenous peoples and colonial subjects worldwide. These differentials are what need to be unpacked, as curators critically aware of unequal conditions stemming from colonialism have envisioned since the 1980s.

Has anything fundamentally changed institutionally speaking since MacGregor articulated his views in 2004? In the case of the Benin Bronzes, the answer is yes, thanks to activists, artists, to scholars who have meticulously documented their history after 1897, and to Nigerian officials who have put pressure on European institutions since Nigeria gained independence from Britain in 1960. The first exhibition of 26 looted treasures, repatriated from the Quai Branly Museum in Paris, went on view in Benin City, Nigeria, in March 2022, while the Smithsonian Institution in the US simultaneously announced plans to return "most" of its looted bronzes, the Humboldt Forum reversed its earlier decision to display its Benin Bronzes, the GRASSI Museum of Ethnology in Leipzig, replaced its display of Benin Bronzes with a critical reflection on restitution, and, in October 2021, Nigeria's cultural minister announced plans to receive over 1,000 Benin Bronzes from Germany in 2022, to be displayed at the new Edo Museum of West African Art in Benin City, an agreement formally ratified in July 2022.[125] The British Museum also announced plans to lend or return its bronzes.[126] The momentum is building and diversifying as museums respond to calls for the repatriation of looted, stolen, and other improperly acquired works of art.[127] Of course, there is no consensus, the issues are complex, every case is different, and looting continues. Even the most ambitious efforts to return burial remains and sacred objects to Native Americans, established in the US in 1990 by the Native American Graves Protection and Repatriation Act (NAGPRA), have been less effective than hoped.[128]

Thankfully, the colonial era of scrambling for treasures and trophies to fill European museums with the rest of the world is regarded very differently today than it was even two decades ago. In fact, the emancipatory potential of the colonialist discourse on art has arguably gone mainstream when the popular journal *National Geographic* can announce in 2023 that the return of "treasures to where they came from is not closing museums, it is opening new doors."[129] Yet the process of restitution is far from straightforward. To continue with the saga of the Benin Bronzes, after a plan was agreed upon to return the Benin Bronzes to be displayed in a new museum designed by the Ghanaian architect David Adjaye, Nigeria's outgoing president Muhammadu Buhari announced that he had transferred ownership to the current Oba, a direct descendant of the Oba who was exiled when the British legion attacked and looted his palace. In March 2023, a new furor arose in- and outside Nigeria about who the rightful owner of the Benin treasures was, what arrangements would be made for their display, and who had a right to make those decisions. The unanticipated reassignment of ownership to the Oba resulted in a backlash that rekindled colonialist justifications that MacGregor offered two decades earlier to retain the material.[130] Critics of the plan for restitution did not consider that, within the Nigerian social structure, the Oba is a public figure, not a private person, so his ownership does not preclude public display. To the contrary, the current Oba, educated at Rutgers University and the University of Wales who had been campaigning for the return of the bronzes for decades, intends to exhibit and travel the collection "as ambassadors" for his kingdom and its culture.[131] Another accusation by a group of African Americans who have filed a lawsuit to stop the return of the Benin Bronzes from the Smithsonian Museum in Washington, DC, was that the rulers of Benin were actively involved in the transatlantic slave trade, therefore descendants of enslaved people should have a right to see the bronzes where they live.[132] Factions in Nigeria are at this writing still arguing on where to display their repatriated cultural patrimony, but agree that "the West" should not meddle.[133]

One of the most important outcomes of this case, like many others, is that restitution is a process, not a singular act, but an ongoing process that can be a fruitful means for opening new perspectives and establishing new relationships. "We have to recognize that decolonization can only be seen as a societal issue and understood as a relational process from which no one is exempt," writes Friedrich von Bose, the former Head of Research and Exhibitions at three ethnological museums that form part of the Dresden State Art Collections who has been involved with the Humboldt Forum and the ethics of display for over a decade.[134] An important task for museums, Bose specifies, is to establish new areas of responsibility and sustainable relationships through networks involving all the stakeholders and knowledge holders. The following Intermezzo takes a closer look at the seventeenth-century European discourse on national styles of artmaking at the height of the colonial period, two centuries before the professionalization of art history on the model of the modern nation-state. Next up will be historical climate theory, but some additional groundwork needs to be established first.

Notes

1 John W. O'Malley, "Trent, Sacred Images, and Catholics' Senses of the Sensuous," In *The Sensuous in the Counter-Reformation Church*, ed. Marcia B. Hall and Tracy E. Cooper (New York: Cambridge University Press, 2012).

2 Jesse M. Locker, *Art and Reform in the Late Renaissance: After Trent* (UK: Routledge, 2018) offers a thorough overview. Criteria applied to prohibited books were considered for music and painted images by the Congregation of the Index in 1587 and 1590, though the Congregation restricted prohibition to printed images: Vittorio Frajese, *Nascita dell'Indice: La censure ecclesiastica dal Rinascimento alla Controriforma* (Brescia: Morcelliana, 2006).

3 "On the Invocation, Veneration, and Relics of Saints, and on Sacred Images," Twenty-fifth Session, *Canons and Decrees of the Council of Trent*. Translation adapted from Norman P. Tanner, ed., *Decrees of the Ecumenical Council*, 2 vols., (Washington, DC, 1990), vol. 2, 774\—776. *Canones et decreta sacrosancti oecumenici Concila tridentini sub Paulo III., lulio III. et Pio IV (*Leipzig, 1866), 175. O'Malley, "Trent, Sacred Images," translates *lascivus* (lasciviousness) as sensual and the term is discussed extensively in the volume (cited in n. 1). According to William McCuaig, translator of Gabriele Paleotti, *Discourse on Sacred and Profane Images*, Intro. Paolo Prodi, trans. William McCuaig (Los Angeles: Getty Research Institute, 2012), 11, the English translator of the Tridentine decree did not understand that painted images were involved – he thought the authors were talking about actions or deeds. I follow O'Malley and McCuaig's translations of the affected text.

4 O'Malley, "Trent, Sacred Images."

5 Wietse de Boer, *Catholic Debates at the Time of Trent: with an Edition and Translation of Key Documents* (Leiden: Brill, 2022). The following discussion is based substantially on De Boer's account.

6 De Boer, *Catholic Debates*, 36, citing the 1540 Latin edition, discusses Martin Perez de Ayala, *De divinis*, preface dated 6 May 1548. Ayala studied first in Salamanca and attended the course of Vitoria then under Juan de Medina Alcala. He was concerned that there be "no superstition or idolomania" (§§ 12,16), insisted that no "divine honors" be offered to images (§§ 13,17), and denounced both the belief that "anything numinous" inhered in them and the adoration of "false powers and heroes" (§ 17). The final section attacked the Thomist interpretation of images receiving same veneration as holy subjects.

7 Thomas Aquinas, *Summa Theologica*, III.q.25,a.3: the same reverence should be shown to an image of Christ as to Christ himself.

8 De Boer, *Catholic Debates*, 23: in the late 1540s Cervini promoted censorship as member of the Holy Office and was probably aware of Carolingian critique of Nicaea II, in the newly discovered and published *Libri Carolini* (Paris, 1549), which influenced Protestant critics of sacred images.

9 De Boer, *Catholic Debates*, 48.

10 De Boer, *Catholic Debates*, 9.

11 See Giuseppe Scavizzi, *The Controversy on Images from Clavin to Baronious* (New York: P. Lang, 1992); and Maria Fabricus Hansen, *The Art of Transformation: Grotesques in Sixteenth-Century Italy* (Rome: Edizioni Quasar, 2018), for a detailed history of the scholarship and extensive illustrations.

12 Carlos M. N. Eire, *War against the Idols: The Reformation of Worship from Erasmus to Calvin* (Cambridge–Sydney: Cambridge University Press, 1986); Lee Palmer Wandel, *Voracious Idols and Violent Hands: Iconoclasm in Reformation Zurich, Strasbourg, and Basel* (Cambridge: Cambridge University Press, 1995).

13 Eire, *War against the Idols*, 84, citing *Huldreich Zwinglis Sämtliche Werke*, ed. E. Egli, W. Köhler, F. Blanke, et al. (Berlin–Zurich: C. A. Schwetschke und Sohn, 1905), vol. 4, 96; W. J. T. Mitchell, "The Rhetoric of Iconoclasm," *Iconology: Image, Text, Ideology* (Chicago: Chicago University Press, 1986), 164, cites Francis Bacon, *The New Organon*, 1620.

14 The clearest, most detailed exposition appears in Zwingli's *Commentary on True and False Religion*, 1525. Eire, *War against the Idols*, 84, 211–220.

15 Mitchell, *Iconology*, 160–208, on Marx's debt to Protestantism.

16 *Sacrifice and Conversion in the Early Modern Atlantic World*, ed. Maria Berbara, I Tatti Research Series 3 (Rome: Officina Libraria, 2022).

17 They were both indebted to Monseigneur Agucchi's unpublished treatise fragment on painting (composed c. 1615, published 1646), first studied by Denis Mahon, Studies in Seicento Art and theory (London: Warburg Institute, University of London, 1947). Comparable statements were made by F. Baldinucci (1767) and others. On the complex history of this scholarship, see Elizabeth Cropper, Introduction, to Craig Hugh Smyth, *Mannerism and Maniera* (Vienna: IRSA, 1992).

18 Donald Posner, Introduction, to Walter Friedlaender, *Mannerism and Anti-Mannerism in Italian Painting* (New York: Schocken Books, 1965), xi–xix, at xii. The term anti-classical was being used at the time to describe contemporary German art (xiii).

19 Chiara Gauna, *La storia pittoria di Luigi Lanzi* (Florence; L. S. Olschki, 2003).

20 Friedländer, *Mannerism and Anti-Mannerism*.

21 Posner, Introduction, to Friedländer, *Mannerism and Anti-Mannerism*, xviii. An analysis of the historiography of the period term Baroque as part of the structuration of the discipline of art history, is beyond the scope of the present study, but see the excellent overview by Helen Hills, "The Baroque: The Grit in the Oyster of Art History," in *Rethinking the Baroque*, ed. Helen Hills (Aldershot: Ashgate Press, 2011), 11–36. Hills' analysis extends the discussion here: "While the Renaissance was central to the development of the history of art, from Vasari on, baroque inhabits its demonic heart, and emerged in contradistinction to its well-mannered counterpart."

22 See Janis Bell, "Introduction," in *Art History in the Age of Bellori: Scholarship and Cultural Politics in Seventeenth-Century Rome*, ed. Janis Bell and Thomas Willette (Cambridge–New York: Cambridge University Press, 2002), 1–52.

23 W. Sauerländer, "From Stilus to Style: Reflections on the Fate of a Notion," *Art History* 6 (1983), 253–270.

24 Hans Belting, *Likeness and Presence: A History of the Image before the Era of Art* (1990 German ed.), trans. Edmund Jephcott (Chicago: Chicago University Press, 1994).

25 Hans Belting, *Florence & Baghdad: Renaissance Art and Arab Science*, trans. Deborah Lucas Schneider (Cambridge, MA–London: The Belknap Press of Harvard University Press, 2011).

26 Belting, *Florence and Baghdad*, 3.

27 Philip Sohm, *Style in the Art Theory of Early Modern Italy* (Cambridge: Cambridge University Press, 2001), 3.

28 David L. Swartz, "Bourdieu's Concept of Field," *Oxford Bibliographies*, accessed 10 April 2023, at www.oxfordbibliographies.com/display/document/obo-9780199756384/obo-9780199756384-0164.xml; Pierre Bourdieu, *The Field of Cultural Production: Essays on Art and Literature* (New York: Columbia University Press, 1993).

29 Randall Johnson, Introduction, in Bourdieu, *The Field of Cultural Production: Essays on Art and Literature*, ed. and intro. Randal Johnson (New York: Columbia University Press, 1993), 2–3.

30 Hall and Cooper, "Introduction," *The Sensuous in the Counter-Reformation Church*, 1, distinguish sensuous, meaning derived from the senses, from sensual, associated with appetites, especially sexual pleasure.

31 Frances S. Connelly, *The Sleep of Reason: Primitivism in Modern European Art and Aesthetics, 1725–1907* (University Park: Pennsylvania State University Press, 1995), 9.

32 Jason Moore, "Introduction," in *Anthropocene or Capitalocene? Nature, History, and the Crisis of Captialism*, ed. Jason W. Moore (Oakland, CA: PM Press, 2016), 1–13.

33 Jorge Cañizares-Esguerra, "On Ignored Global 'Scientific Revolutions,'" *Journal of Early Modern History* 21 (2017): 420–432.
34 Paul Grendler, *The Roman Inquisition and the Venetian Press, 1540–1605* (Princeton: Princeton University Press, 1977), 260–261.
35 On Borromeo's institutional reforms, see Wietse de Boer, *The Conquest of the Soul: Confession, Discipline, and Public Order in Counter-Reformation Milan* (Leiden: Brill, 2001); *Carlo Borromeo L'Opera della "Grande Riforma": Cultura, Religione, e Arti del Governo nella Milano del Pieno Cinqucento*, ed. Franco Buzzi and Danilo Zardin, intro. Gianfranco Ravasi (Milan: Silvana Editoriale, 1997); John Alexander, *From Renaissance to Counter-Reformation: The Architectural Patronage of Carlo Borromeo during the Reign of Pius IV* (Milan: Biblioteca Ambrosiana; Rome: Bulzoni, 2007).
36 *Trattato della pittura di Lionardo da Vinci*, ed. Guglielmo Manzi (Rome: Stamperia de Romanis, 1817). The current critical edition is *Leonardo da Vinci: Libro di pittura*, ed. Carlo Pedretti, transcribed Carlo Vecce. 2 vols. (Florence: Giunti, 1995).
37 Nikolaus Pevsner, *Academies of Art Past and Present* (1940; New York: Da Capo Press, 1973).
38 See *The Fabrication of Leonardo da Vinci's Trattato della Pittura, with a scholarly edition of the Italian editio princeps (1651) and an annotated English Translation*, ed. Claire Farago, Janis Bell, and Carlo Vecce, foreword Martin Kemp, additional contributions by Juliana Barone, Mario Valentino Guffanti, Matthew Landrus, Maria Rascaglia, and Anna Sconza, 2 vols. (Leiden: Brill Press, 2018).
39 See Maria Fabricius Hansen, *The Art of Transformation: Grotesques in Sixteenth-Century Italy* (Rome: Edizioni Quasar, 2018).
40 Anton Francesco Doni, *Disegno* (Venice, 1549), 141v.
41 David Summers, "Michelangelo on Architecture," *The Art Bulletin* 54 (1972): 146–157, at 152.
42 Artists such as Annibale Fontana who was a leading producer of these objects, benefited from Leonardo's writings, drawings, and designs for instruments for working precious materials. Paola Venturelli, *Leonardo da Vinci: Milano tra XV e XVI secolo* (Venice: Marsilio Editori, 2002).
43 Gabriele Paleotti, *Discorso intorno alle imagini sacre e profane* (Bologna, 1582), Book 2, chapter 36.
44 Samuel Y. Edgerton, Jr., *Pictures and Punishment: Art and Criminal Prosecution during the Florentine Renaissance* (Ithaca: Cornell University Press, 1985), 173.
45 Claire Farago, Janis Bell, and Carlo Vecce, *The Fabrication of Leonardo da Vinci's Trattato della Pittura*, foreword Martin Kemp, 2 vols. (Leiden: Brill Press, 2018), provides full documentation of the following discussion.
46 Aristotle's "faculty of discovering the middle term," or *forma agens*. On Avicenna and Scholastic thought, see David Summers, *Judgment of Sense: Renaissance Naturalism and the Rise of Aesthetics* (Cambridge: Cambridge University Press, 1987).
47 Cicero: *Oratore*, 51, 173; 58, 198; 44, 151; *De natura deorum*, 2, 58. David Summers, *Michelangelo and the Language of Art* (Princeton: Princeton University Press, 1981), 355–358.
48 Summers, *The Judgment of Sense*, 97–101.
49 The following analysis draws upon the primary sources assembled and discussed by Summers, "Furia," *Michelangelo*, 60–71. Leonardo draws upon both strands of accounts of *ingegno* without apparent discomfort at their incommensurability.
50 Matthew Landrus, "Leonardo's Lost Book on Painting and Human Movements," in Farago, Bell, and Vecce, *Fabrication*, 1: 183–212.
51 Alexander Marr et al., *Logodaedalus: Word Histories of Ingenuity in Early Modern Europe* (Pittsburgh: University of Pittsburgh Press, 2015).
52 Pamela H. Smith, "Science on the Move: Recent Trends in the History of Early Modern Science," *Renaissance Quarterly* 62 (2009): 345–375.
53 Thomas Cole, *Democritus and the Sources of Greek Anthropology* (Cleveland: Western Reserve University Press, 1967), 35.

54 Roberto Valturio (1405–1475), *De re militari: umanesimo e arte della Guerra tra Medioevo e Rinascimento* (Rimini: Guaraldi; Milan: Y. Press, 2006).
55 E. Cecilia Voelker, "Borromeo's Influence on Sacred Art and Architecture," in *San Carlo Borromeo: Catholic Reform and Ecclesiastical Politics in the Second Half of the Sixteenth Century*, ed. John M. Headley and John B. Tomaro (Washington: Folger Shakespeare Library, 1988).
56 Evelyn Cecilia Voelker, *Charles Borromeo's Instructiones fabricae et supellectilis ecclesiasticae, 1577, with a translation with commentary and analysis*, PhD diss., Syracuse University, 1977 (Ann Arbor: University of Michigan Microfilms, 1980), chapter 17, 228.
57 Anne H. Muraoka, *The Path of Humility*: *Caravaggio and Carlo Borromeo* (New York: Peter Lang, 2015), 121–126.
58 Paolo Prodi, "San Carlo Borromeo e Il Cardinale Gabriele Paleotti: due vescovi della Riforma Cattolica," *Critica Storica* 3/2 (1964): 135–151; Muraoka, *Path of Humility*, 106–111.
59 Pamela Jones, "Art Theory as Ideology: Gabriele Paleotti's Hierarchical Notion of Painting's Universality and Reception," in *Reframing the Renaissance: Visual Culture in Europe and Latin America, 1450–1650*, ed. Claire Farago (London–New Haven: Yale University Press, 1995), 128–129, citing Paleotti, *Discourse*, Book 1, chapter 22. See also, Brenda Deen Schildgen, "Cardinal Paleotti and the *Discorso intorno*," in *Sacred Possessions: Collecting Italian Religious Art, 1500–1900*, ed. Gail Feigenbaum and Sybille Ebert-Schifferer (Los Angeles: Getty Publications, 2011), 8–16.
60 Paleotti, *Discourse*, Book 1, Chapter 22.
61 In 1490, Savonarola delivered sermons on the abuses of poetry in which he followed Thomas Aquinas. Concetta Carestia Greenfield, *Humanist and Scholastic Poetics, 1250–1500* (Lewisburg: Bucknell University Press, 1981), 251.
62 Paleotti, *Discourse*, Book 1, chapter 1, mentions "recent voyages of discovery" and the practice of religion. Book 2, Chapter 33, advises not depicting things from foreign countries that the painter does not know. Book 2, Chapter 36 conjures up images from world maps, travel accounts, cultural geographies.
63 Paleotti, *Discourse*, Book 1, Chapter 1, citing Cicero, *De Legibus [On the Laws*], I, 8.
64 A source text for these characterizations was Gonzalo Fernández de Oviedo y Valdéz, *La natural historia de las Indias* (Toledo, 1526), described by Las Casas as "one of the greatest tyrants, thieves, and destroyers of the Indies, whose Historia contains almost as many lies as pages" (cited by Indalecio Liévano Aguirre, *Los grandes conflictos sociales y económicos de nuestra historia*. Volumes 3–4, Bogotá: Intermedio, 2002, 84).
65 Paleotti, *Discourse*, Book 2, Chapter 37.
66 This is much more tolerant of *grottesche* than Carlo Borromeo, "De Sacris Imaginibus Picturis," Book 1, Chapter 17, cited by Voelker: "The accessories, that is the elements the painters and sculptors usually add to the images for decoration, shall not be profane, nor sensual, nor solely for aesthetic delight, nor incompatible with the sacred picture, such as for example the deformed human heads commonly called "*mascaroni*," or the birds, or the sea, or the green fields painted to please and delight the eye and for decoration. [They may be used] only if they are an integral part of the sacred story represented, or unless they are ex-votos, in which human heads or other things, mentioned above, are painted to explain the meaning." The same arguments were used in New Spain: Sabine MacCormack, "Calderás *La Aurora en Copacabana*: The Conversion of the Incas in Light of Seventeenth-century Spanish Theology, Culture, and Political Theory," *Journal of Theological Studies* 33 (1982): 448–480.
67 Paleotti, *Discourse*, Book 2, Chapter 36, cites the quotation that Aldrovandi himself cited from Plato (*The Republic*, Book 6, 488a), in the same connection: Paleotti contrasts the false fictions of human imagination with the allegories and mysteries of divine revelation.
68 Paleotti, *Discourse*, Book 2, Chapter 36.
69 Cyril Mango, *The Homilies of Photius, Patriarch of Constantinople* (Cambridge, MA: Harvard University Press, 1958), 293–294 for the homily of 867.

70 Paleotti, *Discourse*, Book 1, Chapter 23. Expanding on Aquinas, *Summa Theologica* 3, q. 25, a. 3. The word "anima" (soul) in this sense is a commonplace in the emblem literature where the soul refers to the motto: image and word are the "body" and "soul," alternately the flesh and the spirit joined in the emblem. The meaning of *misteriosamente* was different from modern understanding of mysterious and is in keeping with the emblem tradition where the difficult meaning had to be puzzled out. Steven F. H. Stowell, *The Spiritual Language of Art: Medieval Christian themes in Writings on Art of the Italian Renaissance* (Leiden–Boston: Brill, 2015), 268, notes that Paleotti's discussion of the "soul of the image" (*anima della pittura*) has no precedent in his sources in Aristotle and Aquinas.

71 Paleotti, *Discourse*, Book 1, Chapter 10. See Stowell, *The Spiritual Language of Art*, 266, with further discussion of Lutheran understanding of sanctioned allegorical images like the brazen serpent in the Old Testament.

72 Stowell, *The Spiritual Language of Art*, 268, notes that it is clearly Augustinian. Leonardo made the same claim for painting in polemical arguments in the first part of the *Libro di Pittura* that were eliminated by the unidentified editor, when he argued that the painter's hands "generate a proportioned harmony, as things do in a single glance." *Libro di Pittura*, Chapter 13, translation cited from Claire J. Farago, *Leonardo da Vinci's "Paragone": A Critical Interpretation with a new edition of the text in the Codex Urbinas* (Leiden: E. J. Brill, 1992), 197.

73 Philippe Morel, "Il funziamento simbolico e la critica delle grottesche nella seconda metà del Cinquecento," *Rome e L'Antico nell arte e nella cultura del Cinquecento*, ed. Marcello Fagiolo (Rome: Istituto della Enciclopedia Italiana, 1985), 149–178.

74 Hansen, *The Art of Transformation*, 342.

75 Morel, "*Il funziamento simbolico*," citing Lomazzo, *Rime . . . grottesque*, 1587, 354–357.

76 On Lomazzo's firsthand knowledge of Leonardo's writings, see Julia Chai, ed. and trans., Gian Paolo Lomazzo, *Idea del Tempio della Pittura* (University Park: Pennsylvania State University Press, 2013), 16; Chai, "Introduction," *Lomazzo's Aesthetic Principles Reflected in the Art of His Time*, ed. Lucia Tantardini and Rebecca Norris, intro. Jean Julia Chai (Leiden–Boston: Brill, 2020).

77 Gianpaolo Lomazzo, *Trattato dell'arte de la pittura* (Milan: Pontio, 1584), 108; translation cited from Summers, *Michelangelo and the Language of Art*, 69, n. 35.

78 The Milanese *Accademia della Val di Blenio* was founded by Lomazzo, Ambrogio Brambilla, Ambrogio Figino, and others in 1560. See Giulio Bora, "Milano nell'età di Lomazzo e San Carlo: Riaffermazione e difficoltà di sopravivenza di una cultura," in *Rabisch*, 37–56; Bora, "Da Leonardo all'*Accademia della Val di Blenio*: Giovan Paolo Lomazzo, Aurelio Luini, e I disegni degli accademici," *Raccolta Vinciana* 23 (1989): 73–101.

79 Their response to the social/religious/economic climate involved dissimulation. Despite the subversive character of some of the *Accademia*'s activities, the members conformed in other ways to the new religious climate established by Archbishop Borromeo. One of the *Accademia*'s members, Lomazzo, wrote about his bad experiences with Borromeo and Church regulations regarding his *Grotteschi* (Lomazzo, *Rime*, Milan, 1587, 289, cited by Bora, "Milano nell'età di Lomazzo," 51).

80 Paleotti, *Discourse*, Book 2, Chapter 41.

81 Paolo Sanvito, "Lomazzo's Influence on Decorative Patterns in Sculptural Workshops before and After 1600," in *Lomazzo's Aesthetic Principles*, 152–170. There is direct continuity with the later sculpted masks of Gian Lorenzo Bernini (1598–1680) and Cosimo Fanzago (1591–1678) who both trained in the workshop of Pietro Bernini in Settignano near Florence.

82 Translation cited from Chai, ed., Lomazzo, *Idea del Tempio della Pittura,* 72.

83 *Giovan Pietro Bellori: The Lives of the Modern Painters, Sculptors, and Architects: A New Translation and Critical Edition*, trans. and ed. Alice Sedgewick Wohl, Helmut Wohl, and Tomaso Montanari (Cambridge: Cambridge University Press, 2005), 347; see further Pamela M. Jones, "Leading Pilgrims to Paradise: Guido Reni's Holy Trinity

(1625–26) for the Church of SS. Trinità dei Pellegrini e Convalescenti and the Care of Bodies and Souls," *Altarpieces and Their Viewers in the Churches of Rome from Caravaggio to Guido Reni* (Aldershot: Ashgate, 2008), 261–324.

84 Jones, "Leading Pilgrims to Paradise," 36, notes that even in antiquity, grace was considered a gift with both stylistic and spiritual resonances associated above all with Apelles by writers such as Quintilian, Pliny the Elder, and Plutarch.

85 Jones, "Leading Pilgrims," 261–324.

86 The prominent Seville artist Franciscso Pacheco accused Carducho of plagiarizing five citations of Leonardo's treatise in Chapter 12 of book II of his *El arte de la pintura*, begun c. 1600–1604, submitted for licensing in 1641, appearing only posthumously in 1649. Carducho quoted Leonardo on practice being based on good theory. Pacheco cited 27 passages from an abridged, pre-publication copy of Leonardo's *Libro di Pittura*. Charlene Villasenor-Black, "Pacheco, Velasquez, and the Legacy of Leonardo in Spain," in *Re-Reading Leonardo: The Treatise on Painting across Europe, 1550–1900*, ed. Claire Farago (Aldershot: Ashgate Press, 2009), 349–375.

87 Mary Crawford-Volk, "Vicente Carducho," *Grove Art Online*, updated 2019, accessed on 2 April 2023 at https://doi org.colorado.idm.oclc.org/10.1093/oao/9781884446054.013.90000369568.

88 George Kubler, "Vicente Carducho's Allegories of Painting," *The Art Bulletin* 47/4 (1965): 439–445. Carducho's images are free adaptations of Cesare Ripa's *Iconologia*.

89 In an extraordinary misreading of Carducho, Russo, "An Artistic Humanity," 363, mistakes the clearly labeled image of the *tabula rasa*, which she identifies as occurring on p. 81, as referring to the modern idea of the artist who works on a "blank canvas." In the copy I consulted this image occurs at the very end of the treatise for reasons explained in my description.

90 Aristotle, *De anima*, 429v39–430a1.

91 The poem on folio 162v, p. 450–451, by Doctor Ivan Perez de Montalban ends: "Porque Diios solamente/Pudo dar luz, a luz tan excelente./Y oi Vicencio Carduchi, que es mi Aollo,/Del sol competidor po solo y solo/Ilustra mi hermosura,/Porque sepan, que tiene la Pintura/Un Dios que la fabrique,/Y un Apolo, que al mundo la publique."

92 See further discussion in Farago, "Leonardo's Workshop Procedures and the *Trattato della pittura*," in Farago, Bell, and Vecce, *Fabrication*, 1: 152–183.

93 Carducho, *Dialogos de la pintura*, 172.

94 Pacheco, *Arte de la pintura*, II, 284.

95 Pacheco, *Arte*, 364; Carducho, *Allegories*, 174.

96 My thanks to Carmen Fernández-Salvador for this information.

97 Simon Ditchfield, "Chapter 8, Inquisition and Intimidation," in *Papacy & Peoples: The Making of Roman Catholicism as a World Religion, 1500–1700* (Oxford: Oxford University Press).

98 Davies, *Renaissance Ethnography and the Invention of the Human: New Worlds, Maps and Monsters (*Cambridge: Cambridge University Press, 2016*)*, 227.

99 Maria Berbara, "'They live one hundred and fifty years': The trope of longevity and epidemic diseases across the early modern Atlantic," presentation at the Getty Research Institute Scholars Program, 15 June 2022. Professor Berbara is preparing a book on the topic.

100 Mary Campbell, *The Witness and the Other World: Exotic Eastern Travel Writing 400–1600* (Ithaca, NY–London: Cornell University Press, 1988), 126.

101 Nanne Buurman, "D Is for . . .? *Documenta* and the Politics of (Re)presentation," *Field: A Journal of Engaged Art Criticism* 18/19 (Spring 2021); Tony Bennett, "Exhibition, Truth, Power. Reconsidering 'The Exhibition Complex,'" in *Documenta 14* catalogue (Munich: Prestel, 2017), 346.

102 Kate Brown, "'We Take Ownership and Responsibility': Indonesian Collective Taring Padi Reflects on the Controversy Over their Art That Paralyzed Documenta," *Artnet* Aug 2022, citing Taring Padi member Hestu Nugorhu. https://news.artnet.com/art-world-archives/taring-padi-collective-interview-2155080.

103 Daniela Bleichmar, "Translation, Mobility, and Mediation: The Case of the *Codex Mendoza*," in *Sites of Mediation: Connected Histories of Places, Processes, and Objects in Europe and Beyond, 1450–1650*, ed. Susanna Burghartz, Lucas Burkart, and Christine Göttler (Leiden–Boston: Brill Press, 2016), 240–269. In 1780, the Jesuit Francisco Javier Clavijero suggested that the Codex was commissioned by the first viceroy of New Spain, Antonio de Mendoza (1495–1552), a sketchy provenance at best. There is no evidence that it ever reached Spain, entering the Bodleian Library at Oxford in 1659 at the death of its most recent private owner, John Selden.

104 David Graeber and David Wengrow, *Dawn of Everything: A New History of Humanity* (New York: Farrar, Straus, and Giroux, 2021), 2.

105 Michel de Montaigne, "Des Cannibales," in *Les Essais*, ed. Maurice Rat, 2 vols. (Paris: Garnier, 1962), 1.

106 Jean de Léry, *Histoire d'un voyage faict en la terre du Brésil autrement dite Amerique, le tout recueilli sur les lieux par Jean de Léry* (Geneva/La Rochelle: Antoine Chuppin, 1578).

107 Claude Levi-Strauss, *Tristes tropiques* (Paris: Plon, 1955); translation cited from *Tristes tropiques*, trans. John Russell (New York: Atheneum, 1972).

108 Michel de Certeau, *The Writing of History* (1975), trans. Tom Conley (New York: Columbia University Press, 1988), 5.

109 Claire Farago, "Jean de Léry's Anatomy Lesson: The Persuasive Power of Word and Image in Framing the Ethnographic Subject," *European Iconography East and West: Selected Papers of the Szeged International Conference, June 9–12, 1993*, 1995, 109–127.

110 Amy J. Buono, "'Their Treasures Are the Feathers of Birds': Tupinamba Featherwork and the Image of America," in *Images Take Flight: Feather Art in Mexico and Europe 1400–1700*, ed. Alessandra Russo et al. (Munich: Hirmer Verlag, 2015), 179–189; Buono, "The Crafts of Color: Tupi Tapirage in Early Colonial Brazil," in *The Materiality of Color*, ed. Andrea Feeser et al. (Farnham–Burlington: Ashgate, 2012), 235–249; with references to Buono's earlier publications. Tiago Rogero, "'A beacon of hope': Indigenous peopled reunited with sacred cloak in Brazil," *The Guardian*, 12 September 2024.

111 Jason Moore, "Introduction," in *Anthropocene or Capitalocene? Nature, History, and the Crisis of Captialism*, ed. Jason W. Moore (Oakland, CA: PM Press, 2016), 1–13.

112 Graeber and Wengrow, *Dawn of Everything*, 5.

113 Thomas Cole, *Democritus and the Sources of Greek Anthropology* (Philadelphia: American Philosophical Society, 1967).

114 Cole, *Democitus*, 6–7.

115 Pagden, *Spanish Imperialism*, 140, n. 89.

116 Neil MacGregor, "The whole world in our hands," T*he Guardian*, 23 July 2004; www.theguardian.com/artanddesign/2004/jul/24/heritage.art. In 2007, the directors of four Euro-American museums hosting the major touring exhibition, *Benin Kings and Rituals*, felt justified to claim that, while the military action seems unjustifiable now, "we must recognize the role it played in bringing these works of art to far broader attention." Cited by Dan Hicks, *The Brutish Museums: The Benin Bronzes, Colonial Violence and Cultural Restitution* (London: Pluto Press, 2020 and 2021 [with a new preface]), 164, from the preface to the exhibition catalogue, Christian Feest et al., *Benin Kings and Rituals: Court Arts from Nigeria* (Ghent: Snoek, 2007), 17. Hicks also cites the same MacGregor article, 204–205.

117 Hicks, *The Brutish Museums*, with further references, including the history of the raid recounted here, and a provisional list of identified individual looters/collectors and the hundreds of institutions that received and still hold Benin objects. See also the Digital Benin project, a concerted effort by 137 institutions to preserve Benin cultural knowledge and make objects and archival material available online (initiated by Hamburg's MARKK as an international project alongside efforts for restitution): https://digitalbenin.org/

118 Hicks, *The Brutish Museums*, 63 and citing 154.

119 https://ia804708.us.archive.org/33/items/cmapr4492/20030000%20Information%20Declaration%20on%20the%20Importance%20and%20Value%20of%20Universal%20Museums.pdf
120 H. Glenn Penny, *In Humboldt's Shadow: A Tragic History of German Ethnology* (Princeton–Oxford: Princeton University Press, 2019), 62.
121 Penny, *In Humboldt's Shadow*, 125.
122 Matthew Vollgraff, "A Response to Horst Bredekamp," *Boasblog DCNtR* 3.17.2021; and Vollgraff, "Faustian Bargains: The Legends and Legacies of German 'Liberal Ethnology,'" review of H. Glenn Penny, *Im Schatten Humboldts* (2019), *History of Anthropology Review* 44 (11 July 2020). See further, Susanne Zantop, *Colonial Fantasies: Conquest, Family, and Nation in Precolonial Germany, 1770–1870* (Durham–London: Duke University Press, 1997).
123 See Friedrich von Bose, *Das Humboldt-Forum: Eine Ethnografie seiner Planung* (Berlin: Kulturverlag Kadmos, 2016).
124 Matthew Rampley, *The Seductions of Darwin: Art, Evolution, Neuroscience* (University Park, PA: Pennsylvania State University Press, 2017).
125 www.unesco.org/en/articles/unesco-welcomes-signing-historic-agreement-between-germany-and-nigeria-return-1130-benin-bronzes. Tobi Onabolu, "As 26 Looted Treasures Go on View in Benin Republic, the West African Cultural Community is Asking What Happens Next," *Artnet News*, 11 March 2022; Helen Holmes, "Germany Plans to Return over 1,000 Benin Bronzes to Nigeria in 2022," *Observer*, 14 October 2021; Alex Greenberger, "Museum Won't Show Benin Bronzes, Begins to Pursue Return of Artifacts," *ARTnews*, 22 March 2021; Amah-Rose Abrams, "A Send-Off Exhibition of 179 Looted Objects in Hamburg Marks 'the Beginning of the Return' of Germany's Benin Bronzes to Nigeria," *Artnet News*, 17 December 2021.
126 Mark Brown, "New Museum in Nigeria raises hopes of resolution to Benin bronzes dispute," *The Guardian*, 14 November 2020.
127 On April 22 2022, the Boston Museum of Fine Arts announced that it, too, will return not only its Benin bronzes to Nigeria, but also Mali sculptures and a Dutch painting stolen from a Jewish Hungarian collector during World War II, while the Denver Museum returned four works to Cambodia in 2021; Ted Loos, "A Long Way Home for 'Looted' Art is Getting Shorter," *The New York Times*, 27 April 2022, accessed at www.nytimes.com/2022/04/27/arts/design/victoria-reed-museum-of-fine-arts-stolen-artwork.html?
128 See further discussion of Indigenous environmentalism in Fugue 5.
129 Cover, *National Geographic*, March 2023.
130 See www.theguardian.com/commentisfree/2023/sep/02/british-museum-should-give-back-loot-benin-bronzes)
131 Alex Marshall, *The New York Times*, May 25 2023.
132 Daedria Farmer-Paellmann, Restitution Study Group (RSG) executive director, cited by Francesca Aton, "Restitution Organization Sues to Keep Smithsonian's Benin Bronzes from Returning to Nigeria," *ARTnews*, 6 December 2022. www.artnews.com/art-news/news/smithsonian-sued-over-benin-bronzes-return-to-nigeria-1234649314/#
133 Victor Ehikhamenor, an artist who sits on the board of the trust developing the Edo Museum in Benin City, as cited by Alex Marshall, "Who Owns the Benin Bronzes? The Answer Just Got More Complicated," *The New York Times*, 4 June 2023. See also Philip Ihenacho, "Benin Bronzes: Whose Restitution Is This, Anyway?", *The Art Newspaper*, 31 May 2023, www.theartnewspaper.com/2023/05/31/benin-bronzes-whose-restitution-is-this-anyway
134 Friedrich von Bose, "Nicht-Restitution ist kein neutraler Akt," *Museem in der Verantwortung: Positionem im Umgang mit Raubkunst*, ed. Nikola Doll (Zurich: Rotpunktverlag, 2024), 201–230.

Intermezzo II

WHAT IS "NATIONAL STYLE"?

The European concept of style is another significant component of the entangled discursive relationship between art and humanity introduced in the previous Fugues. What corresponds to "national style" before modern nation-states existed? The nomenclature and significance of nation, people, ethnic group, "raza," and other terms of collective identity remained fluid throughout the preceding era of large dynastic and commonwealth formations. In the early eighteenth century, writing in (allegedly) universal terms, Giambattista Vico (1668–1744) defined a "nation," a word that etymologically means "a birth" or "being born," as having a system of institutions that a group of people share, that are continually changing over time due to internal stresses, giving birth to new institutions and transforming old institutions until the nation reaches maturity. For earlier stages of social evolution, Vico used the Latin term *ges/gentes*, which has the same etymology as *natio*, that is, genesis or birth. Vico speaks of nations as constituting a world, "the world of nations" (*il mondo delle nazioni*), also the "civil world" in Aristotle's sense of a polis and in Augustine's sense of the *City of God*: polity, civility, and humanity are synonymous in Vico's language.[1] The nature of nations, he wrote, will be continuous with the nature of this world in the sense of the Greek *kosmos* and the Latin *mundus*, a beautiful order created out of an ugly chaos. Chaos in Vico's opinion was due to miscegenation, "the confusion of human seeds in the state of the infamous promiscuity of women" among the degenerated, non-Hebraic descendants of Noah.[2] Vico maintained that the cosmos was first that of primitive institutions of religion, marriage, and burial; and later, the whole complex of social institutions that developed out of these primitive ones. Both Vico and his source in Aristotle's *Politics* contend that humans become fully human only in the polis, which requires the creation of institutions (*nomos*, a body of law governing institutions). Vico writes of "rational humanity" as the "true and proper nature of man" when "human

DOI: 10.4324/9781351023429-5

reason fully developed" (gendered male and misogynist in claiming that women caused chaos through miscegenation).

The European discourse on collective style first emerged in seventeenth-century art criticism among writers who distinguished different "manners" of painting by "national" and regional "schools." As mentioned in the second Fugue, among noteworthy contributors to the discourse on "national" style were the Papal diplomat Monseigneur Giovanni Battista Agucchi (1570–1632), who introduced the idea of "schools" modeled after Vasari; the painter/engraver, writer, and Academician Roger de Piles (1635–1709) and the painter, antiquarian, and biographer Giovanni Pietro Bellori (1613–1696). Agucchi's writings are known through a surviving fragment of his *Trattato della pittura* (Bologna, Bib. U., MS 245, published by G. A. Mosini in 1646), while De Piles and Bellori published extensively on the arts. De Piles and Bellori were associated with the branch of the French Royal Academy of Painting and Sculpture in Rome where French artists emulated their Italian counterparts in close contact with one another.

Leonardo da Vinci's Treatise on Painting was an important source of their ideas. One of the reasons readers who did not necessarily share his agenda for painting could still find Leonardo's ideas useful is that it is the product of an active engagement with preexisting ideas on the power of images constructed in conformity with vision. Leonardo taught readers to see with the eyes of an intellectually gifted, scientifically trained artist. Since his text channeled a broad range of existing technology pertaining to painters and sculptors, his writings and their effects provide a focusing lens for many issues relevant to the concept of a national style. Along with epitomes, imitations, and related writings in the same genre, the *Trattato della Pittura*, as the abridged text is most famously known, served state institutions beginning with the Florentine Medici court in the mid-sixteenth century, when copies were circulating in manuscript shortly after the first art academy was established under the patronage of Duke Cosimo de Medici in 1563.

At the end of a complex process involving four generations of editors, multiple manuscript copies, and a series of highly placed patrons, the first printed editions of the Treatise on Painting were published in 1651 in the original Italian and French translation, in close association with the *Académie royale de peinture et de sculpture* conceived by young, ambitious artists in Paris in 1648 who were intent on breaking away from the restrictive, state-supported guild structure.[3] The 1651 publications appeared at the height of a series of French civil wars known as the Fronde (1648–1653), centered in Paris when Louis XIV was still in his minority and the royal court itself was intermittently in exile. The *Académie* was not yet the powerful institution it would become in the mid-1660s. Royal support for the arts was achieved after Jean-Baptiste Colbert (1619–1683) was appointed as Louis XIV's chief minister in 1663. Colbert's strategy for stabilizing the French economy focused on selling in foreign markets, regulating the guilds, founding new academies, raising tariffs, and encouraging public works projects.[4] The great age of French printmaking during the reign of Louis XIV is a testament to the artistic and economic success of his policies.

The *Trattato* and *Traitté* indicate that profit, diplomacy, and what we might today call branding of the French name were all motivating factors. By the time Leonardo's lessons had been digested by various academicians who reissued his complex ideas in more palatable forms, absolutism had yoked artists to a new state apparatus.

The breakdown of divisions between social classes, the mixture of amateurs and intellectuals with painters and sculptors, and the output of the artists themselves, which materially was indistinguishable from that of guild artists, can begin to suggest how discussions about the freedom and nobility of the artist during the formative decades of art academies were social and political activities in an increasingly centralized state bureaucracy. Colbert was pointedly emulating the Plantin-Moretus Press in Antwerp, publisher for the Spanish Habsburg Empire. The art book, illustrated compilations of natural history specimens, and equally lavishly illustrated, large-format cultural geographies attracted a considerable market share by the late sixteenth century, and sales were booming in the 1600s.

Printed, illustrated versions of Leonardo's ideas on painting made possible by this new and rapidly evolving technology in the seventeenth century began their multiforked trek across Europe and the Mediterranean, the Americas, and eventually the entire globe.[5] The same text elicited many different responses as it was translated into Spanish, English, German, Dutch, Polish, and Greek. Case studies emphasize its many socio-political functions before modern nation-states existed.[6] It was read by a diverse network including painters, sculptors, illustrators, printmakers, architects, biographers, theorists, natural philosophers, translators, astronomers, publishers, engineers, theologians, aristocrats, lawyers, politicians, entrepreneurs, and collectors [Figure ii.1].

What became the institutional authority of European art was spread around the world, and its history today deserves to be told differently if we really want to create more inclusive understandings of the past and how it reverberates in the present. As articulated by Roger de Piles (1635–1709) and taken up by many writers in the eighteenth century, the connoisseur's highest calling is to judge the quality of paintings by comparing them to their counterparts in nature. Since the analysis of correct execution depends on knowing how faithful the representation is to nature, the connoisseur had to be familiar with the same principles as the practitioner: he had to understand the scientific underpinnings of effects observed in nature, and he had to be able to articulate what he saw knowledgeably, dispassionately, when judging quality. De Piles' highly successful *L'Abrégé de la vie des peintres . . . avec un traité du peintre parfait* (1699), published in English translation as *The Art of Painting and the Lives of the Painters* (London, 1706), categorized selected artists into schools.

In the seventeenth century, the judgment of quality involved more than scientific analysis of materials and attribution studies, as it does today. Carol Gibson-Wood locates the origins of connoisseurship as a literary genre with De Piles' adversary at the French Art Academy in Paris, Abraham Bosse (1604–1676), infamous player in the history of Leonardo's *Trattato* for his bitter denunciation of the 1651 publication.[7] In his 1649 *Sentimens*, Bosse, who was not a man of letters by education

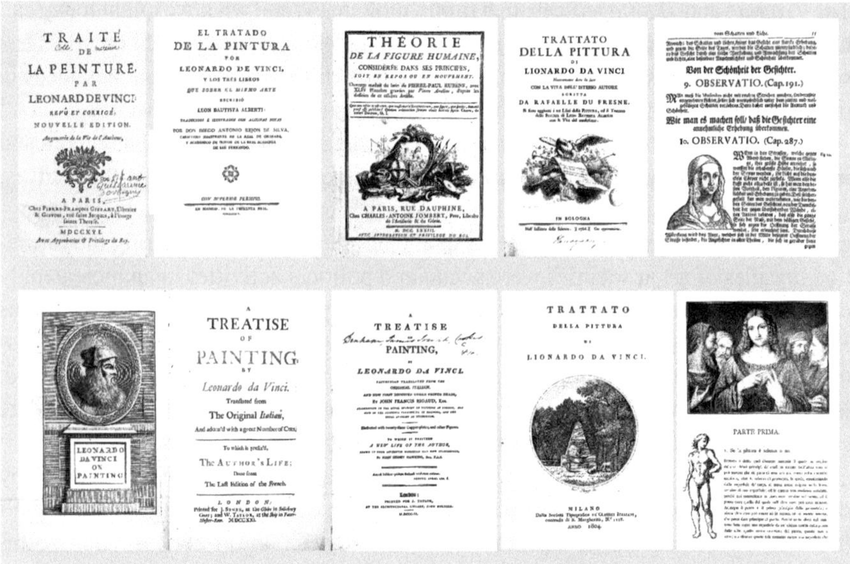

FIGURE II.1 Editions of Leonardo's *Trattato della Pittura* with new visual imagery. Top (left to right): French 1716; Spanish 1786; Rubens 1773; Italian 1786; German 1724; Bottom (left to right): English 1721; English 1802; Italian 1804; Italian 1890, p. 3, "La Disputa" based on Melzi. Photos courtesy of database of Leonardo's Treatises on Painting created by Mario Valentino Guffanti, researcher, Milan, Raccolta Vinciana.

but a highly successful engraver and teacher of perspective at the *Académie royale de peinture et de sculpture,* wrote expressly for non-artists to gain knowledge of art.[8] For Bosse, the issue of quality judgments is related to that of personal manner: the best painters were those with the *least* manner. To be able to judge a picture's quality, therefore, it was necessary to know how correctly it has been executed, that is, how faithful it was to nature and to the laws of perspective in particular. For De Piles, the most difficult aspect of *connoissance* may be mastered by non-painters, but they can attain this skill only by long periods of study of actual works of art.[9] In his most lucid account of "*caractere d'esprit,*" character consists of the manner in which the painter shows the living image of his spirit that moves our imagination ("*la vive image de son Espirit. C'est ce Caractere qui remue notre imagination*"). The systematization of connoisseurship into "schools" begun by Agucchi, Bellori, and Roger de Piles was taken up by major writers on art of the eighteenth century, notably the portraitist and writer Jonathan Richardson (1667–1745), and the collector A. J. Dezallier d'Argenville (1680–1745) who focused on attribution and personal artistic style.

The mirrored symmetry between the judgment of quality by the connoisseur and the judgments made by the artist in the process of fabricating his or her work is key to understanding how this field of cultural production operated. Early modern European writers on art shared the idea that psychological characteristics manifest in concrete works of art were hereditary and transmissible. A century after Agucchi, De Piles, and Bellori formulated the idea of regional "schools," the first theorists of racial science, the French naturalist Comte de Buffon (1707–1788) and Johann Blumenbach (1752–1840), drew on these commonplace notions circulating in the literature on art to develop scientific theories about the "national varieties" of inherited physiognomic characteristics, discussed further in Fugue 3.

Éric Michaud has investigated the racialization of art history during and prior to the nineteenth century.[10] His central thesis is that the real source of the history of art as a discipline was born from German and French attacks on the universalism of the classical ideal promoted by Johannes Winckelmann (1764), who laid the foundation for the biological concept of style, and his predecessors beginning with Giorgio Vasari, whose *Lives* of Italian artists (1550, rev. ed. 1568), is still widely regarded as the foundational text of art history. The Germanic peoples, described as a single population in ancient sources used by eighteenth-century writers, notably by the first-century Roman historian Tacitus (*Germania*, IV), were reimagined as "the new blood of the Northern races . . . that rejuvenated the people of the empire."[11]

The "barbarian invasions" were largely a romantic invention inseparable from the formation of modern nation-states and the rise of nationalism in Europe, Michaud continues, but the history of art fashioned its concepts and tools of interpretation based on this false anthropological paradigm. Even though the groups entering European territory in the fourth and fifth centuries are now recognized as neither homogeneous nor predominantly Germanic, "these tools have survived the collapse of their very own suppositions," and the old assumptions about style continue to be a controversial and sensitive topic among historians.[12] Today, Michaud concludes, "contemporary art practices and 'tourist art' entail a fetishization of art history seen as representative of a collective racial identity." The ideologies that motivated nineteenth-century art historians today sustains the globalized art market.[13]

As discussed in the first Fugue, in the sixteenth century sovereignty was regarded as the universal community to which all civilized Christian humans belong on the basis of Aristotle's *Politics* by both Vitoria and his opponent Sepúlveda in the debates regarding natural slavery held in Valladolid in 1550/51. Their ideas had an enormous historical impact as they circulated widely in Europe through published texts. Sovereignty referred to the internal organization of distinct societies in Las Casas' *Apologética* (1551 and later) that Indigenous peoples formed their own distinct polities, a definition that corresponds with Jean Bodin's (1530–1596) influential climate theory/cultural geography and many others like it which are also based on Aristotle's *Politics*. Bodin is best known for his theory of absolute, undivided sovereignty as distinct from the government through which the sovereign rules. Sovereign states, he theorized, are independent both from the claims of the Holy Roman Empire and the papacy.[14] Bodin was concerned with internal relations of the state at a time when the connotations of the word sovereignty referred to individual rulers, not their dominions or their subjects as sovereignty was understood by European writers in the nineteenth century. The European definition of national sovereignty ultimately derives from traditions of Christian kingship, but it does not apply to all forms of rulership. The theory of state might be better defined transculturally by the term "ascendancy," suggests historian and political theorist Prathama Banerjee, who draws counter examples to European ideas from South Asian history.[15]

As far as the method and aims of the present study are concerned, transculturation is not a matter of creating new universal definitions or categories that apply to all forms of sovereignty or anything else. The challenge undertaken here is to understand how and when certain culturally specific ideas of sovereignty came to be regarded as universal, how they intersected with other ideas of polity historically, and how that history changed over time relevant to where we are now. Transcultural historical inquiry in this sense requires a layered approach that is inevitably recursive. The Treaty of Westphalia (1648) is conventionally recognized as the birth of the incipient nation-state system and a milestone in establishing sovereignty as a regulatory framework for the coexistence of states. However, in the past two decades scholars working on the history of international order in global history, international relations, and international law have reevaluated the traditional account of the Peace of Westphalia and the "Westphalian system" as not only false but diametrically opposed to the historical record.[16]

The "Westphalian system" is a myth created in the nineteenth century by scholars who projected their own investment in the new nation-state onto the past. Their sources have been traced to anti-Hapsburg propaganda from the Thirty Years' War.[17] The original addressees were relatively impervious to the anti-Habsburg propaganda, Andreas Osiander observes in proposing this revisionist history, but the propaganda appealed to the nationalistic and confessional preconceptions of nineteenth- and twentieth-century historians. While the emphasis on territory may be evidence for changing conceptions of the state traditionally concerned with rulership over people, the treaties deal with practicalities internal to the Holy Roman Empire, not the prerogatives of the Holy Roman Emperor or the pope and they did not produce a pan-European charter. The Treaty of Westphalia, actually consisting of two treaties signed by the Holy Roman Emperor in 1648 with the French and Swedish monarchs, who were already rulers of independent states, makes no mention of sovereignty, non-intervention, the balance of power, or a desire to reorganize the European political system as nineteenth-century scholars claimed.

What might be better understood as the *ideology* of sovereignty is a phenomenon of modern nationalism conceived as a unifying and new type of political entity in the nineteenth century. Nineteenth-century legal scholars and historians anachronistically projected their own ideas about sovereignty onto their seventeenth-century sources – just as art historians of the same period did in writing art histories of "national culture" from the perspective of their respective modern nation-states, emphasizing their links with eponymous "nations" of the past while ignoring the past mutual obligations of those polities to the Holy Roman Empire, which was dissolved only in 1806. Until the nineteenth century, the international order consisted of a patchwork of polities even in Europe. Some of these were sovereign states, others were or had been composite formations such as the Holy Roman Empire and the Polish–Lithuanian Commonwealth (1569–1795). The closest contemporary parallel is the European Union.

The myth of Westphalia according to those who accept the revisionist history inflicts serious damage on our ability to think creatively about today's pressing global challenges that transcend borders and all levels of governmental organization from neighborhoods to international institutions. It is important to bear in mind that the dominant forms of collective identity were multiple, clustered in overlapping groups defined by family, profession, religion, and region, with strong visual elements that art historians are beginning to explore in a transcultural framework.

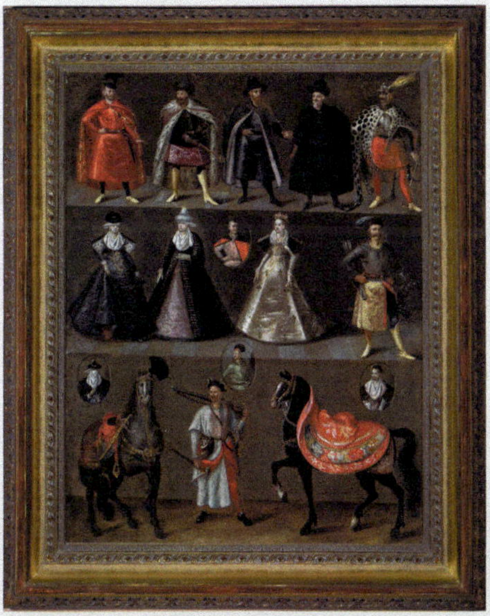

FIGURE II.2 Anonymous, *Variety of Polish Costumes*, 17th century, oil on panel. Poznań, National Museum, Mp 841. Photo Museum.

Sartorial code-switching was a vital aspect of Polish–Lithuanian high society, offering a dynamic way to express cultural affiliation that defied rigid self-definitions. Yet, as this panel [Figure II.2] exemplifies, it may have also sparked concerns about the erosion of Polish traditions in the face of foreign novelties. Echoing costume books of the era, the panel presents a variety of Polish attire worn by the nobility during the Vasa period (1587–1668). It visually constructs an imagined tradition where costume signifies a sense of enduring community, encouraging comparisons with the past through four historical bust portrait vignettes that are virtually indistinguishable in dress. The men, clad in contemporary Ottoman-inspired loose garments, are unified through their emphasis on military prowess (each carrying weapons), while the women are demurely dressed – both depictions contradict other historical evidence. To avoid the perils of cultural essentialism, the study of Polish costume is best undertaken with the acknowledgment that all cultures are inherently heterogeneous, even if this heterogeneity is not immediately apparent.

Tomasz Grusiecki, *Trancultural Things and the Spectre of Orientalism in Early Modern Poland-Lithuania* (Manchester: Manchester University Press, 2023).

Specialized studies already exist that consider visual symbols and material culture associated with sovereignty transculturally. For example, Tomasz Grusiecki has examined the symbolic values attached to certain forms of material culture such as oriental rugs and ethnic costume in the Polish–Lithuanian Commonwealth (see text box).[18] Russia's political system was conceived as non-commensurable in seventeenth-century Europe, yet Russia was recognized as a state based on the symbolic power of its court.[19] Similar arguments have been made regarding the incommensurable concepts of kingship between France and Siam (Thailand) in the late seventeenth century that operated transculturally through symbolic representations of power relationships.[20]

The conventional understanding of sovereignty in Western Europe imagines international law as based on the "sovereign equality of states" but, in fact, international law in the seventeenth century fixed the *unequal* status of humans on the basis of traits associated with civilizational failures and achievements that were under colonial control.[21] In the colonial encounter with other societies European imperial formations created vassal states (viceroyalties) that identified their subjects on a civilizational hierarchy requiring tutelage and coercive surveillance. Drawing upon the work of Antony Anghie and others on international human rights law who are critical of political theory restricted to Western European models, Ann Laura Stoler understands sovereignty as a concept "improvised out of the colonial encounter."[22] Imperial formations (Stolers preferred term, rather than empire) produced "shadow populations, second-class citizens, citizens-in-waiting" who were threatened with expulsion if they did not "submit to a devil's pact for access to basic rights."[23]

Vitoria's initiating argument for treating Indigenous people as Spanish subjects requiring education (that may take centuries to make them fully civilized), fits Anghie's description of how sovereignty and universal rights came to be defined by European political theorists to justify imperialism. Exclusion is fundamental and exemption is key to the organizing principles of imperial formations: claims to universalism (like those made by Vitoria's successors about universal human rights) are the founding principles of imperial inequalities. In including Indigenous people in the category human while excluding them from civilized status, meaning fully realized rational human beings, Vitoria himself was trying to justify Charles V's claims to conquest, settlement, and the extraction of raw material resources in the Americas and elsewhere on juridical grounds through appeals to cosmopolitan hospitality and commerce practiced between discrete polities.

Stoler tracks the shifting categories and moving parts of imperial formations "whose designated borders at any one time were not necessarily the force fields in which they operated," in the colonial expansion of European sovereignties. Sliding scales of basic rights, frequent redrawing of the categories of subject and citizen, and elaborate nomenclatures: these are the discourses of exceptionalism that Edward Said identified as part of the material apparatus and conceptual grammar of imperial states. Stoler never deals with art or material culture, but she emphasizes that written documents are not enough to identify the scope of colonial empires when it comes to the alienation of Indigenous rights. Sara Miglietti has documented the "flexibility and resilience of ancient epistemic paradigms" by studying how the Spanish imperial House of Trade and the Council of the Indies, both located in Seville, gathered geo-ethnographic information by distributing standardized questionnaires to travelers and residents in the American colonies.[24] The focus in many of these questionnaires was on the environmental properties of the site and the character of local native populations. Later known as the *Relaciones de Indias*, the reports took the form of itemized lists of answers initially intended for circulation within the Society of Jesus (the Jesuits) that became best-selling publications describing exotic lands and the peoples they contained.

The historical entanglement of race, art, and environmental theory is part of the unexplored ground on which imperial evaluations of national sovereignty were gradually turned into hegemonic claims for universal human rights. Beyond their popular success as cultural geographies, climate theory enabled European administrators to evaluate the character of Indigenous populations to devise effective strategies of evangelization. The justification for the high degree of standardization (the same twelve or so questions) in gathering geo-ethnographic information on the American colonies was to ensure objectivity and fairness, while the result was an effective tool for collecting information, "a rhetorical strategy in the service of a particular epistemology," to cite Miglietti.[25] She documents how the Royal Society of London sought the information gathered by Jesuit missionaries, decontextualized from their Indigenous colonial location and recontextualized into the two main categories of climate theory, environment and people. The information was then distributed around the globe through extensive networks of correspondents, generating what Miglietti calls a "chain of epistemic consequences that reached the very core of European natural-philosophical thought." As Stoler concludes from her own archival findings, the asserted universal laws of racial classification were insufficient for actual governance where the essentialisms attached to race had to be mobile: concept work studies these slippages in a charged colonial and contemporary environment. It follows that the correlations between historical racism and contemporary practices are not causal but complementary with the capacity and the potential to work through "sedimented and familiar cultural representations and relations of subjugation."[26]

The next Fugue examines cultural representations of peoples according to their climate and geography operating since the sixteenth century for their emancipatory potential in rethinking the relationship of humans to the rest of nature. This body of literature and associated institutions of artistic training and criticism were also fundamentally involved in the transformation of a field of studies into a "discipline" in the nineteenth century or – to use a term historian Hayden White coined to discuss the politics of interpretation – "disciplinization." [27] Fields of study in the human and social sciences, White argues, address and co-produce the context of modern social institutions designed for the regulation of knowledge production. Empirical history – by which White meant the gathering of facts without asking what constitutes a "fact" – acts like a discipline in the physical sciences, but without having developed their characteristic theoretical and methodological regimentation. How history considered as a recovery of the facts of the past is linked to ideology requires an epistemological critique because "[t]he politics of this disciplinization . . . consists in what it marks out for repression for those who wish to claim the authority of the discipline itself for their learning." The repression and exclusion of other forms of artistry from the institutionally sanctioned, academic discourse on art defined as mimesis or imitation of the real world is a classic case in point of White's analysis of the politics of interpretation.

Raymond Williams (1958), the Marxist literary historian, was concerned to define the field of general change that introduced elements "we can point to as distinctly modern."[28] He argued that when culture came to mean a mode of interpreting common experience that refers to an area of personal experience, it affected the meaning and practice of art, which became the "center of defense against the disintegrating tendencies of industrialism." For Williams, the historical transformation in the function of art corresponds in time with theories of cultural relativism beginning with J. G. von Herder (1744–1803). Williams emphasized that Herder was an anti-imperialist who attacked what he called European subjugation and domination of "all quarters of the globe. . . . The very thought of a superior European culture is a blatant insult to the majesty of Nature."[29] Historians of nationalism and of the institutional history of modern academic disciplines, as well as many critics of Eurocentrism, all point out that Herder's idealized notions about cultural integrity and interaction, and the language in which he expressed his ideas, offered an inadequate account of the devastating effects of European colonialism three centuries into the global expansion of European interests. Herder's cultural pluralism was innovative, but the Herderian assumption of a cultural hierarchy and the idea that each culture (and each language) remains discrete and incommensurable with any other has been debunked for some time.

Moreover, the nesting of art/culture/modern society in this manner cannot adequately conceptualize the contribution of transcultural processes to modern notions of art because "art" and "culture" are both historical constructs defined around the same time. Therefore, one cannot provide the foundation for the other. In the eighteenth century, "art" and "culture" were both treated as ontological categories alongside "religion," "biology," "nation," and other European terms to establish what they (mistakenly) imagined to be neutral and universal. As Margaret Hodgen (1964) wrote about sixteenth- and seventeenth-century precursors to modern anthropological texts – cultural geographies and travel literature organized by nations, cities, and continents according to ancient categories such as customs, religious rites, forms of government, costumes, language, and artistic products, provided an important and frequently visual record of what she called emerging "Europocentric" attitudes along the same lines as Herder but two centuries earlier.[30] By reframing other societies according to European categories, making the incommensurable commensurable, as Hodgen was among the first of many to argue, these accounts eliminated from consideration everything that does not fit into these categories.

In a groundbreaking study that redefined the field, political scientist and historian Benedict Anderson (1983) argued that nationalism originated in the American colonies rather than nineteenth-century Europe. Anderson focused on the role of media (the convergence of capitalism and print technology) in defining a "nation" as an "imagined political community," regardless of actual inequalities, that aligns itself with large cultural systems that preceded it, such as a religious community or a dynastic realm.[31] Drawing upon the groundbreaking work of Miroslav Hroch (1986), historian Eric Hobsbawm (1990) identified three criteria for the formation of a modern nation-state: both a long and a recent historical association, a long-established cultural elite with a written national literary and administrative vernacular, and a proven capacity for conquest. An important aspect of Hobsbawm's analysis of nationalism was his rather unexpected finding (surprising because it denies Herder's central assumption) that a common spoken language is rarely present, but a powerful combination of representations – visual symbols of collective practices – "give palpable reality to an otherwise imaginary community."[32]

Williams cites G. F. Klemm as the reference point in the social sciences for the modern sense of culture as a synonym for civilization that emerged in the 1840s. Klemm's *Allgemeine Kulturgeschichte des Menschkeit/General Cultural History of Mankind* (1843–1852), followed by Edward Tylor's *Primitive Culture* (1870), both "traced human development from savagery through domestication to freedom."[33] Herder, Klemm, and Tylor may have been anti-imperialists, but their accounts of cultural history also subscribed to the view that sub-Saharan Africans were less civilized because they were less gifted in their capacity for intellectual progress and more gifted in sensual cognition capable of "sensual animal enjoyment." The claim that works of art embody the collective psychology of entire nations or epochs in perceptible form is no longer taken seriously by most historians of culture. Yet this kind of essentialism is still pervasive both in academic settings and popular culture. In their revision of *Keywords*, sociologist Tony Bennett and his co-authors (2005) refined Williams' analysis by acknowledging that the "waning use of culture as a normative standard" is due to awareness of the tension between the terms "culture" and "civilization" aligned with the development of industrialization in the nineteenth century.[34] The tension is evident in Tylor's arrangement of culture into evolutionary stages, which George Stocking, Jr. already noted in 1968 when he singled out the work of anthropologist Franz Boas (1858–1942) for "translating the non-evolutionary assumptions of German anthropology into the first fully developed statement of the principles of cultural relativism."[35] Bennett and his co-authors compare Boas to historian and Black civil rights activist William Du Bois (1868–1903) who introduced the term "double-consciousness" to describe the identities of African Americans caught in the relations between White and Black cultures (*The Souls of Black Folk*, 1903).

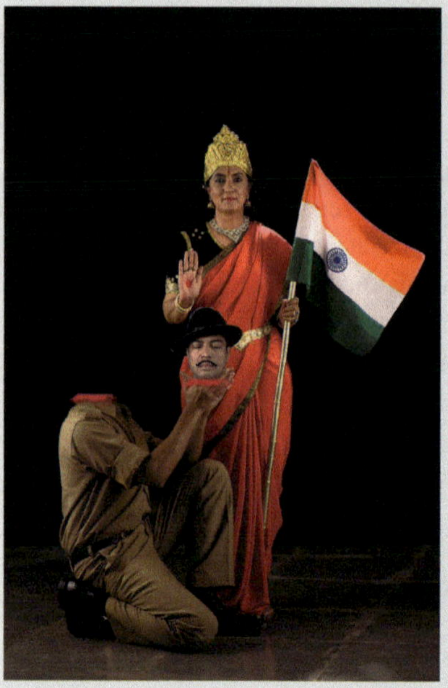

FIGURE II.3 Pushpamala N., *Motherland: The Great Sacrifice* (from an unpublished test shoot), c. 2010, digital image. Cast: Pushpamala N. and Umesh Maddanahalli. Photographer: Clayton Kelton. Photo courtesy of the artist.

Khaki-clad Bhagat Singh, the social revolutionary executed by the British in 1931 – following the trope of ultimate sacrifice (*balidaan*) that can be traced back to the early 1930s – offers up on folded hands his own decapitated head as the martyred son. Mother India graciously accepts the sacrifice of one son and offers encouragement to those who follow. What is at stake when the artist chooses, in a feminist mode, to re-enact the personification of the nation and its attributes as mother and as female icon, and looks out from within the image? Is she "undoing the mother/nation" or redoing it or both? The artist's body is positioned as both agential subject and the object of art: can this double engagement with the artist's body circumvent those exclusions and erasures inherent in the process of creating and upholding nations? Can an artistic act of transgression show the way to re-scripting the national by asking who "we" are and who "belongs" to "our nation"?

How does circulating this object–image transform the contexts to which it travels? In taking on the persona of Mother India as a bejeweled and bountiful goddess, the shining embodiment of the (Hindu) nation, the upper caste, middle-class artist Pushpamala interrupts and interrogates a century and more of visual attempts to picture the novel goddess of an emergent nation, Bharat Mata, originating in the 1870s though timeless for patriots and devotees. Pushpamala's "ludic irreverence" takes place a century after the veritable explosion of Mother India in the anti-colonial politics of the Swadeshi movement, a self-sufficiency movement started in 1905 that Mahatma Gandhi described as the soul of *swaraj* (self-rule). The Indian National Congress used this movement to gain independence in 1947, but as India won independence from the British, it succumbed to a triumphant Hindu nationalism that threatens its very existence as a secular country.

As female artist and secular feminist, Pushpamala's investments in the contradictions of national belonging are performative. She approximates iconic prototypes that circulate in India's visual landscape and puts them in visual "dialogue" through citation and appropriation. As she does so, she reveals that nations are invented, as are national embodiments. The artist bears witness through her photo performances to precarity itself as an existential fact.

Monica Juneja and Sumathi Ramaswamy, "'Entering the Skin of the Other': Woman and Nation in Pushpamala N.'s Motherland," *Motherland: Pushpamala N.'s Woman and Nation* (New Delhi: Roli Books, 2022), published in connection with the eponymous exhibition they curated in collaboration with Robert Bitsch at the Völkerkundemuseum, Heidelberg, Germany, 28 May–31 July 2022.

The universalist assumptions of nineteenth-century German anthropology are being reevaluated again in the framework of decolonization, as the second Fugue has already indicated in the case of repatriating the Benin Bronzes looted by British soldiers in 1896. Social movements have also taken issue with the classed, gendered, racial, and Eurocentric investment in cultural evolutionism that undermine culture's claim to universalism. Meanwhile, increased commodification has blurred the boundaries between "real culture" and the rest, better described today according to Bennett and his co-authors in terms of segmented cultural markets operating with their own internal values. Contemporary cultures are better identified in terms of their "distinct styles of consumption and ways of fashioning behavior," Bennett and his co-authors conclude.

Is there no way out of this hall of mirrors driven by consumerism operating in a globalized, transnational capitalist economy that is destroying the environment? I am arguing for a whole new focus. Systematic attempts to reground the discipline in the historical circumstances of its own making are ongoing in the field of art history for more than three decades. As Edward Said and many other critics of Eurocentrism charged in the 1970s and '80s, cultural domination is the result of consensual assimilation.[36] The impetus for expanding the boundaries of what is culturally intelligible is of course much greater when we take into account our agency as authors who help to construct these histories. In the 1990s, the focus in critiques of imperial histories moved to studying the ways in which colonial categories were always subject to dislocation and transformation. Colonial power had established the dehumanized figure of the '"native," which now, re-reading the colonial archive, directed attention to the violence of colonialism and liminal sites of mixing and crossing. Mahatma Gandhi's *Hind Swaraj* (1908), a severe indictment of modern civilization directed at British rule in India, met French Afro-Caribbean Frantz Fanon's analysis of colonial identities (*Black Skin, White Masks*, 1952), which in turn met other accounts of ambivalent, subaltern agency by postcolonial writers such as Gayatri Spivak and Homi Bhabha in a new, shared discursive space that carved out positions in between authority and victimhood.[37] Across South America, in Palestine, Egypt, Pakistan, Myanmar, Rwanda, Sudan, the Pacific Northwest, and elsewhere, identity is being reinterpreted as a process of ambivalent identification that encourages scholars and activists to seek new sources of knowledge. The dialogue and the interpretations remain contextual and contingent, dialectical and intersectional, relational and horizontal rather than hierarchical, universal, and abstract.[38] It turns out that Hegel and Leibniz read Chinese philosophy, Oxford-educated Gandhi read the Stoics. New histories today are decolonizing narratives of European colonialism by challenging the notion that colonialism defined the American continent and the experiences of those living on it. From a pan-Indigenous perspective, First Nations in North America invested power in kinship. Looking at a broad range of Native American worlds, in most cases they "attempted to bring Europeans into their fold, making them useful."[39]

Amid the current resurgence of nationalism, some criticize Anderson's masculine vison and still others fault his contention that race had nothing to do with nationalism.[40] Already three decades ago, the South Asian political scientist and anthropologist Partha Chatterjee (1993) pushed back against Anderson to argue that European colonialism imposed limits to nationalism.[41] Heterogeneous postcolonial nation-states such as India offer strategic opportunities today for academic and artistic interventions that turn visual symbols of the nation-state into forms of resistance *against* essentialism and colonialism.

Transcultural, longitudinal studies focused on the deployment of visual symbols add considerable complexity to the understanding of nationalist agendas. A borderless approach to culture conceived as a set of flows and relations developed by sociologist Arjun Appadurai (1996) has been widely employed by art historians in case studies moving away from taxonomic exercises that classify cultures as discrete entities. Where does the climate crisis fit in this rewiring of national histories as intersectional and dynamic? Giving priority to the analysis of long-term historical structures is critical for articulating a multiverse approach to the climate emergency that embraces all human and more than human worlds without imposing a teleological narrative of cultural progress or universalizing structures of any kind. Two centuries *avant la lettre*, Academicians at the French Academy rehearsed arguments similar to those that motivated late nineteenth- and early twentieth-century art historians and curators in the circle of the Italian art critic (and political activist) Giovanni Morelli (1816–1891) to establish objective, "scientific" bases for their judgments of quality based on the "correctness" of the image compared with its model in nature (to be discussed in Fugue 4).

The next Fugue takes a closer look at the ways human ingenuity was construed in relation to the environment in historical climate theories. Why does this history matter now? A lot is at stake for the future of cultural memory at a time when humans pose an existential threat to all life on Earth. The shock of meeting one's distorted *doppelgänger* in the mirror of historical climate theory may be an uncanny experience (it certainly has been for me in researching this book) but ignoring the implications for the present does not eliminate their spectral effects. It only makes their assumptions invisible, so they act on our thinking without our even realizing it. The political theory argument for cosmopolitanism to support peaceful coexistence through "commerce" runs throughout European disputes over the construction of new European empires overseas since first contact with the Americas. In fact, European political theorists redeployed Christian humanist arguments for cosmopolitanism by Vitoria and his successors to imagine a possible world order based on trade and exchange. The lived history of cosmopolitan practices requires identifying institutions and events, many of which were associated with international commerce, writes Margaret Jacob who identifies instances of the terms "cosmopolitan" and "citizen of the world" being used in the mid-seventeenth and early-eighteenth centuries.[42] The former was employed by natural philosophers to refer to wider audiences for their works, while the latter was used in the context of the Royal Exchange in London. The self-described "cosmopolitan" natural philosophers primarily interacted with other Europeans, and the term "citizen of the world" was used to emphasize London's role as the economic and political center of the world (Jacob cites *The Spectator*, May 19, 1711).

Neither aligns with the Kantian ideal of cosmopolitanism.[43] By the time Diderot (1751) famously defined cosmopolitans as being "strangers nowhere in the world" because they live both within and beyond the borders of single nations, the term had become a commonplace.[44] To think intersectionally and longitudinally about the climate crisis, cosmopolitanism, the "Scientific Revolution," and European imperialism involves breaching geographical and disciplinary boundaries designated by long-established specializations. "Art" and "techno-science" overlapped in ways that our modern disciplinary formations do not recognize, while "European imperialism" involves studying European behavior outside Europe in the same breath (and breadth) as within. Fugue 3 suggests how focusing on ingenuity offers a significant opportunity to revisit well-known literature with a different interpretive goal.

Notes

1 Thomas Goodard Bergin and Max Harold Fisch, Introduction, *The New Science of Giambattista Vico: Abridged Translation of the third Edition (1744)*, (Ithaca–London: Cornell University Press, 1970), xxv.
2 Vico, *The New Science*, Section VII: [Poetic Physics], chapter 1, 688.
3 Claire Farago, Janis Bell, and Carlo Vecce, *The Fabrication of Leonardo da Vinci's Trattato della Pittura, with a scholarly edition of the Italian editio princeps (1651) and an annotated English Translation*, 2 vols., with additional contributors, foreword Martin Kemp (Leiden: Brill Press, 2018). See my Introduction for this history and further references.

4 See Paola Bertucci, *Artisanal Enlightenment: Science and the Mechanical Arts in Old Regime France* (London– New Haven: Yale University Press, 2017), 34–36, for an excellent discussion of Colbert's projects to revitalize French trade and his mercantilist plan to establish government control over trade and manufacturing to compete in the global economy.
5 Mario Valentino Guffanti, "The Visual Imagery of the Printed Editions of Leonardo's Treatise on Painting," in Farago, Bell, and Vecce, *Fabrication*, 1: 373–411; and Guffanti, "Bibliography of Printed Editions of Leonardo da Vinci's *Treatise on Painting*," in *Re-Reading Leonardo: The Treatise on Painting across Europe, 1550–1900,* ed. and intro. Claire Farago (Farnham–Burlington: Ashgate, 2009), 569–606, which includes a complete list of all printed editions.
6 See *Re-Reading Leonardo*.
7 Carol Gibson-Wood, *Studies in the Theory of Connoisseurship from Vasari to Morelli* (New York: Garland Publishing, 1988), 71–94.
8 Abraham Bosse: *Sentimens sur la distinction des diverses manieres de peinture, dessein, & graveurs* (Paris 1649).
9 Gibson-Woods, *Studies in Connoisseurship*, 61.
10 Éric Michaud, *The Barbarian Invasions: A Genealogy of the History of Art* (2015 French ed.), trans. Nicholas Huckle (Cambridge, MA–London: The MIT Press, 2019).
11 Michaud, *The Barbarian Invasions*, 2.
12 Michaud, *The Barbarian Invasions*, 3.
13 Kamini Vellodi, "Two Histories of Art History: Review of Christopher Wood's *The History of Art History*, Princeton University Press, 2019, and Eric Michaud's, *The Barbarian Invasions A Genealogy of the History of Art*. MIT 2019," *Art History* 44/2 (2021): 409–416.
14 Edward Andrew, "Jean Bodin on Sovereignty." *Republics of Letters: A Journal for the Study of Knowledge, Politics, and the Arts* 2/2 (June 1, 2011): http://rofl.stanford.edu/node/90
15 Prathama Banerjee, "Sovereignty and Ascendancy: South Asian Reflections," in *Thinking the Re-Thinking of the World: Decolonial Challenges to the Humanities and Social Sciences from Africa, Asia and the Middle East*, ed. Kai Kresse and Abdoulaye Sounaye (Berlin–Boston: De Gruyter, 2022), 83–110, https://doi.org/10.1515/9783110733198-004. See further, Banerjee, *Politics of Time: "Primitives" and History Writing in a Colonial Society* (New Delhi: Oxford University Press, 2006).
16 Claire Vergerio, "Beyond the Nation-State," *Boston Review*, 27 May 2021, www.bostonreview.net/articles/beyond-the-nation-state/. See further, Vergerio, *War, States, and International Order: Alerico Gentili and the Foundational Myth of the Laws of War* (Cambridge–New York: Cambridge University Press, 2022).
17 Andreas Osiander, "Sovereignty, International Relations, and the Westphalian Myth," *International Organization* 55/2 (Spring 2001): 251–287; Derek Croxton, "The Peace of Westphalia of 1648 and the Origins of Sovereignty," *The International History Review* 21/3 (Sept 1999): 569–591. The following discussion of the "Westphalian myth" draws on these studies and Vergerio's review cited in the previous note.
18 Tomasz Grusiecki, *Transcultural Things and the Spectre of Orientalism in Early Modern Poland-Lithuania* (Manchester: Manchester University Press, 2023).
19 Jan Hennings, *Russia and Courtly Europe; Ritual and the Culture of Diplomacy, 1648–1725* (Cambridge: Cambridge University Press, 2016).
20 Meredith Martin, "Mirror Reflections: Louis XUV, Phra Narai, and the Material Culture of Kingship," *Art History* 38/4 (September 2015): 652–667.

21 Antony Anghie, *Imperialism, Sovereignty, and the Making of International Law* (Cambridge: Cambridge University Press, 2007), discussed by Stoler, *Duress*, 176–178.
22 Antony Anghie, *Imperialism*, 6.
23 Stoler, *Duress*, 177–178.
24 The institutions of trade and law in the Indies followed a royal proclamation to the Audiencia of Mexico by Charles V in 1533. Sara Miglietti, "New Worlds, Ancient Theories: Reshaping Climate Theory in the Early Colonial Atlantic," in *Translating Nature: Cross-Cultural Histories of Early Modern Science*, ed. Jaime Marroquín Arredondo and Ralph Bauer (Philadelphia: University of Pennsylvania Press, 2019), 203–223.
25 Miglietti, "New Worlds," 218.
26 Stoler, *Duress*, 249.
27 Hayden White, "The Politics of Historical Interpretation: Discipline and De-Sublimation," *Critical Inquiry* 9/1 (September 1982): 113–137, at 121.
28 Raymond Williams, *Culture and Society, 1780–1950* (New York–London: Harper & Row, 1958), 42.
29 Raymond Williams, *Keywords: A Vocabulary of Culture and Society* (1976; rev ed., New York: Oxford University Press, 1983), 89, citing Herder's unfinished *Ideas on the Philosophy of the History of Mankind* (1784–1791), 87–93.
30 Margaret Hodgen, *Early Anthropology in the Sixteenth and Seventeenth Centuries* (Philadelphia: University of Pennsylvania Press, 1964).
31 Benedict Anderson, *Imagined Communities: Reflections on the Origin and Spread of Nationalism* (1982; rev. ed., London–New York: Verso, 1991).
32 Eric Hobsbawm, *Nations and Nationalism since 1780: Programme, Myth, Reality* (Cambridge: Cambridge University Press, 1990), 71. Miroslave Hroch, *Social Preconditons of National Survival in Europe* (Cambridge: Cambridge University Press, 1985).
33 Williams, *Keywords*, 86.
34 *New Keywords: A Revised Vocabulary of Culture and Society*, ed. Tony Bennett, Lawrence Grossberg, and Meaghan Morris (Malden–Oxford–Victoria: Blackwell Publishing, 2005), 63–69.
35 George W. Stocking, Jr., *Race, Culture, and Evolution: Essays in the History of Anthropology* (New York: Free Press, 1968), cited in *New Keywords*, 67.
36 Edward Said, "Opponents, Audiences, Constituencies, and Community," in *The Politics of Interpretation*, ed. WJT Mitchell (Chicago–London: University of Chicago Press, 1983), 7–32; Terry Eagleton, Frederic Jameson, and Edward Said, *Nationalism, Colonialism, and Literature*, intro. S. Deane (Minneapolis: University of Minnesota Press, 1990).
37 Gyan Prakash, "Introduction: After Colonialism" in *After Colonialism: Imperial Histories and Postcolonial Displacements*, ed. Gyan Prakash (Princeton: Princeton University Press, 1995), 3–20.
38 Laura Doyle, "Theoretical Introduction: Between States," *Inter-imperiality: Vying Empires, Gendered Labor, and the Literary Arts of Alliance* (Durham–London: Duke University Press, 2020), 1–32.
39 Pekka Hämälinen, *Indigenous Continent; The Epic Contest for North America* (New York: Liveright Publishing Corporation, 2022), xii. See further discussion in Fugue 5.
40 Samuel Clowes Huneke, "Reading Imagined Communities Amid a Resurgence of Nationalism," *The New Republic*, 10 April 2024.
41 Partha Chatterjee, *Nationalist Thought and the Colonial World: A Derivative Discourse* (Minneapolis: University of Minnesota Press, 1993).

42 Margaret C. Jacob, *Strangers Nowhere in the World: The Rise of Cosmopolitanism in Early Modern Europe* (Philadelphia: University of Pennsylvania Press, 2006).
43 Thanks to Tomasz Grusiecki for offering this succinct evaluation.
44 Denis Diderot, as cited in Thomas J. Schlereth, *The Cosmopolitan Ideal in Enlightenment Thought: Its Form and Function in the Ideas of Franklin, Hume, and Voltaire, 1694–1790* (Notre Dame, Ind.: University of Notre Dame Press, 1977), 47. Cited by Jacob, *Strangers Nowhere*, 3.

FUGUE 3

HAUNTOLOGIES OF ART

"Race," Climate, and Genius

How was the intersection of art, collective social identity, and the environment negotiated by Europeans before the formation of modern nation-states? The ability to gain a rational understanding of the created world came to be regarded as a distinctly human feature practiced to various degrees ranging from the most primitive savages to the most civilized Europeans. This Fugue focuses on major Enlightenment thinkers who maintained that humans could be defined collectively and hierarchically by their intellectual, moral, and aesthetic capabilities. The Eurocentrism of European philosophers has been rehashed *ad infinitum* over the past several decades – what more is to be gained from circling the same drain? Most of the writers I will discuss were harsh critics of European imperialism, believed in universal human rights, and supported the abolition of slavery. Yet they still maintained the longstanding view that humans could be defined collectively and hierarchically by their intellectual, moral, and aesthetic capabilities. This conundrum has been a flashpoint for historians of the Enlightenment. Some categorically deny that Enlightenment philosophers were racists and others have been puzzled by their cognitive dissonance. Why did these eminent philosophers condemn slavery as inhumane and still espouse the view that some humans are inferior to others in apparent violation of their belief in universal human rights? What would be an adequate explanation that unlocks the emancipatory potential of this history? I have already established that contradictory ideas about humanness coexisted because the discussions were transmitted along two different trajectories, one originating in sixteenth-century writings on universal human rights associated with political theory, discussed in the first Fugue, and the other associated with the contemporaneous literature on art and Church reform, discussed in the second Fugue. Yet neither body of evidence explains how the concept of national culture became entangled in the same mix of art and human exceptionalism, which is the subject of this Fugue.

DOI: 10.4324/9781351023429-6

This Fugue reviews the seminal role played by historical theories of climate that Michaud cites for the emergence of modern racial theory, texts that have recently also drawn interest from cultural historians interested in the history of climate theory. A largely unfamiliar story is hidden in plain sight in this familiar literature which held that where you were born and live determines your capabilities. Historical preoccupations with the criteria for what it meant to be human and what it meant to be excluded – the problematic of what it has meant, historically, not to be human, or not to be fully civilized – is part of that discourse, often functioning silently, insidiously. It is not at all exceptional for modern scholars to focus on what is most advanced and still tenable in their inherited texts, while ignoring the rest. However, this approach leaves the dualistic structure of inclusion/exclusion in place while excluding the role of art in establishing those same boundaries. In rethinking those ideas now, my operating premise is that parallel accounts that represent the same events from mutually exclusive points of view do not offer an adequate epistemic critique. Integrated accounts are needed to define the critical issues that produced mutually exclusive narratives. If the objective is to rethink the nature/culture divide, it is imperative to recognize the occluded arguments as part of the process of coming to terms with Eurocentrism. It is also imperative to define an enunciative framework, to borrow Michel Foucault's formulation, much broader than any discipline established in the nineteenth century because their epistemological claims inevitably rest on grounds obscured by their differentiation as distinct subjects of study.

Art, "Race," and Climate Theory

Macro-environmental theories that connect the nature of individuals to their environments appear in numerous genres and contexts based on a wide range of sources. What we now call cultural geography refers to accounts of how place and climate shape body, mind, the character of human beings, and the organization and development of human societies. In the period sources, they are often called cosmographies. Andrew Curran, in his study of primary ethnographic sources since the late seventeenth century, discussed below, offers the alternative term "physio-environmental determinism." Sara Miglietti studies the sixteenth-century literature in relation to contemporary eco-criticism. She proposes "geo-ethnographic inquiry," and notes that the term "environment" is also anachronistic.[1] However, despite semantic shifts in the meaning of the term, "climate theory," as this literature was known in the nineteenth century, offers a convenient shorthand today to describe a wide range of ancient ideas, often employed in some combination by early modern writers.

In addition to the theory of natural slavery, Aristotle's *Politics* also contains a brief account of climate theory favoring Greeks who are located in the allegedly ideal temperate and geographically intermediate region of the Mediterranean. According to Aristotle, whose account is typical of the ancient Mediterranean literature, people in cold countries and Europe are excessively impulsive, unintelligent, or limited in their organizational capacity, independent but incapable of true government; while the peoples of Asia are intelligent and resourceful but morally weak and habitually live in submission and slavery (*Politics* 1327b).[2] Even as the details changed as climate theories were reappraised in light of new empirical evidence, the understanding that geographical location and climate determined the character of peoples established the framework for discussing differences of "genius" at the collective level in Europe beginning in the sixteenth century.

Climate theory developed on the basis of ancient Mediterranean sources became a key ingredient in the way modern Europeans understood their place within the natural world. Winckelmann drew on climate theory to argue for the superiority of Greek art while stressing the proximity of Black people to monkeys.[3] His *Geschichte der Kunst der Alterthums*/*History of Ancient Art* (1764), attributes the fabrication of works of art to a given people, with nature favoring the ancient Greeks above all others. Subsequently, many other writers conflated the life of a style with the life of a people, as Éric Michaud has documented, in conceiving art as the *natural* function of a body of people dependent on their location and climate. Winckelmann and a broad spectrum of writers before and after him employed the term "race" in various roughly interchangeable ways along with the terms "nation," "*maniera*," and "style" (*elocutio* in Latin), the latter two terms initially referring to individual artists.

Even those who rejected the influence of climate and geography framed their arguments in these terms. Drawing upon the ancient sources, Jean Bodin (*Le methode de l'histoire*, 1566; *Six livres de la republique*, 1576), divided the entire globe from poles to the equator into parallel bands to establish uniform climate zones. He discussed diverse forms of government suited to each single people based on their location and climate. Bodin held Aristotelian views articulated in Aristotle's *Politics* on the benefit of cities in the ideal temperate zones and the harm caused everywhere else by their absence, a claim repeated and extended by many others over the next three centuries who invoked racial theories of human difference based on a combination of factors: climate, environment, and human ingenuity. Beyond his ancient sources, Bodin took into account altitude, the direction of the wind, fertility of the soil, paths of communication, and national characteristics arising from these factors.[4] His successors speculated on the physical environment of different "races" using the voluminous data furnished by explorers, ethnographers, and missionaries. Bodin's idea that "all men have become brothers and share miraculously in the universal republic, as if they formed one same city" is indebted to Aristotle's *Politics*, interpreted in the same way as the Catholic Vitoria had. They both rejected Aristotle's idea of natural slavery while promoting the idea that the inhabitants of the American continent were mentally and politically inferior, which Bodin attributed to their physical weakness caused by the climate.[5]

The Hippocratic tradition of medicine recorded by Galen (second century CE) was another significant ingredient in early modern climate theory. The Muslim philosopher and physician Ibn Sina (980–1037 CE), known as Avicenna through Latin translations available since the thirteenth century, wrote in these terms about the balance of bodily humors encompassing physical appearance, personality, mental aptitude, and character resulting from interaction with the climate.[6] The literary tradition based on Pliny the Elder that included St. Augustine (354–430 CE) and Isidore of Seville (early seventh century CE), was also a favorite of many humanists since the fifteenth century. The literary tradition focused on species of monstrous people in distant places, which were also diagrammatically depicted on medieval *mappa mundi* (world maps centered on Jerusalem), portolan atlases used for navigation, the landmark printed publication known as the Nuremberg Chronicle (1493), and incorporated into widely known travel narratives such as the *Travels* of Marco Polo (c. 1254–1324), the Venetian merchant who traveled through Asia in the late thirteenth century; and John Mandeville's enormously popular but fictitious *Travels*, written between 1357 and 1371 [Figures 3.1–3.2].[7]

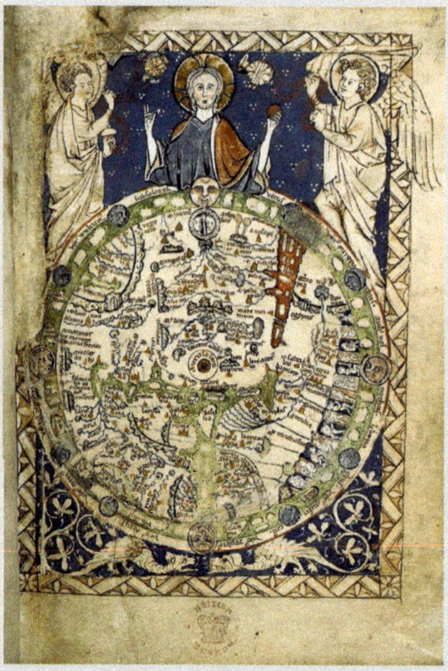

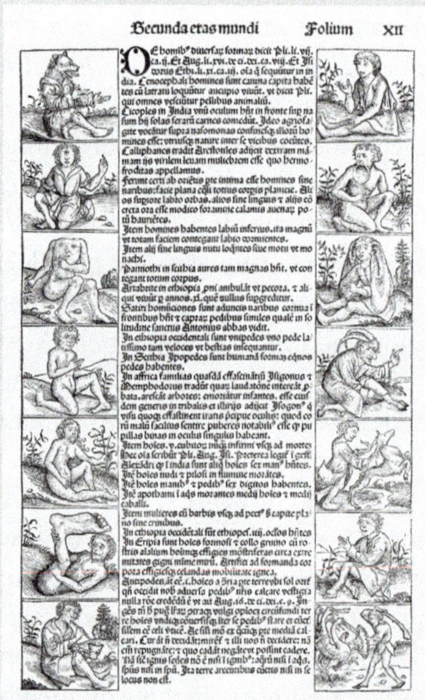
Secunda etas mundi Folium XII

FIGURE 3.1 AND 3.2 (Left) Psalter World Map (*mappa mundi*), c. 1265, parchment. London, British Library. ADD. MS 28681. Photo Maldun Collecton/Alamy Stock Photo; (Right) Nuremburg Chronicle. Hartmann Schedel, *Liber chronicarum/Die Schedelsche Weltchronik/Book of Chronicles*, German trans. George Alt (Nuremberg: Anton Koberger, 1493). Metropolitan Museum of Art, Purchase, Rogers Fund, 1906, transferred from the Library.

In this miniature (6.6 x 4.9 inches), Christ appears in the East, the traditional location of the Garden of Eden, as a figure of salvation giving a blessing. Christ's body is the world that humans inhabit depicted as a history projected onto a geography that names 91 locations, each associated with the text of a psalm. At the bottom edge are fourteen images of monstrous people at the edge of the world. Like its German counterpart, the Ebstorf Map (destroyed in World War II), which had a map area about 12 feet in diameter, this Map Psalter sums up a medieval European–Christian cartographic tradition that began in the sixth century CE.

The *Chronicle* was an enormously popular, profusely illustrated biblical world history divided into eleven world ages, one of the first print publications to successfully integrate illustrations and text. It combines Christian chronology, ancient secular geography, and travel literature including recent information about the west coast of Africa. At the beginning, Schedel laid out an account of the wild races who inhabited the edges of the world, as ancient Greek visitors to India had first reported and Pliny the Elder (23/4–79CE) and many other writers repeated.

Cultural geographies, maps, travel accounts, and other forms of print culture have attracted a great deal of interdisciplinary scholarly attention in the past three decades. The old historical narrative held that the encounter between Europe and the rest of the world since the late fifteenth century, and especially with respect to what Europeans called the discovery of the New World, gradually stripped the inherited sources of their aura of completeness and utility, to cite historian Anthony Grafton.[8] Based on close study of a vast range of illustrated material, Grafton and others have revisited this understanding to argue that European notions of history and civilization remained intact, documented in the pervasive influence of classical texts and ideas in education, scholarship, and science. However, the old Aristotelian categories were stretched beyond their tensile strength by the immense amount of new empirical evidence entering Europe and/or recorded by Europeans traveling abroad. Ancient literary sources had mentioned Africans, Orientals, and Asians, but the Americas were a completely unexpected discovery. Sixteenth-century literary accounts are filled with discussions on the degree to which the Amerindians, unrecorded in any text, are rational creatures worthy of the name human. The earliest visual records often portray the inhabitants of the "New World" according to the medieval stereotypes of wild men, cannibals, rude barbarians, and even entirely distinct species. The study of print culture using a cultural history approach has significantly extended knowledge of the various ways in which Europeans represented peoples of Africa, Asia, and the newly discovered Americas during the first phase of global contact in the sixteenth century. By the first decade of the sixteenth century, some

European printed images, such as those by Hans Burgkmair [Figure 3.3 compare Figure 3.4], soon followed by others, were based on firsthand ethnographic information. Burgkmair's prints, informed by the humanist Konrad Peutlinger, overturned the fabulous armchair travel accounts of John Mandeville and others who had fed the European imaginary for centuries.[9]

Stephanie Leitch argues that printed illustrations, because they established the semblance of an eyewitness account by visual means of persuasion, became suited to ratify claims of empiricism and played an important role in developing

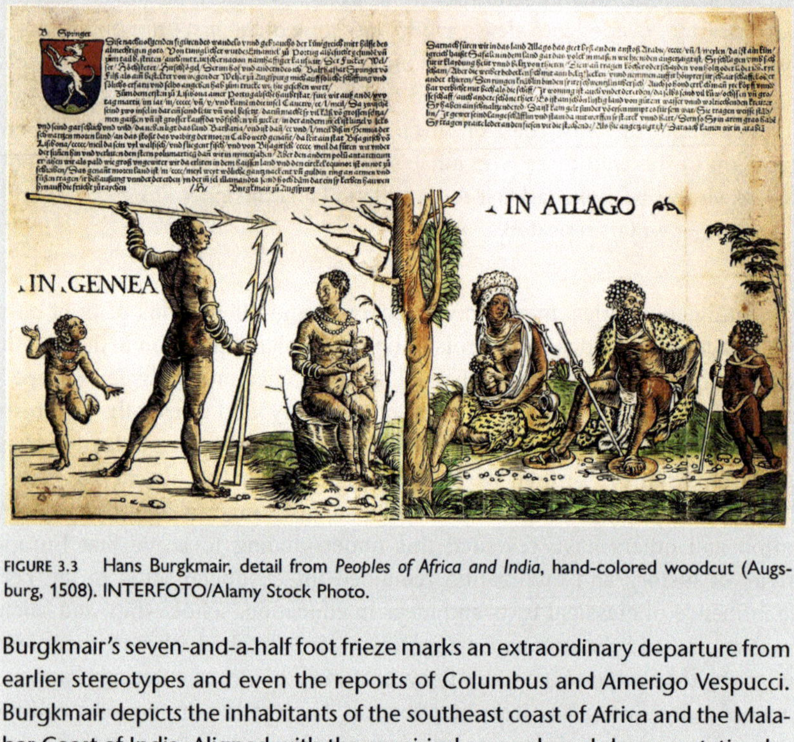

FIGURE 3.3 Hans Burgkmair, detail from *Peoples of Africa and India*, hand-colored woodcut (Augsburg, 1508). INTERFOTO/Alamy Stock Photo.

Burgkmair's seven-and-a-half foot frieze marks an extraordinary departure from earlier stereotypes and even the reports of Columbus and Amerigo Vespucci. Burgkmair depicts the inhabitants of the southeast coast of Africa and the Malabar Coast of India. Aligned with the empirical research and documentation by his humanist colleagues in Augsburg, his detailed visual descriptions of people, animals, and topography were made at the request of the Welser family of merchant bankers who co-sponsored Balthasar Springer, a Tirolese merchant who traveled with the mission that established the first Portuguese viceroyalty in India in 1505/6. The images follow Springer's journey in a series of consecutive frames, with his travel report forming a caption running across the top of the prints.

Stephanie Leitch, *Mapping Ethnography in Early Modern Germany: New Worlds in Print Culture* (New York: Palgrave Macmillan, 2010).

new ideas about the visual representation of truth. The revolution in the forms of knowledge and expression which took place in early modern Europe resulted in tensions between and within texts as they confronted inconsistencies as well as new worlds. Change was complex, yielding paradoxes and continuities in the sources themselves, Grafton concludes, so "[p]erhaps no causal scheme can convey the richness, the complexity, and the frequent self-contradictions of the Western Canon."[10]

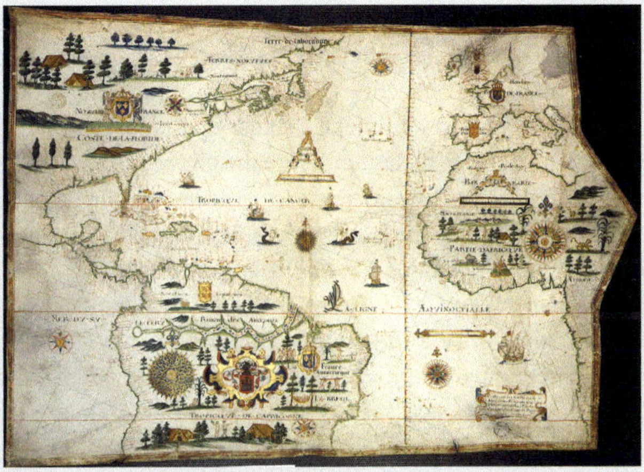

FIGURE 3.4 Pierre DeVaux, Portolan map of Atlantic Ocean showing material resources in Brazil, then Antarctic France, North America, Africa, and elsewhere. 1613. Paris, Bibliothèque nationale de France, Le département des Cartes et plans, CPL GE SH ARCH-6.

"They [the natives] live one hundred and fifty years, and rarely fall ill, and if they do fall victims to any disease, they cure themselves with certain roots and herbs [. . .] The climate there was very temperate and good, and as I was able to learn from their accounts, there was never there any pest or epidemic caused by corruption of the air; and unless they die a violent death they live long." Amerigo Vespucci (attributed), *Mundus Novus* (Latin ed., 1503), trans. George Tyler Northup (Princeton: Princeton University Press, 1916).

Travel writers portrayed Indigenous people in the New World as healthy, happy, and long-living in a land filled with resources for export, but the arrival of Europeans in the Americas in 1492 CE marks the onset of recurring waves of epidemics resulting in the loss of an estimated 56 million people by 1600. (Alexander Koch, Chris Brierley, et al., "Impacts of the European Arrival and Great Dying in the Americas after 1492," *Quaternary Science Reviews* 207 [2019]: 13–36.)

Maria Berbara, "'They live one hundred and fifty years': The trope of longevity and epidemic diseases across the early modern Atlantic," Getty Research Institute Presentation, 15 June 2022. Cited with the author's permission.

How did major thinkers come to hold their views on the role of "climate" as a formative agent for the collective identity of people and art? Ann Laura Stoler's strategy of seeking correlations among constellations of concepts (rather than comparisons or causes) offers a useful methodological tool aligned with Grafton's conclusions for approaching such a vast body of documentation. It allows for the juxtaposition of different genres and contexts of discussion ranging from cultural geographies to political theory to natural philosophy and anatomy, from medical and juridical records and colonial questionnaires to writings for and against chattel slavery. The classic study dealing with the formation of the modern system of the arts by Paul O. Kristeller, published in 1951–1952, is based on European writings on the arts for laymen, treatises comparing the arts, treatises on aesthetics, and discussions of problems of the arts in art academies.[11] Kristeller argued that modern aesthetics conceived in terms of taste and sentiment, genius, originality, and creative imagination did not assume its modern meaning before the eighteenth century. According to his narrative, the unity of the "fine arts" was established on the shared ancient principle of imitation which is also the basis for the modern term "aesthetics." Derived from the ancient Greek αἰσθητικός (*aisthetikos*) meaning sense perception, it was coined by the German philosopher Alexander Gottlieb Baumgarten (1714–1762), whose unfinished Latin work *Aesthetica* was published in the 1750s.[12]

Kristeller never mentioned that his sources also *excluded* people in some regions of the world for lacking the necessary genius due to their climate. Kristeller cites the Abbé Jean-Baptiste Du Bos, *Réflexions critiques sur la poésie et sur la peinture* (first ed., 1719), an amateur author who was, in Kristeller's narrative, among the first to have "a fairly clear notion of the difference between the arts that depend on 'genius' or talent and the sciences based on accumulated knowledge."[13] Du Bos distinguished between the sciences and the professions that "depend more on the talent of inventing and natural genius" (*dépend plus du talent d'inventer et du génie naturel*) in which the ancients excelled.[14] Kristeller accused Du Bos of being unsystematic in the presentation of his ideas, yet character, genius, and climate are the organizing topics of the second volume of Du Bos' *Réflexions*, where he discusses the collective "genius" of people. The order of the opening chapters indicates his principles of organization throughout and his format depends on Scholastic modes of argumentation by offering general propositions, raising objections, and resolving them in favor of the initial proposition. In keeping with this mode of argumentation, the chapter titles that open the second part of Du Bos' *Réflexions* indicate how the concept of "genius" intersected with his ideas about climate as his argument moves from the general to the particular: (1) On Genius in general; (2) On the Genius which forms painters and poets; (3) That the impulse of genius determines men to be painters; (4) Objection against the preceding proposition, and answer to the objection; (5) On the studies and progress of painters and poets; (6) On artisans without genius – and so on until the introduction of climate theory in Chapter 15, entitled "The power of the air over our bodies proved by the different characters of nations." A series of chapters follow on how the "genius of people" is determined by "the variations of the air."

Du Bos, who held that "[i]t has in all times been observed, that the influence of climate is stronger than that of origin and blood," followed Bodin, who had envisioned ways that humans can shield themselves from climatic influence through diet, music, and a liberal arts education. [15] Art historian Thomas Kirchner notes that Du Bos went beyond Bodin and the ancient theorists in making climate responsible for both the character of a nation and the character of its art.[16] Du Bos acknowledged that the peoples of Mexico and Peru were exceptional because they established empires in which the art of painting was cultivated, a frequent trope that had been introduced by missionaries like Las Casas in the early contact period of the sixteenth century. Du Bos writes about their feather mosaics in terms that echo Ginés de Sepúlveda, Charles V's chronicler who translated Aristotle's *Politics* and had applied its theory of natural slavery to the Indigenous peoples of the Americas nearly two centuries earlier in the famous debates at Valladolid (1550/51). According to Du Bos (1719): "But as genius was lacking in these peoples, they were, in spite of the skill of their hands, rude craftsmen. They had neither the simplest rules of drawing, not the first principles of composition, perspective, and chiaroscuro."[17]

Du Bos defined genius as "an aptitude which man has received from nature to perform well and easily, that which others can do but indifferently, with a great deal of pain."[18] He is credited with the idea that we judge artworks by means of sentiments, rather than rule-governed reasoning. Yet in fact, as the cited excerpt from his account of Indigenous artistic practices attests, the "genius" that even the most civilized American cities lacked was not simply absence of inborn capacity. Initially, they also lacked the skilled, theoretically based knowledge of academic artistic representational practices, namely pictorial perspective and chiaroscuro, which are techniques based on geometry, optical theory, and observation for rendering three-dimensional shapes in painting to make them appear volumetric, as recorded at length in Leonardo's abridged treatise on painting and other sources. Du Bos' critique of artistic practices as lacking the ability to master Western representational techniques is ubiquitous. The influential German Jesuit polymath Athanasius Kircher (1602–1680) criticized Chinese painting on similar terms, calling Chinese artists skillful but incapable of perspective (*China monumentis, qua sacris qua profanes . . . illustrata*, Latin ed. 1667; French ed. 1670). There are many others, including assessments by uncomprehending modern scholars faced with images and objects that are products of colliding systems of visual signification. Alessandra Russo has named combinations of classicizing European and Pre-Hispanic sources "untranslatable images."[19] They are not syncretistic fusions or "hybrids," more like palimpsest visual semiotic systems that can be read in multiple ways depending on one's cultural knowledge and values.[20] In keeping with European political theorists of natural law such as Hugo Grotius (1583–1645), who recast the Christian universalist arguments of Vitoria and his successors in secular terms, Du Bos recommended commerce as an alternative to war. Like many others who justified international trade in terms of climate advantages and disadvantages, Du Bos described the transmissible effects of climate in commodities newly available in different parts of the world. For example, wine produced in sunny climates "infuses vigor and delicacy into the blood and the imaginations" of inhabitants of northern countries such as England.[21]

What can we make of these commonalities today? Michaud compares Du Bos' arguments to De Piles' highly influential characterization of the "six tastes of nations" according to their varying degrees of natural and artificial taste arranged in a hierarchy of "schools" with Roman taste at the top because it was the most artificial, by which he meant the most educated. Along similar lines but with opposite value judgments, Michaud writes that all French attempts to classify European schools of painting were inspired by De Piles for a century and played a crucial role in the construction of "national characters" that flourished throughout the eighteenth century. The implication is that taste ideally should be cosmopolitan, though essays on national character comparing European peoples and schools of painting show strong national rivalries for prestige and hegemony even by citizens of the international republic of letters.[22] By the mid-to-late eighteenth century, Du Bos' *Réflexions* was widely known as a textbook in France, and it made an appearance in the expanded 1781 edition of Diderot's *Encyclopédie*. Du Bos' ideas on the fine arts based on climatic conditions were read by Hume, Baumgarten, Herder, Voltaire, Rousseau, Lessing, and other philosophers. His readers included his immediate successor in Kristeller's narrative, the Abbé Batteux whom Kristeller identifies as the first writer to clearly separate the fine arts from the mechanical arts, in 1746.[23] Neither De Piles nor Batteux situated their arguments with direct reference to climate theory, which left De Piles without a foundation, according to Michaud, and enabled Batteaux, according to Kristeller, to take the decisive step toward a clear system of fine arts.

Even when climate theory was not directly referenced, the assumption that human differences could be assessed in terms of geography and climate was never far from sight. Climate theory moved to center stage again with Winckelmann's *History of Ancient Art* (1764), which inaugurated a new biological conception of collective style that assumed peoples to be homogeneous, enduring, and unchanging through time.[24] Winckelmann's stated intention was to provide a system (*Lehrgebäudes*) for studying the "essence of art" as the direct reflection of biological identity. He argued that the ancient Greeks were the "original inventors" of art since they were the first to give human form to their gods, which they allegedly did independently of borrowings from other peoples.[25]

Éric Michaud credits Winckelmann with the idea that writing the life cycle of a style meant writing the biography of a people from first appearance to decline, borrowing metaphors from models of plant and human reproduction as if art were the natural function of a body of a people, a "bodily secretion of the nation as a whole" that guaranteed the self-identity of a people or a race through time through the organ of art. Michaud also cites sources into the nineteenth century on bodily fluids that were thought capable of ensuring a vertical transmission guaranteeing self-identity of a people or race through time.[26] The beauty of the Greek profile by this account was not fashioned by art but produced by nature herself: Nature forms this profile less in a cold climate than in a mild climate like that of Greece. Michaud cites the comparative anatomical studies of the famous Dutch physician, Petrus Camper (1722–1789), whose profile drawings of human and animal physiognomy (1791, cited by Diderot) were inspired by what Camper described as Winckelmann's "national physiognomies." Through these reciprocal connections, Michaud situates the development of German art history in the context of national rivalries and historical notions of "race" in the second half of the eighteenth century when the term was interwoven with many others such as people, tribe, nation, and later "ethnic group." Camper noted morphological similarities between men and apes, and his successor Georges-Louis Leclerc, Comte de Buffon, author of the idea of racial degenerative evolution (1749, also praised by Darwin), considered apes completely devoid of the ability to think. There were many others. Edward Tyson's *Orang-outang, sive homo sylvestris, or Anatomy of a Pygmie compared with that of a Monkey, and Ape, and a Man* (1699), one of the earliest illustrated publications on the comparative anatomy of humans and apes, identifies orangutans as wild men, a conflation of pygmies with apes present in medieval Scholastic texts such as Albertus Magnus that others attached to Indigenous peoples in the nineteenth century as the discussion of Darwin will elaborate in the next Fugue.

A scholar who has studied a wide range of historical texts dealing with climate and race in depth is Antonello Gerbi (1904–1976), whose publication of 1955, translated into English as *The Dispute of the New World: The History of a Polemic, 1750–1900* (1973), deserves to be better known by historians of climate theory. It constitutes the culmination of a life's work to understand why nature in the Americas, and particularly American natives, were considered inferior to Europe up to his own day. His fourth book on the topic spans nearly 800 pages in what Gerbi called a "concertina work" because it could be expanded or contracted at whim. He found that the theme of the "inferiority of the Americas" runs consistently through texts by early travelers, chroniclers (beginning with Oviedo in 1525), naturalists, and missionaries. The idea that the American continent was inferior first assumed a coherent and scientific form in Comte de Buffon's (1707–1788) *Histoire Naturelle*, a massive work almost as popular as Diderot's *Encyclopédie*, that was issued in forty-four volumes and translated in part or whole into numerous European languages by the beginning of the nineteenth century. Analyzing texts from Buffon to Cornelius de Pauw (1739–1799), considered the greatest expert on the Americas during his lifetime, Gerbi provides a broad outline for the uninterrupted history of what he characterized as solid facts turned into value judgments and improper generalizations. "Particulars were illegitimately polarized" into antitheses between the Old World and the New World that have "no existence outside the schemes of an impassioned and systematizing abstract and polemic mentality."[27] Buffon, for example, who did not use precise anatomical data, held that large animals are superior to the small ones found in the Americas, fixed is superior to changeable, and large is more fixed than the small.[28] Even when the animals are almost the same stature, the environment of the American continent is hostile and its "savage" human inhabitants are weaker, with smaller sexual organs, less sensitive, more fearful, lacking vivacity, lifeless in their souls, and motivated purely by hunger and thirst.[29]

Nature, for Buffon, varied according to different climates. Just as the idea of Europe was becoming more fully worked out, he boasted that Europe had shown the way to the rest of the world in the civil arts, technical fields, and its highly civilized social institutions. When Buffon's ideas on the immaturity of animals were taken up by David Hume in his essay, *Of National Characters* (1748), the philosopher explained why "nations that live beyond the polar circles or between the tropics are inferior to the rest of the species."[30] Rousseau's *Émile, ou De l'éducation* (1762), an important source for Kant whom I will discuss below, drew from Buffon's climate theory. Buffon went beyond it to institutionalize belief in the inherited inferiority of Black Africans more explicitly than any other thinker of his generation, Andrew Curran writes, by "suggesting more deterministically that humans living in taxing locations would make poor students because of their brains."[31] Curran views Buffon's understanding of humankind as generating "a new type of 'toxic speculation on the African'" overlaid environmentalism with a "bleak anatomy" and other inherited factors. The concept of Blackness in the eighteenth century was increasingly dissected, handled, measured, and weighed, serving as a demonstrable wedge between human categories defined by its supposed materiality. It testifies to the power of representation and its connections to social reality.

Anthropologists and historians have more recently collaborated with Indigenous experts throughout Latin America in a variety of ways that have benefited native communities, write Ralph Bauer and Marcy Norton (2017) in a wide-ranging literature review on the historiography of such technological entanglements.[32] I agree with their emphasis on recovering Indigenous knowledge in our colonial texts, which also has great potential for examining the nature/culture divide in relation to capitalism and the climate crisis. However, the haunting continues if entangled European and colonial (and other) sources are mined for what is still tenable in them while their untenable epistemological assumptions and framework are simply ignored. With the responsibility to come to terms with the complex legacy of Eurocentrism through epistemological critique in mind, I will discuss one more writer mentioned by Kristeller who followed Batteux's system of the fine arts, was closely read by Winckelmann, and was also a major contributor both to climate theory and the debates on the abolition of slavery. The political theorist Baron de Montesquieu (1689–1755) was a French nobleman whose short essay on taste written for Diderot's *Encyclopédie*, left unfinished at his death, is misleadingly cited by Kristeller as a founding text for aesthetic theory that gave it general currency in Europe. Kristeller cites Montesquieu only in this context, but Montesquieu dealt at great length with climate theory in his *L'esprit des lois/The Spirit of [the] Laws* (1748), an attempt to explain universal human laws and social institutions. His argument continues the conjoined themes of hospitality and commerce as it was introduced into political theory by Vitoria to justify the Spanish Conquest/invasion in the sixteenth century. Montesquieu advocated democracy as opposed to monarchy and despotism. His account of the separation of powers and checks and balances profoundly influenced the design of the US Constitution.[33]

Significant here, writes Trevor Shelley in his analysis of Montesquieu's political theory on which my summary draws, is that "the body and the spirit of a polity are inseparable."[34] There are striking similarities to contemporary ideas of a constitutional republic based on representation and universal suffrage, but there are also significant differences in Montesquieu's underlying assumptions about how the "body and spirit" of a polity are connected. His lengthy discussion of the impact of climate on laws and nations connects the physical nature of a territory to its type of government: for example, Asia is more conducive to despotism and servitude because the continent is so homogeneous, compared with Europe's "genius for liberty" partly due to its topographical unevenness, required for free and moderate government [Figure 3.5].

Montesquieu's views of European republicanism are based on what he perceived as the need for the rule of law and government by a representative elite that would protect the economic interests of the citizen body.[35] He famously censored the

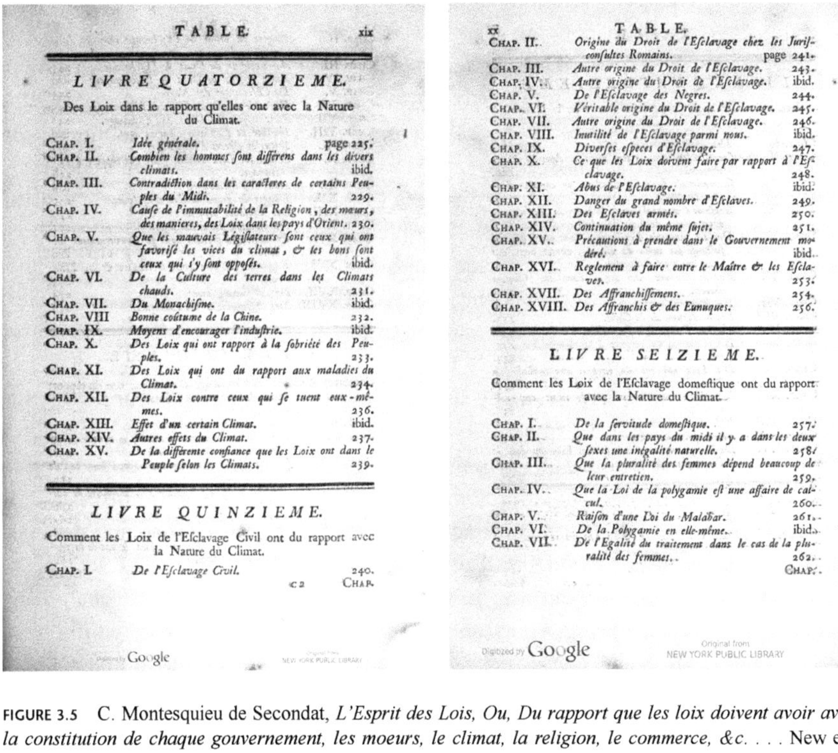

TABLE. xix

LIVRE QUATORZIEME.

Des Loix dans le rapport qu'elles ont avec la Nature du Climat.

LIVRE QUINZIEME.

Comment les Loix de l'Eſclavage Civil ont du rapport avec la Nature du Climat.

C 2 CHAP.

xx TABLE.

LIVRE SEIZIEME.

Comment les Loix de l'Eſclavage domeſtique ont du rapport avec la Nature du Climat.

CHAP.

FIGURE 3.5 C. Montesquieu de Secondat, *L'Esprit des Lois, Ou, Du rapport que les loix doivent avoir avec la constitution de chaque gouvernement, les moeurs, le climat, la religion, le commerce, &c.* . . . New ed. (Geneva: Chez Barillot & fils, 1749).

institution of slavery as a violation of natural law, but at the same time he held that certain people such as Africans were suitable to slavery due to certain physical variables understood as a function of the climate. He also argued similarly to Du Bos and others that the hot climate in Mexico and Peru "nearly always made them slaves" while the "courage of the people of cold climates has kept them free." These are not simply ethnic stereotypes to be overlooked, but constitutive of his entire political theory.

At the same time, Montesquieu's ambivalent view of economic globalization has so much in common with contemporary critiques of unregulated global capitalism that it will be useful to examine his climate/race theory more closely. The history of European republicanism is beyond the scope of this study. My aim here is to articulate some of the fundamental issues raised in Montesquieu's writings about the entanglement of climate theory, race, and art in a global framework in relation to the present. He praised both the modern right of nations and the expansion of commerce for spreading knowledge of the diversity of customs or mores that the laws of commerce can either perfect or ruin (*The Spirit of [the] Laws*, XX.1). This is because the spirit of commerce reduces everything to money so that the very requirements of and for humanity become transactional and reducible to the logic of trade and exchange: while joined at a national level, individuals lose a sense of humanity toward others.

Every nation or people, Montesquieu argues, is a real actor in history with more or less ability to act depending partly on the nature and principle of its government. Wherever peoples of the world have a *higher* degree of communication, there is likely to be *less* hospitality among them. He notes Aristotle's inclusion of banditry (outlaws, brigands) as a means of acquisition that produces a virtue altogether absent among commercial peoples, namely "hospitality." In contrast to Vitoria who argued that commerce and hospitality naturally go hand in hand, Montesquieu split them into opposing camps. "Bandit peoples," such as the Germans described by the ancient Roman historian Tacitus, both offer and receive strangers "with the same humanity."

As Michaud notes, Montesquieu and Tacitus were important sources for the positive reevaluation of Germanic "barbarians" by art historians framed in terms of emerging German nationalism in the early nineteenth century in opposition to Vasari's brand of humanism embracing the revival of classical antiquity. According to Montesquieu, by forming alliances for the purpose of offense and defense, mixed alliances of large and small republics have a better chance at security if they have something in common to dread, like a shared enemy. French King Louis XIV's project of a universal monarchy, Montesquieu writes, "would have been . . . fatal to Europe" had it succeeded because a universal rule of one "cannot fail in one country without failing in all others," just as it eventually failed with the Romans. "Considered as inhabitants of a planet so large," it follows that "different peoples are necessary" due to the broad range of "physical" and "moral" causes that shape peoples "from all these points of view" (I.3, I.1). He concludes by saying that the opening of the universe by commerce does not beget a singular or uniform political solution to the continuing problem of human rule and order (XXIII.25).

Today, the existential threat posed by human degradation of the environment certainly fits Montesquieu's description of a shared enemy, and the differences between peoples and their forms of government corresponds to his observations of how we must act together even though nations have different forms of government. Unfortunately, another point of resonance is that we still lack a rule-governed world order that would rein in commerce, avoid war, and protect rights, as Montesquieu envisioned. Whose planetary rights did Montesquieu envision protecting? Who was excluded, and who was the exception who benefited from that exclusion? Montesquieu's position recalls the way that earlier European political theorists discussed above defined sovereignty and universal rights to justify imperialism, as a closer look at his argument corroborates. *The Spirit of [the] Laws* begins with a chapter on "laws in their relation to the nature of climate" (XIV) and the topic of slavery in relation to the natural environment is central throughout, though Montesquieu recognizes that many factors govern people in conjunction to create "a general spirit" (XIX.4). The physical aspect of some climates is so strong "that morality can do practically nothing" (XVI.8), but human nature can tame nonhuman nature to some extent. Montesquieu introduces by then familiar colonialist themes about the need for European oversight, now pitched in terms of the environment: the less temperate a climate is, the more "good education" is necessary, where success is achieved by attending to climatological factors. A successful commerce of luxury perfects the arts (XXI.6), but luxury is typically the foundation of government by one alone, Montesquieu argues citing Cicero's *De Republica* (4.7), whereas commerce "founded on an economy" cannot be "done by a people among whom luxury is established who spend much and who see only great objects" (XX.4). His argument is a strident critique of despotism and monarchy, but also of consumerism, at least of a certain kind directly relevant to the fine arts – which is part of what makes his argument pertinent today.

Here, I remain focused on connections that Montesquieu draws between climate, commerce, and colonialist policies regarding rights. He argues that politics and "the great enterprises of the traders are always necessarily mixed with the public business" (XX.4). The English have been the most successful in prioritizing commerce over its political interests, but this has required "a constant preparedness for war and a strategy of colonization" (XX.7). The ancient Romans, by contrast, were destroyers whose "genius" was without concern for commerce (XX.14). The discovery of America linked Europe, Asia, and Africa commercially, resulting in Europe's unprecedented power, which may at times require less-than-peaceful approaches to ensure the continuance of commerce (XX.19).

During the same years at the height of the colonial era that Montesquieu was justifying imperialism by developing these chauvinist arguments protective of European commercial interests on a global scale, the slander of American nature including its inhabitants reached a "definitive climax," to cite Gerbi's account of the Dutch expert on the Americas, Cornelius de Pauw, who was a major contributor to the emerging science on race.[36] Curran sets De Pauw into the context of increasing doubts by the 1770s regarding the single-origin theory of humanity. Curran points to a growing list of discernible and measurable anatomical differences separating Blacks from Whites that naturalized these distinctions not as products of the environment alone but as resulting from a biology-based logic.[37] De Pauw claimed that inhospitable climate and poor food explained why non-Whites had come into existence. His *Recherches philosophiques sur les Américains/Philosophical Research on Americans* (Berlin, 1768), an encyclopedic work, cites Sepúlveda's famous polemic on the inferiority of American natives while attacking their defenders like Las Casas.[38] Meanwhile, Las Casas' defense was transformed into proof of the degenerate nature of Americans by others, including the philosopher Voltaire. Voltaire conflated opposing arguments in these sources when he claimed that Indigenous Americans' timid nature made them slaves naturally.[39] De Pauw, whose account was based on Buffon's monogenetic and environmentalist explanation of humankind, was also an important source for Johann Friedrich Blumenbach's *De generis humani varietate nativa* (first ed., 1775), a foundational text for physical anthropology that established a schematic classification of the human species into four or five separate races.

It would be misleading to understand individual writers' evolving views as if they were products of a larger shift within a monolithic, teleological narrative of the Enlightenment, as the first scholars who tried to understand the conflicting images of Africa, Asia, the Americas did. There is a consensus now that the presumed inferiority of others, especially Black Africans due to their discursive presence in both race theory and commerce through the slave trade, played many roles during the eighteenth century. A full consideration of the discourse on race and slavery would take my argument far afield. My purpose here is to understand how, epistemologically, various accounts of human exceptionalism and the discourse on art are mutually co-constructed prior to the nineteenth century. The relationship of natural history (the precursor to biology, a late eighteenth-century coinage) to the discourse on human bondage, writes Curran in *The Anatomy of Blackness* (2011), is multi-faceted and ranges from denunciation to collaboration.[40] He emphasizes that this enormous range of evidence rarely operated in lockstep with science defined as an academic discipline. Curran has examined the complex relationship between natural history and economic justifications for chattel slavery. His findings are useful in the present context because he examines both pro- and anti-slavery arguments to identify discursive formations in a decolonial framework. His argument is briefly sketched below to provide context for evaluating Kant's views, but my account does not do justice to Curran's thorough and highly nuanced study. Differing evaluative criteria for Black Africans included morphology, occupations, institutions, tools, instruments, pastimes, religions, trade practices, sexual mores, and how to get the most work out of their labor force. Curran draws on Foucault and Said to examine the plethora of Africanist documents by identifying a period-crossing, discursive structuring of Africa that "functioned as a form of grammar, as a highly codified nexus of beliefs that gave shape to the overall representation of Africa, mapped onto a larger colonial project of representation and exploitation."[41]

By the 1760s, there was a growing consensus among progressive thinkers that African chattel slavery was a brutal institution at odds with their liberal principles on human rights. These debates were complicated by the rise of a new set of anatomical data regarding Black Africans based on natural history (natural history is the predecessor of the term "biology" coined in the late eighteenth century). Louis de Jaucourt's article on slavery ("Esclavage"), published in Diderot and d'Alembert's *Encyclopédie* in 1755 reflects the tension between natural law dealing with human rights and natural history dealing with race and climatology during these decades. Drawing substantially on Montesquieu's writings that a root cause of slavery could be attributed to a climate-induced suitability to "servitude," Jaucourt emphasized that, according to natural law, everyone must value and treat all human beings as naturally equal to oneself. A decade later, in his entry on "Traite des nègres," Jaucourt offered one of the first real denunciations of the colonial project in French thought by weighing the economic importance of the colonies against the suffering of African slaves.

Yet elsewhere in their geographical and ethnographic entries in the *Encyclopédie*, Jaucourt and Diderot each offered denigrating assessments of Black Africans as lacking in intelligence but not in emotions. They amplified the views of Vico, Hume, and many other writers on Indigenous peoples outside Europe. The earliest anti-slavery accounts after Montesquieu and Jaucourt rejected their physico-geographic determinism and focused the terms of debate, as did the sixteenth-century debates on natural slavery, on forms of government and contact with more advanced peoples, namely Europeans. Europeans could share their knowledge so that in future centuries, some Africans "as ferocious and as savage as the Iroquois" might make their own contributions to humankind."[42]

Within Diderot's *Encyclopédie*, to continue with that influential example, there was a pro-slavery faction using natural history to dehumanize Africans, and an anti-slavery contingent that emphasized a softer view. These differences remained fragmented into different disciplinary treatments depending on whether the context of discussion was universal human rights or a speculative history of humankind, a well-established distinction that is key to understanding Kant's arguments as I will take up in the next section.[43] The 1780 (third) edition of Abbé Guillaume Raynal's *Histoire philosphique et politique du commerce et des établissements des Européens dans les deux Indies/Philosophical and Political History of Commerce and the Establishment of Europeans in the Two Indies* (first ed. 1770), also edited by Diderot, is considered a major turning point in the anti-slavery debates because it argued against slavery by *rejecting* the scientific data for a humoral–anatomical understanding of Blackness, thus joining previously compartmentalized arguments into a single frame of reference. More than a simple recasting of environmentalism, Diderot's third edition of Raynal "provided one of the first entirely coherent anti-slavery arguments in French thought," in the process reasserting a belief in the shared unity of the human species.[44] The *Histoire* was banned by the Paris *parlement* yet it was one of the most popular eighteenth-century "forbidden" publications, published in thirteen editions in seventeen years.

The *Histoire* was a history of Europe's interactions with most of the non-European globe that had been largely subjugated by Europeans since 1492, an ambitious work in ten volumes to which Diderot contributed roughly 700 pages.[45] Diderot refuted the political implications of the colonialist view of Blackness to advance a new biopolitics of essential sameness that recalls the Christian universalism of the sixteenth century.[46] By the late 1780s, anti-slavery writings, including accounts by freed slaves like the Afro-British writer Olaudah Equiano, promoted a new politicized environmentalism that attributed the dehumanizing effects of human bondage to the influence of cruel plantation owners. At the same time, race theorists like the naturalist Georges Cuvier (1769–1832), instrumental in establishing the fields of comparative anatomy and paleontology, continued to emphasize supposed cognitive differences between "races" on zoological grounds. During the 1770s and 1780s, a number of other writers including Kant proposed their own racial classification schemes based on an increasingly physiological, measurable conception of human categories, a new view of anatomy that fixed degeneration in what Curran calls a "hodgepodge of recent anatomical discoveries [conflated] with classical humoral theory."[47] The new science of race replaced Buffon's "varieties" with the idea of species studied in terms of "measurable" variables that had long been associated with the effects of climatic degeneration at the collective level. Curran identifies three categories: differences between "complexion" and color; shape and size; and temperament, nature, and "national genius," the last a key category for examining the intersection of separate discourses on art and human exceptionalism that merged when the modern discipline of art history was framed at the end of the eighteenth century by Germanophone art historians.

By isolating the precise sources of racial differences, the real objective, Curran concludes, was managing such concepts "to establish normal and degenerative categories of humans" that shifted the locus of race from exterior to interior physiology.[48] Between 1775 and 1777 alone, Kant, Johann Christian Polykarp Erxleben, and Eberhardt August Wilhelm von Zimmermann all published schematic renderings of essential human categories largely based on the new view of anatomy and fixed degeneration that French thinkers adopted. One remarkable idea that appears in Kant's writings is the notion that skin color changes permanently in hot climates because excessive heat produces greater agitation in the blood and other humors, so that "the animalistic ether of the mucous bodies will become more saturated with phlogiston," first proposed as a new element in the mid-seventeenth century to explain chemical processes now collectively known as oxidation.[49]

The ability to reason was the key difference between savage and civilized, necessary to master both abstract systems of thought and the tools of illusionism, namely drawing, modeling, perspective, and narrative composition. The primitive imagination unencumbered by reason was widely held to be more powerful than that of an educated European who had learned to subdue the imagination. Primitive imagination could easily fall prey to the senses and passions of the physical body, as attested in the geo-ethnographic accounts based on climate theory studied by Curran, Gerbi, Michaud, and others. Many ethnographic texts dealing with climate theory corroborate the widespread presence of these ideas far beyond the context of art.[50] The relationship between art and moral character that runs through the entire European heritage of thinking about man's place in nature was spelled out in Kant's accounts of geography and anthropology, categories he derived from climate theory, and universalized in his writings on aesthetic judgment. The next section examines the relationship between Kant's anthropological writings and his account of aesthetic judgment as a universal human capability.

Immanuel Kant on Aesthetic Judgment, Genius, and Race

At the core of Immanuel Kant's aesthetic theory is the idea that we judge objects to be beautiful because apprehending their form stimulates the harmonious "free play" of our understanding and imagination, in which we take a distinctive, "disinterested" aesthetic pleasure.[51] The fundamental idea of Kant's critical philosophy is that, since human understanding is the source of the general laws of nature that structure all human experience, "human understanding gives itself the moral law that is the basis of belief in God, freedom, and immortality." All knowledge rests on the foundation of human autonomy, which is also the final end of nature.[52] I bring Kant's idea of human autonomy into the present discussion because he articulated an approach in which human inventiveness keyed to nature plays a central role that systematic attempts to rethink the nature/culture divide today cannot neglect to examine critically. Of course, there is no shortage of writings on the modern idea of "genius" that emerged in the late eighteenth century, most famously defined by Kant in his treatise on aesthetic judgement: "Genius is a talent for producing something for which no determinate rule can be given, not a predisposition consisting of a skill for something that can be learned by following some rule or other."[53]

Kant's *Critique of Judgment* (1790) is contemporaneous with his writings on racial science, which were also widely read and discussed, as scholarship appearing in the past three decades has established.[54] Kant's so-called "precritical" writings on anthropology used to be dismissed as superseded by his analytical philosophy because the latter addressed issues that pertain to all humans. There has been an exponential growth of critical interest in Kant's concept of race beginning with a groundbreaking article published in 1995 by Nigerian-born philosopher Emmanuel Chukwudi Eze (1963–2007) and following the publication of Kant's anthropological lectures in 1997.[55] There have been two main interpretive strategies in the new wave of attention: those, like Eze, who accuse Kant directly of racism argue that it influenced his views of philosophy and universalism, while others continue to treat his analytical philosophy as a separate domain. The question raised by Kant specialists like Pauline Kleingold is whether his racializing ideas are manifest in Kant's philosophical writings on judgment. There is general agreement that Kant's initial concept of race underwent a major change in the 1790s. One thing is for certain, until he retired in 1796, Kant continued to develop ideas on race, concurrent with his philosophical projects, in his writings and public lectures on physical geography and anthropology (the two main categories of climate theory), that he introduced into the university curriculum.

The relationship between Kant's analytical philosophy and his anthropological writings needs to be approached contextually with regard to his position on the challenge to find a natural *system* of nature that could account for both the unity and the diversity of the human species.[56] In his later writings, Kant shifted his discussion from the morals of races to the morals of nations, in keeping with his changing position on slavery and colonialism. In the late treatise, *Perpetual Peace, a Philosophical Sketch* (1795), Kant presents his views on cosmopolitanism in terms distinctly reminiscent of Vitoria, a connection proposed by Anthony Pagden (2000) that has been widely accepted. It is now recognized that Vitoria's sixteenth-century arguments for limited Indigenous sovereignty closely resemble Kant's aspirational views on cosmopolitanism that culminated in a proposal for "perpetual peace" (1795) based on a voluntary investment of all nations in commerce rather than war. Beyond Vitoria, Kant was aware of the "injustice" of European nations toward Indigenous Americans and the "Negro race."[57] His defense of victims of Europe aggression coincides with the appearance of a new anti-slavery discourse, the abolition of slavery by the French Jacobins in 1794, and it follows the appearance of a new literature critical of imperialism, colonialism, and global commerce discussed in the previous section.[58] Kant, Diderot, Montesquieu, and other philosophers who were highly critical of European expansionism envisioned the regulation of global commerce by a set of transnational practices and institutions written by philosophers.

Kant, like Diderot, was also concerned about the negative impact of European imperialism on European society. The historian of political science Sankar Muthu compares Kant's vision of a future cosmopolitan world in *Perpetual Peace* to Diderot's arguments on the limited hospitality due to "guests" who become thieves and murderers if they demand more than sanctuary and sustenance, unless they are allowed to settle and conform with the country's laws and customs.[59] Like Montesquieu, Diderot condemned the increasing importance of luxury goods that imperial activities and the slave trade furnished because it damages the ability of people to empathize with the plight of oppressed non-Europeans.[60] Writing in the 1770s when the French monarchy had lost most of its colonial possessions except for its Caribbean plantations, Diderot advised Europeans to decolonize and rescind their imperial holdings with the hope of forging peaceful and respectful ties of commerce and communication rather than being made to leave by a series of bloody revolts.

Focused on the anti-imperial discourse, Muthu compares Diderot's critique of cosmopolitan hospitality to Kant's understanding of human unity and incommensurable diversity as the basis for his condemnation of imperialism and his cosmopolitan conception of global governance: Kant granted "non-European peoples' freedom to organize their societies and to practice their collective lifestyles in the manner that they see fit."[61] Muthu argues that Kant applied the concept of distinctly human freedom consistently to all human peoples in his anti-imperialist political philosophy.[62] However, because he does not delve into cultural history, Muthu misses the context of Kant's arguments for universal human rights in pre-evolutionary biology which lie at the heart of his concerns to develop a universal account of human development. Fully rational humanity, as Vitoria argued and passed on to later writers on universal human rights based on natural law, is limited to "civilized" human beings (aka highly educated white European men in Kant's case) who have realized their intellectual potential and moral capacity.

Being human and being fully civilized developed as two separate streams in an intersecting discourse, which I have argued is one major reason that authors who advocated for the abolition of slavery still made hierarchical, Eurocentric racial distinctions about collective identity. Hierarchical distinctions of this kind appear throughout Kant's *Anthropology* lectures addressed to a general educated public. Kant assumed that a certain natural pre-disposition (*Anlage*) determines the limitations of the "lower races."[63] His *Anthropology from a Pragmatic Point of View*, based on public lectures spanning three decades from 1771 until his retirement, was published in 1798. Kant never repudiated his concept of racial hierarchy. Gerbi notes that in the 1798 version of his *Lectures on Mankind*, Kant omits the section referring to various races, a point that some contemporary Kant specialists argue is an indication that Kant revised his views by this time. However, in this text, Kant refers readers to the work of H. R. Girtannner, *Über des Kantische Prinzip fur die Naturgeschichte: Ein Versuch diese Wissenschaft philosophisch zu behandeln/On the Kantian Principle for Natural History: An Attempt to Treat this Science Philosophically* (1796), which was an epitome of Kant's racial theories compared with those of Girtanner's teacher Hans Blumenbach, with whom Kant corresponded and exchanged texts while they were both working out their ideas about race and heredity. According to Girtanner, only the climatic region [*Himmelstrich*] can influence heritability or "establish a race." [64]

The English edition of *Anthropology* eliminates these discussions, literally whitewashing Kant's text for modern audiences. During the 1790s and well beyond, Kant's essays on race were repeatedly cited and circulated in other collections, taken up and defended by natural scientists. His opinions were widely known and respected, as indicated in Darwin's positive reference through a

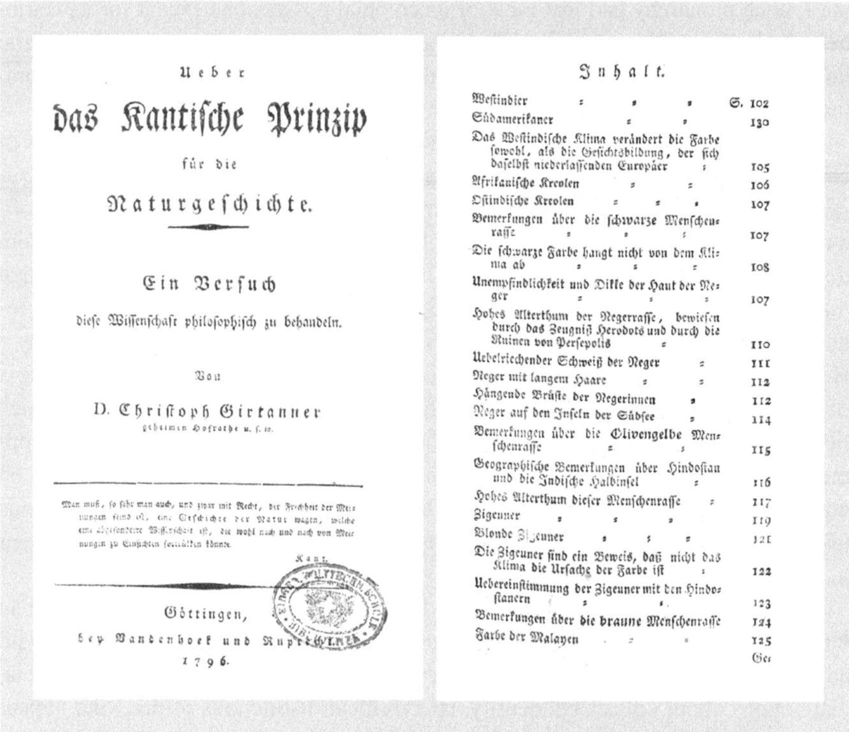

Ueber

das Kantische Prinzip

für die

Naturgeschichte.

Ein Versuch

diese Wissenschaft philosophisch zu behandeln.

Von

D. Christoph Girtanner

geheimen Hofrathe u. s. w.

Man muß, so sehr man auch, und zwar mit Recht, der Frechheit der Meinungen feind ist, eine Geschichte der Natur wagen, welche eine abgesonderte Wissenschaft ist, die wohl nach und nach von Meinungen zu Einsichten fortrücken könnte.

Kant.

Göttingen,

bey Vandenhoek und Ruprecht.

1796.

Inhalt.

Ge=

FIGURE 3.6 Christoph Girtanner, *Über das Kantisch Prinzip für Naturgeschichte* (Göttingen: bey Vandenhoek und Ruprecht, 1796), Table of Contents showing chapters on human races identified by color. Photo ETH-Bibliothek Zürich, Rar 8806. https://doi.org/10.3931/e-rara-42705/Public Domain Mark.

secondary source to Kant's racial theory.[65] His philosophical position on the systematic unity of nature and of knowledge in *Critiques of Reason* and *Practical Reason* developed out of problems in natural history articulated in his theory of race. Kant's discussions of race were divided between two categories derived from climate theory: "physical geography" defined as the study of "the natural condition of the earth and what is contained on it" including humans as part of nature in his external physical ("physiological") aspect; and "anthropology" defined as humans' psychological, moral, and internal ("pragmatic") aspect which "aims at what man makes, can, or should make of himself as a freely acting being."[66] In his study of the human, these two aspects and disciplines intersect, as they do in his own succinct summary of philosophy as seeking answers to two things that fill the mind with admiration and awe, "the starry heavens above and the moral law within."[67]

Beginning with his early publications, Kant argued that all people have the ability to reason using their intuition, but not all peoples have the ability to form abstract concepts, which is his definition of rational thought. His argument is grounded in a philosophical tradition stretching from ancient Greece to his immediate predecessors such as René Descartes (1596–1650), John Locke (1632–1704), and Isaac Newton (1643–1727), whose *Physics* formed part of Kant's teaching curriculum and reinforced his racial thinking. In the early text, *Observations on the Feeling of the Beautiful* (1764), and his early lectures, Kant outlined a classification of four human races conceived as biologically distinct classes, geographically distributed in the tradition of climate theory, with skin color as evidence of racial class: American Indians (red), Africans (black), and Hindus (yellow) were incapable of moral maturity because they lacked talent (*Talente*), which he defined as a gift of nature that lies in the moral nature of man himself.[68] Two decades later, *Menschenkunde, oder philosophisches Anthropologie* (*Human Studies or Philosophical Anthropology*; 1781–1782), is organized as a hierarchical system of classification in which moral qualities are paired with external appearances. Kant writes in the familiar terms of climate theorists about the lesser mental capacity and compromised moral character of extra-European peoples. For example, "Oriental peoples" gain insight according to analogy from the use of their imagination, but do they not have any ability to use pure reason to judge concepts. From this it follows that they lack a pure moral concept.[69] In *Foundations of the Metaphysics of Morals* (1785), Kant famously argued that it is a duty to develop one's talents rather than indulge in pleasure and enjoyment by devoting one's life "to idleness, indulgence, and propagation" like the "South Sea Islanders" who let their talents rust.[70] With some variation as to the cause of these apparent cognitive and behavioral deficiencies, the distinctions themselves remained constant in his later writings, with only the "white race" possessing all the motivating forces and talents in itself.[71] In his lectures and *Zur Verwendung teleologischer Prinzipien in der Philosophie/On the Use of Teleological Principles in Philosophy* (1788), Kant once again adds the moral dimension to his description of races in support of the argument that Indians and people of the "Negroid race" can only acquire slave culture, because they are unable to have enough incentive (i.e., the moral will to initiate action) for free labor.[72] Kant also stresses that Indians and "Negroes" do not have the ability to adapt themselves to the cold climate while he implicitly assumes that the "white race" has no such difficulties migrating to hot climates.[73] Although he abandons the use of the notion of incentive as the distinguishing moral factor, his main argument is only a minor revision of the earlier one in *Menschenkunde/Human Studies*.

Kant maintained the longstanding categorical distinctions between "savage" and "civilized" humans, extolling the latter, denigrating the former, but he also articulated a "universal" theory of aesthetic judgment that acknowledges the ability of all humans to make worlds by knowing nature. In 1790, in *The Critique of Judgment*, Kant defined aesthetic judgment as a universal human faculty analogous to but separate from rational judgment leading to abstract concepts.[74] He elevated the operations of the common sense, traditionally defined as a physical part of the brain where information received from the five special senses is combined and judged, to the faculty of aesthetic judgment as being equal to but distinct from rational thought because it does not go through language and does not involve "concepts."[75] Aesthetic judgment is a "universal" (but not necessarily egalitarian) solution to the conundrum of accounting for mental and moral differences among humans at both the collective and individual level. In the *Critique of Pure Reason* (1781; 2nd ed. 1787), Kant had first set himself the task of explaining how the supersensible "mediates" between nature in itself and nature as it appears to us.[76] Kant objected to what he understood as dogmatism by positing that the laws of nature are not derived from reason alone – nature's laws are also discovered through experience. Kant's objection (inspired by his critical reading of Hume) that sensibility is different in kind from thought is the basis for his account of the aesthetic as a separate faculty on the order of reason or the understanding. For example, he wrote, in geometry judgments describe the world we experience, yet geometry is derived from logic. The only way this can be possible is if we have a priori knowledge of spatial relations that we use in experiencing the world. *Anschauung* refers to this mediation between mind and world. Thus, *Anschauung*, translatable as "visuality," also entails "intuition," and a better translation of his term, Frances Ferguson suggests, might be "the intuitive experience of objects." [77] Kant's *Anschauung* may have unrealized potential as a transcultural concept, but contemporary critical discussions of visuality have misaligned his understanding of the term with the purely visual, rather than with interconnections between consciousness and matter.[78]

As far as Kant's text itself is concerned, he assumed that the artwork's underlying unity or integrity is perceived as being in harmony with nature. He stressed that the judging spectator, that is, the enlightened subject, uses his own faculty of reason to understand and change the world by working in society. The spectator's detachment from the natural world is a mark of his control of his inner nature, making aesthetic and teleological judgments (of beauty and of the sublime in nature, respectively) equally important markers of moral society.[79] The inability to form abstract concepts, by the same argument, is proof of an individual's incapacity for moral autonomy and true freedom: the intelligible by reference to which we demand universal assent in our judgment of taste is the "morally good."[80]

Kant advocated a certain normative interpretation of the world as "harmonious" and accessible to human understanding. It is well known that his remarks on the beautiful are indebted to his immediate predecessors including Baumgarten, G. W. Lessing, Moses Mendelssohn, and Edmund Burke who were also focusing on the general principles of the arts and of human understanding, but these issues have a much longer history worth recalling in the present context. For Kant, figured language interferes with the purpose of philosophy to make the universal become distinct through words. For Leonardo da Vinci and many of his contemporaries, the opposite is true: images *aid* propositional discourse. The painter uses his *ingegno* to "discourse" about the causes of effects he sees in nature and painting embodies harmony in an enduring, simultaneous mode. The viewer is educated in natural philosophy by looking at such images.[81] Seventeenth-century writers such as Giovanni Pietro Bellori (1613–1696), argued that viewers are educated in *moral* character by evaluating such images. However diverse the claims may be, they are all grounded in a neo-Aristotelian theory of cognition based on the model of vision according to which "concrete" sense experience passes to "abstract" rational thought by way of the imagination. In successive stages, the mind abstracts the "ratio," or essential form, embodied in sense impressions that the imagination receives as "images." Thomas Aquinas similarly defined beauty in Aristotelian terms as "a matter of right proportion, for the senses delight in rightly proportioned things as similar to themselves . . . since knowing proceeds by imaging, and images have to do with form, beauty properly involves the notion of form."[82] Aquinas's account of beauty perceived as a cognitive act is indebted to optical theory that analyzes the process of cognition on the model of vision and the action of light. Beauty subsists in the relation of a form to knowledge alone, whereas beautiful things please when they are seen (*visa placent*). For Aquinas, *visio* meant *apprehensio*, an intellectual, conceptual act of comprehension through sight.

Leonardo's ideas grew out of the same geometric theories of optics known to Scholastics like Aquinas (that Leonardo could access in Italian translation) when he described the universal appeal of painting as dependent on the beauty of mathematical "proportionality," which creates a "divine harmony."[83] He described painting as a universal language because its mathematical structure (pictorial perspective based on geometry) is universally accessible to viewers, needing "no interpreters of different languages as letters do."[84] Paleotti had the same idea as did Descartes and many other philosophers who modeled the mind as a mirror of the world. They distinguished the "clarity" or "distinctness" of ideas represented in the mind from "dark" impressions at the "lowest" levels of conscious attention. In the seventeenth century, there were explicit attempts to construct a universal language by classifying all phenomena into a single, cosmic hierarchy on the basis of Aristotelian categories. By the 1690s, universal language projects were relics of the past, but no one questioned the neo-Aristotelian model of cognition that was the basis for making and judging works of art.[85]

We have long since abandoned the model of the mind as a mirror that supported representationalism in both philosophy and the arts. And Kant differs from Leonardo and his contemporaries in insisting that the judgment of beauty itself is subjective and therefore not directly available to universal consent. Nonetheless, it is remarkable that Thomas Aquinas's argument that the perception of beauty as proportionality is a "disinterested" cognitive act exclusive to humans and a mark of rationality itself (*Summa theologiae* 1.91.3 ad 3) anticipates by six centuries Kant's account that aesthetic judgment is based on "disinterested" delight in the form of representation. According to Kant, fine or beautiful art (*schöne Kunst*) elicits pleasure considered as "modes of cognition." It has universal appeal that binds the members of society in a community, or *sensus communis*. The reciprocal communication of ideas is a source of substantial satisfaction desired for its own sake which bridges the difference between "the more cultured and ruder sections of the community."[86]

Like Aquinas and many others since, Kant closely associated two kinds of judgment, aesthetic and moral, to arrive at his understanding of humanity. He argued that every human being has the capacity to know the world through aesthetic judgment, but only those who also have "rational will," meaning the capacity to form abstract concepts (requiring rational thought, including detachment from nature through scientific understanding of it) are fully realized human beings capable of recognizing the beautiful and exercising moral judgment at the highest level. His argument was based on the assumption that art could be viewed as a subject of individual and independent study, as well as the product of collective identity. A Kantian understanding of aesthetic judgment and moral capacity defines rationality on European terms. As richly conceived as Kant's arguments are in articulating the tension between a universalizing structure of value and the acknowledgment that one apprehends the world individually through one's senses, his framework imposes a European ontology on the world.

What accounts for these lasting continuities is the Thomistic neo-Aristotelian notion of judging the beauty of a "work of art" that became a model for individual judgment in general. The "work of art" remained an undifferentiated analogy in the literature on political theory, a paradigm for productive legislation (as the product of deliberation) – to use the language of Thomas Hobbes' 1651 *Leviathan*. Hobbes replaced the Thomistic notion that productive judgment universally rests on objective proportion (because that is how the cosmos is structured) with the far more relativistic notion of form as artifice, in other words art made by humans that is subject to human judgment. Seventeenth-century academic art theory and criticism held that contemplating depictions of right action develops the beholder's moral character. Excellence in art, as in moral conduct, was an individual exercise of judgment based on experience that resulted neither in excess nor in deficiency, but in temperance and in eloquence. The historical entanglement of the discourse on art and political theory was lost from view in the course of the nineteenth century, when art was increasingly defined and treated as the external manifestation of collective mentality.[87]

Kant's arguments on the beautiful and sublime pertain to nature, which is universally the object of human perception and cognition and therefore supports his universal theory of human understanding of the world without having to justify differences between humans at the collective level as his anthropological writings do. There, he deduced the inadequacy of other "races" from their lacks, such as the absence of organized societies, as did Vitoria and others who debated the humanness of Indigenous peoples in the sixteenth century. Kant's philosophical arguments drew connections between moral character and outward appearance, just as he did in his anthropological writings. He claimed that man is the only one capable of an ideal of beauty, and this capability connects reason with the morally good and with great imaginative power, which is "*visible, in bodily expression* (*in körplicher Äusserung*) (*as an effect of what is inward*)."[88] While this general statement is all that remains manifest of his theories on race in his philosophical aesthetics, Kant's writings on physical geography and anthropology show that, even though his ideas about race evolved over time, they still entered into his analytical philosophy as well as his anthropological writings and lectures that he addressed to a broad, educated public until a few years before his death in 1804.

Worldmaking can only deliver its promise when it is capacious enough to encompass all human and more-than-human worlds. Since the disciplinary crises of the humanities in the 1980s and '90s, the very idea of a single comprehensive principle has been thrown into doubt if not completely rejected. In the words of philosopher Jean-Francois Lyotard, we do not necessarily form stable communities, and those that we do form are not necessarily communicable.[89] Philosopher Roland Barthes is less circumspect about hegemonic systems of representation: we need "to *fissure* the very representation of meaning."[90] These arguments anticipate many decolonial writers today who question the ability of any set of values to serve as universal criteria for art or aesthetic judgment or anything else for that matter.

Why should art history bear so much responsibility in conceiving a planetary approach to culture? It is certainly *not* because Kant or anyone else valued art as beautiful or capable of eliciting aesthetic contemplation. It is because certain culturally specific criteria have excluded, devalued, or reframed other artistic practices. Kant's critical philosophy has also been questioned from feminist, sociological, anthropological, deconstructionist, decolonial, transcultural, extra-European, pre-modern, and other positions. Yet many contemporary writers who may not identity with his hegemonic legacy still consider art in terms of aesthetic contemplation assumed to be a universal feature of all art. As nuanced and sophisticated as the Kantian philosophical tradition is, it bends contemporary art to its Eurocentric will if it imposes these norms and/or excludes or devalues other forms of artistic practice.

Emancipatory Transcultural Approaches: Rethinking Kristeller through Hegel

Gerbi locates the "vortex" of writings on the inferiority of the Americas in the philosopher G. W. H. Hegel's "slanderous" descriptions of the Americas as an immature or impotent continent, or otherwise "inferior" to the Old World.[91] Hegel (1770–1831) relied on racialized climate theory to characterize the Americas as too natural, unpolitical, and unspiritual to form an organic state. He also wrote about the slave trade with sympathy for "Old World primitives" whose dark color is a result of climate, heat, and light, who established Haiti as a "state built on Christian principles." Gerbi emphasizes that Hegel's dismissal of the Americas is not an inevitable outgrowth of his system, but the facts on which he based his argument are wrong, and the logical form in which he argued these "facts" are improper, an outgrowth of the same effort as Buffon's attempt to synthesize the "living nature of two worlds into a single principle."

Hegel's historical importance is more complex when viewed in a different transcultural framework supported by historical research on the formation and reception of his ideas, as Susan Buck-Morss has argued Hegel's positive reception in Haiti. Hegel read Abbé Raynal's *History of the Indies* and was informed about Caribbean slavery. Hegel also read the economic theory of Adam Smith, who saw the colonial economy as distorting what he viewed as the natural state of national polity.[92] From Smith, Hegel developed an argument about "borderless" commerce by which a people are "dissolved" and returned to a "state of nature." Buck-Morss glosses Hegel's argument to show that he was not appealing to Aristotle's concept of polity where every class is in its proper place in a hierarchy and slavery is a necessary social institution but theorizing the dehumanization of the worker. Deriving his conceptual vocabulary from everyday experience, "the central Hegelian term 'objectification' (*Entäusserung*) has mundane human labor as its referent."[93] In her reading, Hegel was the first philosopher to describe how consumerism creates social inequality in the deterritorialized world market of the European colonial system where a merchant class of long-distance traders was primarily interested in securing the right to sell. Unlike the contractual relationships that ensure the legal right of possession developed in the political philosophy of Hugo Grotius (1583–1645), Samuel von Pufendorf (1632–1694), and others who contributed to the development of international law indebted to Vitoria's arguments about cosmopolitanism and commerce, the "insatiable desire" of consumers is combined with "inexhaustible production" with no discernible limits.

Hegel, in Buck-Morss's reading, re-interpreted society in the context of dehumanized labor. The apparent dominance of the master reverses itself with awareness that the master is dependent on the slave for the "overabundance" that constitutes his wealth. Hegel's slave was the dehumanized worker. The revolutionary struggle of enslaved Africans in Haiti to overthrow their own servitude to establish a constitutional state adapted Hegel's theoretical argument to their own circumstances and Hegel's connections with Freemasonry, a secret brotherhood with a vast, international communicating network, provided the historical opportunity for access to his text. Buck-Morss' transcultural study of Hegel's reception from both sides of the main cultural divide is a groundbreaking contribution to the historical context of Hegel's philosophy and its positive reception in Haiti not least because of the way she ties philosophy to capitalism. However, as was the case with other anti-imperialists, Hegel understood Africa as immature, the "land of children," "barbarity and wildness," and the more he studied his available European sources, the more he regarded African slavery as "a necessary moment in the education [*Bildung*] of every man."[94]

In writing about the modern system of the fine arts, Kristeller did not consider climate theory, cultural geographies, global trade, the circulation of objects and ideas, or anything remotely resembling the artifacts found in early modern European collections such as *Wunderkammers* and curiosity cabinets that were later recontextualized in ethnological museums. Kristeller also did not mention that while writers were popularizing systematic classifications of the *beaux arts* in the eighteenth century, concurrently, at the French Académie des Inscriptions et Belles-Lettres, Charles de Brosses (one of Hegel's documented sources) argued that "fetishism," defined as the direct worship of earthly material objects "capable of satisfying mundane desires" was the unifying characteristic of primordial religion.[95] For his study of African "fetishism," De Brosses drew on existing discussions of "idols" as false images, such as Francis Bacon's *New Organon* (1620), which in turn drew on sixteenth-century Protestant Reformation writings suspicious of any tendency to venerate images within the Catholic traditions of the time (and Bacon is the source of Marx's concrete metaphor of the fetish).[96] De Brosses' study of non-Christian material culture as religious superstition complemented other Enlightenment contributions to an emerging field of interest in the origins of society, such as David Hume's *Natural History of Religion* (1757) and Giambattista Vico's *La Scienza nuova* (1725). Vico distinguished rational from irrational understandings of the world in the following terms: "for man, by understanding, articulates his own mind and comprehends those things, but by not understanding, he makes those things from himself and, by transforming himself, becomes those things."[97]

Both "aesthetics" and "fetishism" are eighteenth-century neologisms devised to understand the cultures being dominated through European colonization. They developed to theorize certain subjective processes in perceiving "sensuous materiality," as argued in an important series of articles by William Pietz published in the 1980s.[98] In the historical record these two discussions were dependent on one another and yet its authors showed no awareness of their co-constructed relationship, as Pietz recognized. The questionable reasons for the distinction between "art" and "artifact" were subsequently lost from view in the historical record, later tucked into the seams between art history and cultural anthropology. The criteria that define the categories are, in the case of "fetishes," denigrating misrepresentations of their cultures of origin.

By the mid-seventeenth century, ancient Roman wall painting, a major source of *grottesche* invention in the sixteenth century that Paleotti and other art theorists aligned with Roman Church reform condemned, had been rehabilitated through archaeology.[99] Archeological interest in Rome's subterranean catacombs, as evidence of valid early Christian practices not cited in Scripture, was supported by ecclesiastical patronage. Pope Urban VIII's nephew and chief minister of culture, Cardinal Francesco Barberini, sponsored a sumptuous publication documenting early Christian catacombs, Antonio Bosio's *Roma sotteranea* (1632; Latin ed. 1651). Meanwhile, the application of European terms and values to extra-European artistry continued to proliferate in texts like the ones Hegel read to form his demeaning opinions about Africans. Attributing artistic license and freedom of the imagination on European terms to objects made for other purposes in their societies of origin or else manufactured for export is a quintessentially Eurocentric practice – even when they elicit curiosity and admiration, the exoticizing gaze transforms incomprehension into the viewer's fascination and projection. Collectively they disclose much about European predilections.[100] This is especially the case when inventiveness in the design of a painted or sculpted figure, for example, is denied the same status as artistry that conforms to European standards of rationality and legibility. Current research focuses on inventories, letters, travel accounts, descriptions, documents, and a wide range of material evidence that is rewriting the history of cultural exchange and interaction. The next section briefly introduces some ways that technological innovation and past collecting practices are being reframed today in terms of the distributed and entangled agencies of the past.

Transcultural Approaches to Artisanal Knowledge Practices

At the same time that optical naturalism was receiving institutional support in and beyond Europe, extra-European luxury goods were sought by European collectors. To name just one category of highly valued objects, nearly all the Mexican painted manuscripts known today are located in European collections, where they were valued as trophies, gifts, and souvenirs. These colonial productions derived from pre-contact pictorial screenfold books, specifically the divinatory almanac (*tonalamatl* in Nahuatl), a format known in a few copies. None of the indisputably pre-Columbian screenfold manuscripts that survive is Aztec (Nahua). Scholars now stress that the body of colonial Mexican pictorial manuscripts document an active, two-way process of transculturation, not simply acculturation. Some of these composite compilations attest to the operations by which "idolatrous" content unacceptable to Christian compilers became isolated from their "scientific" content admired by the missionaries who directed Indigenous artists and by European collectors [Figures 3.7–3.9].

In the mediated process of passing from a native artifact to its European imitation to a thoroughly Europeanized format, otherness was domesticated, the "grotesque idol" transformed into intriguing artistic inventions. An example illustrated in Figure 3.9 comes from the Codex Ixtlilxochitl assembled by the historian, Fernando de Alva Cortéz Ixtlilxóchitl (c. 1587–1650), a direct descendant of the rulers of Texcoco who was commissioned by the Viceroy of New Spain to record Aztec culture. This section of the manuscript, completed in 1582, was intended to accompany a commissioned census made in response to the *Relaciones geográficas* questionnaire distributed to the colonies by King Philip II of Spain (of the kind studied by Sara Miglietti).[101] The highly revered and greatly feared Tlaloc, the chief supernatural being of the Mexica (Aztec) associated with rain, earthly fertility, and water, the giver of life and sustenance, is recast as if he were a benign figure in a costume book. In the process of reframing the Indigenous material, "idolatry" was initially singled out and then gradually objectified through successive generations of copying until it was eliminated entirely from the reader's consciousness.

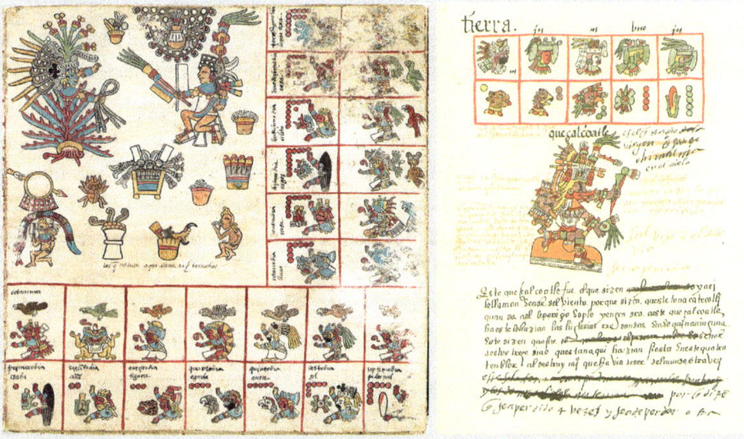

FIGURE 3.7 AND 3.8 (Left) Codex Borbonicus, Mayahuel as patroness of the trecena 1 Malinalli or 1 Grass. Paris, Bibliothèque de l'Assemblée Nationale. Photo Museum; (Right) Codex Telleriano-Ramensis, Quetzelcoatl, 8v, 16th Century. Paris, Bibliothèque nationale de France, MS Mex. 385. Wiki.

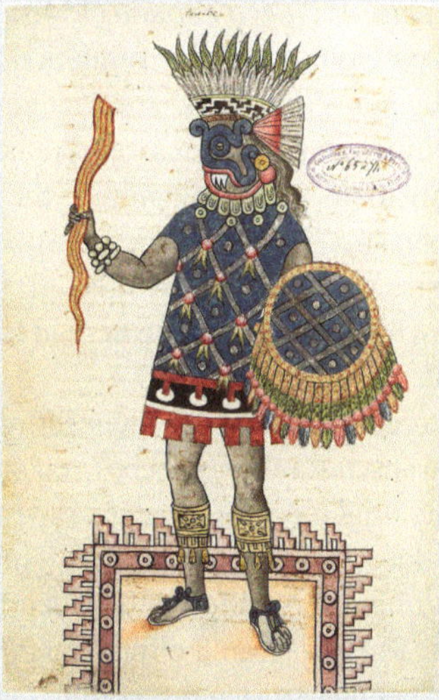

FIGURE 3.9 Fernando da Alva Ixtlilxochitl (1578?–1650), Tlaloc, Codex Ixtlilxochitl, folio 110, 1580-1584. Paris, Bibliothèque nationale de France, MS Mex. 65–71. Photo Library of Congress, https://www.loc.gov/item/2021668123/

Indigenous knowledge became increasingly attenuated and divorced from its cultural context through a process of successive copying and editing, but close analysis shows many points of continuity. The Codex Borbonicus is an unfinished screenfold manuscript made of native bark paper (amatl) consisting of accordion-folded pages containing only pictographs, to which some Spanish commentary has been added. The first section is an intricate divinatory calendar (*tonalamatl*), with each page representing one of twenty thirteen-day periods. Page 13, representing one 13-day period of the 260-day year of the *tonalamatl*, shows the ruling deity Tlazolteotl, wearing a flayed skin, giving birth to Cinteotl. The ruling supernatural identified by glyphs is in the center, the rest of the page consists of day signs and other glyphs and supernaturals used to create horoscopes and divine the future. The Codex Telleriano-Ramensis contains three sections in a European-style book that abandons the glyph system but includes a Nahuatl-style *tonalamatl* painted by an Indigenous scribe, Nahuatl words using a Roman-style alphabet, numerical dates that reposition Aztec dynastic history within a Christian concept of linear time, and an explanatory Spanish text at the bottom of each page. The Codex Ixtlilxochitl, which combines three separate documents, dispenses with the conventional Nahuatl pictorial framework and includes six illustrations intended to accompany Juan Bautista Pomar's 1577 *Relación de Texcoco*, one of which depicts Tláloc, highly regarded as a giver of life and sustenance, in a European style.

Central to the copyist's ambivalent attitude in the case of Mexican colonial pictorial manuscripts is the multivalent, shifting use of the category "grotesque," which has traditionally served to label cultural differences. This is an ethnocentric approach to the pursuit of knowledge because it imposes the ideology of the European observer and occludes other cultural meanings. Missionaries like the Franciscan friar Bernardino da Sahagún (1499–1590) who compiled a monumental ethno-geography, *Historia general de las Cosas de Nueva España* (1545–1590) for King Philip II of Spain, not only preserved precious detailed information about pre-contact worlds contributed by colonial Indigenous artists and knowledge holders, they also document European understanding of Indigenous representations of supernatural beings as fascinating exemplifications of the ridiculous, the monstrous, the abhorrent, the fabulous, and the fantastic – many of these terms were lifted from Horace's *Art of Poetry* and Vitruvius's treatise on architecture where they described hybrid fantastical creatures known in Italy and elsewhere in Europe as *grottesche*, as discussed in the second Fugue.

When the signifying systems of previously unrelated societies intersect in individual works of art, those objects necessitate transcultural approaches sensitive to the process of transformation preserved in the material record. Indigenous artists and knowledge holders in colonial settings also valued these artistic skills highly, but their knowledge and artistic productions had signified very differently in their Indigenous contexts prior to contact with Europeans. Today, research efforts are directed to recovering the agency and worldview of Indigenous artists preserved in colonial images, materials, techniques, and, in some fortunate cases, the multi-lingual texts that accompany them [Figure 3.10].

Latin Americanist Serge Gruzinski argues that the category of "the grotesque" enables Indigenous pictorial traditions to coexist comfortably with ancient European mythological signs, a line of argument that has been pursued by Alessandra Russo as "untranslatable images."[102] It is important to bear in mind that this "coexistence" once positioned Indigenous truth values in a subaltern relationship to European knowledge. The same hierarchical, two-way process of cultural interaction can be discerned in all colonial Mexican painted manuscripts. They are all

As the imagery in the Florentine Codex testifies, the *tlahcuilohqueh* emulated aspects of Western illusionism but they remained fundamentally engaged with their material resources. The *tlahcuilohqueh* visualize themselves in Book 11 on "Earthly Things," in the section dedicated to the procurement and making of color pigments. Ironically, scores of images on color were painted in black and white during or after the 1576 epidemic when pigments were not readily available. Instead, the ever-inventive *tlahcuilohqueh* inserted glyph-like symbols to suggest the original colors.[103]

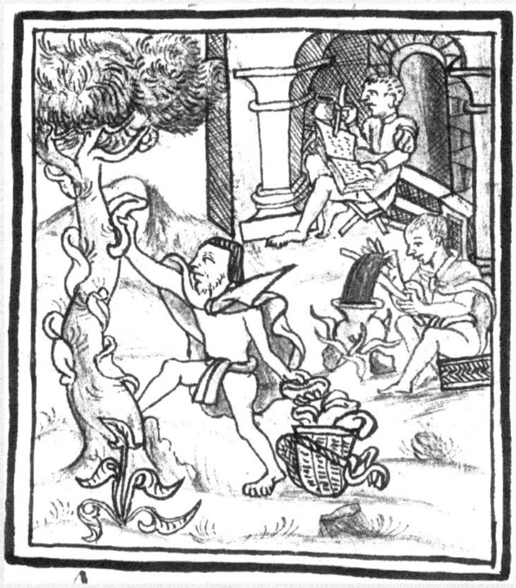

FIGURE 3.10 Bernardino da Sahagún and Nahua collaborators. Nahua Artist E, Assistants procure and prepare Nacazcolotl as a black dye with master *tlahcuiloh* working in the background. Florentine Codex, Bk. 11, fol. 218v, 1577. Florence, Biblioteca Medicea Laurenziana, Ms. Med. Palat. 220, I.11, f. 218v. Under the permission of the MiC. Any further reproduction by any means is prohibited.

bi-cultural documents, compilations of ideas, statements, and representations functioning in an enunciative network driven by the political importance of defining Amerindians.[104] The Mexica regarded the figures of their ritual calendar as sacred, but the Spanish inscribed them as false. While the format and style of the Codex may be European, the order, structure, and message of the ritual calendar are not.

Russo's most recent book, *A New Antiquity: Art and Humanity as Universal, 1400–1600* (2024), still makes no mention of the Catholic Reformation or the historical consequences of extensive sixteenth-century debates regarding artistic license that had both immediate and long-term historical effects.[105] To understand the emancipatory potential of the entangled colonial and colonialist discourse as a dynamic process of transculturation continuing over many generations, this history is crucial. Early modern European ideas of "art" as a form of knowledge were contemporary with the emergence of early modern "science" in European centers of learning. Yet, to avoid projecting anachronistic categories on the evidence, it is important to note that neither art nor science assumed its modern definition overnight. "Art" and "techno-science" were fluid categories that overlapped in ways that our inherited disciplinary formations do not recognize. Historian of science Pamela Smith introduced the term "artisanal epistemology" to focus on the workshops of artisans and other experimental forms of knowledge making that contributed to the Scientific Revolution.[106] The study of nature took many dynamic new forms that have long been linked with the expertise of artisans. Smith suggests that one possible definition of science and technology around the turn of the seventeenth century is simply the interaction of humans with their natural environment and their aspirations to understand it.

Globalization, industrialization, capitalism – the driving forces of colonialization and modernity that Mignolo was among the first to characterize as two aspects of one process – encouraged innovation put to practical purposes. By the mid-eighteenth century, knowledge of mechanics and Newtonian science ushered in what Margaret Jacob calls "the first knowledge economy" by supplying the theoretical underpinnings to technological innovation in mining, manufacturing, and the application of steam power more generally.[107]

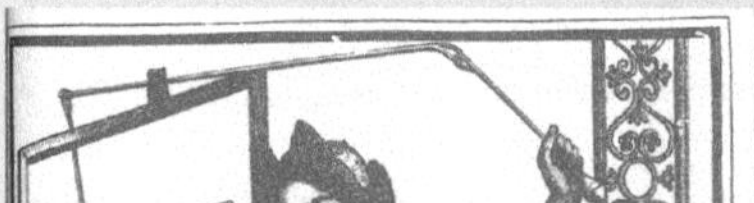

FIGURE 3.11 Nicolas de Larmessin II (c. 1638–1694), *Habit de serrurier (Habitude of a Locksmith)*, from *Costumes grotesques* (Paris, 1695). Paris, Bibliothèque nationale de France. ["Habit" is a double entendre that can refer to dress or behavior.] VTR/Alamy Stock Photo.

In seventeenth- and eighteenth-century Paris, artisans lived at the fringe of state-supported institutions that were notoriously disdainful of their ability to articulate practice in theoretical terms. The new term *artiste* referred to artisans who, in addition to manual skills, boasted of *esprit* (spirit) due to their ingenious ability to combine practical skill, creative design, and inventive intelligence. Diderot codified the philosophe's point of view in his *Encyclopédie* (1751) by distinguishing between artisans who practice the mechanical arts that need the least intelligence and a wide range of professionals who are well versed in the practical part of a science that is also theoretical. How did *artistes* regard themselves? Larmessin II, from a multi-generational family of engravers and print sellers, ingeniously visualized the *esprit* of the *artiste* embodied in a series of seventy satirical *grotesques*, mannequins dressed in and as the tools and works of their trade.

After Paola Bertucci, *Artisanal Enlightenment: Science and the Mechanical Arts in Old Regime France* (New Haven–London: Yale University Press, 2017)

"Art" and "techno-science" overlapped in ways that our modern disciplinary formations do not recognize, while "European imperialism" involves studying European behavior outside Europe in the same breath (and breadth) as within. Jorge Cañizares-Esguerra argues that the Enlightenment concept of cosmopolitanism emerged to denounce Indigenous worlds. Seen transculturally, Kantian cosmopolitanism is "no more than a situated form of local knowledge."[108]

An entirely different history emerges from studying artisanal knowledge longitudinally in a transcultural framework that attends to "the multiplicity of sources, agencies, directions of influence, and modalities of intercultural connectedness," to cite again Ralph Bauer and Marcy Norton in their excellent introduction to a collection of "entangled" case studies of artisanal knowledge.[109] They advocate attending to the mutual effects of contact between colonizing and Indigenous societies by focusing on materiality and technology: most cultures are inherently heterogeneous so "mixing and interaction" are the norm but approaches focused on outcomes tend to miss the "confrontations, shifts, and revision" in the dynamic process of learning and pushback. Aligned with the critical framework of the present study, Bauer, Norton, and their contributors emphasize the necessity of looking beyond the nature/culture binary that has structured Western metaphysics by emphasizing the continuous and unresolved aspects of intercultural exchanges in a historiographic framework.

The perennial challenge is in moving from material processes to signifying practices. Artisanal epistemology offers an analytical concept that emphasizes process and intentionally avoids the existing taxonomies and pattern of binaries in art historical theories and methodologies. The first Europeans assigned Indigenous people to living in a "state of nature." Some of the examples of Indigenous technologies that Norton offers for rewriting history from Indigenous points of view derive from Fernandez de Oviedo's *Historia general de las Indias* (1537, 1547). Among the forms of Indigenous knowledge preserved in Oviedo's text are the red body paste made of *bija*, tobacco, pineapples and other botanicals extracts used for food, healing, and ornamentation; the sowing of maize, preparation of cassava, fishing, hunting and taming instruments; hammocks, henequen fiber, thatching methods, canoes, musical instruments, and weaponry.[110]

One of the principal aims of current research is to develop non-totalizing transcultural approaches to historically documented relationships that rethink how specific technologies of making are interrelated in economic, philosophical, social, and political terms. How do materials and technologies signify, what do they signify, and to whom, when, where, under what conditions do they carry meaning? With these questions and conceptual tools as starting points, an ecological approach to the history of planetary culture is possible without setting humans in a sovereign position apart from the rest of the natural world. Conceiving artistic production in terms of artisanal epistemologies also makes it possible to de-familiarize European conceptions of art and technology, to think its history anew in a global context. The critical question has always been *how* to define the relationship between culture and nature or, in the words of Ingold, "sociobecomings" that bring the social and the biological together into a single frame to rethink the Western metaphysical ontology of scientific inquiry altogether.

Ingold argues that we must move beyond the inherited Western dichotomy between nature and culture to think about the ways that the social and the biological are distributed and entangled.[111] He defines the core of creativity as improvisation – the problem-solving skills needed to fashion matter that are involved in everyday life. (In fact, improvisation and problem-solving are not limited to humans.) The inclusive concept "artisanal epistemology" recognizes art as a more holistic enterprise through which all societies pass on their cultural knowledge, their technology, their rites, and practices. It is not intended to contrast with "artistic" or "scientific knowledge," but to rethink the concept of knowledge in transcultural terms. Various types of local knowledge – including the expertise of farmers, miners, and metalworkers – cut across the modern boundaries that sort the history of art, science, and technology into separate domains. Subaltern scribal literacy wielded by slaves, women, and Indigenous peoples has been ignored too long because they "escape the historiographical categories used to capture the rise of early Atlantic modernity," to cite again Cañizares-Esguerra, who has recovered extensive Indigenous technologies operating in the Iberian and British empires.[112] Studying the knowledge utilized in making things has broad implications for thinking transculturally about knowledge and technology as open systems for understanding the natural world. Such approaches de-center Western "rationality" and "scientificity" as the benchmark criteria by which other cultures' knowledges should be evaluated.[113] They also de-center the commonplace notion of the autonomous artistic "genius" deeply rooted in European concepts of human exceptionalism and relativize the European idea of art as the uniquely human command of material and control of nature.[114]

The next Fugue turns to the ways that ingenuity was construed in relation to the environment in nineteenth-century debates on humanness, once again discovering emancipatory potential in the historical discourse on human exceptionalism. Many contemporary artists have also been working along these lines – rethinking the sole agency of the individual artist built on the Western metaphysical model in favor of a materialist, relational account of distributed agency spread across the entire field of cultural production. In Fugue 5, I will discuss some collective artistic practices in relation to Indigenous knowledge of the environment, climate change, and unregulated, extractive capitalism today.

Notes

1 Sara Miglietti, "Between Nature and Culture: The integrated Ecology of Renaissance Climate Theories," in *Early Modern Ecologies: Beyond English Ecocriticism*, ed. Pauline Goul and Phillip John Usher (Amsterdam: Amsterdam University Press, 2020), 137–160; Miglietti, "Introduction: The Past and Present of Climate Theory," *MLN* 132/4 (September 2017): 902–911.

2 Antonello Gerbi, *The Dispute of the New World: The History of a Polemic, 1750–1900* (1955 Italian ed.), trans. Jeremy Moyle (Pittsburgh: University of Pittsburgh Press, 1973).

3 Michaud, *Barbarian Invasions*, 57–61.

4 Gerbi, *The Dispute of the New World*, 38. Jean Bodin, *Methodus ad facilem historiarum cognitionem*. ed. and trans. Sara Miglietti (Pisa: Edizioni della Normale, 2013).

5 Bodin, *La Méthode de l'histoire* (1566), trans. and intro. Pierre Mesnard (Paris: Société d'édition "Les Belles Lettres," 1941), 198, as cited by Gerbi, *Dispute*, 38.

6 Nancy Siraisi, *Avicenna in Renaissance Italy: The Canon and Medical Teaching in Italian Universities after 1500* (Princeton: Princeton University Press,1987).
7 Mary B. Campbell, *The Witness and the Other World: Exotic European Travel Writing, 400–1600* (Ithaca: Cornell University Press, 1988).
8 Anthony Grafton, Introduction in Anthony Grafton with April Shelford and Nancy Siraisi, *New Worlds, Ancient Texts: The Power of Tradition and the Shock of Discovery* (Cambridge: Belknap Press of Harvard University Press, 1995), 5.
9 Stephanie Leitch, *Mapping Ethnography in Early Modern Germany: New Worlds in Print Culture* (New York; Palgrave Macmillan, 2010).
10 Grafton, "Epilogue," *New Worlds, Ancient Texts*, 254.
11 Paul O. Kristeller, "The Modern System of the Arts: A Study in the History of Aesthetics," *Journal of the History of Ideas* 12 (1951), 496–527 (Part 1); 13 (1952), 17–46 (Part 2).
12 Alexander Gottlieb Baumgarten, *Aesthetica*, 2 vols. (Frankfurt an der Oder: Ioannis Christiani Kleyb, 1750–1758).
13 Kristeller, "The Modern System," *Part 2*, 19.
14 Abbé Jean-Baptiste Du Bos, *Réflexions critiques sur la poésie et sur la peinture*, 4th ed., 3 vols (Paris, 1740), II, 558ff., as cited by Kristeller, "The Modern System," *Part 2*, 19.
15 Michaud, *Barbarian Invasions*, 20. Du Bos, *Réflexions critiques* (1719; 1755 ed.), intro. Dominique Désirat (Paris: École nationale supérieure des beaux-arts, 1993), Part 2, Section 15.
16 Thomas Kirchner, "Migration, National Art, and the Climate," unpublished manuscript (2023), cited with the author's permission.
17 Du Bos, *Réflexions critiques,* Part 2, Section 13, 223.
18 Du Bos, *Réflexions critiques*, Part 2, Section 1, 173.
19 Alessandra Russo, *The Untranslatable Image: A Mestizo History of the Arts in New Spain, 1500–1600,* trans. Susan Emanuel (Austin: University of Texas Press, 2014).
20 Claire Farago, "The Semiotics of Images and Political Realities," in Claire Farago and Donna Pierce, *Transforming images: New Mexican Santos In-between Worlds* (Pennsylvania Park: Pennsylvania State University Press, 2006), 26–43.
21 Du Bos, *Réflexions critiques*, Part 2, Section 17, 265.
22 Michaud, *Barbarian Invasions*, 19 and 60.
23 Kristeller, "Modern System of the Arts," Part 2, 20.
24 Michaud, *Barbarian Invasions*, 3.
25 Michaud, *Barbarian Invasions*, 30.
26 Michaud, *Barbarian Invasions*, 32.
27 Gerbi, "Preface," *The Dispute of the New World*, xvii.
28 Comte de Buffon, *On the Degenerations of Animals* (1766), in *Histoire Naturelle, Générale et Particulière*, 36 vols. (Paris: Imprimerie Royale, 1749–1788), vol. 14; see also vol. 9.
29 Gerbi, *The Dispute of the New World*, 8.
30 Hume wrote that "I am apt to suspect the negroes and in general all the other species of men (for there are four or five different kinds) to be naturally inferior to the white. There was never a civilized nation of any other complexion than white . . . not even individuals . . . such a uniform and constant difference could not happen in so many countries and ages if nature had not made an original distinction between these breeds of men." Cited by Ibram X. Kendi, *Stamped from the Beginning: The Definitive History of Racist Ideas in America* (New York: Bold Type Books, 2016), 95.
31 Andrew S. Curran, *The Anatomy of Blackness: Science & Slavery in the Age of Enlightenment* (Baltimore: The Johns Hopkins University Press, 2011), 219–224.
32 Ralph Bauer and Marcy Norton, "Introduction: Entangled Trajectories: Indigenous and European Histories," *Colonial Latin American Review* 26/1 (March 2017): 1–17.
33 National Constitution Center, accessed on 17 October 2023, at https://constitutioncenter.org/the-constitution/historic-document-library/detail/montesquieuthe-spirit-of-the-laws-1748#:~:text=In%20particular%2C%20Montesquieu%27s%20discussion%20of,design%20of%20the%20U.S.%20Constitution.

34 Trevor Shelley, *Globalization and Liberalism: Montesquieu, Tocqueville, and Manent* (Notre Dame: University of Notre Dame Press, 2020), 63.
35 Anthony Pagden, Introduction, *The Idea of Europe: From Antiquity to the European Union*, ed. Anthony Pagden (Washington, DC: Woodrow Wilson Center Press; Cambridge–New York: Cambridge University Press, 2002), 5.
36 Gerbi, *The Dispute of the New World*, 52.
37 Curran, *The Anatomy of Blackness*, 20.
38 Pedtro Leturia, "Maior y Vitoria ante la conquista de America," *Estudio Eclesiasticos*, 11/1 (Jan 1932), 44–82.
39 Voltaire, *Essai sur les moeurs*, 1756, chapter 148, cited by Gerbi, *The Dispute of the New World*, 71.
40 The earliest use of the term "biology" in its modern sense, distinct from physics, appears in the work of the Göttingen naturalist Gottfried Reinhold Treviranus (1776–1837), but it was not widely used until August Comte (1798–1857) popularized it. Jon M. Mikkelsen, trans. and ed., *Kant and the Concept of Race* (Albany: State University of New York Press, 2013), 3–4, 302, n. 9.
41 Curran, *Anatomy of Blackness*, 27.
42 Curran, *Anatomy of Blackness*, 187–190, citing Jean-François de Saint-Lambert, *Zimeo*, 1760.
43 Curran, *Anatomy of Blackness*, 184, notes that in his sole outburst against the slave trade, Diderot writes that "Africans have little intelligence but they are far from lacking in emotions."
44 Curran, *Anatomy of Blackness*, 25, 194–199.
45 Robert Darnton, *The Forbidden Best-Sellers of Pre-revolutionary France* (New York: Norton, 1996), 22–82.
46 Ann Thomson, "Didertot, e máterialisme et la division de l'espèce humaine," *Recherches sur Diderot et sur l'Encyclopédie* 26 (1999): 197–211, compared passages in the different editions, which show that Diderot adapted the work of physiocrat Abbé Pierre Roubaud (Curran, *Anatomy of Blackness*, 196–199).
47 Curran, *Anatomy of Blackness*, 181.
48 Curran, *Anatomy of Blackness*, 175, cites the following authors.
49 Abbé Nauton, "*Essai sur la cause physique de la couleur des différents habitants de la Terre,*" 1781, cited by Curran, *Anatomy of Blackness*, 173–174, as a widely influential text. The word phlogiston, meaning to inflame, may have been used even earlier: John Henry White, *The History of Phlogiston Theory* (New York: AMS Press, Inc., 1973).
50 Curran lists his ethnographic sources. See also Hannah Murphy, "Re-writing Race in Early Modern European Medicine," *History Compass* 19 (11), e12692, with further references. https://doi.org/10.1111/hic3.12692.
51 Citations from Kant's texts refer to volume and page numbers in the Akademie German edition of Kant's works: *Königlichen Preußischen (later Deutschen) Akademie der Wissenschaften* (ed.), 1900–, *Kants gesammelte Schriften* (Berlin: Georg Reimer [Walter De Gruyter, 1902–]). For the English translation, I used Immanuel Kant, *Critique of Judgment* (1790), trans. and intro. Werner S. Pluhar, foreword Mary J. Gregor (Indianapolis: Hackett Publishing Co., 1987), Part 1, §§ 1–3 (pp. 44–48), § 9 (pp. 61–63), and § 35 (150–152). Volume 5: Ak. 204–207, 217–218, 287.
52 Michael Rohlf, "Immanuel Kant," *Stanford Encyclopedia of Philosophy*, rev. 28 July 2020, https://plato.stanford.edu/entries/kant/
53 Kant, *Critique of Judgment*, Part 1, § 46, Ak. 307–308. Pluhar, ed., *Critique*, 174–175.
54 For a balanced literature review, see Alexey Zhavoronkow and Alexey Salikov, "The Concept of Race in Kant's Lectures on Anthropology," *Cont-Textos Kantianos, International Journal of Philosophy* 7 (June 2018): 275–292. See also, less evenhanded, Jon Mikkelsen, "Translator's Introduction," *Kant and the Concept of Race: Late Eighteenth-Century Writings*, ed. Jon Mikkelson (Albany: SUNY Press, 2013), 1–40. The contributions I have found most useful for the following discussion are Emmanuel Chukwudi Eze "The Color of Reason: The Idea of 'Race' in Kant's Anthropology," *The Bucknell Review* 38/2 (January 1995): 200–241; Robert Bernasconi, "Who Invented

the Concept of Race? – Kant's Role in the Enlightenment Construction of Race," in *Race*, ed. Robert Bernasconi (Oxford: Blackwell, 2001), 11–36; Bernasconi, "Kant as an Unfamiliar Source of Racism," in T. Lott, J. Ward (eds.), *Philosophers on Race* (Oxford: Oxford University Press, New York, 2002), 145–166; Pauline Kleingeld, "Kant's Second Thoughts on Race," *The Philosophical Quarterly* 57/229 (2007): 573–592; and *Kant and Colonialism: Historical and Critical Perspectives*, ed. Karin Flikschuh and Lea Ypi (Oxford: Oxford University Press, 2014).

55 Eze, "The Color of Reason." *Kant's Anthropology from the Pragmatic Point of View*, ed. and comm. Reinhard Brandt (Cambridge University Press, 1999); and see *Kant's Lectures on Anthropology: A Critical Guide*, ed. Alix Cohen (Cambridge: Cambridge University Press, 2014).

56 Stella Sanford, "Kant, Race, and Natural History," *Philosophy and Social Criticism* 44/9 (2018): 950–977.

57 Immanuel Kant, *Gesammelte Schriften*, vol. 25, *Vorlesungen über Anthropologie*, ed. and intro. R. Brandt and W. Stark (Berlin: De Gruyter, 1997), VIII, 358. Anthony Pagden, "Stoicism, Cosmopolitanism, and the Legacy of European Imperialism," *Constellations* 7/1 (2000): 3–22; Pagden, "The Law of Continuity: Conquest and Settlement within the Limits of Kant's International Right," in *Kant and Colonialism*, 19–42.

58 French officials emancipated the enslaved people in the colony of Saint-Domingue on 21 June 1793 (uprisings began in 1791) and the French National Convention in Paris abolished slavery in all its colonies on 4 February 1794. Richard D. Popkin, *You Are All Free: The Haitian Revolution and the Abolition of Slavery* (Cambridge: Cambridge University Press, 2010).

59 Sankar Muthu, *Enlightenment against Empire* (Princeton: Princeton University Press, 2003), 102–104, cites Diderot, Raynal, Montesquieu, and Kant, and focuses on the anti-imperialist discourse. See also Margaret C. Jacob, *The Radical Enlightenment: Pantheists, Freemasons, and Republicans*, 2nd rev. ed. (Lafayette, LA: Cornerstone Book Publishers, 2006).

60 Muthu, *Enlightenment*, 108–111, citing Diderot, in Raynal, *Histoire*.

61 Muthu, *Enlightenment*, 124. This is Muthu's central argument.

62 Muthu, *Enlightenment*, 312, for this succinct formulation of his argument.

63 Eze, "The Color of Reason," concludes that *Anthropology* is a sympathetic study of European humanity taken as humanity in itself, superior to all others, consistent with color–racial distinctions in his other writings.

64 I cite Mikkelsen's translation of Girtanner, at 216 (see below). Muthu, *Enlightenment Against Empire*, 184, mistakenly claims that Girtanner applied Kant's hereditary theories only to non-human species, whereas Girtanner was interested in "the laws of generation in [all] organized bodies." (Mikkelsen, 232). Girtanner was a physician with a medical practice in Göttingen, a prolific writer on the natural sciences, a popularizer of anti-phlogistic chemistry, an early advocate of epigenesis (the theory that the embryo develops progressively from an undifferentiated egg cell), and an anti-revolutionary chronicler of the French Revolution. On Girtanner, see Robert Bernasconi, "Kant and Blumenbach's Polyps: A Neglected Chapter in the History of the Concept of Race," in *The German Invention of Race*, ed. Sara Eigen and Mark Larrimore (Albany: State University of New York Press, 2006), 73–90; Sandford, "Kant, Race, and Natural History"; and Mikkelsen, *Kant and the Concept of Race*, 209–232, with an English translation of the first section of *Kantische Prinzip*, "Theory: Presentation of the Basic Principles [*Grundsätze*]." Mikkelsen takes issue with Eze's interpretation and that of another pathbreaking African philosopher from the 1990s, Tsenay Serequeberhan (see 4-9). See the book review by John H. Zamminto, "Kant and the Concept of Race: Late Eighteenth-Century Writings," *Notre Dame Philosophical Reviews* 10 January 2014, https://ndpr.nd.edu/reviews/kant-and-the-concept-of-race-late-eighteenth-century-writings, accessed 5 October 2024.

65 Darwin, "On the Races of Man," *The Descent of Man*, vol. 1, chapter 7, names Kant as author of the theory of four races, citing Waitz, "Introduction to Anthropology," 1863, 198–208, 227; and H. Tuttle, "Origin of Antiquity of Physical Man," Boston, 1866, 35. Kant's views developed in response to Herder's position that climatic differences

are genetic forces, and with direct reference to Buffon's distinction between race and variety: Phillip R. Sloan, "Performing the Categories: Eighteenth-Century Generation Theory and the Biological Roots of Kant's A Priori," *Journal of the History of Philosophy* 40/2 (2002): 229–253.

66 Kant, *Anthropology*, 3, cited by Eze, "The Color of Reason," 234, n. 26: this is where Kant's idea of anthropology is woven into his critical philosophy.

67 Kant, *Critique of Practical Reason*, 1788. Eze, "The Color of Reason," 204–205, n. 29. On the importance of this phrase for neo-Kantian art historians, see Karen Lang, "The Dialectics of Decay: Rereading the Kantian Subject" *The Art Bulletin* 79 (September 1997): 413–439, at 421: "In the *Critique of Judgment*, the starry heavens will be replaced by an object whose vastness or might will initially overwhelm the subject; the "moral law within" will be translated into the ideas of a higher purposiveness, occasioned by the experience of the sublime. Just as "the moral law within" lifts the subject out of his own animal nature, so in the experience of the sublime the subject discovers his superiority over and above nature. In Kant's second and third Critiques, mortality gives way to morality as nature is traded for reason." See further, Lang, *Chaos and Cosmos: On the Image in Aesthetics and Art History* (Ithaca–London: Cornell University Press, 2006).

68 Kant, *Observations on the Feeling of the Beautiful and Sublime*, section 4, "On National Characteristics," (1764), trans. Paul Guyer, in Immanuel Kant, *Anthropology, History, and Education*, ed. Günter Zöller and Robert B. Louden, trans. Mary Gregor et al. (Cambridge: Cambridge University Press, 2007), 18–62. Eze, "The Color of Reason," argues that Kant's concept of talent, derived from Hume and Rousseau, is a concrete reaction to the primitivism and anticolonialism of his time. See also Catherine Wilson, "Savagery and the Supersensible: Kant's Universalism in Historical context," *History of European Ideas* 24/4–5 (1999): 315–330.

69 Zhavoronkow and Salikov, "The Concept of Race," 284–285, note that already in *VA-Friedländer* (XXV, 552), Kant makes a major statement concerning the differences between Occidental Europeans and "Oriental peoples" (1781–1782), assuming that the latter cognize from images but not from "pure concepts, which is the pure use of reason" so they are lacking in their morality. "All Oriental peoples belong to this part." Kant, "Anthropology Friedländer (1775–1776)," trans. G. Felicitas Munzel, in *Lectures on Anthropology*, ed. and trans. Robert B. Louden and Allen W. Wood (Cambridge: Cambridge University Press, 2012, 0nline 2013), 111 (25: 552) https://doi.org/10.1017/CBO9781139028639

70 Kant, "Foundations of the Metaphysics of Morals" (AA 4: 423), cited by Wilson, "Savagery and the Supersensible," 316–317. I suspect that Kant's choice of the word "rust" is an allusion to phlogiston.

71 Eze, "The Color of Reason," 223, n. 77, citing *Kants philosophische Anthropologie: Nach handscriftlichen Vorlesungen*, ed. Friedrich Christian Starke (Leipzig, 1831), 353; Eze's translation. See also Robert R. Louden, *Kant's Impure Ethics: From Rational Beings to Human Beings* (New York: Oxford University Press, 2000).

72 Kant, AA 8: 174.

73 Du Bos and others disagreed on this point; Kirchner, "Migration." The framework of discussion remains the same.

74 In the first section, "Analytic of the Beautiful," which distinguishes judgments of beauty from other cognitive kinds of judgment.

75 Summers, *The Judgment of Sense*, 71–108; 106–109 on Kant.

76 He referred his concerns to David Hume's *Enquiry Concerning Human Understanding* (1748), which claimed that a priori truths derived from logic can tell us nothing about the world, because the world is accessed empirically, through experience. Pluhar, "Translator's Introduction," in Kant, *Critique of Judgment* (1987), xxxi. The distinction between a phenomenal world and a world in itself was used previously by Leibniz and Christian Wolff, for whom the latter was simply the former perceived through sensation, construed as a "confused" rather than a "distinct" kind of thought. The terminology of "confused" versus "distinct" cognition derives from ibn al'Hatham's theory of vision.

77 As recognized by Martin Heidegger, *Kant and the Problem of Metaphysics (1929)*, cited by Frances Ferguson, *Solitude and the Sublime: Romanticism and the Aesthetics of Individuation* (New York–London: Routledge, 1992), 6.
78 Central to discussions by Hal Foster, Jonathan Crary, and others is Theodor Adorno's interpretation of Kant's term, according to which the "bourgeois mind" clings to pure visuality (*Anschaulichkeit*) as if art's only virtue were to copy reality. See Claire Farago, "Understanding Visuality," in *Seeing across Cultures*, ed. Jeanette Peterson and Dana Leibsohn (Aldershot: Ashgate Press, 2012), 239–256.
79 Kant defines the sublime as exceeding the ability of the senses to function but inducing in the beholder an understanding of the purposiveness of nature beyond human understanding. See Lang, "Dialectics of Decay."
80 Pluhar, "Translator's Introduction," in Kant, *Critique of Judgment* (1987), xliii.
81 Leonardo da Vinci, Parte Prima, *Libro di Pittura*, is filled with such statements, beginning with the definition of painting as a science born of first principles (geometry) and experience, based on optical theory. See Farago, *Leonardo da Vinci's "Paragone."*
82 Umberto Eco, *Art and Beauty in the Middle Ages*, trans. Hugh Bredin (New Haven–London: Yale University Press, 1986), 70–73, citing Thomas Aquinas, *Summa Theologica*, I, 5, 4 ad 1, for the passage cited.
83 Leonardo da Vinci, *Libro di Pittura*, n. 13 (Farago, *Paragone*, 196–197).
84 Leonardo da Vinci, *Libro di Pittura*, n. 7 (Farago, *Paragone*, 184–187).
85 M. M. Slaughter, *Universal Languages and Scientific Taxonomy in the Seventeenth Century* (Cambridge: Cambridge University Press, 1982), 40–42.
86 Kant, *Critique of Judgment:* "Taste . . . is, in the ultimate analysis, a critical faculty that judges of the rendering (*Versimlichung*) of moral ideas in terms of sense." Members of society who experience this satisfaction in communication exhibit a *sensus communis* (AA 40: 293).
87 I have discussed the connection between Burckhardt and political theory elsewhere: "The Status of the 'State as a Work of Art': Re-Viewing Burckhardt's Renaissance from the Borderlines," in *Cultural Exchange between European Nations during the Renaissance*, Acta Universitatis Upsaliensis, ed. Gunnar Sorelius and Michael Srigley (Uppsala: Almqvist & Wiksell, 1994), 17–32, and in *Reframing the Renaissance*, 68–70.
88 Kant, "On the Ideal of Beauty," *Critique of Judgment*, § 17 (Pluhar ed., 79–84, at 84); AK5: 231–236.
89 Jean-François Lyotard, *The Postmodern Condition: A report on Knowledge*, trans. Geoff Bennington and Michael Massumi, foreword Frederic Jameson (Minneapolis: University of Minnesota Press, 1984).
90 Roland Barthes, "Changing the Object Itself," *Image, Music, Text*, ed. and trans. Stephen Heath (New York: Hill and Wang, 1977), 167, emphasis added.
91 Gerbi, *The Dispute of the New World*, 433–438.
92 Susan Buck-Morss, *Hegel, Haiti, and Universal History* (Pittsburgh: University of Pittsburgh Press, 2009).
93 Buck-Morss, *Hegel*, 6.
94 Buck-Morss, *Hegel*, 75.
95 Charles De Brosses, *Du culte des dieux fétiches, ou Parallèle de l'ancienne religion de l'Égypte avec la religion actuelle de Nigritie* (Paris: [Fayard], 1760).
96 Mitchell, *Iconology*, 163–164.
97 Giambattisa Vico, *The New Science*, 3rd ed. (1744), trans. and ed. Jason Taylor and Robert Miner, intro. Giuseppe Mazotta (New Haven–London: Yale University Press, 2020), 149.
98 William Pietz, "Fetish," in *Critical Terms for Art History*, 2nd ed., ed. 2003, 306–317, with further references.
99 Christian Hecht, *Katholische Bildertheologie der Frühen Neizeit: Studien zu Traktaten von Johannes Molanus, Gabriele Paleotti, und anderen Autoren* (Berlin: Gebr. Mann Verlag, 2012), 356–359.
100 Eloise Qniñones Keber, "Collecting Cultures: A Mexican Manuscript in the Vatican Library," in *Reframing the Renaissance*, 228–242.

101 Howard F. Cline, "The *Relaciones Géograficas* of the Spanish Indies, 1*577–1586," Hispanic American Historical Review 44/3 (1964): 341–374.* See the discussion of these reports studied by Sara Miglietti in Intermezzo II. Elizabeth Boone, "Ixtlilxochitl, Codex," *The Oxford Encyclopedia of Mesoamerican Cultures* (Oxford: Oxford University Press, 2006).

102 Serge Grusinski, *The Mestizo Mind: The Intellectual Dynamics of Colonization and Globalization*, trans. Deke Dusinberre (New York: Routledge, Taylor & Francis Group, 2002). Alessandra Russo, *The Untranslatable Image: A Mestizo History of the Arts in New Spain, 1500–1600*, trans. Susan Emanuel (Austin: University of Texas Press, 2014). See my discussion of Carducho in Fugue 2.

103 Jeanette Favrot Peterson, "Artisanal Authority and Indigenous Knowledge in the Book Culture of Sixteenth-century Mexico," in *Transcultural Histories of Art and Artisanal Epistemologies: Knowledge to Be Made*, ed. Claire Farago, Susan Lowish, and Jens Baumgarten (London: Routledge, 2025).

104 Michel Foucault, *The Archaeology of Knowledge and the Discourse of Language* (1969), trans. A. M. Sheridan Smith (New York: Pantheon Books, 1972), 91.

105 Alessandra Russo, *A New Antiquity: Art and Humanity as Universal, 1400–1600* (University Park, PA: Pennsylvania State University Press, 2024).

106 Pamela H. Smith, "Science on the Move: Recent Trends in the History of Early Modern Science," *Renaissance Quarterly* 62 (2009): 345–375; Smith, "Epistemology, Artisanal," *Renaissance Encyclopedia of Philosophy*, ed. Marco Sgarbi (Cham: Springer, 2022), 1118–1124. Smith has published extensively on artisanal epistemology, often in collaboration with others, including the *Making and Knowing* project at Columbia University, New York (www.makingandknowing.org)

107 Margaret C. Jacob, *The First Knowledge Economy: Human Capital and the European Economy, 1750–1850* (Cambridge: Cambridge University Press, 2014). See further, Paola Bertucci, *Artisanal Enlightenment: Science and the Mechanical Arts in Old Regime France* (New Haven–London: Yale University Press, 2017); John R. Pannaker, "Representing Mechanical Arts in Diderot's *'Encyclopédie*,'" *Technology and Culture* 39/1 (January 1998): 33–73.

108 Jorge Cañizares-Esguerra, "Imperial, Global (Cosmopolitan) Dimensions of Nonelite Colonial Scribal Cultures in the Early Modern Iberian Atlantic," in *Cosmopolitanism and the Enlightenment*, ed. Joan-Pau Rubiés and Neil Safier (Cambridge: Cambridge University Press, 2023), 144–176. DOI: https://doi.org/10.1017/9781009305372.007

109 Ralph Bauer and Marcy Norton, "Introduction: Entangled Trajectories: Indigenous and European Histories," *Colonial Latin American Review* 26/1 (March 2017): 1–17.

110 Marcy Norton, "Subaltern technologies and early modernity in the Atlantic World," *Colonial Latin American Review* 26:1 (March 2017), 18–38, DOI: 10.1080/10609164.2017.1287322.

111 As argued in numerous publications. For example, Tim Ingold, *Making: Anthropology, Archaeology, Art, and Architecture* (London–New York: Routledge, 2013); Tim Ingold and Elizabeth Hallam, "Creativity and Cultural Improvisation: An Introduction," in *Creativity and Cultural Improvisation*, ed. Elizabeth Hallam and Tim Ingold (Oxford–New York: Berg, 2007), 1–25. See also the discussion in my Introduction.

112 Cañizares-Esguerra, "Imperial, Global (Cosmopolitan) Dimensions," 146.

113 Helen Watson-Verran and David Turnbull, "Science and Other Indigenous Knowledge Systems," in David Turnbull et al., *Research in Science and Technology Studies: Knowledge Systems* (Stamford, CT: Jai Press, 1998), 115–139. Trevor H. J. Marchand, "Making Knowledge: Explorations of the Indissoluble Relation between Minds, Bodies, and Environment," *Journal of the Royal Anthropological Institute* 16, no. 1 (April 2010): 1–21.

114 See further, *Transcultural Histories of Art and Artisanal Epistemologies: Knowledge to Be Made*, ed. Claire Farago, Susan Lowish, and Jens Baumgarten (New York–London: Routledge, 2025).

FUGUE 4

A TRANSCULTURAL APPROACH TO HISTORIES OF VISION

As the preceding Fugues have argued, human exceptionalism and racial thinking are two facets of the same Aristotelian legacy. In this Fugue, I begin with the sea change in European thinking marked by Charles Darwin's theory of evolution, which was unprecedented in arguing for the continuity between humans and other animals. Few realize today that Darwin was still indebted to Aristotelian/Christian theories of humanity when he situated the so-called "lower races" and "savages" to fill the gap between humans and lower animals.[1] How did Darwin come to hold these views given that he questioned so many other aspects of received authority on humanity's place in nature? While there is no indication that Darwin the naturalist was personally interested in material culture or cultural practices, philosophical aesthetics, or art criticism, he argued that natural selection was no longer a major factor once modern humans could adapt to their environment through their inventiveness. It is amazing how persistent the distinction between humans and other animals on the grounds of their different inventive capacities remained: In 1871, when he was talking about different "races" of humans, Darwin made the same Aristotelian claim for human inventiveness as Aquinas. Darwin's account of human inventiveness as technological superiority retained the two ubiquitous endpoints of "civilized" and "savage" in relation to moral character. Why would Darwin invoke such a static model of absolute human differences to formulate a theory of human evolution when his close studies of biological specimens indicated just the opposite for all other animals?

From Da Vinci's Dream to Darwin's Dilemma

Darwin used the so-called "lower races" and "savages" to fill the gap between humans and lower animals. He believed in the "brotherhood of man" and found

DOI: 10.4324/9781351023429-7

slavery repugnant, but Darwin still located modern humans in a racial hierarchy. He imagined the history of humans beginning with all individuals as racially alike and argued that racial traits arose very early in the prehistory of man and were not biologically adaptive. Darwin's debts to racial science, along with those of other founding figures of evolutionism, have been examined systematically and in depth. Matthew Rampley has recently examined the response to Darwin since the nineteenth century with a focus on art history in a comprehensive book-length study provocatively titled *The Seductions of Darwin* (2017), but his interest is different: Rampley's stated aim is to address the following question: "how can knowledge of the general and universal laws of the biological sciences inform our engagement with the images and artifacts that spur our interest in art?"[2]

What has not been a topic of discussion is the significant role played by the concept of inventiveness in Darwin's accounts of human difference at the collective level. Darwin's general theory of evolution, *On the Origin of Species by Means of Natural Selection, or the Preservation of Favoured Races in the Struggle for Life* (1859), introduced the idea that populations evolve over the course of generations through a process of natural selection. As far as human development is concerned, Darwin relied on pre-evolutionary theory, including climate theory and the Christian "great chain of being," which holds that all species were created distinct and occupy a specific place in the divine hierarchy.[3] By the 1850s, the notion that races formed a graded series with Europeans at the top and sub-Saharan dark-skinned peoples ("Negroes") invariably at the bottom had become one of the cornerstones of racial science.[4] In rethinking those ideas now, it is essential to know that, in Christian doctrine, no creature could be explained in terms of evolution as we think today, because this would have implied that something capable of existence had been omitted from the divine plan devised according to God's complete freedom of will. Each link in this model contained the positive attributes of the previous link. Gaps between animal types in nature were not considered missing links but distinct species: every type of being was in its proper place in a great chain of being, conceived as a hierarchy with God at the top and minerals at the bottom. Creatures on the borderline between man and beast, according to Albertus Magnus (c. 1200–1280) commenting on Aristotle, held that pygmies and apes are intermediaries in this sense: only man forms universals and distinguishes virtue from vice, but even apes and pygmies learn from past experience, speak, and possess a kind of imitation of art and of reason.[5] According to a myth widespread in medieval literature and art, the wild man was not created in his present lowly state, but had instead been brought to this condition by outrageous hardships.[6] This subhuman status was reached not by a gradual ascent from lower animals but by a descent – a loss of civilization defined in Christian terms. The loss or absence of human faculties such as rationality, speech, and the power to recognize the Divinity – accompanied by other bestial endowments like gigantic size, enormous strength, derangement, hairiness, and cannibalism – could be partially rehabilitated through the teachings of the Christian religion. Knowledge of God was the prerequisite and basis for any further mental activity.[7]

The definition of "species" was an unstable signifier in modern accounts of human difference partly because interpretations derived from *both* Christian accounts and modern science based on empirical evidence. Christian polygenists argued that the different races of humans were so different in physical, mental, and moral attributes as to form not merely varieties of a single species, but several distinct biological species. Polygenesis had always been the popular answer to why different races exist, but by the 1850s racial science, which initially rejected polygenesis, accepted its assumptions and described them in the language of science.[8] Darwin followed many earlier writers who were indebted to the Christian idea of universality articulated as the great chain of being based on the biblical creation story in the book of Genesis. Although evolutionists were monogenists by conviction, they adopted polygenist styles of typological analysis used by physical anthropologists who were committed to a science of fixed and unchanging essences assigned to different racial "types."[9] To a typologist, every individual belonged to an underlying essence and bore its characteristic features: the task of the scientist was to explore the stable essences behind variation, to reconstruct the pure and distinct racial stocks that comprise contemporary mixed populations. The historian of cultural anthropology, George Stocking and historian Nancy Stepan, who has studied the critical role played by the idea of race in Great Britain, identify the following tension in Darwinian evolutionary theory: evolution is a theory of continual change, so it is opposed to typological or essentialist thinking. The following discussion focuses on how Darwin himself dealt with this contradiction.

Darwin entered contentious debates belatedly on the formation of human races with the publication of *The Descent of Man and Selection in Relation to Sex* (first edition, 1871).[10] His earlier account of general evolution had been positively received, but the traditional Christian view of humanity's unique place in nature was still dominant in scientific circles, including his own London-based scene.[11] Darwin devoted the first seven chapters to showing that the physical, mental, and moral nature of modern humans could be explained by evolutionary theory, the first two objectives of his book. Darwin's third objective was to consider "the value of the differences between the so-called races of man."[12] Arguing that animals showed greater moral and mental capacities than many naturalists allowed, he provided largely anecdotal evidence that resembles the claims made by contemporary evolutionary biologists such as Carl Safina that animals think, feel, and socialize in ways that differ from modern *Homo sapiens* only in degree, not in kind (dogs were frequently the protagonists in Darwin's stories).[13]

The main point of Darwin's argument in 1871, and the main preoccupation of the first seven chapters, was that evolution could account for the development of human mental and moral capacity. Darwin responded to objections raised by his Christian scientist colleagues that "natural selection" was not enough to explain the evolution of *Homo sapiens* from lower forms of animals on the matter of moral character. He incorporated many elements of pre-evolutionary climate theory into his account of human development in arguing that human evolution was due to man's inventiveness to adapt to different environments. He also drew on the most recent anthropological literature that largely agreed with art historians like Winckelmann and natural philosophers a century earlier who conceived of artistry as the natural function of a body of a people. The differences between "savage" and "civilized man" must be due to their cultural adaptation to specific circumstances, Darwin argued, understood as differences of degree rather than kind, depending upon inborn capacity and a variety of environmental factors.

In the second part of *Descent of Man*, Darwin invoked sexual selection rather than natural selection to explain traits that were found in animal species that were not useful in the struggle for life. He thought racial traits appeared by spontaneous variation but, in savage life, man was governed by instinct so sexual selection could account for evolution. As human populations divided into small groups and spread into new parts of the globe, different physical traits appeared by spontaneous variation, and then proceeded by natural selection based on sexual preferences to develop the physical, racial diversity of humankind. Some of Darwin's readers questioned his theory of sexual selection because they imagined European ideals of beauty to be universal. It was in this context of defending and demonstrating his general theory of continuous evolution that Darwin compared some contemporary African "savages" unfavorably with certain animals (birds) for their aesthetic and artistic capabilities.[14]

Darwin argued that natural selection was no longer a major factor once modern humans could adapt to their environment through their inventiveness. Yet this single statement does not do justice to the many factors he considered important, which were not inherited differences alone but mental capacity and environmental conditions far more complex and nuanced than any previous theory about climate or geographic location or racial essence. Darwin's main theoretical investment was in continuity and gradation to support his dynamic evolutionary theory: cultural factors were not necessarily linked to biological progression. He questioned received authority from his firsthand contacts with Fuegans, "Negroes," and individuals of mixed ancestry whom he met on his far-ranging travels. Darwin also did not define species as fixed entities endowed with natural essences by the Creator, and natural selection does not homogenize the individuals of a species.

Montesquieu and Darwin (and many others) rejected climate theory as the cause of racial difference such as skin color (once hotly debated) but they did not reject its underlying assumptions and epistemological structures. Darwin accepted the deeply entrenched idea that absolute human differences could be classified by "race." Here is an excerpt from the widely cited conclusion to his defense of monogenism in the *Descent of Man*, an eyewitness reprise of his encounter with the Indigenous inhabitants of Tierra del Fuego, in the southernmost tip of South America, the "lowest savages of the present time," that retains the categories and tropes of climate theory:

> But there can hardly be a doubt that we are descended from barbarians. The astonishment which I felt on first seeing a party of wild Fuegians on a wild and broken shore will never be forgotten by me, for the reflection at once rushed into my mind— such were our ancestors. These men were absolutely naked and bedaubed with paint, their long hair was tangled, their mouths frothed with excitement, and their expression was wild, startled, and distrustful. They possessed hardly any arts, and like wild animals lived on what they could catch; they had no government, and were merciless to everyone not of their own small tribe.[15]

Darwin never acknowledged that "civilized man" destroyed the lives and lifeways of so-called "savage" or "barbarous" Indigenous peoples. He did deal at some length with attempts to civilize them that had resulted in death and degradation, but he attributed the massive loss of life to the suddenly changed conditions under colonialism that "civilized races" were better able to resist. Darwin also supported an international discourse mounted in Europe that had established Indigenous peoples as living examples of primordial humans.[16] Nineteenth-century reconstructions of Neanderthal physiognomy were actually based on comparisons with modern Indigenous Australian specimens, the anatomical evidence reinforced by circular arguments about the "primitive state" of Aboriginal culture. The most widely known "reconstruction" was by comparative anatomist Thomas Henry Huxley, entitled *Evidence as to Man's Place in Nature* (1863), published in support of Darwin's theory of evolution nearly a decade before the appearance of *The Descent of Man* (1871). In 1873, when Darwin was preparing a new edition, Huxley assisted him with an update on ape-brain inheritance.

In two publications of 1863, Huxley had laid the foundation for associating modern Indigenous Australians with ancient Europeans on anatomical grounds.[17] Huxley provided the first detailed descriptions of a Neanderthal skull based on a fragment that he compared to the skulls of a chimpanzee, ancient and modern Europeans, and a number of modern Indigenous Australians. To illustrate the developmental sequence of humans from apes and monkeys, Huxley used a modern Australian skull (even though he had an ancient Neanderthal specimen on hand) because he considered it had more "profound" meaning, drawing on existing hierarchical views of humanity rather than his own anatomical measurements [Figure 4.1].

Many others made similar claims including James Hunt, President of the Anthropological Society of London he founded in 1863, who believed in polygenesis. For Hunt, the idea that the ancient primitive race of Europe resembled modern Australians was "disgusting" and "all theories founded thereon as

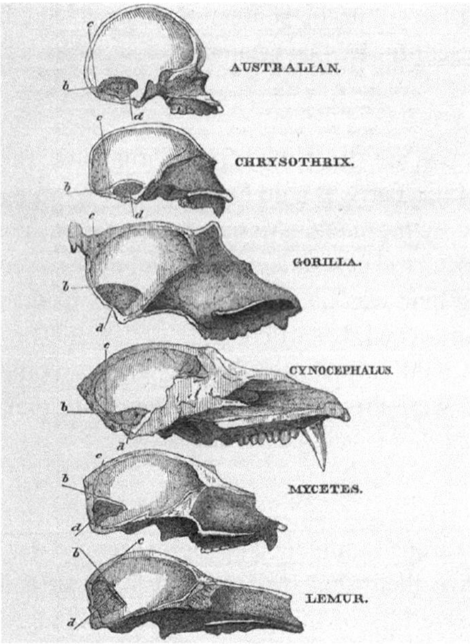

FIGURE 4.1 Primate evolutionary sequence, after T. H. Huxley, *Evidence as to Man's Place in Nature* (London: Williams & Norgate, 1863), fig. 17. London, Wellcome Collection.

to the extreme savage state of the primitive inhabitants of Europe are utterly worthless."[18] The most popular book promoting these ideas was a bestseller written by Huxley's associate, the banker and politician John Lubbock, *Pre-Historic Times: As Illustrated by Ancient Remains, and the Manners and Customs of Modern Savages* (1865), for whom the ancientness of "savages" could only be measured "by their works." Lubbock compared ancient European stone tools with nineteenth-century Tasmanian stone tools, a comparison taken up by two of the most influential anthropologists, the British academic Edward B. Tylor and the American Lewis Henry Morgan, who extended the comparison to present-day Native North Americans as "an exemplification of the experience of our own ancestors."[19] The academic tradition "says more about notions of savagery and ideology than it does about evolutionary relationships," observe Ian McNiven and Lynette Russell, both leading specialists in Indigenous Australian studies. In their fine-grained, incisive review of the European and Australian literature from ancient theories of cultural progress to the present day, the co-authors point out that at the same time that Europeans were "fine-tuning" their views on what characteristics constitute the lowest and most primitive form of humanity, Europeans were engaged in the violent colonization of Australia, committing atrocities aided by prevailing ideologies and mainstream scientific theories that made it "far easier on the conscience" to kill a Stone Age primitive savage who might even be another species than killing a fellow human being of equal standing.[20] Moreover, these evolutionist theories were embraced by right-wing capitalists pushing ideas of liberal individualism and progressivism based on Adam Smith's moralizing view of the economy in which markets are a self-regulating "laissez faire" system ensuring the rights of natural law.[21] Smith's egalitarian commitment to individual self-interest (an "invisible hand" controls the "free market") in *Inquiry in the Nature and Causes of the Wealth of Nations* (1776) was enthusiastically embraced and its arguments inverted to benefit the wealthy by Milton Friedman (1912–2006), recipient of a 1976 Nobel Memorial Prize in Economic Sciences, and the Chicago School of Economics.[22] Rising social and economic inequality have been driving political polarization and populist nationalism globally since c. 1980, most of all in advanced and major emerging economies, due to lack of regulation of the so-called free markets.[23]

We (scholars, artists, critics, scientists, students) are not innocent bystanders but part of the polity or state apparatus. The instability of race as a scientific category, conflated with ethnicity, a cultural category, was endemic to Darwin's account and the consequences as well as the possibilities it opened up are still with us today. Scientists in the nineteenth century and beyond interpreted evolution in a way that made natural selection no longer operative on physical humans because their theories preserved the idea that racial types were extremely old and fixed. By contrast, Gregor Mendel (1822–1884) and Rosalind Franklin (1920–1958), posthumously recognized as the founders of modern genetic science, were able to establish the actions of "invisible" genes in transmitting the traits of organisms. Mendelians believed that the fundamental laws of inheritance would be discovered by experimental breeding and the study of cells, not the statistical study of the complex traits of individual organisms, which is the approach taken by racial scientists. A synthetic theory of evolution that unites genetics and evolution by natural selection did not develop until the 1930s and '40s, primarily because many biologists accepted Darwin's claim that once archaic humans became truly human, they escaped the force of natural selection through their inventiveness.[24] If he had argued otherwise, that in fact the fully human race(s) continued to evolve, would that argument have been any better, given his acceptance of the idea of separate races reluctant though it might have been? Darwin accepted the theory of cultural progression from savage to civilized. "Race" (as distinguished from concentrations of population) is an irredeemable concept unsupported by today's scientific evidence. Now the origins of *Homo sapiens* have become a complex issue again, as I discuss in the Intermezzo following this Fugue.

Provincializing Art

Darwin's understanding of inventiveness is firmly planted in climate theory-cum-science of race as it was entangled with Christian theories of creation in his day in London. Anyone who read Darwin was faced with a conundrum: he emphatically rejected post-*Homo sapiens* human evolution (race theory), but he promoted the idea that humans advanced culturally through their inventive engagement with their environment. In his general theory of evolution, Darwin situated the so-called "lower races" and "savages" to fill the gap between humans and lower animals. His account of cultural change as the inventive engagement of *Homo sapiens* with the environment, combined with this positioning of some modern humans in this gap, re-introduced in rather convoluted form the question of who was fully human, on what basis. Darwin's inconsistent but probative account of cultural evolution left that question in limbo. Where did Africans and Native Americans fit into the scheme of evolution if they were "savages" located in the gap? On the other hand, Darwin's account also seemed to free cultural history from evolutionism while retaining the environmentalism inherited from climate theory.

The premise of this book is that we can get past our past only by confronting the epistemological structures and ontological framework of the nature/culture divide of European (or "Western" or Euro-Mediterranean) origin. Today, what might be called Darwin's environmentalist account of race is mostly ignored, but in a book that advocates attending to the climate catastrophe in our midst by unpacking the historically entangled relationship of art, human exceptionalism, colonialism, imperialism, and economic globalization, it is imperative to re-examine the reception of Darwin's theory of human evolution by the European founders of the discipline of art history. The fundamental question was whether racial differences in mental ability existed – and if so, how were they inherited: could cultural acquisitions be passed on from one generation to the next? Chevalier de Lamarck, a well-known early nineteenth-century pre-Darwinian biologist, proposed that genetic characteristics are culturally acquired. Lamarck searched for perceptible characteristics that could measure human intelligence on a vertical scale classified by "race." In contrast to the developmentalists (Darwinians), Lamarckians believed that genetic improvements in "races" would result from providing individuals with a better social environment. In 1866, generalizing from embryological comparisons, the Darwinist Ernst Haeckel formulated his famous thesis that *ontogeny recapitulates phylogeny*, a "biogenetic law" he declared valid not only in the growth of the embryo, but also in the psychology of peoples.[25] "In order to understand correctly the highly differentiated, delicate mental life of civilized man," Haeckel argued, "we must . . . observe not only its gradual awakening in the child, but also its step-by-step development in lower, primitive peoples and in invertebrates."[26] Haeckel was a key proponent of social Darwinism and scientific racism who believed that the characteristics of an organism were acquired through interactions with the environment.[27]

Given the context of the mid-nineteenth-century debates about racial inheritance – whether cultural acquisitions could be passed on to affect mental capability from one generation to the next – Darwin's unresolved dilemma almost begged to be reinserted into some sort of Lamarckian scheme of social environmentalism. In German, French, and Anglo-American discussions, the emerging category of "art" as a universal human practice provided a new means for reformulating the Enlightenment theory of the essential unity of mankind. Writing in 1968, George Stocking showed that many writers at the end of the nineteenth century combined elements of Lamarckian, pre-Darwinian thinking with some of Darwin's ideas.[28] An impressive number of fine-grained studies have since clarified and complicated Stocking's conclusions with regard to world histories of art proposed by the founders of the modern disciplines of art history and anthropology (or ethnology, the preferred term in German discussions).

The following discussion focuses on the relationship of inventiveness to the environment, but the introduction of evolutionary theory into nineteenth-century accounts of cultural history during this formative era is difficult to sort out chronologically because older ideas were often reintroduced, newer ideas were sometimes ignored, and at other times older and newer ideas were intermingled as Stocking observed. And there were many sources for broadly disseminated ideas, a methodological challenge to which my focus on "thought structures" is one coping strategy. The situation then is comparable to our own challenges: there is no siloed discipline for channeling the arguments from one author to another and the potential reading list of the de-centered field is so vast that no one can be responsible for, or even familiar with, all of it. In these circumstances, the discourse is especially recursive and consequently difficult to narrate.

Today, as in the nineteenth century, there are deep tensions between the liberal ideals of ethnological and cultural universalism, on the one hand ("we are all one," "humanity at large"), and racial and cultural injustice on the other (treating Indigenous societies as "primitive" stages in a cultural "evolution"). The German art historian Franz Kugler described "art as a possibility of all peoples," a framework that has understandably attracted renewed interest recently for conceiving an all-encompassing field for the study of human material culture. Horst Bredekamp praises Kugler's expansive concept, also embodied in the Ethnology Museum in Leipzig that opened in 1843 and the Neues Museum in Berlin conceptualized in the same year, because it

> grasps the entire pictorial inventory of human artifacts as one cosmos in which, from the beginning, *form is tied to semantics*: in which, in *a universal Aristotelianism*, the intrinsic connection is emphasized in such a way that the art-historical methods are applied in genuine self-evidence, and not merely in coincidental bridge-building [between the earliest artifacts and modern art]. [emphasis added][29]

However, there is a slight problem with this argument because Aristotle's universal system of classification is *not* universal: many societies have other ways of understanding their "cultural belongings," to use the term preferred by Ruth Phillips, a specialist on Indigenous North American material culture who has worked closely with Indigenous communities for decades to build mutual trust. In this pan-human characterization of what constitutes the artifactual history of the planet, the values used to define the "origins" of human artifacts remained unexamined. Kugler, his contemporaries, and successors treated extra-European cultures as intermediate stages between the "childhood" of humanity and the "true art" of modern European civilization. The principal criteria invoked, "the individual," "beauty" (described in terms of harmony and symmetry), and "form" tied to "semantics" (the cognitive structure of meaning), all derive from the longstanding European discourse on art. Where Bredekamp and others today understand Kugler's definition of aesthetic consciousness as universally valid, one can also observe the continuation of old ideas and the construction of new hierarchical cultural boundaries.

When the first attempts were made to define art history as a unified subject area, there existed centuries of accounts of human geography linked to both culture and the environment encompassing the entire planet. The world art histories of the nineteenth century, in other words, were not completely unprecedented. Their widespread popularity is partly explained through Foucault's concept of a "discursive formation" that reanimates already existing themes "making it possible, with a particular set of concepts, to play different games . . . [to] define a field of strategic possibilities."[30] Beginning in the latter part of the eighteenth century, climate theory was often replaced by accounts of absolute human difference supported by objectifying criteria of the kind that natural philosophers and medical doctors sought in empirical, comparative studies of shared human features such as brain size, constitution of blood, and anatomical structure as measures of human mental capacity.

Climate theory was also still cited by some writers well into the twentieth century. The relation of humans to their environment that had been a central feature of climate theory dropped out of these discussions, but the structure and categories they established remained as the basis for making new claims about degrees of humanness, as did the fundamental premise inherited from classical antiquity that humans progressed from savage to civilized, from hunter–gatherers to agriculturalists to urban dwellers. This too is disputed by the archeological data recently published by David Graeber and David Wengrow, in *The Dawn of Everything: A New History of Humanity* (2023), noted in the second Fugue. Their empirical archaeological evidence leaves no doubt that the linear model of social evolution is a philosophical construct. For a start, settlements preceded agriculture, early farming sometimes included a mix of food-producing activities to avoid getting trapped or endangered by the demands of fragile ecological conditions, many large cities show no sign of centralized administration, democratic institutions did not begin just once in Athens, and the state itself may not be inevitable.[31]

As discussed in the third Fugue, Winckelmann (*History of Ancient Art*, 1764) initiated the idea that the life of a style is indistinguishable from the life of a people, borrowing from pre-Darwinian theories of evolution and climate theory, as studied by Éric Michaud. Michaud argues that when artistic style could be written like the biography of a whole people from its first appearance to its decline, it laid the foundation for a biological concept of style.[32] In the nineteenth century, it became routine to associate art with the nation even before the publication of Darwin's theories or the creation of the modern bureaucratic nation-state – the nation-state of Germany was established in 1871. Writers argued on the basis of Herder's idea that every people has a unique "spirit" or *Volkgeist*, amplified in Hegel's lectures on the fine arts in the 1820s which claimed that the subject attains self-consciousness through reproducing the self in works of art. Art is "the most faithful consciousness of a people" because "the finest and most characteristic traits of the soul of a people can only be known by its artistic creations," according to the German art historian Karl Schnaase (1798–1875), author of another early world art history (1843) who explicitly held that the historian of art was an expert mediator trained to make works of art intelligible to a broader public.[33]

The first histories and atlases of *Weltkunstgeschichte* also contributed to the organization of ethnological museums, created to serve as laboratories for studying the world's earliest cultures on a systematic, scientific foundation. Franz Kugler himself drew upon material in Alexander von Humboldt's collection of ancient Mexican sculptures and the art cabinet (*Kunstkammer*) housed in Berlin's City Palace, which also provided objects for Berlin's Altes Museum, the Berlin Museum of Decorative Arts, and Berlin University's collections.[34] The ethnologist and librarian, Gustav Friedrich Klemm (1802–1867), author of a ten-volume cultural history of mankind, *Allgemeine Kulturgeschichte der Menschheit* (*Universal Cultural History of Humankind*; 1843–1852), whose collection became the core of the Ethnology Museum of Leipzig, established in 1843, included a short text on the founding of a museum for all cultures that grasps the entire pictorial inventory of human artifacts as one cosmos in which the same art historical methods could be applied to elucidate the progress of humanity from savage to civilized.[35]

Disagreements over epistemological assumptions once considered progressive arose at the end of the nineteenth century when art history and ethnology (aka cultural anthropology) were not the distinct disciplinary practices they are today. In the second Fugue, I discussed ethnographic museums as part of a colonialist enterprise central to decolonial efforts today that span art history and museology. Here, I provide a few key examples from the ongoing debates to indicate how climate theory and evolutionism played out in the decades around 1900. In Germany, *Welkunstgeschichte* gained fresh momentum in the 1870s in the wake of Darwinian thought when it was argued that all cultures or peoples produce "art." The formation of new ethnographic museums that absorbed older Wunderkammers, increased archaeological activity, growing trade in artifacts, competition among nation-states to acquire material for universal public museums, and the introduction of railroads, were all contributing factors.[36] H. Glenn Penny defends nineteenth-century German ethnologists, arguing that they were "anti-racists" practicing "cosmopolitan ideals" in "generating theories about the essential nature of human beings through their museums' collections."[37] The moral mission of nineteenth-century ethnographers was to preserve and study that which was about to be destroyed (by colonizing European imperialists) based on the assumption that certain elementary ideas [*Elementargedanken*] structured all human thought ramified into ethnically specific ideas [*Völkergedanken*] that appear incomprehensible "unless perceived as being part of a cosmic harmony," to cite Adolf Bastian (1826–1905), the German explorer, ethnologist, and voracious collector who served as a founder and first Director of the Königliches Museum für Völkerkunde in Berlin (today the Ethnologisches Museum, otherwise known as the Humboldt Forum, discussed in the second Fugue) where he assembled material culture of every kind – texts, legends, grammars, sculptures, tools, idols – as a universal scientific project in the spirit of Herder and Alexander von Humboldt's *Kosmos*.[38] In Bastian's updated version of climate theory, focused like Herder's on collective mentality ("folk ideas"), the world was divided into "geographical provinces" differentiated by their environment, each of which passed through the same stages of evolutionary development that could be studied comparatively, a view that was reinforced by Bastian's successor, Felix von Luschan, whose great appreciation for the Benin Bronzes I already mentioned, also in the second Fugue.[39]

According to Ulrich Pfisterer writing in 2007 about these world art schemes, it was simply "easier" to study "primitive" human beings such as prehistoric and Indigenous peoples and children than complex European high cultures.[40] The central argument of Ernst Grosse's (1862–1927) influential book, *Die Anfänge der Kunst* (*The Beginnings of Art*; 1894; English ed. 1904), was that the aesthetic properties of the world's art could be classified according to stages of cultural and aesthetic development ranging from "savage" to "civilized."[41] According to Pfisterer, Grosse's text "pleaded most explicitly for a worldwide art history and the end of Eurocentric aesthetic categories."[42] The arguments Pfisterer made two decades ago have evolved into a more critical understanding of these early world art schemes. Monica Juneja reassesses Grosse's central argument that the aesthetic properties of the world's art could be inferred from their visual properties according to stages of cultural and aesthetic development.[43] Most troubling of all, Grosse deployed the Eurocentric concept of the "primitive" to designate the *Naturvölker* (literally "peoples close to nature") of the present who could serve as available models to understand humanity's phased cultural development, including the contemporary Indigenous peoples of Australia, Africa, Oceania, and the Americas.

Du Bos' *Reflexions* (1719) and Herder were directly cited by Grosse who was interested in formulating a unified concept of art for all humanity. *Die Anfänge der Kunst/The Beginnings of Art*, the first German language text on "primitive art," was a major source of ideas for his colleagues, along with a slightly earlier essay on the relationship between aesthetics and ethnology, *Ethnologie und Ästhetik* (1891), in which Grosse explained developmental differences in art among various peoples by appealing to climate theory.[44] He defined "aesthetic drive" as the common feature of all humanity. His understanding that "aesthetic drive" is a shared feature of humanity is indebted not only to Du Bos but to a number of other eighteenth-century writers on aesthetics including Alexander Baumgarten, who invented the term *aesthetica*; Herder, Friedrich Schiller, and Immanuel Kant, whose ideas on aesthetic judgment I discussed at the end of the third Fugue. Grosse's "aesthetic drive" is realized differently according to the type of society imagined as a technological evolution from hunters to gatherers to farmers. An honorary curator of the archaeological and ethnographical university collections of Freiburg, Germany, from 1889–1905, Grosse conformed with the narrative of cultural evolution shared by many writers around 1900.

I draw from the close readings of texts by Grosse and others by Susanne Leeb that suggest how writers around 1900 dealt with Darwin's theory of continuous evolution by turning to Schiller's (1795) idea of a "ludic drive," evident in the writings of Grosse and Karl Woermann (1844–1933), Director of the collection of new masters at Dresden's Royal Painting Academy and the author of another universal history of art, entitled *Die Geschichte der Kunst aller Völker und Zeiten* (*History of Art of all Peoples and Times*; 1900). Woermann cited Grosse's evolutionist history and was especially interested in the "architectural arts" of animals.[45] Leeb describes how Grosse and his contemporaries conceived of two fundamental divisions, the difference between animals and humans, and the difference between "peoples of nature" and "peoples of culture."[46] Grosse defined ethnology broadly as the "science of peoples and nations" that would foster a scientific approach to the study of aesthetic matters beginning with the category of "ornament" found on engraved bones from the Stone Age as well as modern Australian shields.

Both Grosse and Woermann (and others) were in search of general laws of human development, and both assigned the "art" of primitive peoples to the realm of natural history. Leeb situates their writings and those of some of their contemporaries in the distinction between the peoples of nature (*Naturvölker*), who were peoples without history denied individual agency and memory, and the peoples of culture (*Culturvölker*), who progress continuously, a distinction she traces to Karl Biedermann's entry on "culture" in his *Staatslexicon* of 1860, which assigned the highest development to Germany in particular. However, I have argued that these distinctions were also made by Darwin and they proliferated on the basis of much older "thought structures." Drawing on the work of nineteenth-century evolutionists, Woermann also considered whether the "architecture" of animals is art and concluded in familiar Aristotelian terms that animal art is only a "blind natural drive" while "free art" (a phrase derived directly from Schiller) separates all humans from animals. Grosse and Woermann joined other prominent German writers on art including Wilhelm Wundt, Leo Frobenius, Alfred Vierkandt, Aloïs Riegl, and Aby Warburg, all of whom defended a linear history of progress from primitive to civilized and equated modern "primitive" peoples with the historic primitive past of humanity.[47] They held that primitive hunting peoples in Australia, America, and Africa offer good material for such an analysis, to cite the ethnologist Leo Frobenius in *Der Ursprung der Afrikanischen Kultur/On the Origins of African Culture* (1898).[48]

To summarize the foregoing argument, at the end of the nineteenth century, the epistemological distinction between nature and culture, interpreted as the distinction between different peoples at different stages of cultural evolution, hardened into one of the most important criteria for discussing the arts of extra-European cultures and societies. The art of animals, understood in neo-Aristotelian terms as due to a "blind natural drive," became another active issue in the debates.[49] The nineteenth-century literature is filled with variations on these interrelated themes that were built into the foundation of the modern discipline of art history when it sought legitimacy as an empirical science.[50] The distinctions that the founders of the discipline of art history drew between primitive and civilized, and between humans and animals, based on their art, still adheres to Aristotelian psychology and ancient Mediterranean accounts of technology, as discussed in the first two Fugues, filtered through Darwin's theory of evolution. Whereas

Darwin spoke about the aesthetic capacities of the "lower races" compared with certain animals, they drew on earlier sources on aesthetics in part because Darwin discussed aesthetic capacity as part of the evolutionary process but left the historical development of culture unresolved. While it is not certain that they actually read Darwin closely, art historians and ethnologists certainly participated in neo-Aristotelian debates about distinctions between humans and other animals based on art and aesthetics.

The notion that all cultures produce art (not merely artifacts or useful products) emerged gradually over several generations of nineteenth-century art historical writing. It displaced Greco-Roman culture from the normative position it had held without exception since the early humanist revival of ancient letters in the fourteenth century. Leeb, Juneja, and other critics of Eurocentrism argue that the nineteenth-century idea of art as a cosmopolitan, universal, ontological category is not a viable alternative to postcolonial thinking as their present-day advocates claim because the Germanophone founders of the disciplines of art history and anthropology embraced the epistemological hierarchy that post- and decolonial scholars have been rejecting since the early 1980s. The next section takes a closer look at these arguments by circling back to the introduction of the category "primitive art" in the mid-nineteenth century at the intersection of Germanophone and Anglophone writings, where climate theory continued to play a central role.

From Primitive Art to Indigenous Environmental Concerns

The introduction of the category "primitive art" in the nineteenth century has been credited to the prominent German architect and historian Gottfried Semper (180–1879) writing a few years before Edward Tylor's *Primitive Culture* (1871), which appeared in the same year as Darwin's *Descent of Man* (1871).[51] Tylor, a professor at Oxford University, did not reject race as a category but he emphasized geographical distribution (a feature of climate theory) and archeological evidence to account for the history of human development as a cultural progression through which every region passes, comparable region by region.[52] According to Stocking, Tylor set the stage for relativist definitions of culture as a universal phenomenon by suggesting that all areas of culture can be comprehended as one natural process rooted in "primitive savagery," so that cultural differences can be explained in terms of degrees of cultural progress through which every society [actually, in his text, every region] passes. In the introduction to his massive two-volume work, densely packed with concrete information, Tylor explains his methodology in which mechanical invention plays a key role in measuring cultural progress:

> For the present purpose it appears both possible and desirable to eliminate considerations of hereditary varieties or races of man, and to treat mankind as homogeneous in nature, though placed in different grades of civilization. . . . A first step in the study of civilizations is to dissect it into details, and to classify

> these in their proper groups. . . . The geographical distribution of these things, and their transmission from region to region, have to be studied as the naturalist studies the geography of his botanical and zoological species. . . . *Mechanical invention supplies apt examples of the kinds of development which affects civilization at large. . . .* By comparing the various stages of civilization among races known to history, with the aid of archaeological inference from the remains of pre-historic tribes, it seems possible to judge in a rough way of an *early general condition of man, which from our point of view is to be regarded as a primitive condition [that] . . . corresponds in a considerable degree to that of modern savage tribes.*[53] [emphasis added]

The sense in which Herder had emphasized distinct national and traditional cultures (which he ordered hierarchically on the basis of climate theory) and Darwin later employed to speak about invention at the collective level was now used by Tylor to distinguish between "material" and "spiritual" development without appealing to racial theory.[54] The equation of ancient primitive humans with "modern savage tribes" was a significant innovation in Tylor's argument as far as the universal concept of art is concerned. For him "spiritual progress" encompassed technology and the crafts as well as the fine arts. Tylor was familiar with Klemm's multi-volume *Allgemeine Kulturgeschichte der Menschkeit/General Cultural History of Mankind* (1843–1852).[55] The concept of art as a universal and simultaneously "spiritual" phenomenon, still tied to the environment and the progression from savage to civilized, frequently encountered since the sixteenth century and rooted in ancient Mediterranean writings, was reconceived by Tylor as stages through which each *region* passes. These ideas were widely disseminated through Tylor's publications. Writings associated with the British Arts and Crafts movement, notably Owen Jones (1809–1876), *The Grammar of Ornament* (1856), also popularized Semper's similar ideas on "primitive art."[56] Semper, who engaged in a running debate with Kugler for many years on this issue, insisted that all the arts, including the utilitarian crafts, are concerned with beauty.[57] His view that weaving is the fundamental source of aesthetic development argued, like Tylor's theory of "primitive culture," for the fundamentally spiritual nature of all human artistic production.

Semper explicitly criticized the exaggerated claims that were made for technology at the expense of the spiritual nature of all artistic endeavor. Like Jones and other members of the British Arts and Crafts circle with whom he associated during his stay in London in the 1850s, Semper praised "natural instinct" for harmonious design in "primitive" societies like those of Native Americans. His thesis (which still followed Vico, Winckelmann, Alexander von Humboldt, and Herder, among others, and was aligned with later discussions of ornament by Ernst Grosse and Karl Woermann), is a climatic theory of human development combined with an Aristotelian analogy between nature and art: populations imitate nature in various ways, but always derive their aesthetic preferences from their natural environment.

The literature on primitivism and modern art is enormous – it requires a Herculean effort to review it that is far beyond the scope of this book. While my brief summary cannot do justice to her nuanced argument, I would like to emphasize some key points in Juneja's account of primitivism relevant to my own claim that environmental concerns have always been central to the history of art: the issue is how to understand this problematic legacy to open it up to the future in an inclusive way that rethinks the relationship of humans to the rest of nature. Juneja provides an in-depth critical analysis of the broader, transcultural historiographical and historical context in which debates on "primitive art" took place in Europe, the US, and India that involved artists, architects, and art historians since the mid-nineteenth century. She treats "primitivism" as a migrant concept, a resilient trope that has still "not relinquished its hold over the imaginations of scholars and curators."[58] Important to her transcultural, conceptual methodology, vital to art history she argues, is its ability to bring lexical definitions into play with the visual and material records to account for signifying practices. The intersection of the two categories "primitive" and "modernist art" forms the core of her critical global art history which engages with multiple modalities ranging from individual artists and writers to institutional practices.

First, as Juneja writes, in line with my foregoing discussion, in the second half of the nineteenth century, the ideologically charged, denigrating term "primitive" morphed into a capacious conceptual container for diverse, unrelated visual traditions. Drawing on a wide range of sources myself, I have argued that the category grotesque is one such shape-shifting container for the primitive that has been in operation since the early sixteenth century, capable of being understood in diametrically opposite ways. Either it was a sign of artistic imagination and invention or it was a sign of irrationality, even demonic possession. Historically and conceptually, the "grotesque" served as the necessary supplement to classicism, that is, Western representationalism taught in academies and schools of art since the latter part of the sixteenth century.

Second, Juneja argues that, with the notable exception of an article by the American art historian Meyer Schapiro (1937), the question of artistic primitivism's complicity with colonialism resurfaced only in 1984, with controversies triggered by the infamous exhibition at the New York Museum of Modern Art, *Primitivism in 20th Century Art: Affinity of the Tribal and the Modern.*[59] Curators William Rubin and Kirk Varnedoe relied on formal resemblances between named and dated modernist paintings and objects labeled "tribal" that were treated as nameless and timeless. The underlying epistemic violence of this framework (and outmoded methodology) became the focus of heated debates, but even the most critical discussion of artistic modernism, Juneja emphasizes, generally remained confined to the domain of "art," whether visual, literary, or musical, while the institutional separation of Art [capital A] from artifact stayed in place, became even more rigid. Thus, the evolutionary classification of the world's cultures from savage to civilized continued to provide the conceptual language because the taxonomic principles separating these two overarching categories still guided the production of artistic knowledge about the world – even as close material study of migrant objects made their reframing as objects of knowledge possible.

Juneja argues that Modernist experiments such as Cubism and Expressionism are best viewed as nodal points in an Ariadne-like web.[60] She borrows this metaphor from Bruno Latour's materialist "actor network theory" (ANT) in which all the agents that act and produce effects, human and otherwise, are connected like nodes in a network that refers only to their connections without considerations of space or time.[61] Regarding the primitive/civilized dichotomy, it is worth extending the web metaphor to Latour's earlier well-known account of the transactions that maintain partitions between the natural world and human culture [Figure 4.2].

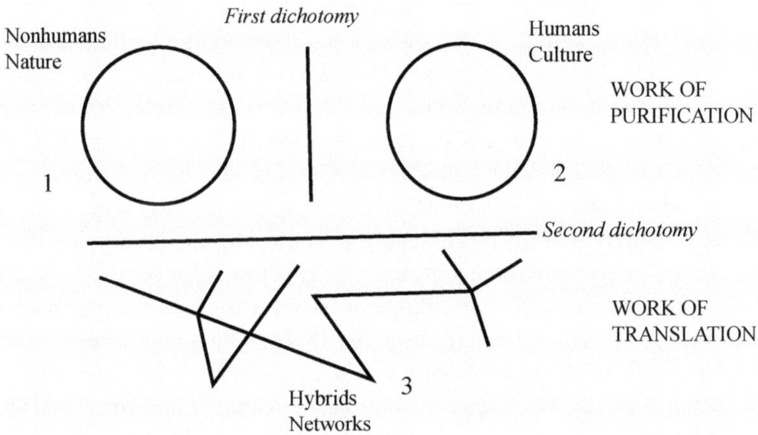

FIGURE 4.2 Diagram after Bruno Latour, "Purification and Translation," *We Have Never Been Modern* (Cambridge, MA: Harvard University Press,1993), p. 11.

The shared matrix of constantly proliferating, unruly, "hybrid" transactions (Latour's "work of translation") is denied in maintaining the separation between nonhuman nature and human culture (the "work of purification" in Latour's account). Two dichotomies are involved: nonhuman nature versus human culture and the simultaneous processes of purification/translation that sort things (such as Art and artifact) into different institutional and scholarly spaces.

James Clifford offered a similar analysis of the "art–culture system" that he called a "machine for making authenticity" to explain how a historically specific, contestable field of meanings and institutions operates. The system classifies objects and assigns them relative value, establishing "contexts" in which they properly belong and between which they circulate. Objects move in two directions in a "semiotic square" consisting of two sets of oppositions: authentic/inauthentic and masterpiece/artifact. Things of historical value may be promoted to the status of fine art, or they can move in an inverse direction, as in the case that a masterwork is culturally and historical contextualized.[62] Any initial binary opposition can generate a much larger field of terms while remaining locked in the initial, closed system. Writing in

1993, Latour identified the dialogical tension that I have also discussed, building on the work of Frances Connelly, as the binary of classicizing naturalism and the grotesque, the normative and its necessary supplement. In his meta-analysis, Latour distinguished between purified "modern" categories and what he called the unrecognized "proliferation of monsters" in acts of translation. ANT treats everything as part of the same unbounded network, but this model does not acknowledge the tension that his earlier scheme identified. Both ways of thinking about connectivity in relational terms are relevant, and they are effectively used together.

Juneja makes a convincing case that treating the primitive as the subject of representational knowledge was a precondition for the production of modernist histories and subjectivities. She identifies two main trends in the extensive nineteenth- and twentieth-century literature. One trend approached the contemporary crisis of culture at the turn of the nineteenth/twentieth century by discovering spiritual affinities between modernism and societies understood as primitive, unspoiled, untouched. The other trend was more clearly informed by evolutionist theory. The French philosopher Lucien Lévy-Bruhl (1857–1939), whose ideas circulated widely in French, German and English, proposed the notion of "other thinking" described as primitive, pre-logical, savage, mystical, incapable of differentiating or analyzing phenomena, thus endowing abstract, "primitive art" with autonomous meaning.[63] This new idea of primitive artistic creation corresponded with the cultural relativism of American anthropology initiated in the writings of Franz Boas in the 1890s, which in turn resonated with contemporaneous writings promoting world art history (*Weltkunstgeschichte*).[64] Art historian Wilhelm Worringer introduced the concept of empathy (1907/8), now simply assuming the "psychic unity of mankind" and arguing that empathy was a precondition for understanding the artistic creations of an entirely different world.[65]

A key point of Juneja's analysis is that none of the individuals or events questioned the epistemological foundations of the colonialist knowledge they were complicit in generating. Furthermore, they shared a concern to *overlook* the transformative effects of colonialism on the societies through which they traveled literally and figuratively, often relying on print culture, museums, world fairs, and other forms of vicarious travel. In fact, the coevalness denied to Indigenous societies in the conventional narrative of Modernist art is now being restored by drawing on the research of scholars who, like Juneja herself, are showing that the histories of African, Indian, and other art considered formative for European modernists also embody *responses* to colonial modernity. For example, "primitive" African art was commissioned and produced in the colonies since the early twentieth century for Western markets. Objects ranging from bark paintings to canoes that salvage anthropologists such as Donald Thomson collected in the Australian outback in the 1930s and '40s were similarly made for him for to buy and collect.[66] Juneja developed the argument that "primitive" is a "migrant concept" through her research on the reception of European ideas by Indian art historians during an active period of decolonization and modern nation-state formation. The literature is extensive and even more diffused if analyses of "tourist art" are included.

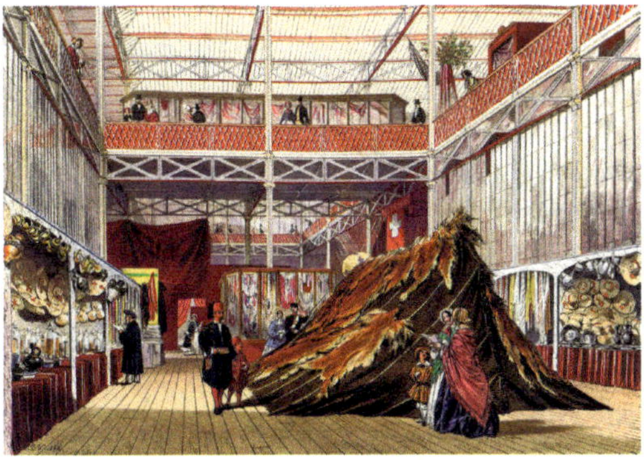

FIGURE 4.3 Joseph Nash, *Tunisia and Switzerland at the Great Exhibition*, color lithograph, Crystal Palace, London, 1851. incamerastock/Alamy Stock Photo.

Modernist art, cultural anthropology/ethnology, and art history are three expressions of the same problematic epistemology, crossing numerous geographical and temporal borders and subdisciplinary boundaries. It is imperative to unpack the paths of transculturation by practicing "epistemic disobedience," to cite Walter Mignolo.[67] For they bring to light, as Juneja emphasizes, deep epistemic ambivalences. Transculturation is also an emancipatory project for rewriting this history and the material record without feigning amnesia and without reproducing the power structures built into institutionally supported practices as scholars, curators, artists, critics, the public. Nineteenth-century German art histories and atlases of *Weltkunstgeschichte* designated material culture beyond the European fine arts of painting, sculpture, and architecture. In the decades surrounding the beginning of the twentieth century, leading scientists, progressive academics, curators, and other intellectuals promoted racial ideas as a means of educating the middle and working classes of the modern, secular nation-state. Many scholars have written about, and continue to study, the complicity of ethnographic museums and world fairs with colonialist enterprises that, at the same time, widened European conceptions of artmaking practices, beginning with the Great Exhibition at the Crystal Palace in London (1851) [Figure 4.3]. The notion of an educational practice based on careful observation and study of artifactual material came primarily from a left middle-class intelligentsia who believed that it was essential for museums to be seen as addressing a broad public. The concept of a national culture was, in fact, a construct that public museums, like the more ephemeral world fairs, made possible. At the same time, these forms of vicarious tourism had the inverse effect of accentuating the distance between Europeans and their counterparts elsewhere.

The binary structure contrasting primitive with civilized that identifies works of human manufacture directly with the mentality of their makers *and* the relationship of self to the world remained a constant for centuries, as did the Aristotelian distinction between human and animal art, even as the arguments expanded with new permutations and different emphases. Semper's *De Stil* (1861–1863) is informed by his experience of the London Great Exhibition (he also designed some of the pavilions in the Crystal Palace) and research in Paris before he moved to Zürich in 1855. Like Owen Jones' *Grammar of Ornament* (1856), Semper understood art as the creative principle shared by all humans that finds its purest expression as "ornament." Both publications remained seminal reading for artists and students of art and architecture for many decades.[68]

However, art continued to be explained in terms of the neo-Aristotelian theory of cognition that rational knowledge of the world begins with sense experience, with the sense of sight defined within the European tradition as the most noble of five senses. "Ornament" has been widely understood since the mid-nineteenth century as an abstract principle of design tied to the environment, regardless of the significance attributed to such "ornament" and "decoration" in other practices of artmaking with different signifying properties. Even when positive critical

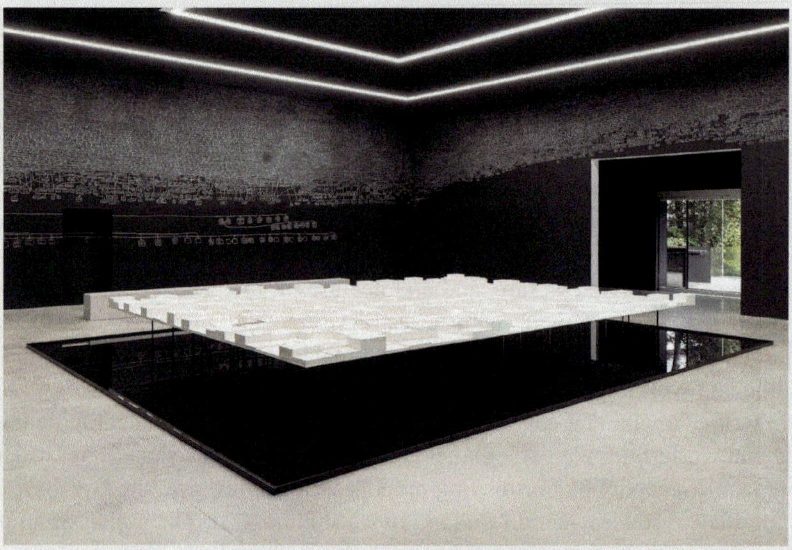

FIGURE 4.4 Archie Moore, *kith and kin*, 2024, ink on polyester, water, composite board, paint, aluminium, steel, pigment and clay crayon, methyl acetate. Venice installation. Australia Pavilion at the 60th International Art Exhibition of the Venice Biennale. Commissioner: Creative Australia. Curator: Ellie Buttrose. Photo: Andrea Rossetti, Courtesy The Commercial, Sydney. Winner of the Golden Lion, top prize.

The Brisbane-based Kamilaroi/Bigambul artist depicts his family tree of 3,484 people. More than 500 documents stacked on a table above a black reflective pool in the middle of the room record recent police brutality against Indigenous Australians. See further www.abc.net.au/news/2024-05-12/archie-moore-venice-biennale-up-close/103789292

> While the work in the pavilion is Archie's family it also includes and importantly speaks to the way that First Nations people consider the landscape, the waterways, the trees and all the animals as part of their kinship system as well. Archie's talking about his own family is very much entwined with the history of Australia that goes back 65,000 years, but he's also saying that everyone in the world is kin.

Ellie Buttrose, Curator, quoted in Rudi Bremer, et al., "Australia, according to Archie Moore," www.abc.net.au/news/2024-05-12/archie-moore-venice-biennale-up-close/103789292. (Accessed 20 September 2024.)

Both globalization and biennialization have their roots in nineteenth-century capitalism's competitive and colonial drives that figured most clearly in the world's fairs and universal exhibitions that developed in London in 1851 and spread across Europe, North America and Australasia in subsequent decades, culminating in the formation of the Venice Biennale and Pittsburgh's Carnegie Annual in the mid-1890s. As sites for social dialogue and cross-disciplinary exchange to contest what curator of *documenta* 11 (2002), Okwui Enwezor, called "the numbing logic of spectacular capitalism," these exhibitions suggest that the colonial-era format of the biennial could be transformed from within, redirected so as to regenerate local cultural infrastructure. Thus, biennials epitomize how the deep histories of colonialism could not be disavowed because they were central to connecting the cultures of the South through "the link of our tragedies," to reiterate Beatriz Bustos Oyanedel's words, and more importantly to finding ways to overcome them.

Okwui Enwezor, "On Mega-Exhibitions and the Antinomies of a Transnational Global Form," *Documents* 23 (spring 2004): 2–19, at 2. Cited by Andrew Gardner and Charles Green, "Biennials of the South on the Edges of the Global," *Third Text* 27/4 (2013): 442–455, at 43. www.tandfonline.com/doi/abs/10.1080/09528822.2013.810892. See the important discussion of Enwezor's *Documenta 11* (2002) by Charles Green and Anthony Gardner, *Biennials, Triennials, and Documenta: The Exhibitions that Created Contemporary Art* (Oxford: Wiley Blackwell, 2016), 183–206.

values were associated with abstract design, the same epistemology remained in place in assuming that other kinds of signifying practices were merely ornamental and decorative [Figure 4.5].

Avant-garde artists were also responsive to the newly published anthologies and facsimiles of the personal notebooks of Leonardo da Vinci, including his

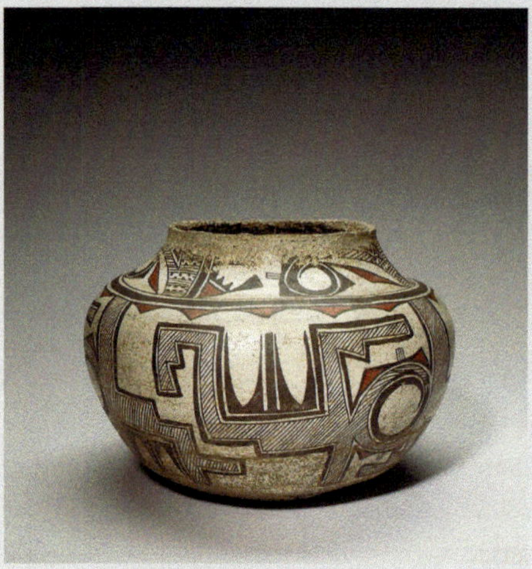

FIGURE 4.5 A'shiwi (Zuni) polyrchrome olla with "Rain Bird" design, c. 1880–95. Minneapolis, Minneapolis Institute of Art, bequest of Frank J. Sorauf 2014.97. Photo Minneapolis Institute of Art.

The bold graphic elements of the "rain bird' design occur in ceramics as early as 1000 CE. In the early nineteenth-century, the A'shiwi (Zuni) were among the first Pueblo communities to integrate these ancient designs into contemporary wares that linked New Mexico in the northernmost reach of New Spain to a global network of commerce. When pictorial conventions change, the same content may be carried in altered form. In this case, the abstract rain bird motif resonates with naturalistic bird designs derived from new European sources introduced after New Mexico became a US territory in 1848.

praise of the artist's active imagination and freedom to invent that had been eliminated from the *Libro di Pittura* by an editor aligned with the Catholic Reformation's narrow view of artistic license.[69] In the generation after Semper and Jones, interest in the creative process included writings by Conrad Fiedler (1876), Adolph von Hildebrand (1893), and Alois Riegl (1893–) who promoted the idea that "art," regardless of appearance, techniques, and materials, is a universal human category based on perception.[70] Translating Aristotle's theory of cognition and Kant's account of aesthetic judgment into a physiological account of the nervous system, these writings define perception as a cognitive function involving the subject's organization, identification, and interpretation of sensory information to understand their environment.[71] The conceptual basis of these theories lay in physiological explanations of aesthetic judgment by Hermann Lotze and others who revised Kant's notion of space as an a priori form of intuition.[72] Riegl's influential *Stilfragen: Grundlegungen zu einer Geschichte der Ornamentik/Problems of Style: Foundations for a History of Ornament* (1893) recast the earlier notion of "aesthetic" capacity (Baumgarten) or "ludic drive " (Friedrich Schiller) as the universal principle of a *Kunstwollen* (literally, will to make art). Riegl described a continuous history of ornament based on principles of design in competition with nature.

Modern ideas of art as synonymous with the creative process established many of the most fundamental premises about the relationship between ethnicity and style that were initially formulated in late nineteenth- and early twentieth-century attempts to establish the study of art on scientific methods and empirical evidence. Europeans had long defined themselves as destined to exploit the God-given resources of nature for the good of mankind. The ancient Greek idea that the first humans were hunter–gatherers was first applied to modern humans in the sixteenth century by Europeans based on perceived cultural absences.[73] The Indigenous peoples of the Americas were said to lack *techne*, lack agriculture, lack cities, lack both the technology and the desire to exploit their own natural resources. In the sixteenth century, Christian theories of human universality linked to cultural progress proliferated on the foundation of ancient authority to justify the seizure of Indigenous lands and material resources without concern for environmental damage. In the late nineteenth century, Indigenous arts were integrated into a "primitive art system" that included contemporary Australian Aboriginal and Inuit arts along with Paleolithic cave paintings from Europe and Africa. The category "Indian" (or *indigene*, indigenous, or native) had initially been imposed on many different contact-period groups by colonial settlers in the Americas because it simplified administrative procedures, writes Jorge Klor de Alva, who notes that "genetic and cultural mixing came to constitute the assumed distinct 'ethnicity' of almost every one of the American nations that had a large native population at contact." Yet the former parts of empires are not interchangeable: "Mexico is not another version of India, Brazil is not one more type of Indonesia, and Latinos in the US . . . are neither like Algerians in France, Pakistanis in Britain, or Palestinians in Israel."[74]

Precontact peoples identified themselves primarily by their ethnic or "national" names. The question of naming for Indigenous peoples, their descendants, and communities for whom the violence of colonization remains very real, writes British historian Caroline Dodds Pennock in an extensive account of the inconsistent terminology, "is far from homogeneous in their attitudes and outlooks." "Savage" is a racial slur that she, as a white, privileged academic, deliberately inverts in her book title, *On Savage Shores*, to retell the history of European imperialism from the standpoint of Indigenous peoples by "centering their voices and perspectives."[75] In recent years, the term "Indigenous art" has become increasingly popular with artists around the world and the academic community, write the authors of a forthcoming study charting the use of the term to describe Inuit and Australian Aboriginal art since the nineteenth century.[76] Indigenous artists have started to promote Indigenous–to–Indigenous dialogue across the globe as a radical critique of the concept of "primitive art" which, as I have argued, was used to assert that Indigenous groups were at a very early stage of cultural development, "living fossils" descended from prehistoric European populations. The strategic use of identities as effects of power, rather than thinking of them as fixed entities bound by common traits or practices, is a pragmatic maneuver to advocate collectively for common needs, writes Klor de Alva (citing Gayatri Spivak and Derrida) who proposes (as I am also advocating) tethering the term to the poststructuralist rejection of linear, teleological historical processes rather than the condition of dependency and oppositional binaries of inclusion/exclusion that characterize the colonial condition.

The category "primitive art" began to be questioned in the 1950s but it was still used until the 1980s, when, as discussed above, the term was widely denounced as Eurocentric. This new critical awareness led to various alternatives such as "First Nations" and "First Peoples" that are still considered acceptable and widely used. The term "Indigenous art," although not universally accepted, has been embraced by Indigenous artists who have formed transnational networks across the world following successive waves of decolonization accompanied by reconciliation and treaty-making processes. Based on their common experience of colonialism and appropriation, self-identified Indigenous artists are redefining their cultural heritage on their own terms linked to the environment.[77] As a powerful critique of the concept of "primitive art," the modern idea of "Indigenous art" acknowledges that "the variety of Indigenous arts around the world cannot be reduced to a single label or a single explanatory principle."[78]

Simply expanding the number or kinds of objects studied within a European/North American-centered art history have proven insufficient to address some of the most urgent contemporary questions and challenges that Nancy Marie Mithlo, a Chiricahua Apache curator, writer, and cultural anthropologist, articulates in the following terms:

> an Indigenous rejection of non-Native contexts such as museums, cultural centers, galleries, and scholarly texts—contexts that imbue fine arts with the Western values of individualism, commercialism, objectivism, and competition, as framed by an elitist point of reference. . . . A rejection of the term 'art' is then a rejection of Western culture as capitalist, patriarchal, and, ultimately, shallow, one that does not value the central principles of Indigenous identity, such as land, language, family, and spirituality. A refusal to be co-opted into a more narrow definition of what is an intrinsically more holistic enterprise is also a refusal to be named. It is an effort toward self-determination. This distinction between the naming and the named is of course a distinction of power—who controls the avenues of expression and communication.[79]

The "no word for art" orientation was reified in the *Oxford History of Art* series, in which Janet Berlo and Ruth Phillips observe, "When speaking of historical Native objects, the statement is often made that Native languages have no exact equivalent for the post-Renaissance Western term 'art,'" noting that "in Native traditions the purely material and visual features of an object are not necessarily the most important in establishing its relative value, as they have come to be in the

West."[80] The problem of inclusion/exclusion in the practice of art history is treated similarly by the Maori art historian Ngarino Ellis who offers that

> the practice of Art History has been alive and kicking in communities across the globe throughout time. Certainly, the terms, methodologies, artists, artworks, and forms are distinct, but the goal of understanding history and culture through analysis and discussion of the art of those communities is the same.[81]

Ellis rejects the "patriarchy and Eurocentrism" inherent in European-based art historical classifications of Maori art in favor of choosing "our own methodologies to come to understand our own practices of Art History," as has been the case among Maori writers, curators, artists, and academics since the 1960s.[82]

Ontological Openings

As Derrida observed about the nature of structures, what counts as origin depends on how the categories are construed. It is a hermeneutic conundrum long discussed by historians. The question of what constitutes the earliest evidence was understandably also important to those nineteenth-century Eurocentric models of world art once considered progressive whose value is still debated today. This section takes another look at these nineteenth-century narratives from an ontological perspective.

Bredekamp, Penny, and others find Kugler's ideas compelling now because they were not limited to the more contentious question of what "phase of human development marks the beginning of what we can genuinely speak of as art" that characterized art history after c. 1900.[83] Nonetheless, Kugler began his history with intentionally collected stones as the earliest known evidence of "the mental penetration of material that leads to form" arranged in a manner that achieves "the more general impressions of sublimity, proportion, and even harmony."[84] Others thinking along similar lines, from Kugler's contemporary Alexander von Humboldt (1759–1869) to Heinrich Klotz who worked recently with the excavations of ruins of Catal Höyük, have characterized the stone handaxe as an "image" that established the human species as *homo faber* for its "artificiality, its harmonious regularity, and its symmetry": according to Klotz, "the artificiality of the stone axe is also art, and its functionality is also beauty."[85] Horst Bredekamp cites these and other, more recently discovered ancient examples of form-consciousness, including the remarkable discovery of a carved ivory figure from a cave in Hohlstein-Stadel, featuring a mythical creature that is part human and part animal, datable c. 32,000 years ago, and a series of forty-one Nassarius shells with drilled holes showing signs of wear that must have been the components of a jewelry chain, recovered from Blombos Cave on the coastline of the southern tip of Africa, datable c. 75,000 years ago, which "shifts the question of the birth of the individual" into the archaic human record.[86]

Despite the protestation that they were "not marking the beginning of what we can genuinely speak of as art," Kugler, his contemporaries, and successors were creating exactly such a history conceived in an expanded field to include all of humanity. Less happily, these nineteenth-century practitioners also ranked cultural artifacts in a developmental hierarchy ranging from primitive to civilized. As I already noted, Kugler treated ancient Amerindian monuments as an intermediate stage between the "childhood" of humanity and "true art." The perniciousness of embracing such equations between "primitive" and "child," only become obvious when we also consider their appearance in nineteenth-century racial theory, where the modern adult "primitive" was widely believed to be as evolved as the white European child on the basis of his artistic productions and assumed aesthetic capabilities.

If the earliest surviving evidence of made artifacts on the planet were the starting point for a *non-totalizing* planetary history of art and material culture, pride of place would still be given to that strange enigma of prehistory called a handaxe that also fascinates Bredekamp [Figure 4.6]. The size and shape of the "handaxe" fits perfectly into the palm and outstretched fingers of an adult hand; it consists of two convex faces, artificially shaped by removing flakes from an original bulb-shaped core, using a technique that exploits the tendency of flint to break off in slivers at the point of impact when struck at an oblique angle near a protruding edge.[87] The *bi-face*, as it is called in the technical literature, is most often described as a "general purpose tool," but its actual function cannot be determined (it is definitely not an axe). Throughout the anthropological literature, this class of artifact is appreciated for its formal beauty, praised for its "artificiality, its harmonious regularity, and its symmetry." The descriptions conform to the Aristotelian model of Kugler's remarks on the origins of art linking "form" with the fabrication of

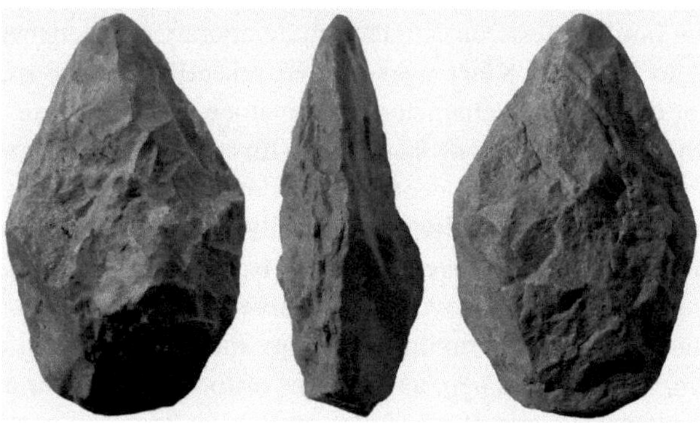

FIGURE 4.6 Archulean "Handaxe." From a superficial site in Valladolid Province, Spain, valley of the Douro River. Wiki/José-Manuel Benito Álvarez (España).

beautiful objects as evidence of the maker's mental capacity. Prehistoric specimens were first discovered in the 1830s at the site of Saint Acheul in northern France (hence the official name of the *bi-face* is "the Acheulean"), but they have since been found in Europe, Africa, the near East, and South Asia, dated to periods spanning well over a million years, with the oldest specimens recovered from East African sites dating 1.7–1.6 million years ago, and the most recent artifacts manufactured in Europe c. 128,000 years ago.

What can account for the stability of this artifact type spanning three continents and enduring more than a million years, extending far into the archaic human past? In contrast to Kugler and Bredekamp, Ingold argues that understanding the enigma of the *bi-face* requires abandoning explanatory models which hold that the mental design precedes the manufacture of the artifact, that "form" is imprinted on matter like a signet ring on a wax tablet, to use Aristotle's own analogy for the way images are recorded in the imagination (*De anima* 412b17). This explanation of the *bi-face* also depends on the Aristotelian assumption of categorical differences between man and animal which posit that the human brain is uniquely able to envision forms in advance of their realization in material form. Such a distinction is, moreover, ill-suited to describe the ways in which humans and non-humans alike come to know what they know "through a process of growth and guided discovery." The processes of the individual organism as it matures, its ontogenesis, is primary, Ingold writes, so beings are better described as becomings whose life task is to create oneself, "weaving a kind of tapestry that is never complete."[88]

Ingold's alternative explanation of the Archeulean does not rely on Western metaphysics. Instead, he describes the design of the *bi-face* in terms of process. The design grows as "an emergent outcome of the process of flake removal" resulting in an instrument that fits neatly into the palm of a human hand. Ingold's account conceives the process of making as a flow, a journey, an event understood in Deleuzian/Bergsonian terms as duration. Understanding design as emerging during the event of fabrication provides an elegant solution to the puzzle posed by the formal stability of the *bi-face* across such a vast temporal span and geographical range. Tool and yet not-tool, human and yet non-human, these artificially shaped rocks depend upon a complex interplay of forces both internal and external to the material: "to understand the form as emergent is to recognize that it is generated in the very unfolding of this force field . . . the properties of the material are directly implicated in the form-generating process."[89] So it appears that the ur-object of the planet's material cultural history can be explained without depending on the problematic Aristotelian assumption that a mental image precedes its material fabrication. This is not to say, as some have argued, that the "handaxe" is a product of instinct, but that the pragmatic relationship of *Homo erectus* to the environment led to producing the same kind of artifact in many locations over a long period of time.

Kugler was the most widely read and influential scholar in the field of general art history anywhere in Europe in the nineteenth century. His *Handbuch* was imitated by others and translated into English, where, in concert with the ideas of Giovanni Morelli, it played an influential role in the formation of the London National Gallery collection under the direction of Charles Eastlake (who translated Kugler into English) and the establishment of modern methods of art historical description and museological practice by Anglophone and Germanophone writers. By the end of the nineteenth century, "visual art" was defined as a universal phenomenon by many influential writers who retained the formalist orientation of racial theories of cultural evolution and their underlying assumption that the defining characteristics of different nationalities could be accessed visually, above all in their artistic productions.[90]

The shifting, unstable senses of *techne* between the sixteenth and nineteenth century await further study. To stay with the key text, Kugler's *Handbuch* evolved in subsequent editions with the assistance of his student Jacob Burckhardt, whose cultural history of the Renaissance (1860) is one of the principal texts that established the category Renaissance at the center of the modern discipline of art history. Burckhardt provided additional text and supervised the illustrations for the second edition of Kugler's *Handbuch* (1848).[91] The collaboration between Kugler and Burckhardt extending over many years provides an unusual opportunity to eavesdrop on the construction of modern sub-disciplinary boundaries drawn along cultural lines that, in the final analysis, granted European culture the upper hand.

Kugler is a watershed figure for establishing art history as a unified field of study, given that the distinction between the utilitarian and leisure arts is the Aristotelian foundation on which accounts of differences between the mechanical and liberal arts were built for a millennium. The same distinction remained the basis for the categorical differences between "art" and "artifact" that are embedded in the modern disciplines of art history and cultural anthropology respectively. Current efforts to rehabilitate the entire genre of *Weltkunstgeschichte*, point to their inclusiveness and lack of hierarchy. Still, it would be self-defeating to take their understanding of "world art" at face value if the objective is to develop an inclusive (but not totalizing) history of material culture, which is the subject of the next section.

Worlding Cosmopolitanism

At the end of the nineteenth century, works of human manufacture were systematically defined as products of perception and objects of vision by a loosely affiliated group of Germanophone art historians who asserted that "vision" has its own history, preserved in works of art. Conrad Fiedler (1876) for example, defined the perceptual powers of the entire human race in terms of the assumed visualness of art as a "peculiar power of the human mind" which is "forced to the attempt by his very nature."[92] One of the main advantages to treating "visuality" and categories associated with it as specific cultural constructs and not as universals valid for all space and time, as Fiedler and his colleagues did, is that such exercises raise awareness of how cultural values are projected onto whatever subject matter is at hand. Formalist concerns with the visual appearance of works of art emerged in the late nineteenth-century writings of art historians who borrowed concepts from the social and natural sciences.[93] They promoted the idea that art is universal because it is visual, because sight and perception are capabilities that all [physically unimpaired] humans share alike. On this basis, Heinrich Wölfflin (1864–1945) articulated widely influential arguments about collective identity in terms such as "Germanic," "Mediterranean," "classical," "Late antique," and "Romantic," which were said to define the "essential" content of specific works of art.[94] The visual characteristics of works of art were held to manifest collective psychology but, as his muddled distinctions suggest, the categories "race," epoch, and national identity were often interchanged and conflated as they had been in the eighteenth century before racial science and the modern nation-state gave these categories distinct referential designations.

Dissatisfied with both earlier cosmopolitan views that privileged Greek antiquity and the singular focus on documents in the practice of *Kunstgeschichte* (art history) by their contemporaries, this contingent of art historians and their followers developed the concept of *Kunstwissenschaft*, translatable as the scientific study of art (bearing in mind that science has a broader meaning in German). They practiced methods alternating between the historically and empirically specific, on the one hand, and the abstracted and aesthetic, on the other. The proponents of *Kunstwissenschaft* were sympathetic to empirical studies but they were not fully positivistic (i.e., looking for principles of causality based on direct observation measured with instruments), precisely because they were committed to the study of introspective and intuitive processes. However, they emulated the way research scientists conducted experiments under controlled laboratory conditions focused on observable phenomena. Wölfflin sought out terminology and notions of synchronic comparison and diachronic sequencing, including ideas borrowed from racial science, in his aspiration to write a formalist history of art "without names."[95] What Wöllflin called *Rassencharakter* was something held to be the source of all structures of feeling and thought, naturally determined by blood and intellect, a shared assumption over and above the individual.

Giovanni Morelli (1816–1891), widely considered the founder of formal stylistic analysis, proposed "race" as a criterion for connoisseurs. Jaynie Anderson and others have documented how Morelli's early scientific interests were directed to comparative anatomy and paleontology.[96] In 1837, Morelli registered in a course on comparative anatomy at the University of Erlangen – his professor Rudolf Wagner had studied with Georges Cuvier in Paris. Cuvier, who described comparative anatomy as "the jewel of our epoch," is an important source of Morelli's notion of the "organic" nature of an artist's style. Morelli wrote a dissertation on the history of physiology following Cuvier's principle of the "correlation of the parts" in the organization of the whole form, in which each form was unique and perfect in itself at the same time that it belonged to the whole. In contemporary terms, we might understand Cuvier's correlation between part and whole as scalar or fractal in nature: the structure of the whole is conveyed in the structure of each part within it.

Morelli (like Edward Tylor) adapted theory developed to describe natural organisms to the classification and description of human artifacts, potentially a problematic move. The measurements of faculties based on the hard facts of comparative anatomy rested in actuality upon the interpretation of equivocal signs.[97] Cuvier was especially interested in the correlation between the structure of the nervous system and intelligence – he reasoned that the more complex, higher degrees of centralization correlated with greater degrees of intelligence and choice.[98] Morelli was not interested in hierarchies of intelligence in the same way as Cuvier and other racial scientists were, but similar assumptions about the correlation of external signs to inward nature are implicit in his interests in what can be seen and inferred from the close study of concrete specimens.[99] On the biological model of an organism that develops in accordance with its environment, Morelli believed that the work of art could be understood as responsive to climate and geography.[100] His understanding that the painting of each region had its own independent pattern of development was based on the assumption that people of various regions of Italy were of different "races," each with their own distinctive characteristics due to their physical environment. The character of each area's art was held to be similar to the "character" of its people and, on this basis, Morelli compared regional styles to local spoken dialects. His morphological approach assumed that the relevant factors in determining attribution were physical contiguities between cultural productions and the inward states of their makers. He treated the relationship between the artist and his work as an indexical relationship as direct as that between a foot and its footprint. According to Morelli, each object is rooted in the artistic personality of its maker, which is in turn rooted in a specific geographical location.

Morelli's empirical observations linking art, artist, and environment were designed to assign every object a specific, unique address in space and time. His explanatory model is highly reductive in that it does not take into account that artists traveled and appropriated elements from various sources, regardless of origin, or that workshops were often in contact with one another rather than developing along separate trajectories. Morelli believed that the work of art could be understood as responsive to climate and geography while remaining unaffected by social or political conditions. He conflated evolutionary deep time with the short time span of animal life and freely adapted ideas from racial theory to suit his practice of connoisseurship. Morelli's assumptions about the causal relationship between genetic and climatic determinations of "race" and "art" identify his ideas with historical climate theory. What is still of contemporary interest is Morelli's interest in individuation through the use of material evidence. Morelli's *Kunstwissenschaft* kindled an ambitious younger generation of art historians, especially in Vienna, where a new "school" of art history emerged at the end of the nineteenth century.[101]

The history of the idea of style discernible by formal analysis is complicated and I have only briefly sketched Morelli's basic premises to make the longstanding affiliation with racial/climate theory clear. In the early twentieth century, when avant-garde movements rejected the academic art system and embraced "primitive art," the same epistemology remained in place – the critical values were merely inverted, much as they had been in different circumstances during the sixteenth century under pressure from Church reform. By the 1970s, many art historians had a vexed relationship with the discipline's foundational concept of style. Since the 1980s, "visual culture" studies, journals, departments, websites, and so on have given the category a material presence far beyond the disciplinary debates that originated the terminology. The lingering effects of the widespread but deeply problematic assumption that "vision" is a natural rather than a cultural category haunt current efforts to imagine history as a pluriverse rather than a universe defined on European terms.

In bringing this Fugue to a close and opening the discussion that follows, I would like to suggest how an ecological theory of all kinds of material culture including performance practices might be configured to foreground what some linguists and anthropologists call "multimodal integration of the body and the environment." Products of cultural interaction are a focus of research today partly because they raise fundamental questions about the nature of signification and visual communication, encouraging theoretical concern with the unstable and shifting signification of signs. One of the main advantages to treating "visuality" and other categories associated with the "five senses" as specific cultural constructs and not as universals valid for all space and time is that such exercises raise awareness of how cultural values are projected onto whatever subject matter is at hand. Indigenous Australian storytelling provides researchers with an excellent case study of how perceptual activity works by integrating the senses within the field of movement. Anthropologist Nancy Munn's groundbreaking study of Warlpiri iconography extensively documented a highly elaborated, well-defined system of signification, in paintings and body ornament, storytelling, dance, and so on.[102] The sand story is built up of a series of visual frames or scenes that cycle in the manner of a movie in multi-modal face-to-face interactions. Following Munn, linguist Jennifer Green, a specialist in Arandic spoken and signed languages, studies how closely integrated the senses of touch and sight, sound and movement are in women's sand drawings. She prefers to speak of these performances as "communicative events" that involve "multimodal semiotic systems." Using relational terms such as vocal/auditory and kinesic/visual modalities involved in storytelling in the sand, Green considers all contrastive and variant aspects of the "sensory" signal – sound, touch, visual material, and so on – to study distinctions between conventional sign and spontaneous gesture that are far from straightforward.[103]

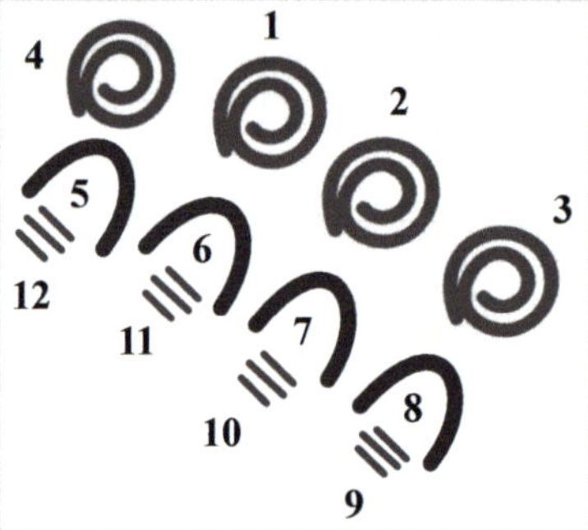

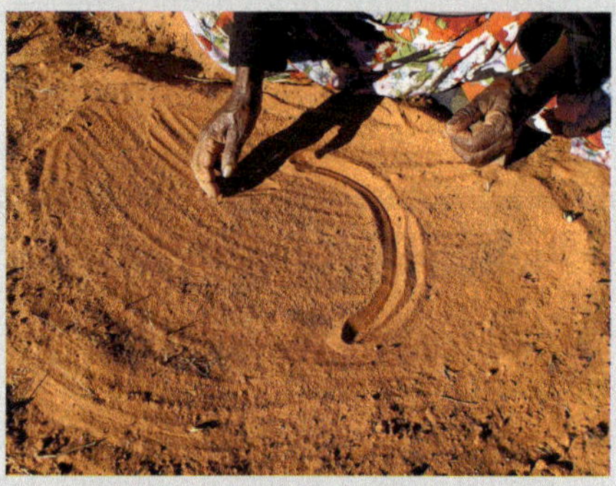

FIGURE 4.7 AND 4.8 (Left) Signs used in storytelling. Jennifer Green, *Drawn from the Ground*, 168, fig. 6.1. In a story about collecting desert raisins, sequential elements 1–4 represent "shade," followed by 5–8, representing "women," and 9–12, representing "children."; (Right) Eileen Pwerrerl Campbell narrating an Anmatyerr sand story, Ti Tree, Northern Territory, Australia, 2012. Photo J. Green.

An understanding of a multi-modal event relies on a complex decoding of conventional symbols, contextual cues, and so on. The performance of Arandic sand stories (called *tyepety* in some Arandic languages) is a traditional form of visual storytelling in which co-speech graphics form an essential part of a composite utterance. Sand stories are a form of rhetorical art in which a skilled narrator incorporates multiple semiotic systems and uses the potentials within these systems to great creative effect. A sand story performance is multimodal to its core, and it exists in the framework of several interlocking spatial fields.

Jennifer Green, *Drawn from the Ground: Sound, Sign, and Inscription in Central Australian Sand Stories*, 2014.

We are still addressing the question of what it means to historicize vision. The "visual" is not exclusively a European prerogative and, by the same token, another culture's "visual" is still not European. Moreover, it requires careful analysis of images, material objects, and broader cultural contexts of use to see processes of inscription, accommodation, resistance, reframing, and so on at work in the "event" of cultural interaction. A growing number of studies take on the visual/visuality from extra-European points of view. In one important contribution, Latin Americanists Jeanette Favrot Peterson and Dana Leibsohn co-edited a collection of case studies, *Visuality across Cultures* (2012), that put into question European understandings of visuality and our "stereotypes of the

Other" as they are connected to political actualities. For example, in a chapter that has since been expanded into a book, Patrick Thomas Hajovsky studied Mexica representations of the sacred ruler Moctezuma II.[104] He argues that the fundamental paradigm or model operating in Mesoamerican thought acknowledges only one principle of being, thus the concept that sight resembles smells, which in turn resemble sounds, was intended to convey "phenomenological associations between essences" that can be accessed through language and visual art. Nahuatl metaphors and metonyms go beyond the visual and aural registers to convey a synaesthetic paradigm very different from Western conceptions of the discreetly functioning special senses. Within a Mesoamerican context, multi-sensorial experiences convey the fundamental principle of being, which missionaries like Diego Durán and mestizo historians such as Fernando de Alvarado Tezozomoc (mis)understand in terms commensurate with European notions of historical truth.

In the convergence of Indigenous American, European, African, and Asian cultures, "coloniality" and "visuality" together emphasize the burgeoning commerce and collecting of material culture since the sixteenth century. Not only are conventional labels of artistic identity often rendered irrelevant in the face of such massive and impersonal cultural collaborations, but the scale of trade and hierarchies of social power implicated are mind-boggling. To give a quantified example, as many as ten million Chinese porcelains were sold in Brazil alone between the sixteenth and nineteenth centuries – Chinese pottery was so plentiful that they were given to slaves, used as chamber pots, and their shards were plastered on church steeples and domes.[105]

Peripatetic lifestyles and transcultural processes characterize artists as well as their art, even if individual identities are difficult to document. Nor does cultural mixing always result in visual features, as Carolyn Dean and Dana Leibsohn emphasize in a widely cited essay on the terminology in use to describe visual culture in Colonial Spanish America that rejects the term "hybrid" on these grounds.[106] Some forms of cultural interaction elicited no comments that have been preserved in the historical record – such as the absence of response by Indigenous people to the mixing itself. Meanwhile, other aspects, such as collecting practices, have left varied and often contradictory traces in archives and museums. More complex than either of these possibilities is what Dean and Leibsohn call the "deceit of visibility" that has effaced the presence of those dispossessed by colonial authority. The effacement during the initial process of contact is repeated in modern historical accounts that deny the existence of Indigenous activity altogether, for example in building practices in the colonial world, unless the result "looks" indigenous.[107] "Visuality" as opposed to the universalizing term "visual" is a critical category well-positioned to include the study of those traces of mixing that are not apparent on the surface, and to articulate the historical processes of misrecognition that favor political and social hierarchies of power.

First and foremost, the construction of knowledge itself – its production and consumption – aligns *Writing Borderless Histories of Art* with interdisciplinary studies in the history of science that explore ways in which knowledge was more holistically conceived before modern distinctions between art, science, and religion in the eighteenth century. By looking at the intersection of different cultural practices, stressing their complex intersections, multiple filters, and numerous transfers demonstrates that nothing studied in the context of global networks of commerce is a binary operation. The importance of studying visuality in the *longue durée* with adequate cultural grounding is essential to understanding the complex, recursive processes of cultural interaction, inscription, transformation, appropriation, and so on that self-reflexive historical writing requires.

The formal vocabulary of art history, like modernist concerns with the language of the text that developed around the same time, rendered these assumptions implicit. In the formative stages of the modern discipline of art history that have been the subject of this Fugue, the principles of evolution were widely discussed and utilized to provide an explanatory framework for cultural differences. Scientific theories of racial difference, that is, the division of humans into biological groups, appeared promising in part because they explained cultural difference at the collective level through the empirical study of individual specimens. At the end of the nineteenth century, nearly all human, behavioral, and biomedical sciences had adopted race, the dominant scientific paradigm of their day, as a primary explanatory concept. Regardless of which discipline claimed it for its object domain, writers posited direct (one-to-one) connections between genetic, environmental, and cultural identity. That reductive, representational account of identity remains one of the most intractable epistemological problems and ethical challenges for revising the discipline of art history.

The critical question has always been *how* to define the relationship between culture and nature. Our modernities and their museologies are *by definition* bound up with one another. As Donald Preziosi has observed, the relationship between them is commonly conceived as an imaginary fulfillment of some essential nature we would wish ourselves to be descended from but which is now obscured, lost, or stolen: a past to which we will always have a relationship simultaneously centrifugal and centripetal. Social existence in the modern nation-state and even more so in its contemporary transnational corporatist permutations involves an inherently unstable and fragile *triangulation* between the present moment which is always slipping into the past, its past, and its future, all of which are subject to interpretation.[108]

This grammar of time parsed into past, present, and future is itself a cultural construct. The fundamental problem of conceiving art as a universal category in the most general and far-reaching sense is the seemingly inherent presumption that art is or can only be a *representational artifact* in the literal sense. However, no matter how strongly anyone insists that things "represent" who and what we imagine ourselves truly to be, something will always be missing. Ecological approaches must now originate from the position of what is *missing*, but lack of coverage was never the only problem with the Eurocentric paradigm of art. Many solutions to the perceived problems have in fact perpetuated the same problems but under different guises. They invariably share a fundamental thesis – that art is primarily a *representation* and that museums are as "natural" as the "specimens" they preserve, rather than an institution for the construction, legitimization, and maintenance of cultural realities. In such a world, the question of "representation" (adequate or otherwise) is, to say the least, very complex.[109]

Contemporary critical concepts of cosmopolitanism as "worlding," initially derived from Heidegger's term for creating one's own worlds of meaning, significance, and interpretation, distance themselves from the historiography I have been discussing in this Fugue.[110] The contemporary concept of cosmopolitanism is opposed to philosophies that make ontological assumptions about the world or cosmos and how to live together. Instead, they offer "a democratisation of the subject position of the cosmopolitan . . . [to show how] an engagement with world is built up from relationships and meanings that are socially and subjectively localized."[111] "Worlding" from the perspective of creolization theory as it first emerged in Caribbean studies redefines what it might mean to live in the world from the standpoint of colonized "natives" as they rise up and reclaim their lands and their human dignity. Creolization always entails questions of power and issues of entanglement between power and its others in uneven terrain.[112] Debates initiated by Caribbeanists on cultural heterogeneity have centered on the notion of creolization as "forced transculturation" arising in concrete social, economic, political, and cultural conditions. In creolization, to cite Stuart Hall, the Jamaican-born founding member of the Birmingham School of Cultural Studies, "the process of 'fusion' occurs in circumstances of massive disparities of power and the exercise of a brutal cultural dominance."[113]

The process of "creolization," now extended to many other cultural geographies, is a concept developed in the writings of the Freudian psychoanalyst turned political philosopher and revolutionary activist, Frantz Fanon (1925–1961).[114] Born in Martinique, educated in Europe, Fanon used his privileged education and social status to speak for the oppressed. He embraced the roles of hybridity (according to his definition, humans are simultaneously storytelling and biological beings) and creolization (stressing cultural continuities, not binary oppositions). Creolization theory builds non-assimilationist connections across cultures and understands the human in terms of praxis, to cite Sylvia Wynter.[115] Fanon's call to decolonize societies by creating new literatures has been taken up by artists and intellectuals around the world. Maori scholar Linda Tuhiwai Smith has written *Decolonizing Methodologies* to support Indigenous research agendas and resurgent Indigenous sovereignty movements that will not reproduce the dehumanizing effects that have been the subject of my critical analysis throughout this book (so far).[116]

For some time, live performance and collective art practices have also been interrogating heteronymic identity, institutional authority, and conventional

Western notions of the autonomous [sovereign, singular] artist in ways aligned with the understanding of humanness as praxis, as the extensive work of Amelia Jones, her students, and followers exemplify.[117] As writers from different subaltern positions across the arts and humanities insist, the world cannot be reduced to a mere resource if subject and object are deeply interconnected. Such an approach requires that whatever the object of knowledge is, it is treated as an actor and an agent, not a passive screen, ground, or resource: the world encountered in knowledge projects is an active entity whose boundaries are not fixed.[118] "Worlding" in this sense acknowledges the ongoing contemporary effects of the violent past in an emancipatory framework. Indigenous ontologies offer useful paradigms for questioning the division between the biological and social realms as long as the history of colonization as a process that dispossessed Indigenous peoples and their lands is taken into account. The "ecological Indian" was a largely fictitious symbol of responsible environmentalism born in the counterculture of the 1960s, writes Dina Gilio-Whitaker, a member of the Colville Confederated Tribes in northeastern Washington state. She studies decolonization and environmental justice through a scholarly framework known as "Indigenized Environmental Justice." Gilio-Whitaker credits more extensive dialogue, better education about harmful stereotypes, and laws that protect tribal sovereignty for contributing to closer working relationships between environmentalists and Native Americans today.[119]

Situated "planetarity" in the visual and performing arts means to think globally and act locally or regionally. It means defining the position from which one speaks in order to identify the blind spots of historical disciplinary formations from different angles and disciplinary backgrounds as "decolonizing art historical knowledge and replacing binary epistemological models . . . with more relational approaches focusing on contacts, flows, and circulations, as well as global relations of production."[120] [see Figure 4.9]

Cultural memories tie the immediate community to the outside world in multifaceted ways. Every case is different, but many kinds of individual and collaborative efforts in the arts are transforming the past into a new reality that includes the more than human and recognizes the enduring cosmopolitan principles of exchange and hospitality in a transcultural *and* decolonizing framework. Without invoking universalizing schemes or even unified worlds, the objective is to "allow us to live together as the global tribe we have become" by respecting difference and once again embracing multiple forms of identification, to cite philosopher Kwame Anthony Appiah's appeal to the ethics of cosmopolitanism.[121]

"Cosmopolitanism" in Appiah's sense, it should be noted, has been contested for coming from a personal position of extreme social privilege in Ashanti and British colonial society in Ghana. By contrast, the exploitation of colonial subjects and destruction of their lifeways, environments, and material resources since the initial phase of economic globalization is the historical basis for what anthropologist James Clifford calls "discrepant cosmopolitanism," an involuntary form of cosmopolitanism and economic globalization "from below."[122] The discussion throughout this book is intended to show that the critical examination of the historical discourse on art has a lot to offer for rethinking the planetary human community not as singular, as universalism was defined from the sixteenth to the nineteenth century and beyond, but grounded in many different, intersecting local and regional worlds that can resist economic globalization and the coloniality of knowledge historically associated with it.

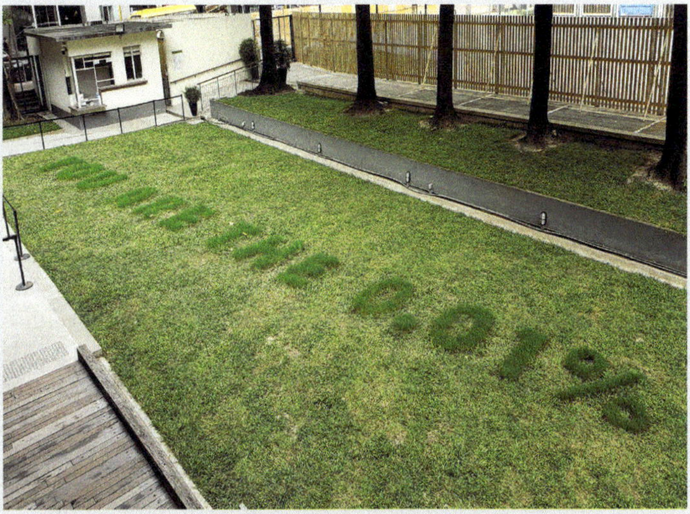

FIGURE 4.9 Zheng Bo, *YOU ARE THE 0.01%*, 2019, living installation at Oil Street Art Space, Hong Kong. Photo courtesy of the artist.

How can we inhabit the planet with other species in a conscious manner? Zheng Bo is one among a growing number of artists in the Sinophone world who investigate different forms of cohabitation and interspecies relationships to consider what planetary thinking means in relation to being locally situated. He uses grass as an organic medium to create a living sculpture of the shockingly small number of humans (0.01% of the earth's biomass) that stands in complete disproportion to our disastrous impact on Earth. Our symposium focused on artistic practices regarding cohabitation as a spatially defined, interspecies related response to this challenge in the greater Chinese region by questioning the discursive and institutionalized power of nationalist, regionalist, and civilizational framings in the arts.

Franziska Koch with Cila Brosius and Nora Wölfing, *Cohabitation – Worlding the Sinophonecene and Planetary Aesthetics in Contemporary Art*. 2nd International Gathering of the Research Network for Modern and Contemporary Chinese Art (ReNetMoCoCA). 3 June 2023. Online, co-hosted by the Heidelberg Centre for Transcultural Studies and Heinrich-Heine-Universität Düsseldorf, and forthcoming book.

In many communities, the word "museum" is a reminder of what has been lost to Indigenous and other colonized peoples, not what has been preserved. As both a scholar and a museum director with over forty years of professional experience, Ruth B. Phillips has been deeply engaged with First Nations communities and artists in Canada and beyond as a key shaper of new curatorial practices and institutional cultures. Advocating for a case-by-case approach attentive to local contexts, she has raised the fundamental question of whether the revived ethos of cosmopolitan values signaled by Appiah supports the Indigenization of museums or serves neo-imperial attempts to defend their current holdings.[123] She urges all sides with vested interests to take advantage of opportunities for cross-cultural connections by conceiving of these objects not as "cultural property" but in Indigenous terms as ambassadors with "the capacity to forge new ties with peoples in distant lands" through loans, traveling exhibitions, websites, exchanges between people including conferences, and "through ways of sharing that we have not yet invented."

Phillips presents the case of a chief's robe made by the Mi'kmaq of Canada, legally acquired by a Canadian writer and amateur ethnologist who emigrated to Australia and bequeathed his notes and extensive collection of North American Indigenous materials to what is now the Melbourne Museum in Melbourne, Australia. Modern-day Mi'kmaq initially requested the loan of their ceremonial regalia which incorporates traditional techniques and designs with symbolic associations fabricated in manufactured materials. However, because the request invoked neither illegality nor sacredness nor the rubric of cultural property, it fell into a grey area that does not meet the legal criteria established during the early 1990s for the repatriation of Indigenous artifacts – categories of illegality, sacrality, and cultural patrimony that many Indigenous people find either too restrictive or not comprehensive enough.

A clear claim for rightful possession was legally necessary to repatriate the regalia to a specific modern-day band in Canada, which is different from the circumstances that existed when the ceremonial outfit was made. As Phillips carefully documents, the repatriation process entailed extensive provenance research and a complex balancing act to consider the needs of the pluralist societies in which we all live today. There is extensive circumstantial evidence but no consensus on the provenance, yet all the stakeholders agreed that the Mi'kmaq people have rights to their regalia. The dialogue involved Mi'kmaq Chiefs and museum curators in both Canada and Australia. In 2023, after twenty years of negotiation, the Melbourne Museum voluntarily returned the legally acquired ceremonial outfit permanently to the first Mi'kmaq facility built to modern museum standards, the Millbrook Cultural and Heritage Centre whose mission is to "communicate to the public the history of the Mi'kmaq nation." The fact that these negotiations succeeded establishes a precedent for other First Nation peoples and museums caught in legal tangles that reduce belonging to property rights, essentialize identity, and encourage exclusive claims to ownership in this case regarding a cultural heritage that belongs *with* all the Mi'kmaq people.[124]

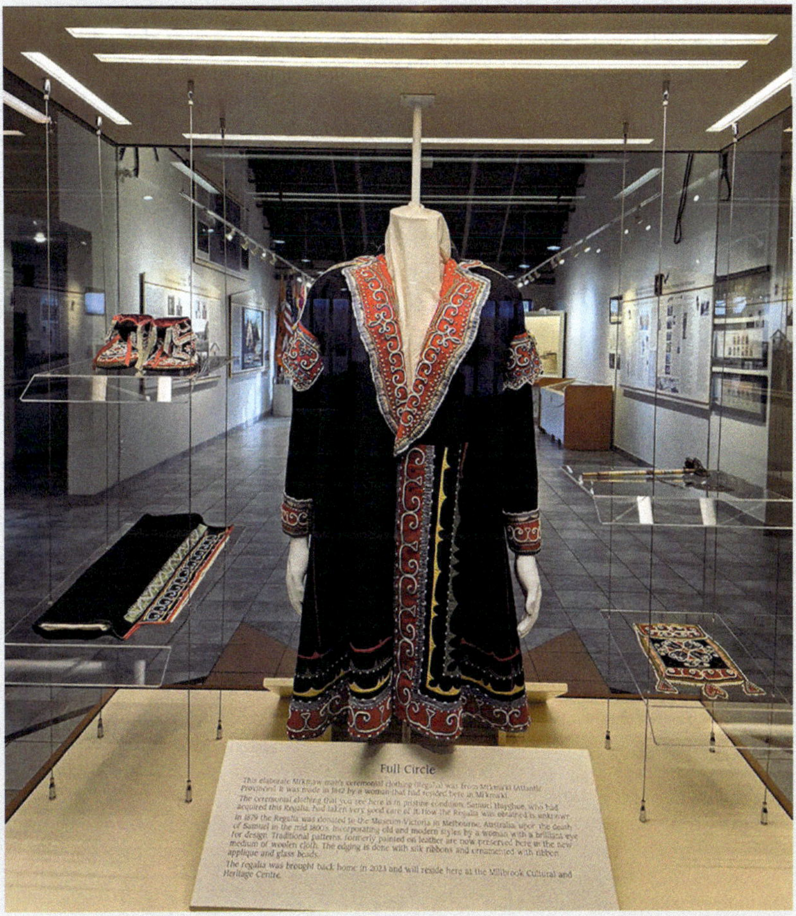

FIGURE 4.10 Mi'kmaq Ceremonial Clothing, c. 1840. Cloth ornamented with appliquéd cloth, silk ribbon, and bead embroidery. Collected by S.D.S. Huyghe before 1848. Millbrook Cultural and Heritage Centre, Truro, Nova Scotia, Canada. Photo: Heather Stevens.

The ceremonial regalia, legally donated to the Victoria Museum in Melbourne, Australia, in 1879, is a material embodiment of diplomatic exchanges that once extended the presence of the Mi'kmaq to distant places. The persistent efforts of the Millbrook band resulted in its repatriation to their modern museum and cultural center, celebrated on 21 June 2023, National Indigenous Peoples Day. The regalia, shown here on public display, is now accessible to Mi'kmaq throughout the region and serve once again as cultural ambassadors.

Homi K. Bhabha, a founding theorist in postcolonial studies, argues that only by embracing both "possession" and "dispossession" can there be "a discourse of heritage that truly understands the trials and tribulations . . . of the ethical obligation of cultural transmission."[125] Bhabha defines a "vernacular cosmopolitanism" by drawing a contrast between hostility and hospitality: hostility brings us closer to our neighbors in a deadly embrace than hospitality ever does in keeping "the gates of oppression and destruction open," not by yearning for the return of a past compliant with its categories of influence, tradition, convention, and custom but by maintaining a "resistant hope that these unsettled energies of place and displacement will settle into a design for living with shared borders and contrapuntual histories." When museum collections become auxiliary sites of memory, they can enable access to a wide variety of cultural practices that were lost from view through the act of building those collections. The final Fugue reconsiders the planetary history of material artifacts in an ontologically pluralistic framework, but first another Intermezzo reviews current understanding of human evolution based on the analysis of genomes.

Notes

1 Nancy Stepan, *Idea of Race in Science: Great Britain 1800–1960* (Hamden, CN: Archon Books and London–Basingstoke: The Macmillan Press, 1982), 47–59.
2 Matthew Rampley, The *Seductions of Darwin: Art/Evolution/Neuroscience* (University Park, PA: Pennsylvania State University Press, 2017), 137.
3 Arthur O. Lovejoy, *The Great Chain of Being: A Study in the History of an Idea* (Cambridge, MA: Harvard University Press, 1964).
4 Stepan, *The Idea of Race*, 5. The term "negro" was adopted from Spanish and Portuguese and first recorded in the mid-sixteenth century. It remained the standard term until the Black Power/Civil Rights movement of the 1960s, when Black and African-American were favored. Today the term "Negro" is offensive to some and still preferred by other Americans. I put the word in quotes for this reason.
5 Albertus Magnus, "Symia," *De animalibus*, cited by H. W. Janson, *Apes and Ape Lore in the Middle Ages and the Renaissance* (London: Warburg Institute, University of London, 1952), 83–88, who notes that most of Albertus's data derives from Aristotle.
6 Richard Bernheimer, *Wild Men in the Middle Ages: A Study in Art, Sentiment, and Demonology* (Cambridge, MA: Harvard University Press, 1952).
7 Bernheimer, *Wild Men*, 12.
8 Stepan, *The Idea of Race*, 29.
9 George W. Stocking, Jr., *Race, Culture, and Evolution: Essays in the History of Anthropology* (1968), rev. ed. (Chicago: University of Chicago Press, 1982).
10 The revised edition was published on 13 November 1874 and is the edition most commonly reprinted, the one on which my own discussion is based.
11 Stepan, *The Idea of Race*, 174. Evelleen Richards, *Darwin and the Making of Sexual Selection* (Chicago: University of Chicago Press, 2017), locates Darwin's adherence to the polygenist idea among members of the Anthropological Society of London, which supported the Confederacy in the US Civil War. Even today, the untenable aspects of Darwin's racial account are minimized: see Dan Falk, "How Darwin's *Descent of Man* Holds Up," *Smithsonian Magazine*, 24 February 2021.
12 Charles Darwin, *The Descent of Man and Selection in Relation to Sex*, rev. ed. (London: John Murray, 1874), Part 1.
13 On Safina, see the Introduction.
14 Darwin, *The Descent of Man*, Part I, Chapter 3, 93: "Judging from the hideous ornaments and the equally hideous music admired by most savages, it might be argued that their aesthetic faculty was not so highly developed as in certain animals, for instance, as in birds."

15 Darwin, *The Descent of Man*, Part III, Chapter 21. Ian Duncan, "Darwin and the Savages," *Yale Journal of Criticism* 4/2 (1991):13–45, discusses Darwin's recurring accounts of the Fuegians and cites this passage, 24 and n. 26, with reference to Darwin's published *Journal of Researches . . ., 1832–1836* (London, 1839) describing the Fuegians at the bottom rung of his scale of humanness "that became canonical largely thanks to Darwin." The passage is also discussed by Richards, *Darwin and the Making of Sexual Selection*, 7; Stocking, *Race, Culture, and Evolution*, 114–116.

16 Ian J. McNiven and Lynette Russell, *Appropriated Pasts: Indigenous Peoples and the Colonial Culture of Archaeology* (Lanham–Oxford: Altamira Press, 2005).

17 Thomas Huxley, *Evidence as to Man's Place in Nature* (1863), 155–159, cited from McNiven and Russell, *Appropriated Pasts*, 58–87, at 59. The following account of Huxley and his contemporaries and successors is based on McNiven and Russell.

18 James Hunt, Editor's preface to Carl Vogt, *Lectures on Man: His Place in Creation, and in the History of the Earth* (London: Longman, Green, Longman & Roberts,1864), xv.

19 Lewis Henry Morgan, *Ancient Society or Research in the Lines of Human Progress from Savagery through to Barbarism to Civilization* (1877; Cleveland: Meridian Books, 1963), 151–152, cited by McNiven and Russell, *Appropriated Pasts*, 66.

20 McNiven and Russell, *Appropriated Pasts*, 76–77, citing A. B. Kehoe, *The Land of Prehistory: A Critical History of American Archaeology* (New York: Routledge, 1998), 46, that many of these texts were readable and available to the general public.

21 C. D. Goodwin, "Evolution Theory in Australian Social Thought," *Journal of the History of Ideas* 25/3 (1964): 393–416; cited by McNiven and Russell, *Appropriated Pasts*, 77.

22 Friedman shaped the "freemarket" policies of US President Ronald Reagan (1981–1989) and UK Prime Minister Margaret Thatcher (1979–1990), which also defunded education. Gloria M. Liu, *Adam Smith's America: How a Scottish Philosopher Became an Icon of American Capitalism* (Princeton: Princeton University Press, 2022); Kim Phillips-Fein, "The Betrayal of Adam Smith," *The New Republic*, 27 February 2023.

23 Zia Quresi, "Rising Inequality: A Major Issue of Our Time," *Brookings*, 16 May 2023; Wendy Brown, *In the Ruins of Neoliberalism: The Rise of Antidemocratic Politics in the West* (New York: Columbia University Press, 2019).

24 Stepan, *The Idea of Race*, 87.

25 Matthew Vollgraff, *The Imperial Childhood of World Art* (New York: Bard Graduate Center, forthcoming). My thanks to the author for sharing his important study of Karl Lamprecht's career before publication.

26 Ernst Haeckel, *The Evolution of Man* (London, 1879 [1874]), 18, cited by Vollgraff, *The Imperial Childhood.*

27 See Stephen Jay Gould, *Ontogeny and Phylogeny* (Cambridge, MA: The Belknap Press of Harvard University Press, 1977). Riegl called Haeckel out by name when he condemned social Darwinism in 1893; Farago, "'Vision Itself His Its History': 'Race,' Nation, and Renaissance Art History," in *Reframing the Renaissance*, 78–90. See further, Michaud, *The Barbarian Invasions*, on heredity and style, 151–199, on the racialization of art history with reference to Haeckel, Riegl, and others, 156–157, 13–119.

28 Stocking, *Race, Culture, and Evolution.* See my longer discussion, "'Vision Itself Has its History': 'Race,' Nation, and Renaissance Art History," in *Reframing the Renaissance*, 67–88; and the excellent discussion of nineteenth- and early twentieth-century German art history by Juneja, *Can Art Be Made Global?*, 41–78.

29 Horst Bredekamp, "Franz Kugler and the Concept of World Art History," in *Cultural Histories of the Material World*, ed. Peter N. Miller (Ann Arbor: U. Michigan Press, 2013), 249–262.

30 Michel Foucault, *The Archaeology of Knowledge* (1969; New York: Pantheon,1982), cited by Stoler, *Duress*, 255.

31 David Graeber and David Wengrow, in *The Dawn of Everything: A New History of Humanity* (New York: Farrar, Strauss, and Giroux, 2023). I cite William Deresiewicz, "Human History gets a Rewrite," *The Atlantic*, 10 October 2021, accessed on line 22 April 2022. An exceptionally thorough and balanced review of the book's reception

is published by Wikipedia, accessed 24 June 2024 at https://en.wikipedia.org/wiki/The_Dawn_of_Everything

32 Éric Michaud, "Barbarian Invasions and the Racialization of Art History," trans. Hélène Amal, *October* 139 (Winter 2012), 68–69, called this "racial attributionism," expanded in his book, *Barbarian Invasions*.

33 Michaud, *The Barbarian Invasions*, 122–123, citing Karl Schnaase, *Niederländishe Brief* (Stuttgart and Tübingen: Corta, 1834), 148–149; and Schnaase, *Geschichte der bildenden Künste*, vol 1 (Duüsseldorf: Julius Buddeus, 1843), 86–87.

34 Bredekamp, "Franz Kugler." Franz Theodor Kugler, *Beschreibung der in der Königl. Kunstkammer zu Berlin vorhandenen Kunst-Sammlung* (Berlin: Carl Heymann Verlag, 1838); Kugler, *Handbuch der Kunstgeschichte*, 2 Bde. (Stuttgart, 1842), ix–xi.

35 The Leipzig Museum is based on the collection of Gustav Friedrich Klemm, a project very similar to Kugler's, as discussed by Peter Miller, "The Missing Link: 'Antiquarianism,' 'Material Culture,' and 'Cultural Science' in the Work of G. F. Klemm," in *Cultural Histories of the Material World*, 263–281.

36 Juneja, *Can Art History Be Made Global?*, Chapter 1.

37 H. Glenn Penny, *In Humboldt's Shadow: A Tragic History of German Ethnology* (2019 German ed.; Princeton-Oxford: Princeton University Press, 2021). See discussion in Fugue 2. *History of Anthropology Review*, 44 (2020) https://histanthro.org/reviews/faustianbargains/.

38 Adolf Bastian, *Den Mensch in der Geschichte* (Leipzig, 1860), 10, translated by K. Köpping, *Adolf Bastian and the Psychic Unity of Mankind* (Munster: Lit. Verlag, 1983), 180. Bastian also proposed a "genetic principle" by which societies develop their sociocultural institutions from simple to complex.

39 Penny, *In Humboldt's Shadow*.

40 Ulrich Pfisterer, "Origins and Principles of World Art History: 1900 (and 2000)," *in World Art Studies: Exploring Concepts and Approaches*, ed. Kitty Zijlmans and Wilfried van Damme (Amsterdam: Valiz, 2008), 69–89.

41 Ernst Grosse, *Die Anfänge der Kunst* (Freiburg–Leipzig: J. C. B. Mohr, 1894) and *The Beginnings of Art*, trans. F. Starr (New York: Appleton, 1897). Pfisterer, "Origins and Principles," 73.

42 Pfisterer, "Origins and Principles," 77, 79.

43 Juneja, *Can Art History Be Made Global?*, 57–63.

44 Ernst Grosse, "Ethnologie und Ästhetik," *Vierteljahrsschrift fu¨r Wissenschaftliche Philosophie*, 15 (1881): 392–417.

45 Susanne Leeb, "Primitivism and Humanist Teleology in Art History around 1900," *Journal of Art Historiography* 12 (June 2015), citing Friedrich Schiller, *Über die Ästhetische Erziehung des Menschen in einer Reihe von Briefen* (1795).

46 Leeb, "Primitivism." See further, Leeb, *Die Kunst der Anderen: "Weltkunst" und die anthropologische Konfiguration der Moderne* (Berlin: b_books Verlag, 2015).

47 Wilhelm Wundt, *Elemente der Völkerpsychologie. Grundlinien einer Psychologischen Entwicklungsgeschichte der Menschheit* (Leipzig: Kröner, 1912); Leo Frobenius, *Der Ursprung der Afrikanischen Kultur* (Berlin: Borntraeger, 1898); Alfred Vierkandt, Naturvölker und Kulturvölker. Ein Beitrag zur Socialpsychologie (Leipzig: Duncker und Humboldt, 1896); Alois Riegl, *Stilfragen, Grundlegungen zu einer Geschichte der Ornamentik* (Berlin: Siemens, 1893); and (based on Warburg's trip to the American Southwest in 1896) Aby Warburg, trans. William Mainland, "A Lecture on Serpent Ritual," *Journal of the Warburg Institute*, 2/4 (April 1939): 277–292.

48 Leo Frobenius, *Der Ursprung*, 350, cited by Leeb, "Primitivism," 3, n. 6.

49 Leeb, "Primitivism," citing Karl Biedermann's *Staatslexikon*, 1860; Woodruff Donald Smith, *Politics and the Sciences of Culture in Germany 1840–1920* (New York–Oxford: Oxford University Press, 1991), 69–70.

50 Regine Prange, *Die Geburt der Kunstgeschichte, Philosophische Ästhetik und Empirische Wissenschaft* (Cologne: Deubner, 2004); Friedhelm Solms, *Disciplina*

Aesthetica. Zur Fru¨hgeschichte der Ästhetischen Theorie bei Baumgarten und Herder (Stuttgart: Klett-Cotta, 1990); Christoph Menke, 'Subjektivität', in Karlheinz Barck, *Ästhetische Grundbegriffe. Historisches Wörterbuch in Sieben Bänden*, ed. Martin Fontius and Dieter Schlenstedt (Stuttgart and Weimar: Metzler, 2003), vol. 5, 734–786, especially 752–753; and Menke, *Kraft. Ein Grundbegriff Ästhetischer Anthropologie* (Frankfurt am Main: Suhrkamp Verlag, 2008).

51 H. F. Mallgrave, "Introduction," Gottfried Semper, *The Four Elements of Architecture and Other Writings*, trans. H. F. Mallgrave and W. Hermann, intro. H. F. Mallgrave (Cambridge: Cambridge University Press, 1989).

52 Edward B. Tylor was the author of many anthropological writings, including *Primitive Culture: Researches into the Development of Mythology, Philosophy, Religion, Art, and Custom*, 2 vols. (London: John Murray, 1871). His foundational textbook, *Anthropology* (1881) outlines a three-stage history of humanity similar to Lewis Henry Morgan's *Ancient Society* (1877). He became the first professor of Anthropology in Great Britain in 1896. Tylor also compared Tasmanians to "paleolithic man" (Tylor, 1894, 1899, ix). McNiven and Russell, *Appropriated Pasts*, 66–67.

53 Tylor, "The Science of Culture," *Primitive Culture*, 6–7, 13, 19.

54 Raymond Williams, *Keywords: A Vocabulary of Culture and Society*, rev. ed. (New York: Oxford University Press, 1983), 89–90.

55 Williams, *Keywords*, 90.

56 Semper, *De Stil* in *den technischen und tektonischen Künsten oder Praktische Ästhetik* (1861, 1863). Owen Jones opened his study of ornament with an extensively illustrated chapter on "The Ornaments of Savage Tribes," arguing that all humans share the urge to create which was more transparently discernible in the "ornament of a savage tribe" than in highly advanced civilization. Owen Jones, *The Grammar of Ornament* (1856; London: Quarich, 1910), 13–18.

57 Semper, *The Four Elements of Architecture*, 89, citing Kugler.

58 Juneja, *Can Art History Be Made Global*, 180.The following is indebted to her analysis, 180–200.

59 Meyer Schapiro, "The Nature of Abstract Art," *Marxist Quarterly* I/1 (1937): 77–98. William Rubin (ed.), *"Primitivism" and 20th Century Art: Affinity of the Tribal and the Modern*, 2 vols (New York: Harry N. Abrams, 1984).

60 Juneja, *Can Art History Be Made Global?*, 184.

61 Bruno Latour, *We Have Never Been Modern* (1991 French ed.), trans. Catherine Porter (Cambridge, MA: Harvard University Press, 1993), 11–12. Latour's most extensive account of ANT is *Reassembling the Social: An Introduction to Actor–Network Theory* (Oxford: Oxford University Press, 2005).

62 James Clifford, *The Predicament of Culture: Twentieth-Century Ethnography, Literature, and Art* (Cambridge–London: Harvard University Press, 1988), 222–227.

63 Lucien Lévy-Bruhl, *La Mentalité primitive (*1922) and *L'âme primitive* (1927). His ideas were also formative for Deleuze and Guattari, Derrida, and others: John Tresch, "Leroi-Gourhan's Hall of Gestures," in *Energies in the Arts*, ed. Douglas Kahn (Cambridge–London: The MIT Press, 2019), 193–238.

64 See Farago in *Reframing the Renaissance*, 76–83. *Art History and Anthropology: Modern Encounters, 1870–1970*, ed. Peter Probst and Joseph Imorde (Los Angeles: Getty Research Institute, 2023), examines connections (and disconnections) between anthropology and art history through the category "primitive art" in a wide-ranging set of case studies. *Mapping Modernisms: Art, Indigeneity, Colonialism*, ed. Elizabeth Harney and Ruth B. Phillips (Durham–London: Duke University Press, 2018).

65 Wilhelm Worringer, Abstraktion und Einfühlung: ein Beitrag zur Stilpyschologie, published dissertation, Neuwied, 1907 (Munich: R. Piper, 1908) and Abstraction and Empathy, trans. Michael Bullock (New York: International University Press, 1953).

66 Donald Thomson, *Donald Thomson in Arnhem Land*, ed. and intro. Nicolas Peterson, rev. ed. (Melbourne: Miegunyah Press, 2003).

67 Walter D. Mignolo, "Epistemic Disobedience, Independent Thought, and Decolonial Freedom," *Theory, Culture, and Society* 26/7–8 (2009): 159–181, DOI: 10.1177/0263276409349275; Mignolo, "Epistemic Disobedience and the Decolonial Option: A Manifesto," *TRANSMODERNITY: Journal of Peripheral Cultural Production of the Luso-Hispanic World*, 1/2 (2011): 44–66. DOI: 10.5070/T412011807.
68 Juneja, *Can Art History Be Made Global?*, 186–187.
69 See Fugue 2.
70 Conrad Fiedler, *Über die Beuteilung con Werken der bildenden Kunst* (1876; Wuppertal: A. Henn, 1970); *Judging Works of Visual Art*, trans. H. Schaefer-Simmern and F. Mood (Berkeley–London: University of California Press, 1978). Adolf Hildebrand, *Das Problem der Form in der bildenden Kunst* (1893; Strasburg: Heitz, 1901). Alois Riegl, *Stilfragen: Grundlegungen zu einer Geschichte der Ornamentik* (1893; Hildesheim–New York: Georg Olms, 1975); *Problems of Style: Foundations for a History of Ornament*, trans. E. Kain, notes and intro. H. Zerner (Princeton: Princeton University Press, 1992).
71 Perception involves signals that go through the nervous system, shaped by learning, memory, expectation, and attention. J. J. Gibson, *The Senses Considered as Perceptual Systems* (Houghton Mifflin, 1966); Rudolf Arnheim, *Visual Thinking* (Berkeley: University of California Press, 1969).
72 See Matthew Rampley, "From Symbol to Allegory: Aby Warburg's Theory of Art," *The Art Bulletiin* 77/1 (1995): 41–55. For the effects of the neo-Kantian account on other art historians, see Karen Lang, "The Dialectics of Decay: Rereading the Kantian Subject," *The Art Bulletin* 79/3 (September 1997): 413–439; and, further, Lang, *Chaos and Cosmos: On the Image in Aesthetics and Art History* (Ithaca–London: Cornell University Press, 2006*)*.
73 See discussion in the first Fugue.
74 J. Jorge Klor de Alva, "The Postcolonization of the (Latin) American Experience: A Reconsideration of 'Colonialism,' 'Postcolonialism,' and 'Mestizaje,'" in *After Colonialism: Imperial Histories and Postcolonial Displacements*, ed. Gyan Prakash (Princeton: Princeton University Press, 1994), 241–278.
75 Caroline Dodds Pennock, *On Savage Shores: How Indigenous Americans Discovered Europe* (London: Weidenfield & Nicolson, 2022), xiii–xvi.
76 Oscar Moro Abadia, Bryn Tapper, and Susan Lowish, "From 'Primitive' to 'Indigenous': Some comments on the History of Inuit and Aboriginal Arts," forthcoming. My thanks to the authors for making their essay available before publication. See also Susan Lowish, "Evolutionists and Australian Aboriginal Art: 1885–1915," *Journal of Art Historiography* (2015/12): 1–35; Adam Kuper, *The Reinvention of Primitive Society: Transformations of a Myth* (London: Routledge, 2017).
77 Caroline Dodds Pennock, *On Savage Shores: How Indigenous Americans Discovered Europe* (London: Wiedenfeld and Nicolson, 2022); Pekka Hämäläinen, *Indigenous Continent: The Epic Contest for North America* (New York: Livergate Publishing, 2022).
78 Abadia, Tapper, and Lowish, "From 'Primitive' to 'Indigenous.'"
79 Nancy Marie Mithlo, "No Word for Art in Our Language? Old Questions, New Paradigms," *Wicazo Sa Review* 27/1 (Spring 2012): 111–126, at 113.
80 Janet Berlo and Ruth B. Phillips, *Native North American Art* (Oxford: Oxford University Press, 1998), 9, as cited by Mithlo, p. 113.
81 Ngarino Ellis, "*Te ao hurihuri o ngä taonga tuku iho*: The Evolving Worlds of Our Ancestral Treasures," *Biography* 39/3 (Summer 2016): 438–460.
82 Ellis, "Evolving Worlds," 440–441.
83 Ulrich Pfisterer, "Altamira – oder: Afänge von Kunst und Kunstwissen-schaft," in *Vortrage aus dem Wärburg-Haus*, vol 10 (Berlin: Academie Verlag, 2007), 13–80.
84 Kugler, *Handbuch*, 4, cited by Bredekamp, "Franz Kugler," 251.

85 Heinrich Klotz, *Die Entdeckung von Catal Höyuk: Der Archäologische Jahrhundertfund* (Munich: C. H. Beck, 1997),13.
86 The site was first excavated in 1991 by Christopher S. Henshilwood and fieldwork is ongoing since 1997. On the Nassarius shell jewelry, "Shell Beads from South Africa Show Modern Human Behavior 75,000 Years Ago," *National Science Foundation*, news release, 15 April 2004.
87 Tim Ingold, *Making: Anthropology, Archeology, Art, and Architecture* (London: Routledge, 2013), 33–35. The following account of the *bi-face* is based on Ingold's description.
88 Ingold, "Prospect," in *Biosocial Becomings: Intregrating Social and Biological Anthropology*, ed. Tim Ingold and Gisli Palsson (Cambridge: Cambridge University Press, 2013), 6–8, cites Giles Deleuze and Félix Guattari, *A Thousand Plateaus: Capitalism and Schizophrenia*, trans. Brian Massumi (London: Continuum, 2004), 323, on life as a perpetual task of creating ourselves, a "line of becoming" understood not as a corpus of received tradition but as a path to be followed, which others will follow in turn.
89 Ingold, *Making*, 44–45.
90 Similar claims had been made earlier by Jacob Burckhardt (1860), Jules Michelet (1855), and Hippolyte Taine. Francis Haskell, *History and Its Images: Art and the Interpretation of the Past* (New Haven–London: Yale University Press, 1993), 226–253.
91 Haskell, *History and its Images*, 335.
92 Fiedler, *On Judging Works of Visual Art*, 43–44.
93 Matthew Rampley, *The Vienna School of Art History: Empire and the Politics of Scholarship, 1847–1918* (University Park, PA: Pennsylvania State University Press, 2013.
94 Heinrich Wölfflin, *Kunstgeschichte Grundebegriffe* (Munich: F. Bruckmann, 1929), 12; Wölfflin, *The Principles of Art History: The Problem of the Development of Style in Later Art*, trans. M Hottinger (1932; New York: Dover Publications, 1950), 11. Surprisingly, the most recent English translation of Wölfflin's text dismisses the racializing and teleological elements of his ideas: Tristan Weddigen, "Approaching Wölfflin's *Principles*," 48–50, in Heinrich Wölfflin, *Principles of Art History: The Problem of the Development of Style in Early Modern Art*, ed. Evonne Levy and Tristan Weddigen, trans. Jonathan Blower (Los Angeles: Getty Research Institute, 2015), with a thorough history of the editions.
95 Mitchell Frank and Daniel Adler, Introduction, *German Art History and Scientific Thought: Beyond Formalism*, ed. Mitchell B. Frank and Daniel Adler (Farnham, UK–Burlinton, VT: Ashgate, 2012).
96 Jaynie Anderson, *The Life of Giovanni Morelli in Risorgimento Italy* (Milan: Officina Libraria, 2019).
97 Karl M. Figlio, "The Metaphor of Organization: An Historiographical Perspective on the Biomedical Sciences of the Early Nineteenth Century," *History of Science* 14 (1976): 17–53.
98 The taxonomic systems derived by Cuvier and Chevalier de Lamarck were very different from one another, but share the same motive to find the organizational rationale for a scale of intelligence. Stepan, *The Idea of Race*, 13.
99 His 1874 article on Leonardo's followers remains one of his most original contributions. Jaynie Anderson, "Dietro lo Pseudonimo," in *Giovanni Morelli, Della Pittura Italiana studii storico-critici. Le Gallerie Borghese e Doria Pamphili in Roma*, ed. Jaynie Anderson (Milan: Adelphi Edizioni, 1991). In the first of his four-part 1874 article on the Borghese Gallery, "Die Galerien Roms: Ein kritischer Versuch. I: Die Galerie Borghese," *Zeitschrift fur bildende kunst* 9 (1874): 1–11, Morelli described his procedure as consisting of three parts: (1) the position and movement of human body, the form of the face, the general impression; (2) the details; and (3) the idiosyncrasies of each painter – only the last is his famous morphological method.

100 Gibson-Wood, *Studies in the Theory of Connoisseurship*, 212. See also Michaud, *Barbarian Invasions*, 44–48.
101 Rampley, *Viennese School*. Stefan Muthesius, "Towards an 'exacte *Kunstwissenschaft*' (?): A report on Some Recent German Books on the Progress of Mid-19th Century Art History," *Journal of Art Historiography*, 9 (December 2012) reviews the German-language scholarship appearing since 2000.
102 Nancy D. Munn, *Walbiri Iconography: Graphic Representation and Cultural Symbolism in a Central Australian Society* (Ithaca–New York: Cornell University Press, 1973).
103 Jennifer Green, *Drawn from the Ground: Sound, Sign, and Inscription in Central Australian Sand Stories* (New York: Cambridge University Press, 2014), at 163.
104 Patrick Thomas Hajovsky, "Without a Face: Voicing Moctezuma II's Image as Chapultepec Park, Mexico City," in *Seeing Across Cultures in the Early Modern World*, ed. Dana Leibsohn and Jeanette Favrot Peterson (Farnham, UK: Ashgate, 2012), 171–192; Hajovsky, *On the Lips of Others: Moteuczoma's Fame in Aztec Monuments and Rituals* (Austin: University of Texas Press, 2015).
105 Gauvin Alexander Bailey, "Asia in the Arts of Colonial Latin America," in Joseph J. Rishel with Suzanne Stratton-Pruitt, *The Arts in Latin America 1492–1820*, exh. cat., Philadelphia Museum of Art (New Haven–London: Yale University Press, 2006), 57–69,
106 Carolyn Dean and Dana Leibsohn, "Hybridity and Its Discontents: Considering Visual Culture in Colonial Spanish America," *Colonial Latin American Review* 12/1 (2003): 5–35. DOI: 10.1080/10609160302341.
107 Dean and Leibsohn, "Hybridity," 15–16. Susan Verdi Webster has published extensively on the contribution of Indigenous artisans to the design and construction of colonial architecture and altars documented in archival records and the built environment, for example, "Masters of the Trade: Native Artisans, Guilds, and the Construction of Colonial Quito," *Journal of the Society of Architectural Historians* 68/1 (2009/3):1029.
108 Donald Preziosi, *Rethinking Art History: Meditations on a Coy Science* (New Haven–London: Yale University Press, 1989); Preziosi, *Brain of the Earth's Body: Art, Museum, and the Phantasms of Modernity* ((Minneapolis–London: University of Minnesota Press, 2003); Preziosi, "Art History: Making the Visible Legible," in *The Art of Art History: A Critical Anthology*, ed. Donald Preziosi, 2nd ed. (Oxford: Oxford University Press, 2009), 7–21.
109 See further, *Grasping the World: The Idea of the Museum*, ed. Donald Preziosi and Claire Farago (Aldershot: Ashgate 2004; reprinted, Routledge 2019); and Donald Preziosi and Claire Farago, *Art Is Not What You think It Is* (Oxford: Blackwells, 2012).
110 Heidegger's distinction between a phenomenal world and a world in itself was used previously by Leibniz and Christian Wolff. See Fugue 3.
111 Huon Wardle, "Caribbean Cosmopolitanism: The View from Ethnography," *Routledge International Handbook of Caribbean Studies*, 2nd ed. (New York–London: Routledge, 2018), 455–466, at 462.
112 Stuart Hall, "Creolization, Diaspora, and Hybridity in the Context of Globalization," in *Créolité amd Creolization* ed. Okwei Enwezor et al. (Ostfildern-Ruit: Hatje Cabtze, 2003), 185–198.
113 Stuart Hall, "Créolité and the Power of Creolization," in *Créolité amd Creolization*, 27–41.
114 *The Creolization of Theory,* ed. Françoise Lionnet and Shu-meo Shih (Durham: Duke University Press, 2001).
115 Sylvia Wynter, "Unparalleled Catastrophe for our Species—Or, to Give Humanness a Different Future: Conversations," Katherine McKittrick, ed., *Sylvia Wynter: On Being Human as Praxis* (Durham, NC: Duke University Press, 2015), 45.
116 Tracey Nicholls, "Frantz Fanon," *Internet Encyclopedia of Philosophy* (2023), citing Linda Tuhiwai Smith, *Decolonizing Methodologies: Research and Indigenous Peoples* (London: Zed Books, 2012). Other publications along similar lines are Silvia

Rivera, *Cusicanqui, Ch'ixinakax utxiwa: On Practices and Discourses of Decolonization* (2010 Spanish ed.), trans. Molly Geidel (Medford, MA: Polity Presss, 2020); Clara-Sue Kidwell, *Native American Knowledge Systems* (London–Singapore: Balestier Press, 2019). And dealing specifically with art in a national context, Amy Lonetree, *Decolonizing Museums: Representing Native America in National and Tribal Museums* (Chapel Hill, NC: University of North Carolina Press, 2012).

117 Amelia Jones, *Seeing Differently: A History and Theory of Identity and the Visual Arts* (New York and London: Routledge, 2012), with further references; Jones, "Who is an Artist?: Identity, Individualism, and the Neoliberalism of the Art World," *Arts* 12/6 (November 2023), https://doi.org/10.3390/arts12060234; and see, *A Companion to Contemporary Art in a Global Framework*, ed. Jane Chin Davidson and Amelia Jones (West Sussex: Wiley Blackwell, 2024).

118 Sylvia Wynter, "Unparalleled Catastrophe for our Species—Or, to Give Humanness a Different Future: Conversations," in *Sylvia Wynter: On Being Human as Praxis*, ed. Katherine McKittrick (Durham, NC: Duke University Press, 2015), 45.

119 Dina Gilio-Whitaker, "The Problem with the Ecological Indian Stereotype," *PBS SoCal*, 7 Feburary 2017, accessed on 20 May 2024, at www.pbssocal.org/shows/tending-the-wild/the-problem-with-the-ecological-indian-stereotype

120 *Situating Global Art: Topologies, Temporalities, Trajectories*, ed. and intro. Sarah Dornhof, Nanne Buurman, Birgit Hopfener, and Barbara Lutz (Bielefeld: Transcript Verlag, 2018), Introduction,12 and 19.

121 Kwame Anthony Appiah, *Cosmopolitanism: Ethics in a World of Strangers* (New York–London: W. W. Norton & Co, 2006), xiii.

122 James Clifford, "Mixed Feelings," in *Cosmopolitics: Thinking and Feeling beyond the Nation*, ed. Pheng Cheah and Bruce Robbins (Minneapolis: University of Minnesota Press, 1998), 362–371, at 365; Clifford, "Traveling Cultures," in *Cultural Studies: Now and in the Future*, ed. Larry Grossberg, Cary Nelson, and Paula A. Treichler (New York: Routledge, 1992), 96–112.

123 Direct citations are taken from Ruth B. Phillips, "The Travels of a Mi'kmaq Coat: A Nineteenth-Century World Art History and Twenty-First-Century Cultural Politics," in *Crossing Cultures: Conflict, Migration, and Convergence: The Proceedings of the 32nd International Congress in the History of Art*, ed. Jaynie Anderson (Carlton [Australia]: Miegunyah Press, Melbourne University Publishing, 2009), 26–30. For full documentation, see Phillips, "The Global Travels of a Mi'kmaq Coat; Colonial Legacies, Repatriation, and the New Cosmopolitanism," *Museum Pieces: Toward the Indigenization of Canadian Museums* (Montreal–Ithaca; McGill-Queen's University Press, 2011), 132–156, at 153.

124 A video on the Melbourne Museum's website documents the repatriation efforts by the Manager of the Millbrook Center, Heather Stevens: https://museumsvictoria.com.au/article/mi-kmaq-regalia-repatriated/

125 Homi K. Bhabha, "On Global Memory: Reflections on Barbaric Transmission," in *Crossing Cultures*, 46–56.

Intermezzo III

DEEP HISTORY

Disentangling "Race" and Genetic Science

Where the Darwinian model of evolution originally stressed the interconnectedness of life in terms of the anatomy of individual organisms, the current understanding of evolution defines identity at the molecular level. Darwin had suggested that the history of life could be drawn as a tree, with all creatures originating in a single trunk, then diverging into lineages akin to the tree's major limbs, branches, twigs, and leaves. A different way of thinking about the interconnectedness of all life at the molecular level is indebted to Carl Woese, the microbiologist who in 1977 discovered the existence of the third kingdom of life. Woese referred to the long molecules containing linear sequences of units of DNA, RNA, and proteins as the cell's "internal fossil record."[1] Comparing variations in sequences in different creatures allowed him to deduce the "ancient ancestor sequences" from which those molecules had diverged, a method for establishing relationships that is fundamental to the genome analysis of ancient DNA. In studying the process that later became known as molecular phylogenetics, Woese found that a tiny molecular mechanism common to all forms of cellular life, called the ribosome, translates genetic information into proteins, turning genetic codes into living bodies. In Darwin's system, the elements of the tree continue to diverge. Comparing the molecular structures of DNA sequences, Woese found that the branches of evolution sometimes converge, that is, DNA can move across barriers from one kind of creature into another. Genes can move sideways from one lineage of life into another, even when the gene was absent from their common ancestor, and not only in the case of bacteria, studied by Woese, but among plants and animals. When portions of a genome of a certain tiny invertebrate animal known as a rotifer were sequenced, for example, scientists found at least 22 genes from other creatures, and a few of those genes were still functional. Other cases include insects.[2]

DOI: 10.4324/9781351023429-8

From the systematic observations of behavioral scientists and from Woese's discovery and subsequent genetic research, we know that environmental forces can alter the genomes of organisms passed on from one generation to another. At first Woese's conclusions that gene transfer was affected by environment were rejected but, by the 1990s, the role of the process known as horizontal gene transfer (HGT) was being widely studied, enabled by new, more powerful computers to carry out the genome sequencing. Darwin's metaphor of an evolutionary tree has been amended to accommodate the DNA evidence that genes flow not only vertically from parents to offspring, but can also be traded across species boundaries.[3]

There is extensive human and artifactual evidence of the deep history of the planet that was not available when the field of art history was conceptualized in the nineteenth century. The ongoing study of large populations of ancient DNA enabled by technological advances in genome sequencing since 2013 is showing that the development of human life on this planet was gradual, complex, and lateral – not the linear evolution that nineteenth-century science proposed, but something that can be described as a complexly ramified structure in which human groups left Africa at many intervals and migrated in many directions, mixing and evolving to create many different outcomes. The estimated date of the earliest skeletal evidence for the spread of humans (*Homo erectus*) from Africa to Euroasia is 1.4–1.9 million years ago.[4] Connections emerging from the genetic study of ancient human populations indicate that humans moved across the planet for hundreds of thousands of years in complex waves that have been described metaphorically as a "trellis, branching and remixing far back into the distant past."[5] Today, scientists estimate that the average proportion of Neanderthal ancestry in non-sub-Saharan African modern human populations is about 2% (Neanderthals were native to Europe although a few came into contact with sub-Saharan Africans).[6] In some unusual places in the genome, more than 50% of DNA sequences are from Neanderthals. The labels themselves are provisional: a better way to view these ancient human populations is as members of a loosely related family who inhabited a vast region of Eurasia.

Population clusters have always been dynamic, and people have always been on the move. Evidence for extensive mixing in the ancestry of humans is growing stronger as the entire genome of more ancient skeletal remains is sequenced. The new scientific model of identity based on genomic structure is highly significant for cultural studies. The central question that the nineteenth-century founders of modern art historical methods addressed is once again on the table for discussion: are biological traits culturally manifested? The relationship between biological and cultural identity in the history of the planet, the former based on DNA and the latter based on artifactual evidence, is currently the subject of intense debate among genetic scientists, anthropologists, and archeologists. The perennial problem that archaeologists and anthropologists try to answer is whether the artifactual evidence of change is due to the migration of people or the transfer of ideas, or some combination of both. Studies of ancient DNA have disputed the longstanding hypothesis that farming spread into Europe from Anatolia through the transfer of technology.[7] The Anatolian farmers were thought to be ancestors of modern Europeans and the first speakers of proto-Indo-European languages. According to prominent geneticist David Reich, the whole genome analysis undertaken by his laboratory at Harvard University working in collaboration with scientists elsewhere, shows something entirely different: soon after 5000 years ago, people of the Yamnaya culture originating in the steppes of central Asia swept across central and western Europe replacing existing hunter–gatherer populations. The first farmers even in the remote reaches of Europe had very little hunter–gatherer related ancestry.[8] Reich contends that the existing population must have been replaced by the Yamnaya who brought farming and other technologies with them, introducing wheeled vehicles, horses, oxen, the practice of clearing land, along with the so-called Corded Ware with its distinctive decorative patterns.[9] In the Near East, the same cultural features were due to the spread of ideas because the artifactual evidence extends across genetically very different groups.[10]

How definitive is this hypothesis? DNA has emerged as central to the new synthesis of genetics, archaeology, and linguistics. Do we know for certain that the Yamnaya were the exclusive source of agriculture and introduced Indo-European languages into Western Europe? There is consensus among geneticists and anthropologists that major cultural shifts took place during the Bronze Age in Europe and Asia, but it remains a matter of debate whether the changes are due to migration or cultural diffusion among settled groups, and whether the spread of Indo-European languages was linked to these events or predates them. Genome data is a more powerful way to cluster present-day human populations than physical features. However, populations can be traced only if enough data from enough people can be obtained. Various genetic tools have been used for many years to trace the histories of human populations, including blood group substances, enzyme variations (polymorphisms), mitochondrial DNA, and other characters that show variation from one individual to another. The analysis of whole genomes shows that the people who live in a particular place today almost never exclusively descend from the people who lived there in the past.[11] Thanks to advances in computer technology and the preparation of genome specimens, the data is currently outstripping publication; as of August 2017, the genomes of more than 3000 ancient individuals had been published.[12] In April 2023, the ancient genome count surpassed 10,000.[13] The future will yield much more evidence and many surprises.

Some of the current controversies growing out of these findings are not with the DNA evidence, but with its interpretation as an indicator of cultural identity. The complexity of human interbreeding and the numerous sites of evolution/change that are beginning to be documented using whole genome analysis shows that there was considerable diversity among *Homo sapiens* populations but they are the product of many genetic factors. To date, studies seeking differences at the genetic level document more variation within groups than between them. As one critic put it, since the 1960s archaeologists had been trained never to assume the purity or coherence of a people, a slippery slope to the conclusion that certain peoples came by their advantages "naturally."[14] Even when the genetic and artifactual evidence corroborate one another, the correlation is strictly circumstantial. Human genome variation supplements the traditional toolkit of archaeology, but because it is often impossible to distinguish between genetic and cultural factors in the material record, collaboration between historians and biologists is imperative, even and especially when genetic scientists find themselves in the domain of history, interpreting skeletal remains for signs of cultural identity.

As exciting and revolutionary as the new information unlocked through the analysis of ancient DNA is, documenting successive waves of migration and dynamic mixing among different gene pools reaching back in time, the genetic record and its relationship to the artifactual record are not clear-cut. Another international group of scientists, working with anthropologists and historians, supported by the Danish National Research Foundation Center for GeoGenetics in Copenhagen, agrees that a new social and economic formation corresponds to the genetic record of Yamnaya migration, which they date to c. 3000 BCE, but they diverge from Reich in arguing that the cultural history is more complex, not a one-to-one fit between genetic and cultural identity as the older, racial models asserted. A new class of master artisans (known as the Sintashta culture emerging from the Ural Mountains around 2000 BCE), brought chariots, horses, and new weapons to Europe and Asia, and they were replaced in the Late Bronze Age, c. 1500, by three other cultures that could have resulted from migration or diffusion among settled groups.[15] The Danish-led team therefore argues, contra Reich, that the Corded Ware culture in Europe resulted from migration of the Yamnaya combined with the local Neolithic people, while migrations during the Early Bronze Age are probably responsible for the spread of Indo-European languages, in line with reconstructions based on archaeological and historical linguistic data.[16]

The emerging evidence that modern human population groups are mixtures of mixtures receding into the archaic human record should have made scientists reject all comparison of their findings to racial theories, but instead just the opposite happened in some cases. In the first place, some scientists, including David Reich, are not sufficiently familiar with the history of racial theory and its untenable assumptions, which Darwin supported, that racial essence was not subject to evolution. [17] Furthermore, the central arguments of scientific racial theories since their appearance in the late eighteenth century are claims far beyond simple biological difference about the correlation between outward appearance and mental capacity. As argued in Fugues 3 and 4, they are often combined with geographical and climatic factors to support arguments about European cultural superiority (always the subtext). The new genetic science has definitively disproven these assumptions: all human populations are mixtures of earlier populations, there was never a single trunk population or "pure," independent branches of human development, and outward appearances are not reliable indicators of genetic make-up. Any resemblance to nineteenth-century theories of polygenesis is purely superficial because the diverse groups of the past have interbred over time until modern population clusters are different and diverse within themselves.

The claim that the new DNA evidence confirms the existence of separate human races as has been argued by Reich and others reintroduces long discredited arguments, including the racial claim that some human populations are cognitively superior to others. "Race" theory ranked different populations hierarchically based on cognitive and physical differences that science has *disproven* time and again since the end of the nineteenth century. The study of ancient DNA supports the idea of genetic differences among populations, but the complexity of past intermixing disproves the fundamental tenets of racial theory. It is certainly not necessary to use the discredited term "race" to discuss biological difference. Whatever terminology is developed in the future to describe the rich diversity of humans collectively according to variations in their genetic make-up, if such generalizations could ever be made, the tragic consequences of the loaded term "race" and related concepts such as "polygenesis" should disqualify them out of hand.

Populations are dynamic and complex, and their cultural identity is an independent factor that is equally dynamic and complex. The correlation between genetic and cultural identity must be determined from the material record on a case-by-case basis. A better system of biological classification is that proposed by anthropologist Frank Livingston, whose term "clines" describes human genetic variation characterized by gradual geographic gradients that reflect interbreeding among neighbors.[18] But even this model does not fit all the genetic histories coming to light, such as the complex case of the Indian subcontinent where small groups living side by side have retained separate genomes due in part to the caste system, in part to the practice of infanticide for those who transgress caste hierarchies.[19] Moreover "clines" do not describe genetic similarities occurring over great distances and times, such as the finding that more ancestry is shared by present-day Native North Americans and people living in France today than with any other modern population.[20] Another recently introduced taxonomical concept, one that has revolutionized biological classification, is the "clade" (from Ancient Greek, klados, "branch"). A clade defines a group of organisms with a common ancestor. Clades can occur at any scale (kingdom, species, individual, etc.) and they are nested, one in another as each branch splits into smaller branches, as populations diverged and evolved independently. The splits refer to evolutionary history as populations diverged and evolved separately.

Conclusions drawn on limited or inappropriate evidence is another problem. Reich has been criticized for claiming the existence of mass migratory patterns on the basis of very few specimens, as in the case of theorizing the origins of people on Vanuatu based on three samples from one site on one island and contemporary comparisons that were not from Vanuatu.[21] Even with extensive genome data, matching skeletal remains to their archaeological sites is not always possible – for example, when analyzing bone from museum specimens. Radiocarbon dating depends on comparing objects at an archeological site, also not always possible. To propose viable hypotheses linking culture and genetics in the archaeological record, which is indisputably

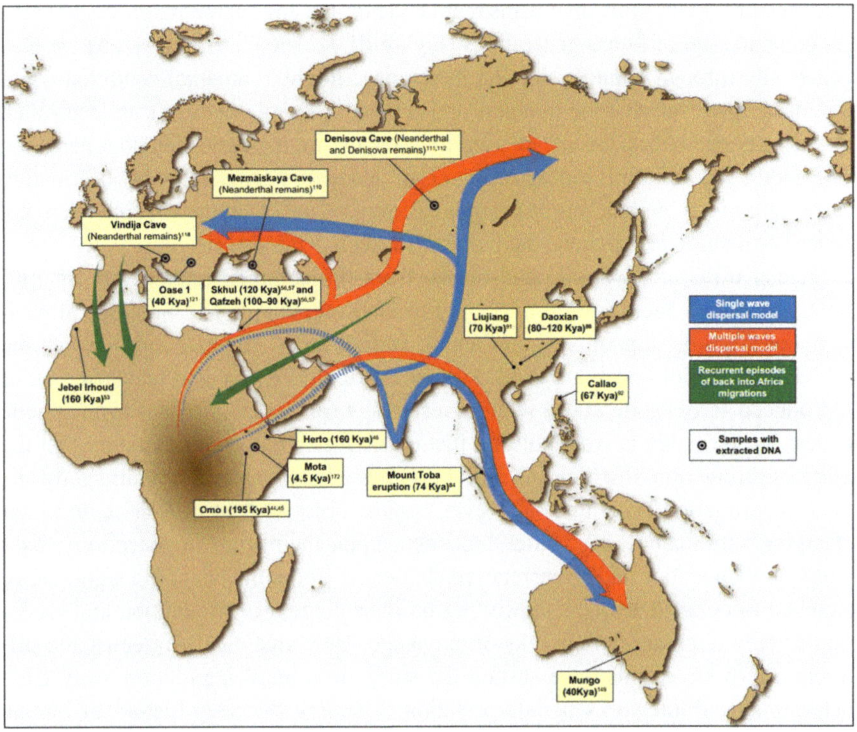

FIGURE III.1 Putative migration waves out of Africa and location of some of the most relevant ancient human remains and archeological sites. After Saloa López, Lucy van Dorp, and Garrett Hellenthal, "Human Dispersal Out of Africa: A Lasting Debate," *Evolutionary Bioinformatics Online* 11 (Suppl 2 2015): 57–68. Creative Commons Attribution 3.0 Unported, Wiki/Saioa López, Lucy van Dorp and Garrett Hellenthal. Copyright © 2015 the author(s), publisher and licensee Libertas Academica Ltd. This is an open-access article distributed under the terms of the Creative Commons CC-BY 3.0 License.

the trajectory of fieldwork today, the key questions are, how many individual specimens with artifactual contexts were analyzed? How many are needed to draw general conclusions?

Keeping in mind these revolutionary developments and cautionary concerns about ancient DNA studies, let's return to the question posed at the beginning of this book of what would be entailed in revisiting the foundational project of art history to study cultural production based on scientific understandings of collective identity. To summarize the preceding discussion briefly, scientific concepts of biological identity are now formulated at the molecular level connecting all life forms. Depending on how culture is defined, there is no conceptual basis to exclude archaic humans and other animals from the planetary history of world culture. Darwin's metaphor of a tree that defines the shape of evolutionary development is now re-conceptualized for ancient human evolution as a rhizomatic structure spreading laterally, with increasing evidence of the ways that organisms regulated through environmental forces alter the genetic make-up of future generations [Figure III.2]. The idea that humans evolved genetically through natural selection in response to environmental conditions does not mean, however, that the thoughts and actions of living organisms are controlled by their genetic codes. Genes are a limiting factor, not a prognostic about behavior. The notion that culture is biologically transmitted across generations by information carried around in our heads is based on a category mistake: nature and culture are not neutral or natural designations but cultural concepts with histories.[22]

Human traits are dynamic and derive from the complex intersection of multiple genes with their natural and cultural environments.[23] The ontological divisions between the domains of the human and all other animals, and between the social and the biological, are fluid. Particular conditions can also be carried on or reproduced across generations without resorting to an explanation based on genetic codes – in fact, that is what cultural history is. It has long been assumed that the unity of production, distribution, and consumption are essential conditions for the local reproduction of culture. However, mobile objects show otherwise and their changing significance over time, dependent upon their point of reception, raises many new questions and interpretative challenges about the changing significance attached to cultural artifacts depending on their context of production and reception as they circulate in networks of exchange. New analytical strategies and different interpretive aims have shifted the study of cultural interaction away from deterministic frameworks of interpretation. Mapping the deep history of human migration and the circulation of cultural artifacts as two independent structures of connectivity operating at vastly different scales, networks of connectivity form the basis for a topological approach to the history of art and material culture. The terms of discussion often slip from culturally determined categories to presumably universal perceptual categories. The Western tradition of writings about perception, cognition, and representation is itself culturally specific, not universal. Depending on the viewer's cultural orientation, visual similarities with very different cultural resonances could combine in a variety of different ways: we can sometimes reconstruct the range of meanings an image, object, or practice might have held for a viewer, but it would be impossible – and pointless – to offer a definitive interpretation for an image that embodies such irreducible semiotic equivocations.

Notes

1 David Quammen, "How the Microbiologist Carl Woese Fundamentally Changed the Way We Think About Evolution and the Origins of Life," *New York Times Magazine*, 13 August 2018. Carl Woese, *The Genetic Code: The Molecular Basis for Genetic Expression* (New York: Harper & Row, 1967).

2 David Quammen, *The Tangled Tree: A Radical New History of Life* (New York–New Delhi: Simon & Schuster Paperbacks, 2018).

3 David Reich, *Who We Are and How We Got Here: Ancient DNA and the New Science of the Human Past* (New York: Pantheon Books, 2018).

4 Reich, *Who We Are*, 67. The following discussion is based on Reich, unless otherwise noted. Modern humans separated from Denisovans and Neanderthals c. 770,000–550,000 years ago; Denisovans split from Neanderthals c. 470,000–380,000 years ago. These figures derive from estimates of the mutation rate of genes. It is also possible that these splits happened in Eurasia, descending from the original *Homo erectus*. The nomenclature used for archaic humans refers to a loosely related family of highly evolved archaic humans who inhabited a vast region of Eurasia (Reich, 74).
5 A. R. Templeton, "Biological Races in Humans," *Studies in History and Philosophy of Biological and Biomedical Science* 44 (2013): 262–271.
6 Miguel Cortés-Sánchez, Francisco Jiménez-Espejo, Maria D. Simón-Vallejo, et al. "An Early Aurignacian Arrival in Southwestern Europe," *Nature Ecology & Evolution* 3 (2019), 207–212. https://doi.org/10.1038/s41559-018-0753-6
7 Morton E. Allentoft et al., "Population Genomics of Bronze Age Eurasia," *Nature* 522 (11 June 2015): 167, noting that "The processes that created the genetic landscape of contemporary human populations of Europe and Asia remain contentious."
8 Reich, *Who We Are*, xi, 238–40.
9 David Anthony, *The Horse, Wheel, and Language: How People from the Eurasian Steppes Shaped the Modern World* (Princeton: Princeton University Press, 2008).
10 Reich, *Who We Are*, 95, contends that these groups would have been categorized as "races" if they had lived 10,000 years ago. Reich defends his conflation of biology and culture, regarding language diffusion: DNA cannot reveal what languages people spoke, but it can establish that migrations occurred, so genetics allows the tracing of potential spreads of culture and language.
11 Reich, *Who We Are*, xi.
12 Stephen Mithen, "Neanderthals, Denisovans and Modern Humans," review of David Reich, *Who We Are and How We Got Here: Ancient DNA and the New Science of the Human Past*, *London Review of Books* 40/17 (13 September 2018): 3, 5–6.
13 Ewen Callaway, "'Truly Gobsmacked': Ancient-human Genomes Count Surpasses 10,000," *Nature*, 24 April 2023.
14 Gideon Lewis-Kraus, "Game of Bones," *The New York Times Sunday Magazine*, 17 January 2019, 45.
15 Allentoft et al., "Population Genomics," 171.
16 Allentoft et al., "Population Genomics," 171.
17 Unfortunately, James Watson, discoverer of the DNA helix along with Rosalind Franklin and Francis Crick, is the worst offender of all, making outright racist claims that have been severely censored. Reich, *Who We Are*, 249, objects to the consensus view that "race" is a social construct because it has morphed into an orthodoxy that biological differences should be ignored and the issues are too fraught. The evidence he cites indicates that Reich is unfamiliar with the historical biological science of race.
18 F. B. Livingstone, "On the Non-existence of Human Races," *Current Anthropology* 3 (1962): 279, cited by Reich, *Who We Are*, 252. The cline describes the transition portion of intermixing. D. Serre and S. Pääbo, "Evidence for Gradients of Human Genetic Diversity within and among Continents," *Genome Research* 14 (2004): 1679–1685. Svente Pääbo was awarded the Nobel Prize in 2022 for his discoveries concerning the genomes of extinct hominims and human evolution.
19 Reich, *Who We Are*, 143, argues that many Indian groups might be the products of a culture of social isolation as embodied in the caste system, important for millennia, creating a large number of small populations living side by side but not mixing. He did not consider the widespread practice of infanticide which includes mixed-caste births. See Pramod Kumar Srivastava, "Female Infanticide in 19th-Century India: A Genocide?," *Advances in Historical Studies* 3/5 (December 2014): 269–284. 10.4236/ahs.2014.35022.

20 Mithen, "Neanderthals," notes that the finger bone of a boy living 24,000 years ago in Mal'ta, central Siberia, showed a stronger affinity to Native Americans and Europeans than to Siberians, indicating that he belonged to what had previously been identified as an "entirely ghostly ancient North Eurasians."

21 Gideon Lewis-Kraus, "Game of Bones."

22 Rampley, *Seductions of Darwin*, 53–58, offers a devastating critique of Richard Dawkins' thesis.

23 Mithen, "Neanderthals."

FUGUE 5

BORDERLESS THINKING ON OUR ANIMAL PLANET

On the Future of the Past

Could planetary cultural history conceived at a grand scale avoid an overarching framework, Eurocentric or otherwise? Until quite recently, most philosophers in the Western tradition maintained the old Aristotelian distinction that humans have certain capacities denied to all other animals. The contemporary reference point is frequently the claim by Martin Heidegger (1889–1976) that the stone is worldless, the animal poor in world, and the human world-forming or world-building.[1] Certain Indigenous ontologies reject these assertions, which are still based on the Aristotelian distinction that humans are exceptional due to their cognitive abilities, including their unique capacity to make art and invent tools, to make worlds associated with reason and reminiscence, while the cognitive powers of all other animals are associated with instinct and a retentive memory.

Among contemporary philosophers who have questioned Heidegger's contention that only humans form worlds, the towering figure is Jacques Derrida (1930–2004). Derrida's life's work might be described succinctly as an ongoing and wide-ranging critique of structural unity and authorial genesis. Simply stated, Derrida argues through many different texts, his own and close readings of others', that every structural phenomenon has a history, and its structure cannot be understood without understanding its genesis. *But therein lies a conundrum: the point of origin must already be structured in order to be the genesis of something.*[2]

Derrida's last books and seminars trained this mode of critique on the Heideggerian claim that only the human has a relationship to death as such while the animal simply perishes. The question of the animal was central to his thinking throughout his career but at the time he was preparing these writings and presenting them in his seminars, Derrida was suffering from the pancreatic cancer that took his

DOI: 10.4324/9781351023429-9

life. In the posthumously published book entitled *The Animal That Therefore I Am*, Derrida asks, with characteristic mix of wry wit and intellectual rigor, what logic generates "the limit between Man with a capital M and Animal with a capital A":

> [T]he whole history of the self that man recounts to himself, that is to say, the thesis of a limit as rupture or abyss between those who say "we men," "I, a human," and what this man among men who say "we," what he calls the animal or animals. I shan't for a single moment venture to contest that thesis, nor the rupture or abyss between this "I-we" and what we call animals. To suppose that I, or anyone else for that matter, could ignore that rupture, indeed that abyss, would mean first of all blinding oneself to so much contrary evidence.[3]

Derrida continues, tongue in cheek, that to deny or ignore the rupture would be "more asinine than any beast" (*plus bête que les bêtes*): the discussion worth having is not whether or not there is a limit that produces a discontinuity, but "what are the edges of *a limit that grows and multiplies by feeding on an abyss*."[4] The limit exists because humans have instituted it through language, but how is it maintained today, how does the process of inclusion/exclusion morph while continuing to produce the same structure with humans on one side and the rest of the entire animal kingdom on the other? Derrida offers a thesis in three steps for working out this dubious inheritance: first, recognize that the abyssal rupture doesn't describe two edges (Man and Animal in general); second, be aware that this rupture has a history; and third, understand that beyond the edge of the so-called human there is already a "heterogeneous multiplicity of the living" that leaves no room for "any simple exteriority of one term with respect to another."

Derrida's thesis offers a prime lesson in borderless thinking about human-ness. The issue is not that the distinction between Human and Animal can ever be eliminated – Derrida writes – its existence is so widely attested in the history of [Western] thought that to make such a claim would be bestial, stupid, undercutting the claim being made for human intelligence. We can instead recognize in this pair of categories the values that humans *invented* to define themselves in distinction from every other creature which, Derrida offers, humans reduced to just one word, *animôt* (his coinage derives from *môt* [word], and is a verbal play on the plural, *animaux*). The categories themselves are not mutually exclusive (one is not exterior to the other) because each one comprises a "heterogeneous multiplicity of the living." There are many kinds of animals (including humans linked into the archaic human past, I would add), many kinds of cultural artifacts, and their co-existence is always embedded in a multitude of contexts that become meaningful only in relation to events.[5]

A "borderless" approach to cultural history in this sense of questioning inherited structures encourages conceptualizing the transformation of things through shifts in time and space – that is, a "borderless" approach is focused on the changeability of things and the instability of their signifying power. Jae Emerling, historian of contemporary art interested in temporality, draws upon the work of Gilles Deleuze and Michel Foucault to describe such an approach in which the ontology of the work of art is understood as a temporal passage. He imagines an art historical mode of inquiry capable of encountering the artwork as a material force, its emergence understood as a dated event that continues to produce effects into the future that alter and change the past. Emerling calls for a "diagrammatic" art history as a practice of temporal and other multiplicities in which "diagram" refers to the way the always present gap between the sensible and the intelligible is theorized as a threshold within history. Transmissibility, for Emerling, gets at the complications of temporality (survival, anachronism, memory, becoming), shuttling us between aesthetic labor and cultural reception.[6] I understand his gap or "threshold" as I do Derrida's abyss: a limit imposed by language that is legitimately the subject of investigation. However, the terms "sensible" and "intelligible" and their pairing carry a long cultural signature in the Western tradition. There are many other ways to partition the multi-modal sensorium. Derrida's abyss is an opening in his text – a place for thinking – that inserting those categories shuts down.

In his larger argument, Derrida does not proceed as the scientists have in documenting cognitive abilities and behaviors in animals that were formerly ascribed only to humans. Derrida takes the opposite tack of observing humanity's *lack* of rationality and abundance of animalistic traits including his own possible lapse into bestial behavior were he simply to deny the existence of the categories themselves. Derrida practices a playful but nonetheless deadly serious strategy by reaching into the abyss (the threshold) to breach the flimsy wall that humans maintain between themselves and all the other animals. To which we might add: what justifies the mass destruction of undomesticated animals if they form emotional bonds, build worlds, suffer pain, and die just like us? The implication for writing responsibly about the history of culture in an expanded field is that we need to value narratives of identity that *connect* humans with the rest of the planet.

Borderless Organizational Strategies

Derrida was not only a consummate logician, he was also an historian, a label he used to describe himself when he studied the history of structures, in this case the loaded history of the distinction between Man and Animal. Derrida's concerns with language to identify and unpack hegemonic structures are aligned with numerous contemporary artists and art collectives who give voice to the perspective of undocumented migrants, for example, where the mainstream media and government view characterizes them as a threat to social order. Artists, curators, critics, and historians can all act as agents in a very similar manner, de-centering their own role and intensifying the process of interchange between members of a community. The "art event" has served as the mediator in countless projects since the mid-1990s. Artists, critics, and historians have drawn attention to many forms of artistry that consciously emphasize dialogic, participatory, or interactive processes focused on socially engaged practices.[7] Changes in artistic practice, exhibition, and marketing have resulted in "a shift from the production of images [for the market, for aesthetic contemplation] to the initiation of scenes for the replaying of social relations" writes the Australian cultural theorist Nikos Papastergiadis. He sees a spontaneous, global art movement toward collaborative artistic practices that critically evaluate the relation of commodities to capital. These art practices "reignite the hope" that art can provide meaningful insight rather than merely "colonizing the lifeworld of consumers."[8] He draws upon Derrida's "abyssal problem" of language, which possesses a "structure of alienation without alienation" that in turn encourages translators to invent their own language. Papastergiadis points to the body of contemporary work produced by Western Desert painters in Australia as such a form of cultural translation committed to imagining an alternative community. He draws upon cultural theorist Paul Carter's description of the Papunya Tula movement that began in 1971: a diverse group of displaced people who had been relocated to a desolate government camp were mobilized by the desire for transporting cultural meanings across their differences. Their collaboration opened up "another space . . . in and round the painting room, another ground of exchange. To look at the paintings made there . . . is also to ponder the terms of a non-assimilationist political future."[9] Papastergiadis cites the Mangkaja (Western Australian) artist Jakuna Mona Chugunga: painting involves "*ngalkara*," which means "spreading the word . . . to let people know . . . I have never lost the idea and feeling for my country, where I came from. It is all still in my brain. It is right here. We have that story all of the time."[10]

Indigenous Australian identity is construed in terms of a fluid combination of space and time that is always moving, in which personal identity is tied to a series of places understood as events linking the past with the present.[11] In the desert region at the center of the continent, this cosmology is in keeping with a lifestyle that may entail navigating 4000 square kilometers in a single year in search of food and water. Yet the travelling is not undertaken solely for sustenance, because the journey is the source of a lifeworld where all consciousness and meaning, all sense of place and belonging, as well as all individual historicity, are generated, in the never-ceasing movement through space. *Tjukurrpa*, a Walpiri word that is usually translated as dreamings – and there are many others in the 250 or so native languages of Australia – designates the creative principle that saturates the world with meaning, as manifested in the topography of the land, its life forms, its law-codes of social behavior. *Tjukurrpa* take the form of inherited narratives about the creation of sacred places, land, people, vegetation, and animals, and they comprise a complex network of knowledge informing all aspects of an individual's life by tying his or her existence to prior events. Upon birth, the child is considered a special custodian of that part of his country where the mother stood when the child first moved in the womb, the place from which his or her spirit came as his or her dreaming. The named landscape features of this geography are said to be created "as the result of the activity of a Dreamtime hero in the distant past."[12] The ancient beings are present all around, in *this* world, and their stories are the Western Desert peoples' geography.

However, when it comes to the manner in which Indigenous Australian representations of the places inside/outside become packaged, commodified, and moved around the world, the precarious nature of living off the land especially during the present era of desertification pressed by climate change, raises the question of who controls that space. In the late 1960s, the Australian government removed several groups of Indigenous peoples living on cattle lands in the Western Desert region of the Northern Territory to Papunya, the government relocation center established 240 kilometers northwest of Alice Springs that gave birth to the painting movement Carter and Papastergiadis describe at its inception. When Western Desert acrylic painting became an artistic sensation and economic goldmine in the Australian and international art industry in the 1980s, the symbolic markings characteristic of the "style" were viewed within the framework of high modernist abstraction. "Aboriginal art" succeeded commercially in the 1990s when High Modernism was critically passé, although it was, as it still is, a profitable share of the art market. From the standpoint of art as a high-end commodity form, it became a new product on an old shelf, a novel variant of an existing genre that invigorated a tired market. The enigmatic nature of the abstraction enhances its noumenal value in the marketplace, and the marketplace is where its actual economic value is determined and maintained according to a system far removed from the artist's actual intentions. And even farther removed from the abject poverty of the desert art centers, where the majority of artists dependent upon and feeding the thriving art market in "Aboriginal art" live out their lives. Lives which are often cut short by health problems due to poor nutrition, lack of adequate access to the health care system, and by poor coping skills most commonly manifesting as alcoholism, lifestyle diseases such as diabetes, and domestic violence.[13]

Profiteering is also directly connected to the devastating effects of climate change that are destroying the lives and homelands of Indigenous people around the world, creating an unprecedented ecological and humanitarian crisis that replays the history of colonial global capitalism in the present at "warp speed" to cite Star Trek technology, only this is not science fiction. To give a salient example of the apocalyptic conditions unfolding before our eyes that would benefit from Indigenous knowledge: Naomi Klein, whose well-known book, *The Shock Doctrine: The Rise of Disaster Capitalism* (2007) exposed the well-worn tactic of exploiting moments of extreme collective trauma to benefit a small capitalist elite, and her co-author Kapua'ala Sproat, Professor of Law at the University of Hawaii and Director of the Ka Huli Ao Native Hawaiian Law Center for Excellence in Native Hawaiian Law and the Environmental Law Program, published a devastating analysis of why firefighters ran out of water battling unprecedented wildfires in August 2023 on Maui, a Hawaiian island whose main source of income derives from the tourist industry. The water rights of Native Hawaiians have been stifled for two centuries by "a long parade of plantations, real estate developers, and luxury resorts."[14] Water across the western region of the island has been extracted to benefit outside interests from large sugar plantations (where flammable non-native grasses now grow) to their corporate successors who have exploited the island's natural resources to develop colonial-style residential subdivisions, luxury resorts, and golf courses, draining Indigenous ecologies of their natural moisture. The historical town of Lahaina, completely destroyed by fire in August 2023, had already been transformed into a parched desert, drying up the freshwater fishpond that was at the seat of the Hawaiian Kingdom in the early 1900s. The mass media also profit when catastrophes are passively consumed as aesthetic images. As contemporary art historian and cultural theorist Terry Smith argues about the way viral images shape contemporary life, "countering spectacle, en route to planetary worldmaking, remains the essential task" [Figure 5.1].[15]

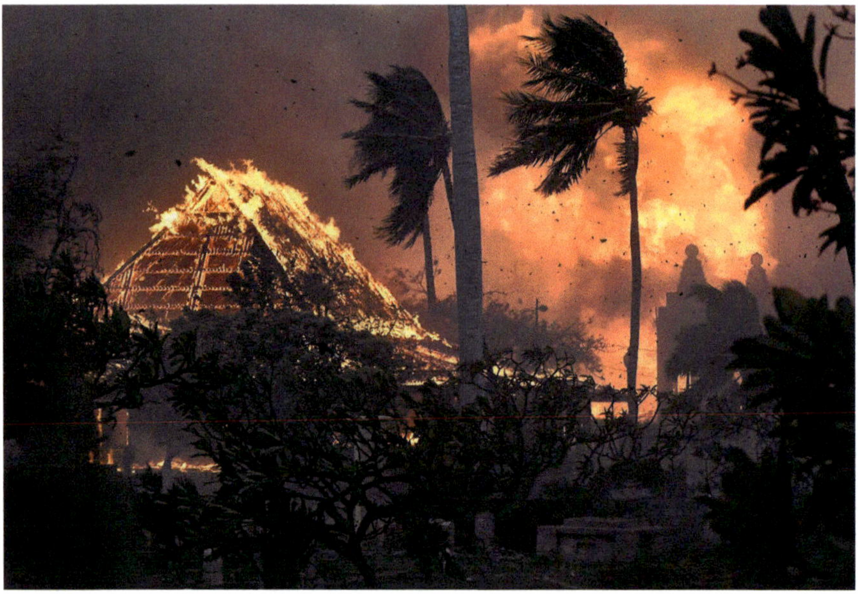

FIGURE 5.1 The hall of historic Waialua Church and nearbv Lahaina Hongwanji Mission are engulfed in flames along Wainee Street on August 8, 2023, in Lahaina, Maui. Photo Matthew Thayer, *The Maui News*, AP. Associated Press/Alamy Stock Photo.

Many Native Hawaiian communities indigenous to this region, Maui Komohana, were cut off from water for their basic needs, including drinking, laundry, and traditional crop irrigation. Streams that once flowed through their valley were diverted for luxury subdivisions that often occupy plantation-controlled lands, leaving many Native families without access to county water lines, fire hydrants, and paved roads to escape the fires. Companies such as the West Maui Land Company control the water commission, diverting the water to service affluent estates while alleging there is not enough water to both sell to its customers and comply with the water commission's stream protection standard. The climate emergency has intensified these conditions and tensions, leading to Indigenous efforts in pursuit of restorative justice to regain the right to manage their own water, a fight that resulted in a historic victory in 2022 to institute a new permitting system. Ironically, the deadline to submit permit applications to the water commission was 7 August 2023, one day before the fire that devoured Lahaina. The governor's administration issued emergency proclamations that suspended a series of laws, including the state water code, in the process removing civil servants who opposed the administration's pro-developer agenda – while the search for survivors was still underway with 1000 persons missing and fires still burning in many parts of Maui. As of 25 April 2024, portions of Lahaina remained under an unsafe water advisory.[16]

On 2 August 2024, a year after the disaster, survivors of the catastrophe reached a settlement with Hawaii's largest utility company which agreed to compensate more than 10,000 plaintiffs. It is a mixed outcome: the governor pushed for a single global agreement to compensate the fire victims quickly while avoiding the bankruptcy of Hawaiian Electric, which would financially devastate Maui County. The utility is expected to pay less than half of the settlement based on the estimated cost of the damages and the settlement does not include any admission of liability.[17]

The Native communities know that they have the rights to stay on their ancestral lands, where their biocultural knowledge "is needed to navigate the path forward in a time of climate crisis." The future of Maui physically *and* culturally depends on who controls the water. Five centuries into extractive capitalism practiced on a massive scale, the environmental determinism of historical climate theory and its companion/sequel, racial science, has been turned on its head. Instead of Europeans classifying the mental capacities and moral character of people based on where they were born and presumed to still live, while characterizing their natural resources in terms of their profitability to capitalists, the planet now looks (or should look) to native knowledge holders to mitigate the environmental degradation that colonialist/capitalist/neoliberal practices have wrought.

As the artist collective Postcommodity articulates what is at stake for the planet, people who are the continuation of the first peoples on their land are the "ongoing knowledge keepers of the first peoples of the Western Hemisphere . . . we use *Indigenous American* as a term for building this hemispheric discourse."[18] Indigenous or First Nation individuals, aware that they have greater agency by joining forces, are forming new globalized connections based on a shared sense of purpose outside the frame of colonization, the main experience that they have in common, writes Indigenous artist/author/curator Gerald McMaster, Director of the Wapatah Center for Indigenous Visual Knowledge in Toronto, Canada, and a Plains Cree member of the Siksika Nation. McMaster's collaborative book coauthored with Nina Vincent and accompanying exhibition, *Arctic/Amazon: Networks of Indigeneity* (2023), is the outgrowth of an international symposium in 2019. It includes artists and writers from "supranational cultural groups that exceed the boundaries of modern nation-states."[19] The Amazon presents a cultural history different from the Circumpolar Arctic, which is relatively homogenous by comparison. The Amazon Forest covers nearly five million square miles and is home to 1.5 million Indigenous individuals comprising 385 diverse ethnic groups that include descendants of fugitive enslaved Africans and of workers who migrated from other regions to supply the rubber extraction industry.[20] The rubber industry, which left poverty in its wake, boomed in the early twentieth century but collapsed by 1945, when cheaper latex became available in Southeast Asia – another instantiation of mobile "commodity frontiers" as Jason Moore describes the dynamics of extractive capitalism operating globally since the sixteenth century.[21] This mixing of peoples over centuries produced a local Amazonian culture influenced by Indigenous habits and beliefs, strongly connected to the forest that they defend today from corporate interests supported by the federal State.

The colonial history of environmental destruction is *continuous* at least since the mid-fifteenth century when the Portuguese colonized the Azore archipelago in the North Atlantic between 1427 and 1452 while searching for new routes to Asia.[22] The long-distance exchanges between Southeast Asia, Central America, and Europe that galleon transport made possible beginning in the sixteenth century depended on connections between places that were not physically contiguous [Figure 5.2].

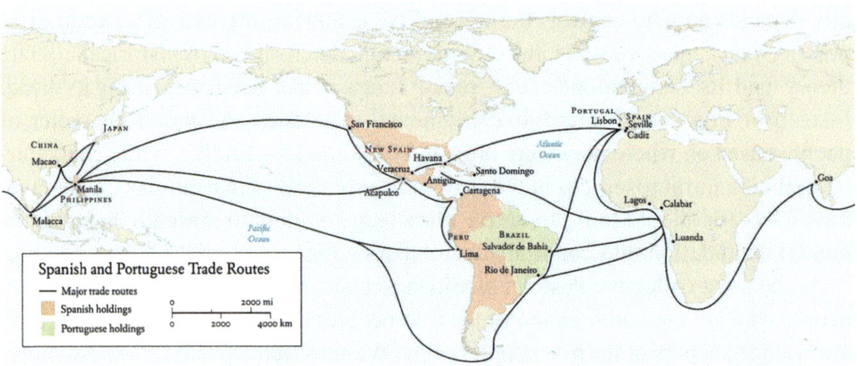

FIGURE 5.2 Spanish and Portuguese Trade Routes. After Anandaroop Roy, in Joseph J. Rishel with Suzanne Stratton-Pruitt, *Tesoros/Treasures/Tesouros: The Arts of Latin America, 1492–1820*, exh. cat. (Philadelphia: Philadelphia Museum of Art in Association with Yale University Press, 2006), p. xxiii. Map courtesy of Anandaroop Roy.

The speed of destruction stands out as a unique feature of the "commodity frontiers" approach taken by Spanish, Dutch, English, and other colonizers and traders once long-distance navigation and shipbuilding technology developed at this scale in the sixteenth century.

What Indigenous knowledge holders recognize as tradition is analogous to history writing. The most compelling rebuttal to teleological, linear accounts of history comes from those actually existing Indigenous individuals who act in solidarity precisely because it gives the worldviews of Indigenous peoples greater agency to change both the discourse and the actual relationship of humans to the rest of nature *now*. Examining how Indigenous artists, writers, and activists describe their "ecological imagination" encourages tackling complex environmental crises by turning toward reciprocity and relationships, as Maori art historian Linda Tuhiwai Smith has identified new principles for research.[23] Many Indigenous writers argue that the current challenges around the globe cannot be approached using one philosophical, epistemological, or ontological lens.[24] Brazilian anthropologist Nina Vincent writes that the goal is not to create a common world, but to act in a world in common.[25] The cosmos encompasses everything but it cannot be comprehended by a single interpretation.[26] Different worldviews offer ways to engage in political and ecological debate through practices that are not grounded in the Western division of nature and culture.

A cosmopolitics, to use Isabelle Stengers' term, must not only be based in an equality of knowledge but also be sustained through the acknowledgment of a diversity of worlds.[27] Many Indigenous cultures do not have a particular word to designate "art" in the Western sense, but this is exactly where art and the climate crisis come together for the sake of the planet we share. In the Amazon, Vincent writes, art in its broadest sense is "intentionally and carefully created to sustain the aesthetic of an everyday symbiotic life" connected to nature, a sensibility that is called "el buen vivir" [*sumak kawsay* in Quecha] in many Latin American Indigenous traditions – meaning the constant pursuit of a balanced, fair, and harmonic *collective* life that also serves as an important political model for the region.[28] Based on Afro-Indigenous principles and vernacular practices, *el buen vivir* refers to an active consciousness that incorporates the potential to live in consonance with the Earth: plants mediate between the natural, the human, and the supernatural.[29] However, writes Macarena Gómez-Barris, in Ecuador and Bolivia, presidents Rafael Correa (served 2007–2017) and Evo Morales (served 2006–2019), respectively, instrumentalized the use of *el buen vivir* as a rhetorical cover for the state that "prioritizes capitalist agendas while diminishing the reach of actual decolonization." Both presidents promoted Indigenous agendas to get elected only to convert legally protected territories into extractable commodities.[30] The distinction between human and non-human, and the alienation of people from the Forest by forced migration that turns them into laborers living in favelas (slums or ghettoes) in urban peripheries and regards them a "natural resource" is the product of colonization that "denies the plurality of life forms of existence and habits," writes artist and activist Ailton Krenak, who speaks from his own village community in the Krenak Indigenous reserve in the State of Minas Gerais in southeastern Brazil.[31]

Gathering Indigenous North and South to talk openly about issues and ideas in a generative way reconnects people who may have been separated for a long time, McMaster observes, awakening them to a futurity in a clarion call to action. Reconnecting Indigenous peoples around the world provides an important sense of shared agency, creating an Indigenous contact zone through a different lens than the colonial sovereignties that first divided Indigenous cultures. The Arctic/Amazon project that McMaster and Vincent describe is focused on connecting Indigenous communities from the Global North and South so that new networks are built, connections are created, and common ground is achieved. Krenak considers the idea of global indigeneity as a way to expand the subjective horizons of the planet by understanding that humans are not the only ones who have subjectivity and a perspective on existence. He writes that it may be possible to preserve the visions and the poetics of existence by recognizing that the experience of diversity, not humanity, is the true richness of the world.[32] Several artists have begun a new discussion of environmental protection in both the Arctic and Amazon, to think more holistically about the environment in two regions that are viewed as critical in the discourse on global climate change. The Amazon is not a wild jungle, but a cultural forest maintained by people who have inhabited the region for at least 11,000 years, intervening in the ecosystem using traditional knowledge which shows that the environment is inextricably connected to people and the more than human world.[33]

It is important not to treat Indigenous knowledge as another resource for extractive processes. Artist Pitseolak Pfeifer, born and raised in Iqaluit, Nunavut (formerly known as Frobisher Bay, Northwest Territories, Canada) pointedly asks, what is the return to us when scientists seek Indigenous opinions and advice? How can knowledge be decolonized so that Indigenous knowledge holders do not "become co-opted to the advantage of the dominant order – even in reconciliation," because reconciliation itself needs to be defined.[34] Pfeifer endorses the diversity and inclusiveness of knowledge made possible by social media: Facebook has been an extraordinary platform connecting Inuit individuals interested in reclaiming their language and culture, their connection to the land. When they post publicly for everyone, family and their wider community, "it's good for the heart" and each little video is an act of resistance.

Extensive knowledge of the local environment, as the traditional knowledge holders in Maui emphasized after drought and fire destroyed their ancestral homeland in August 2023, is essential for stabilizing nature. Professor of Humanities and the Environment Rob Nixon describes the process of alienation in concrete terms when he outlines the stages of dehumanization in the "petroleum nation-state" of Saudi Arabia, where the inhabitants of the oasis (*wadi*) first experience the oil's blessings as violation when the oil-extracting machinery destroys the habitat of their anchored communities. In the second phase, the now homeless people get displaced to a coastal refinery town, where they are housed in metal shacks and remade as laborers in a wage economy under foreign control. Thus, an economy dispersed around nodal oases is suddenly transformed into a centralized, client nation-state presided over by an oil corporation.[35] The "blessing of oil" becomes institutionalized as class distinction and racial segregation. Alongside the loss of lives, habitat, and human dignity, is the wholesale destruction of millennia of cultural knowledge.

We may not be able to bend capitalism to our will, but until we (artists, scholars, students, activists, social critics, politicians, scientists, readers of these words) change the discourse that *is* within our power to change, we will remain complicit with divisive old paradigms when we could be ushering in new, healthier ways to develop the future of sustainable life on Earth. Lacking adequate government response, desperate scientists advocate grassroots acts of resistance such as "environmental direct action, resistance taken from outside the dominant culture, as in protests, blockades, and sabotage by Indigenous peoples, workers, anarchists, and other activist groups."[36] Their exhortations to practice civil disobedience bring to mind Agamben's sober injunction on "the coming community": "The novelty of the coming politics is that it will no longer be a struggle for the conquest or control of the State, but a struggle between the State and the non-State (humanity)."[37]

Naomi Klein writes that imagining the world we want is the hardest work of all, but it is our only hope. The aftermath of the Great Depression and World War II became periods of massive social transformation, and so the climate crisis *could* become an opportunity for social and economic change. She advocates mapping the "intersectional agendas of competing visions that can push forward on multiple fronts."[38] The drama of a global humanity linked by peaceful trade, digital communication, and international institutions, has been compromised by right-wing nationalism, neoliberalism, trade wars, withdrawals from multilateralism, and the reconfiguration of historical alliances. The "re-shoring" and scaling down of globally dispersed supply chains involving globe-spanning processes of extraction, production, distribution, and finance, is a bewilderingly complex task, writes Laurie Parsons arguing against "one world" approaches to mitigating the climate crisis. Focusing on textile waste in the global clothing industry, Parsons documents supply chains so complex that they are impossible to regulate, thus "greenwashing" is a major contributor to the climate crisis. Major companies who claim compliance with environmental standards outsource their manufacturing processes in a complex chain of factories in poor countries that do not even have the means to regulate their polluting practices.[39]

Putting it Altogether: Borderless Organizational Strategies

The project of writing planetary histories of culture in the plural invites collaboration across various disciplinary platforms working in the shadow of catastrophic climate change, diminishing biodiversity, and their many collateral effects. Indigenous/First Nation artists are not alone in actively addressing environmental issues with non-totalizing, transcultural approaches to art. It is beyond the scope of the present study to review the burgeoning but fragmented literature on contemporary art devoted to climate justice, but maybe I can suggest the flavor of these efforts through a few key examples without wishing to imply that they are "representative" of what is a de-centered field of inquiry. Some of the most exciting projects involve collaborations between scientists and artists.

Victoria Vesna, who is Director of the UCLA Art|Sci Center in Los Angeles, is among the leading sci/artists collaborating with scientists on equal footing in which each side changes the other and something new emerges. Sound, not visuals, are the foundation of Vesna's creative process. This is an important difference between "visual" strategies and "visualizing" strategies. In a neuro-sound meditation for *Noise Aquarium* with sound artist Anna Nacher, breathing and drumming provide the rhythm of sound and silence that quiets the brain to meditate with the awareness. Vesna stresses that harmony or balance is the dynamic life force that connects the individual with the creatures of the ocean. The physical experience triggers the viewer's compassion through immersion in an artificial environment composed of enhanced sight and sound collected from the natural environment. The spectator is sensorily engaged in understanding how the entire ecosystem of the planet is connected and depends on the tiniest creatures in the ocean that produce the oxygen we breathe. Learning about stranded whales breaks our hearts, but focusing on the entire ecosystem informs us about what is going on in order to take action [Figure 5.3].

Lisa E. Bloom, a prominent critical voice who works with case studies, links gendered, sexual, and racial discriminatory violence to wide environmental destruction using "an intersectional feminist perspective and an environmental justice framework." In a recent review essay, Bloom emphasizes the changes wrought by the Covid-19 pandemic to rethink what it means to be part of an arts community. She focuses on one artist and an art media collective who emphasize message-delivering over the "formal concerns of object-based art."[40] At the opposite end of the methodological spectrum, in an ambitiously comprehensive and theoretically well-informed survey text that also registers the impact of the pandemic, curators Maja and Reuben Fowkes approach climate change as a planetary process that "demands a radical rethinking of the human in the terrestrial order." They focus on "research-based and situated artistic approaches that uncover particular socio-environmental matters in sites of crisis yet engage in an international conversation that spans geographies and connects with planetary questions."[41] Their material is organized thematically, an approach that is still based on taxonomic classification but one that foregrounds process rather than essential traits. Five sections document the work of 155 artists and art collectives: artists who scrutinize the anthropogenic causes of climate change, artists who investigate how these changes affect natural entities; artists who engage with the vegetal world; artists who consider animal and human relations threatened by climate change; and artists who rethink the position of the human within the terrestrial order.

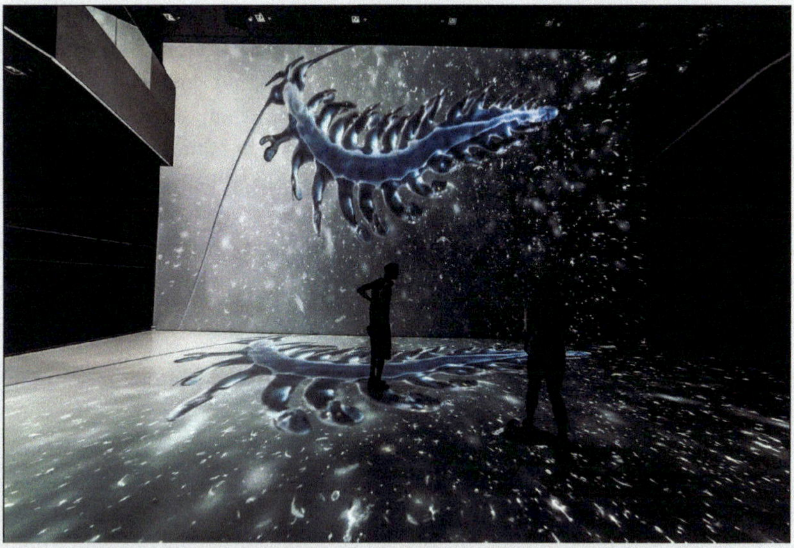

FIGURE 5.3 Victoria Vesna, *Noise Aquarium*, multimedia installation, 2016–present. Photo Ars Electronica Deep Space 2018, Glenn Bristol. See further Vesna's Website: http://noiseaquarium.com

Plankton serve as one of the primary bases of the marine food chain and are as a result a crucial component of the Earth's ecosystem. Scientists believe that phytoplankton contribute between 50 to 85% of the oxygen in Earth's atmosphere. *Noise Aquarium* utilizes 3D scans of these micro creatures obtained with unique scientific imaging techniques and immerses the audience in the 3D "aquarium" of diverse planktons projected as large as whales. The fully evolved project offers the participant the possibility of interacting with the projection by balancing on a platform – out of balance creates underwater noises and when the participant is fully centered the plankton (bottom of the food chain) appear and we hear whale songs (top of the food chain).

"Ecology is one of the most important sites for rethinking temporality within the humanities," write Birgit Hopfener and Karin Zitzewitz in their introduction to a collection of critical essays on ways to reconceptualize art history's universalizing temporal frameworks by adopting a "multi-temporal pluriverse" approach to the world.[42] Focusing on the Asian context, they argue that the decolonial concept of the pluriverse plays a crucial role in the distinction between an engaged thought project designed to link to political activism in the present and, on the other hand, what they characterize as the merely critical approach taken by postcolonial thought.[43] Conceiving of knowledge as relational and situated, the editors selected contributors who advocate an approach that "attends to specific regional and historical contexts and how they relate to each other, while continuously scaling back and forth between multiple and entangled perspectives" to examine processes through which forms and discourses emerge in local contexts within circuits of exchange.[44] At the beginning of *Writing Borderless Histories of Art*, I noted the important work of T. J. Demos, who writes about artists working at the intersections of art, environmental activism, and political ecology. In this arena, acting collaboratively is essential to cover the bases of expertise. In 2021, joining efforts with the environmental humanities but remaining distinct from them, Demos, Emily Eliza Scott, and Subhankar Banerjee, also leading specialists on contemporary art and ecology, edited a collection of essays at the intersection of contemporary art, visual culture, and climate breakdown. They bring together nearly fifty contributors whose diverse voices provide, in the words of the editors' opening statement, "a vital site of intervention, complementary and alternative to the earth sciences, engineering design, and economics, which have popularly defined climate-change discourse and policy." They stress the importance of including art and visual culture in the discourse and policy to mitigate the effects of the climate crisis. They emphasize the need to assess the representational politics of climate transformation beyond the techno-scientific discourse that currently dominates public perception. The key issues that structure their book are: Extractivism, Climate Violence, Sensing Climates, In/Visibilities, Multispecies Justice, and Ruptures/Insurgencies/Worldings.

Demos, Scott, and Banerjee insist that colonization of the Americas since 1492 was an inaugural event, but the "derangement of natural systems" cannot be defined by isolated events. Instead:

> We have attempted to center in the book's diverse inclusions the perspectives, experiences, and voices of underrepresented and under-resourced frontline communities who have historically suffered (and in many cases continue to suffer) an outsized proportion of climate-related vulnerabilities, bearing the brunt of the unequal social dynamics that have further exacerbated those vulnerabilities.[45]

Regardless of emphasis or methodology, contemporary artists and those who write about the underrepresented advocate political activism. The main targets of their critiques are unregulated extractive capitalism and linear historical narratives based on Eurocentric ideas about the rest of the world. Existing accounts of the past often use the same problematic epistemological categories and teleological narratives that transcultural studies are trying to eliminate. Historians who study the objects and texts of the past are also re-writing the history of the past in the present. As I have argued throughout *Writing Borderless Histories of Art*, processes of environmental destruction on a global scale identified in these transcultural approaches began long before the Industrial era of capitalism usually associated with the Anthropocene. This re-written history deserves to be at the table of discussion of contemporary art and the climate emergency too. To do otherwise is to exclude the historian as yet another voiceless, marginalized, dispossessed subject. (How) could a planetary history of art include all artifacts in a non-totalizing, non-Eurocentric framework? It would, by definition, include the earliest artifactual evidence (of course, narratives can be organized in many different ways).

On the Origins of Culture

Given the historical division of human material culture into the categories of art versus artifact, studied respectively by art historians and anthropologists and archaeologists, it is important to reunite them in developing an inclusive approach to planetary culture. Structurally speaking, the paired categories of art and artifact present an abyssal problem analogous to that of "animal" and "human." We would be tilting at windmills to deny their existence – there is an enormous amount of evidence showing that and how the categories exist – but these categorical differences are imposed on "a heterogeneous multiplicity" of cultural materials, to cite Derrida's pertinent objection.[46] The categories themselves are not mutually exclusive (one is not exterior to the other) because each one comprises a "heterogeneous multiplicity of the living." There are many kinds of animals (including humans linked into the archaic human past, I would add), many kinds of cultural artifacts, and their co-existence is always embedded in a multitude of contexts that become meaningful only in relation to events.[47]

A "borderless" approach to cultural history in this sense of questioning inherited structures encourages conceptualizing the transformation of things through shifts in time and space – that is, a "borderless" approach is focused on the changeability of things and the instability of their signifying power. A "borderless" approach to the origins of planetary culture in the sense I have defined it throughout this book acknowledges the history of the categories "art" and "artifact" but it focuses on the "abyss" between them that maintains the distinction discursively.

The record of humans emerging out of their environmental matrix is preserved in material culture and the built environment. De-centering of the human makes it easier to imagine cultural and behavioral continuities with the rest of the animal world. Accounts of the planet's artifactual history also need to be flexible, to admit new information as it emerges along the animal/human interface and elsewhere in the subsequent record of human migration and settlement. To put the development of material culture on Earth into the context of planetary history, scientists have documented five significant ice ages, of which the most recent is called the Quaternary beginning 2.6 million years ago and continuing into the present. Approximately a dozen glaciations have occurred over the past million years, the largest of which peaked 650,000 years ago and lasted for 50,000 years.[48]

The most recent glaciation period reached peak conditions c. 30,000 years ago, ending with the interglacial Holocene epoch that began c. 11,700 years ago. The earliest fossil hominids are about three million years old, but significant remains of material culture coincide roughly with the Last Glacial Maximum (26,500–19,000 years ago). This is the period when the earliest presence of Native Americans is conventionally documented, corroborated recently by a genome study based on human remains and computer modeling published in 2018 which, the authors argue, confirm the theory that Native Americans descended from a single founding population that migrated across Beringia, a land bridge connecting Asia and North America 20,000 years ago.[49] That claim has been disputed by archaeological evidence published in 2020 that people traveled by boat to North America more than 30,000 years ago, based on hundreds of dates obtained from 42 archaeological sites that were combined statistically along with stratigraphic information from the deposits to estimate the period of human occupation.[50] Another study (2017) found evidence of human presence in North America 130,000 years ago.[51]

The Bering Strait theory has long been disputed by Native American oral traditions considered to preserve real cultural memory of lived experience on the American continent. Vine Deloria, Jr. (1933–2005), a respected Sioux elder, theologian, historian, legal scholar, university professor, and activist for Native American rights, argued that the Bering Strait theory is a leftover of cultural evolutionism.[52] Worldwide, a large number of cultural sites have been discovered dating from or shortly before the Last Glacial Maximum, such as the spectacular multi-chambered painted caves in what are now southern France and northern Spain [Figure 5.4].

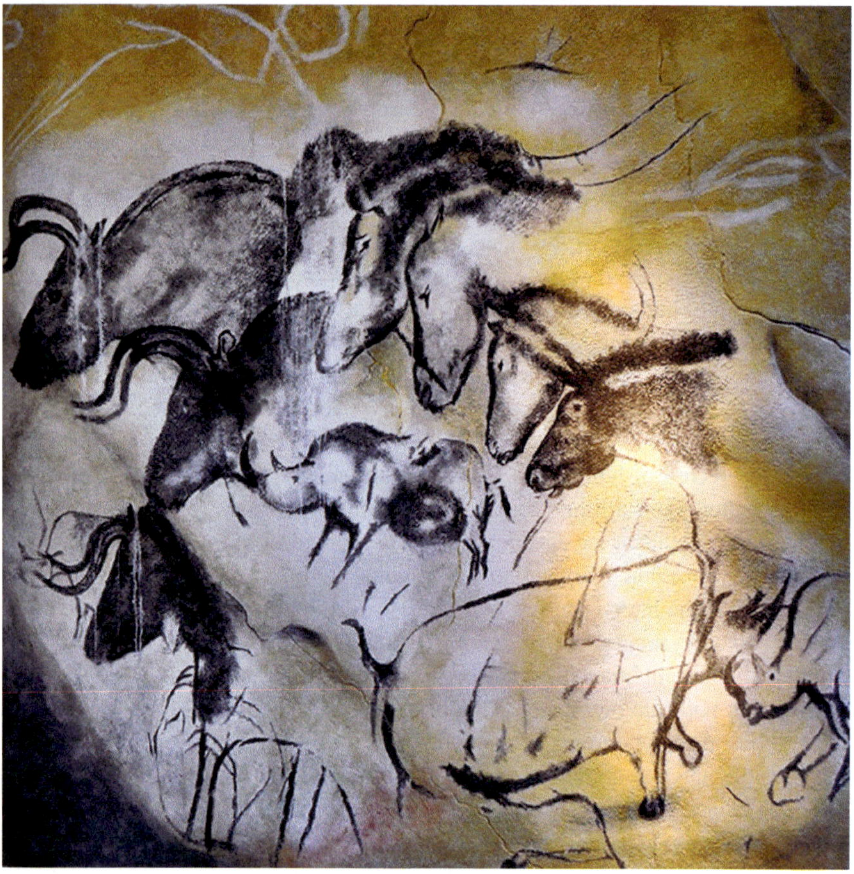

FIGURE 5.4 Painted horses from Chauvet Cave, Ardèche, France, detail, c. 37,000–33,500 years ago. Part of an 11-meter-long fresco with rhinoceros, mammoths, and big cats different from horse, bison, and deer dominant in later Ice Age art, Photo L. Guichard, 2006. Creative Commons Attribution-Share Alike 2.0 Generic, Wiki/FunkMonk/Thomas T. https://www.flickr.com/photos/theadventurouseye/5602930382/

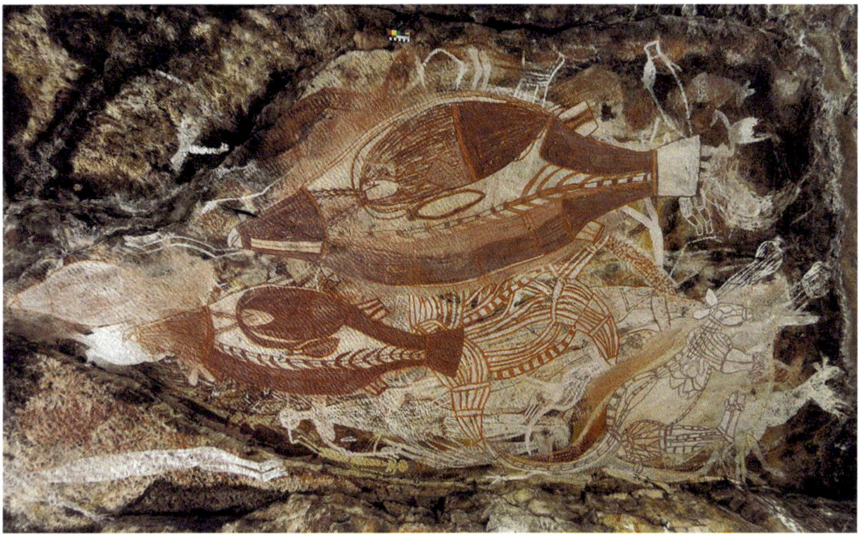

FIGURE 5.5 Australia, Ceiling panel E1 from Narwala Gabarnmang rock shelter, Arnhem Land plateau, Australia, dated 28,000 years ago, on a site inhabited by humans 45,000 years BP. Photo R. Gunn with permission of the late M. Katherine.

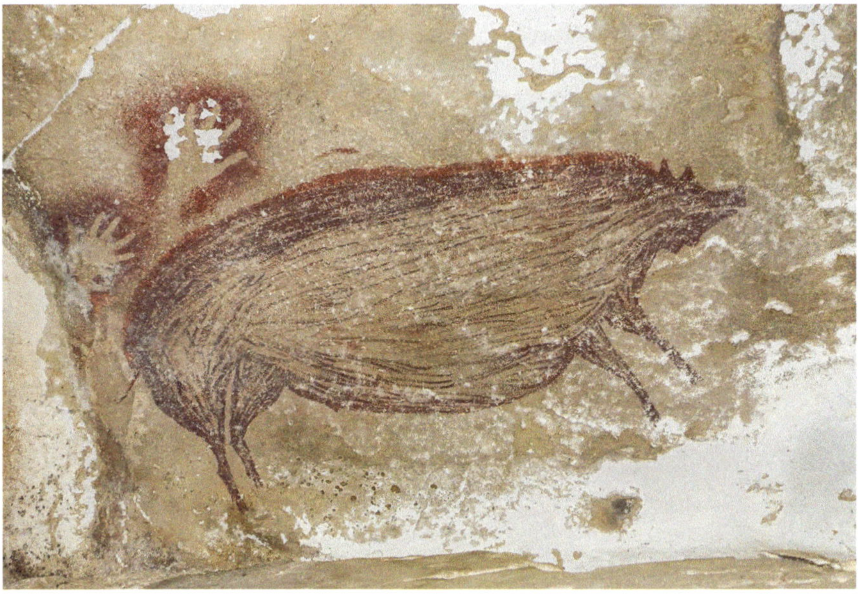

FIGURE 5.6 Warty Pig facing two other pigs, partially preserved (not shown), dark ochre pigment, 53 x 21 inches, Leang Tedongnge Cave, Sulawesi Island, Indonesia, at least 45,500 years BP. Image credit: Brumm et al., doi: 10.1126/sciadv.abd4648. Photo Maxime Aubert.

While controversies about dating remain, it appears that the oldest of these European sites, paintings of megafauna from Chauvet Cave in southern France dating from about 37,000–33,500–CE, are roughly contemporaneous with awe-inspiring rock paintings in northern Australia (Narwala Gabarnmang rock shelter, southwestern Arnhem Land, Northern Territory, datable 28,000 BCE), at least 10,000 years later than the naturalistic cave paintings recently discovered in Indonesia [Figure 5.6], and 40,000 years later than the oldest known drawing, discovered in 2018 in Blombos Cave in South Africa, dated 73,000 years ago [Figure 5.7]. Two ochre-processing toolkits from the same site were discovered in the 100,000 year-old levels.

There are other extensive cultural remains from the last Ice Age occurring on every continent. "Origin" and "first" are constantly changing and will continue to do so as the planet heats up to reveal more evidence of planetary co-habitation under the ice and frozen tundra. Archaeologists working in Zambia in central Africa have discovered evidence of the world's currently oldest-known wood structure, consisting of two interlocking logs joined by a notch. Markings on the logs show they were cut and chopped with a range of tools about 476,000 years ago, predating the rise of *Homo sapiens* about 300,000 years ago [Figure 5.8].[54]

If we were to map the earliest cultural artifacts on earth, the result would look like a globe that lights up in many different places. Europe is brightly lit but it is not at the center of the light show. Such a cultural map might correspond to the numerous migrations out of Africa, back and forth across Eurasia, into and out of Australia, spreading further over time, but the history of humans populating the planet is developing so rapidly and is so complex, as the new genomic science of ancient DNA analysis is documenting, that it may never be possible to see patterns or identify regions of cultural interaction in this distant past.

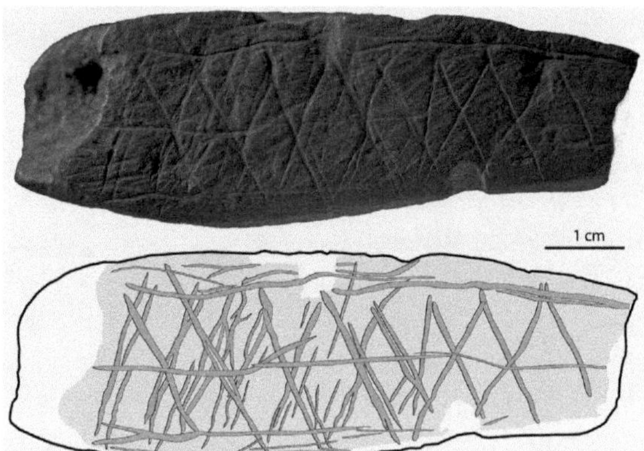

FIGURE 5.7 Engraved ochre stone found at Biombos cave site, South Africa, dated c. 70,000 years BP. Image courtesy of Professor Christopher Henshilwood. Photo Francesco d'Errico.[53]

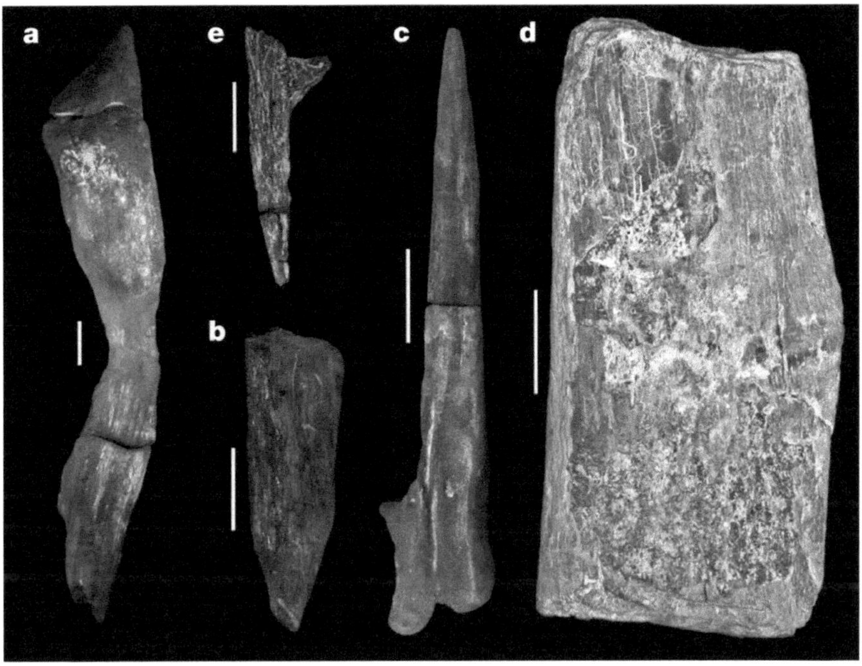

FIGURE 5.8 Archaic human. Modified wood tools. Excavated in 2019 at site BLB, Kalambo Falls, near border of Zambia and Tanzania, c. 390,000–324,000 BP. (a. BLB5 structural element [object 1033]. b, BLB3 'wedge' [object 660]. c, BLB2 'digging stick' [object 219]. d, BLB4 cut log. e, BLB4, tapered piece with single chop-mark.) Scale bars, 10 cm. The earliest known wooden structure (not illustrated), part of a platform, was found in this area, cut and chopped with stone tools, c. 476,000 years BP. L. Barham, G. A. T. Duller, I. Candy, et al., "Evidence for the earliest structural use of wood at least 476,000 years ago," *Nature* 622 (2023): 107–111. https://doi.org/10.1038/s41586-023-06557-9

The earliest documented large-scale trading regions date after the end of the last Ice Age, triggered about 20,000 years ago by an orbital shift in the Earth's rotation which brought more summer sunlight to the northern hemisphere, reshaped the planet's wind belts, and increased the levels of carbon dioxide in the atmosphere.[55] As in the case of the "handaxe," the reinterpretation of existing paradigms is driven in part by a stream of new data and in part by increasing awareness of Eurocentric assumptions in the existing literature. Nordic Bronze Age archaeologist Kristian Kristiansen writes about recent changes in writing the prehistory of northern Europe during the first and second millennia BCE which, in archaeological terms, encompasses the Bronze Age and the Early Iron Age. This era is key to understanding world history because it accounts for the first industrialization in the history of Europe and produced some of the "most stunning works of artistic and technical mastery in bronze and gold ever seen."[56] Echoing Derrida's observations about the nature of origins (and perfectly aligned with *Writing Borderless Histories of Art*), Kristiansen writes that the way we structure and use historical knowledge is largely shaped by present concerns.

Archaeology, charged with interpreting the past through material remains, was initially framed in terms of European nation-states and national identities during the nineteenth and early twentieth centuries.

It has become increasingly clear over the past quarter century, Kristiansen writes, that historical changes operated at a much larger scale than regional research traditions and the prehistoric cultures themselves. He emphasizes the need to abandon "the arbitrary and ideological basis of traditional research" that considers Europe and its regions as natural, self-contained units, by setting them into wider networks of interacting regional systems. During the Bronze Age, an international network of metal trade and exchange emerged, making all regions dependent on each other, thus calling for the development of broader interpretative theoretical frameworks able to account for this complexity. Events that favored new regional traditions in Northern and Central Europe operated at a much larger historical and geographical scale than the traditional barriers of chronological and cultural classifications, spanning categories ranging from tribal societies to archaic states – and producing a complex play of relations that Kristiansen, writing in 1998, characterized as "center–periphery" relations, but which might be better described today in terms of circulation or flows.

Kristiansen concludes that the Bronze Age introduced new forms of interaction and interdependence that can only be grasped by taking a "world system" approach to studying how supplies of metal and know-how passed between different regions. He argues that exchange must have proceeded on a common stock of knowledge and accompanying social and religious value systems:

> the genesis of the Roman Empire, and consequently of much of later European history, is to be sought in the two millennia preceding it . . . [in] historical and structural regularities that characterized the integration of Europe into a Bronze Age world system, which gradually transformed Europe north of the Mediterranean and created a structural hierarchy of regional traditions.[57]

Interacting prehistoric societies able to create the conditions for their own transformation resulted in the formation and collapse of large-scale networks of exchange and trade, and migrations. These waxing and waning trading networks created new conditions for interaction with other societies and regions ranging from pastoral nomads of the Eurasian steppes to civilizations of the Near East and Mediterranean. To give one significant example of the new ways of understanding regions as part of much larger trading networks, archaeologist Flemming Kaul studies the rich evidence of long-distance exchange and communication between southern Scandinavia and the Mediterranean in the second millennium BCE. Evidence of these long-distance exchanges appears to be documented by the appearance of new types of artefacts such as single-edge razors and new iconographic motifs including the presence of specific types of ships, two-wheeled chariots, and folding stools of Mediterranean origin in Nordic Late Bronze Age rock carvings.[58] Kaul interprets the sun chariot as being pulled over the heavens by a divine horse. The sun image, covered in gold foil incised with radial grooves only on one side, and the horse were placed on wheels to demonstrate the movement of the sun. The horse faces right on the radiant side of the sun disk, moving in the direction that the sun is seen to travel from the northern hemisphere, while on the darker side, the horse faces left as if the sun had to return to its starting point by sunrise. The sun horse as an independent motif, with a line running from the horse's neck to the sun as was once the case for the Sun Chariot, should probably be seen as a sign manifesting the sun or its movement. The ships (also depicted on razors as in the example shown in Figure 5.11) are more than transporters of the sun, they also represent a certain flow of time conveying the idea of cosmological order. Kaul makes the important point that stylization of a motif does not make it meaningless as long as the abstract patterns can be "read" in their context, even if the borderline line between decoration without meaning and decoration with meaning remains uncertain for us [Figures 5.10–5.12].[59]

Demands for metal created long distance exchange systems – copper was exclusively imported from far away sources in the Alps, the Carpathians, even Cyprus. Cornwall was an important source of tin. Sourcing of raw materials for manufacturing bronze was part of a two-way exchange that involved exporting amber found along the coasts of the Baltic Sea, including Scania in Sweden, some of the Danish islands, and North Sea coast of the Jutland Peninsula [Figure 5.13]. The most distant connections, not shown on this map, are documented by the extraordinary find of Egyptian blue glass beads placed in rich Danish burial mounds from 1400–1100 BCE (Nordic period II and III). Non-invasive plasma-spectrometry analyses of twenty-three glass beads from Denmark show that the glass originates from the same workshops that supplied Egyptian Pharaoh Tutankhamun's grave in 1323 BCE. Were there also links between the Egyptian sun cult and the Nordic sun cult [Figure 5.9]?[60]

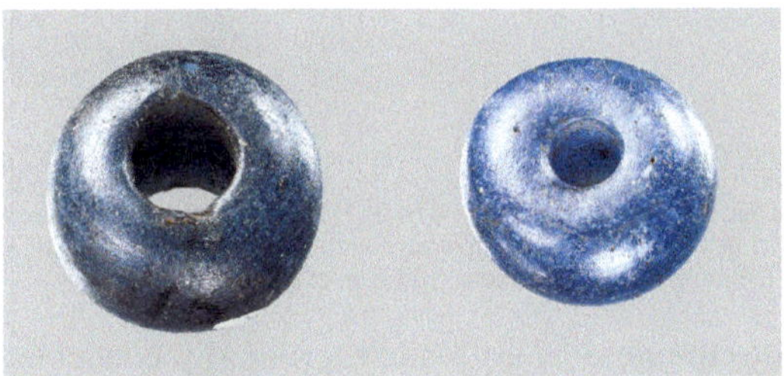

FIGURE 5.9 Two glass beads of Egyptian cobalt colored glass, from burial mounds in Hesselager, Funen, and Ølby, Zealand, Denmark, Nordic Bronze Age II, c. 1400 BCE. Photo: A. Mikkelsen, The National Museum of Denmark.

The first period of intensive global contact developed in the sixteenth century and this "fact" has been one

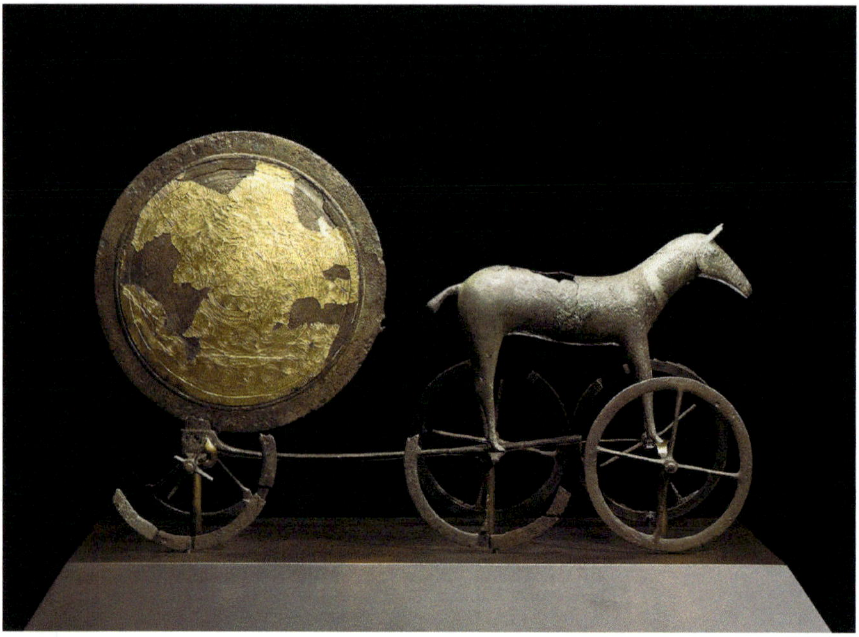

FIGURE 5.10 Sun Chariot, recovered from the former bog Trundholm Mose, northwestern Zealand, bronze and gold, c. 1400 BCE. The horse was made using a sophisticated Nordic lost wax casting method that might have been introduced from areas far to the South, along with knowledge of horse handling and breeding. Copenhagen, The National Museum of Denmark. Photo: CC BY-SA, Roberto Fortuna & Kira Ursem, The National Museum of Denmark.

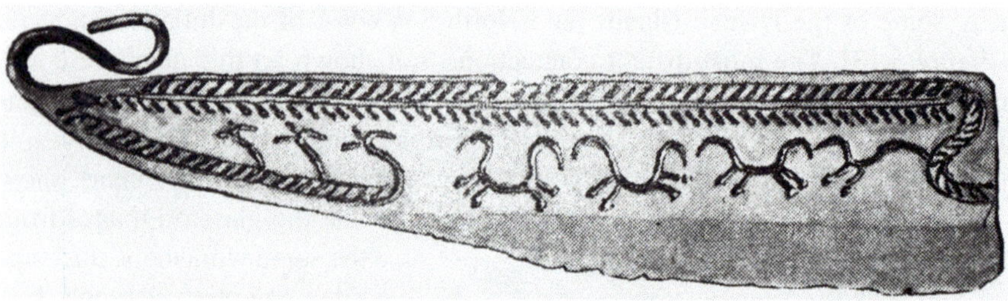

FIGURE 5.11 Single-edged, asymmetrical razor with double horses related to a horse-headed ship of a type introduced c. 1400 BCE. From Sennels, northwest Jutland, Denmark, 1100–900 BCE. If the S-shaped handle is also a stylized horse's head, the whole razor may refer to a ship. This type of razor was introduced just before 1400 BCE from the Mycenaean/Minoan world. Photo: Flemming Kaul, The National Museum of Denmark.

of the justifications for expanding the field of art history, originally conceived with Renaissance art as its core, to a global arena. However, it is misleading to imagine trading networks conforming to the periodization of art or artifacts, as the foregoing discussion has already emphasized. A trade route connecting the North Sea to the Mediterranean was still active in the ninth century. In a now classic study, *Before European Hegemony: The World System AD 1250–1350* (1989), Janet Abu-Lughod argues that failure to begin the story early enough

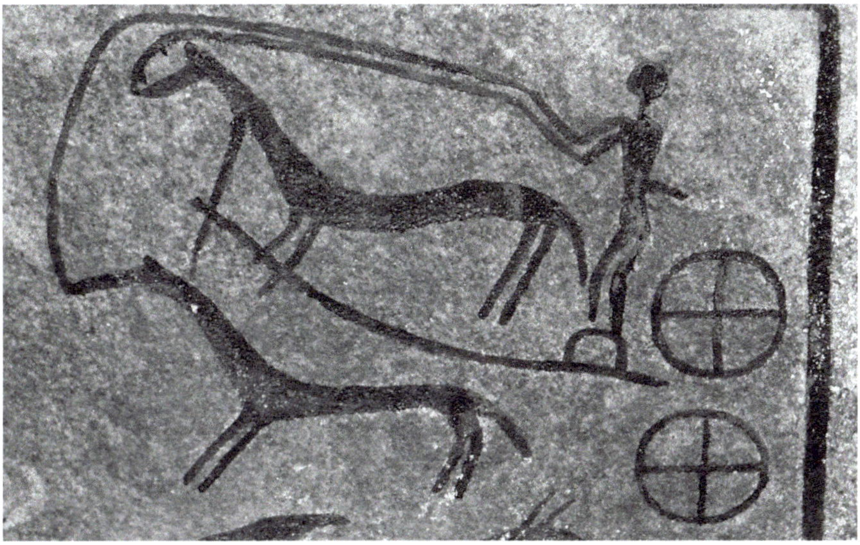

FIGURE 5.12 Chariot driving, rock art in Bredarör, Kivik, Scania, South Sweden, 1400–1300 BCE. These should be regarded as evidence of the use of chariots in south Scandinavia, probably for processional purposes. Photo: Flemming Kaul, The National Museum of Denmark.

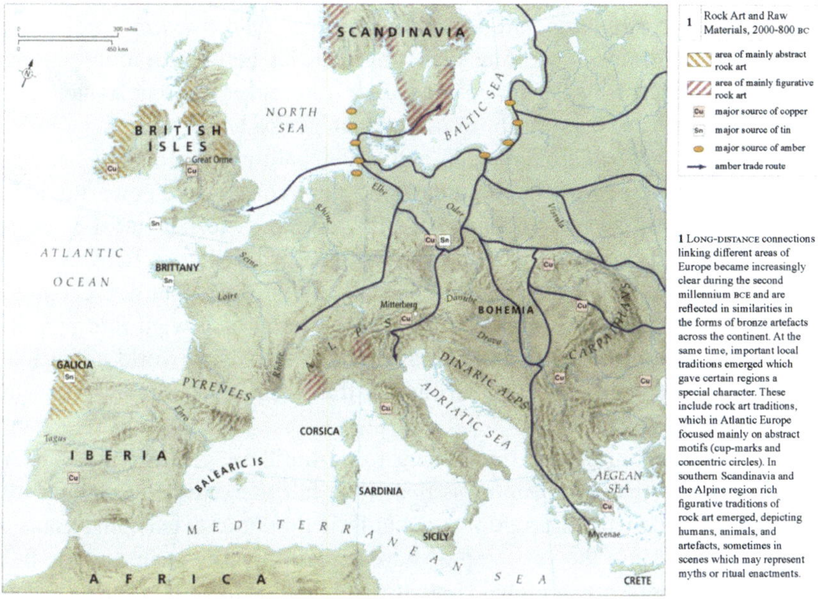

FIGURE 5.13 Map, long distance connections showing circulation of raw materials between Scandinavia and Mycanae, 2000–800 BCE. After *The Art Atlas*, ed. John Onians (New York–London: Abbeville Press, 2008), p. 30.

has resulted in a "truncated and distorted causal explanation for the rise of the West."[61] Abu-Lughod's critique of modern understandings of an East/West divide does not imply that the trading network was equally developed in all places, or that all manufactured goods participated equally in it. Drawing upon a wide range of more specialized studies and taking issue with the world-systems approaches of Braudel, Wallerstein, and others organized in terms of center and periphery, in Abu-Lughod's view changes in a trading network in which manufactured goods were central stretched from China to northwestern Europe between the thirteenth and sixteenth centuries, made Europe's rise possible. By c.1300, the "old world" was linked into a common commercial network of production and exchange beyond the subsistence economies of all the participating regions. As widely recognized, this large and complex network in which surplus goods circulated was built on the foundation of an earlier system that existed by the second century CE.

It is important to bear in mind that Abu-Lughod avoids a center–periphery model by charting the circulation of raw materials, trade goods, and people. In the international trade economy Abu-Lughod examines, the Middle East was the heartland region linking the eastern Mediterranean with the Indian Ocean by both sea and land, while Europe at that time was a peripheral region.[62] Abu-Lughod argues that the rapid increase in agriculture, mining, and manufacturing in northwestern Europe during the twelfth and thirteenth centuries must be attributed, at least in part, to the expansion of its horizons and heightened opportunities for trade generated by the Crusades. One research finding that Abu-Lughod identifies as striking is that similarities between trading partners in the thirteenth century far outweighed their differences: among Asian, Arab, and Western forms of capitalism, to use her categories and terminology, manufactured goods were dominant, land and water pathways were longstanding, recognized currencies were in use, independent merchants were powerful, and a labor force was utilized to produce goods for foreign trade. The most cataclysmic event to disrupt that network was the spread of the plague between 1348 and 1351. The sudden contraction of the population had complex economic effects that fragmented the system so that many parts of it went into simultaneous decline. Fragmentation and decline created fluidity in world conditions, Abu-Lughod argues, that facilitated radical transformations, among them the rise of European hegemony.

The immediate implication in seeking to de-limit the global temporally in some historically justified fashion, is that if we fail to examine the longer history of world trade when Europe was not at the fulcrum of events, historians of culture could fall into the very trap of Eurocentrism that de-centering the field by expanding its reach to a global context was intended to avoid. The American territories, particularly the viceroyalties of New Spain and Peru, played a crucial role in establishing transoceanic trade in luxury objects from 1565, when the first galleon bound for Manila set sail, until 1815, when the last galleon left Acapulco for the Philippines. Yet this new commerce of unprecedented scale also benefited from long established maritime trade routes in Southeast Asia. Excavations of shipwrecks show that bulk trade in ceramics from China, for example, began in the early ninth century, with fluctuations in intensive trade cycles due to changing political regimes. When the Portuguese and Spanish arrived in Southeast Asia in 1511 and 1521, respectively, they entered the region during a cycle of increased trade.[63] Land- and waterways link the Mediterranean and Indian Ocean trading networks since the most ancient times of human settlement. Roman gold coins have been found in Pudukottai, India: one such coin shows the head of Caesar Augustus, the first Roman emperor (reigned 27 BCE–14 CE) [Figure 5.14].

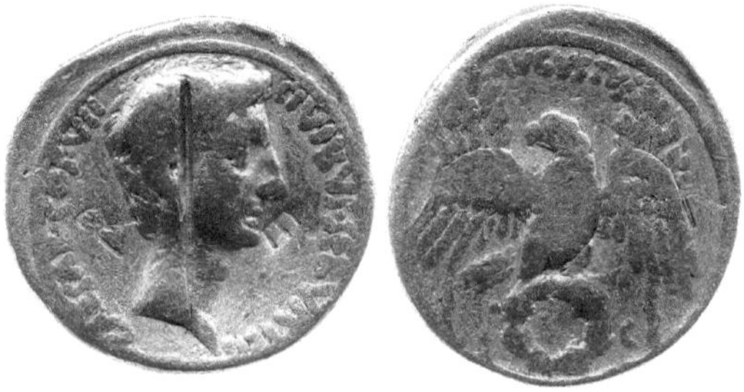

FIGURE 5.14 Roman gold coin minted in Italy, collected in Pudukottai, India: Head of Augustus (obverse). Eagle with spread wings facing left standing on oak wreath flanked by two laurel branches (reverse). 27 BCE, British Museum, 1898.0803.4. © The Trustees of the British Museum.

Long distance commercial relations are also documented in settlements on the East coast of Africa since the first century CE. An array of exotic imports from the ninth to the fourteenth century have been excavated, including ceramics and glass beads as far inland as the fourteenth-century city of Great Zimbabwe located 300 miles from the Mozambican coast, capital of a twelfth-century state that controlled large goldfields which made it important to Indian Ocean trade.[64]

The trading network approach to cultural connectivity encourages many new questions about the circulation of goods and ideas. The ecological model of regional "connectivity" developed by Peregrine Horden and Nicholas Purcell in their account of the Mediterranean (*The Corrupting Sea*, 2000) is a useful model that moves away from questions of fixed identity to a multifaceted understanding of the dynamic processes of identity formation, articulating historical alternatives to monolithic ideas of culture. The stability of regions in this view is sustained by systems of local exchange based on shared environmental, biological, and anthropological factors that maintain a delicate balance between separation and connection.[65] This approach is useful also because it connects local perspectives with regional and ultimately global systems of production and exchange. The trading network model encourages thinking about cultural production in terms of scale – a fractal mode of organization that admits many different approaches and methodologies as well as consideration of place at different scales, depending on the object of study. The trading network model also avoids the anachronistic organization of premodern material culture by nation-state.

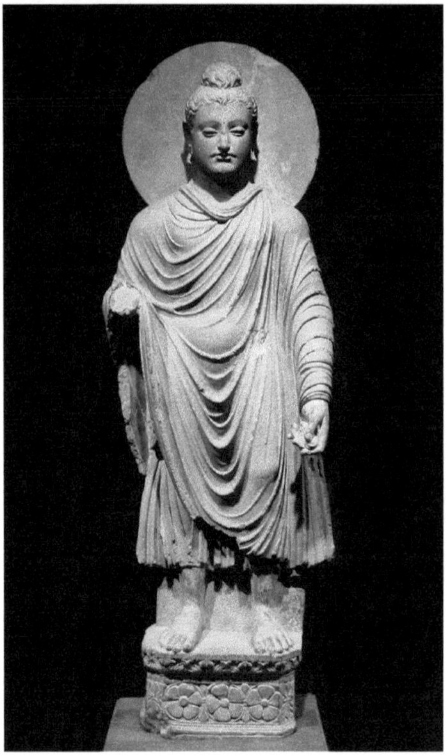

FIGURE 5.15 Kushan Empire, Gandharan Buddha, schist rock, first to second century CE. Tokyo National Museum TC-733. Wiki/TC-733 (Tokyo National Museum).

For example, conflicts with Chinese expansion to central Asia beginning in the first century BCE interrupted existing commerce in the complexly ramified trading network known as the Silk Road (another nineteenth-century term), so that merchants moved south, creating the maritime routes of the Indian Ocean and the Persian Gulf. The Roman government expanded its shipping into the Indian Ocean but when Alexander the Great withdrew from the Indian subcontinent in 326 BCE, trade increased again across the west Asian subcontinent, creating among other things the phenomenon of monumental Gandharan sculpture, a Greco-Buddhist style that flourished from the first to the fifth century CE [Figure 5.15].

It is unclassifiable by the monolithic models of culture fashioned in the nineteenth century and therefore excluded from conventional surveys despite their aesthetic and historical significance. The question of whether Gandharan sculptures (and many other products of the Silk Road network) are Mediterranean or Indian or Chinese is a taxonomic conundrum. If the question instead is what conditions made these types of productions at the intersections of different cultural traditions possible, it opens a history of entanglements instead of parallel trajectories.

Exchanges between the Nordic region and the Mediterranean in the second millennium BCE, when metallurgy developed into a “world system” of knowledge sharing and trade, were still operating in the early eighth century CE. Development of the cloisonné technique that claims the Sutton Hoo purse lid and other burial objects in the British Isles as prized national treasures in conventional art historical narratives organized by period, “style,” and national culture, may have resulted from contact between Nordic and Byzantine traders in the Mediterranean where cloisonné techniques are first documented.[66] The ceremonial Oseberg longship (not intended for long-distance travel) excavated from a burial mound near Tørnsberg, Norway, dated around 800 CE, has a bow and stern elaborately decorated with complex woodcarvings and cloisonné details. A bucket handle in the shape of a person sitting with crossed legs is strikingly similar in pose to a seated Buddha figure. Remarkably, its resemblance to images of the Buddha is supported by the recovery of a small bronze statue of a Buddha from the sixth century CE from another Viking burial, on Helgo Island, Lake Mälaren, Sweden, which was an important Viking trading and manufacturing center from the sixth to the eleventh centuries CE. We may never be able to discover what significance Viking traders attached to the imagery of the meditating Buddha, which was probably made in Kashmir today on the India/Pakistan border, but obviously it was valued in their burial practices [Figures 5.16 and 5.17].

Entirely different histories emerge when the itineraries of objects are the focus of study rather than the histories of modern nation-states.[67] The study of complex, nuanced questions of cultural transmission takes place at the level of strategic case studies, but these case studies are not limited to single objects. Considering the global trading network established in the sixteenth century in

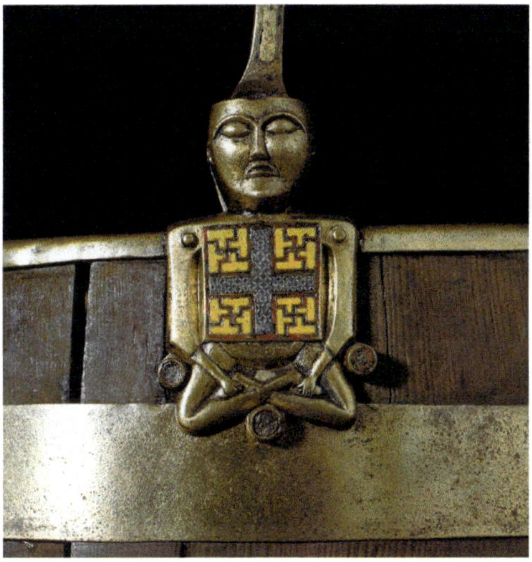

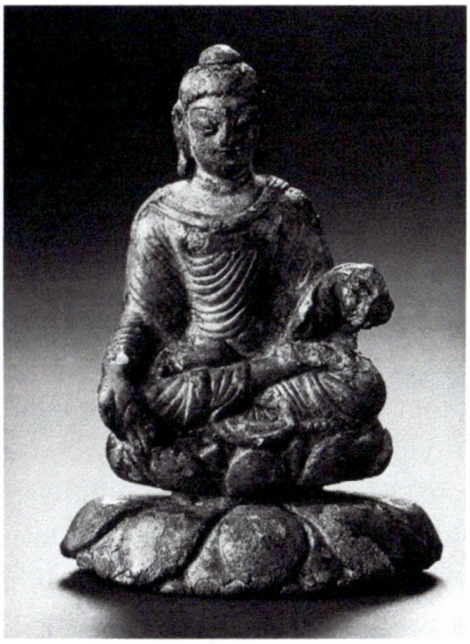

FIGURE 5.16 AND 5.17 (Left) "Buddha" detail of bucket handle, the Oseberg Ship, cloisonné enamel. Bygdøy, Viking Ship Museum, © Museum of Cultural History, University of Oslo, Norway. Photographer: Eirik Irgens Johnsen. See further: https://en.wikipedia.org/wiki/Oseberg_Ship; (Right) Statue of a Buddha, sixth century CE, bronze, from a Viking burial on Helgo Island, Lake Mälaren, Sweden. Source: Employee at SHM, Historiska museet/SHM (CC BY 4.0).

a longer historical context effectively de-centers the dominant role attributed to Europe since the era of colonialism. A de-centered concept of cultural interrelationships is very useful for understanding the complex processes that bind broader, waxing and waning networks of cultural exchange to regional and local trading regions. Network models of connectivity are currently widely used by art historians to account for products of global exchange especially for those that do not fit European categories such as artist, patron, place of origin. To cite Sussan Babaie, co-editor of a recent (2019) anthology on exchange in the Islamicate world, the trade routes collectively known today as the Silk Roads, crisscrossed Asia and connected it to Europe and Africa since antiquity even though modern perception of these mercantile movements is most clearly visible in polities that arose after the Mongol invasions in the thirteenth century. Babaie follows historians who urge rewriting the history of the world through these mercantile networks of connectivity where the spread of Islam was a "crucially important common denominator." Their consequences for our modern conditions are extraordinarily complex and lead away from national narratives and their geopolitical frameworks.[68]

Entangling history by re-imagining lines of transmission that go in multiple directions, treating geographical and period boundaries as porous, heuristic categories, reading canonical works against the grain, and bringing to the fore important cultural artifacts marginalized by the nineteenth-century categories still in use also leads to new considerations of interrelatedness at large scale. Conceiving of agency in a network of agents and quasi-agents that includes the materiality of the object itself; understanding regional trading networks as porous, interconnecting with other networks; studying long periods of time in porous regional trading networks: these are some of the main components for thinking with but also beyond borders about cultural memory on the planet we share.

The global theme inspires fundamental epistemological revisions at *every* scale. Coastal regions, islands, and other geographical features defined important points of exchange in maritime and inland routes of trade very differently from modern conceptions of culture configured in terms of land masses. In fact, dividing the world's culture by continents postdates the moment of initial global contact and is another initially European idea in need of critical study.[69] This trading networks approach is also useful because it connects local perspectives with regional and ultimately global systems of production and exchange. It encourages thinking about cultural production in terms of scale – it is a capacious, fractal model that admits many different approaches and methodologies.

Art historians who focus on maritime trade emphasize the value of leaving behind "arguments framed through the lenses of derivation, imitation, and influence, favoring more nuanced understandings of visual negotiation, cultural appropriation, and multi-sited meaning-making," writes Nancy Um, who has traced the complex routes of commodities including furniture, silver, ceramics, and coffee beyond economic models of supply and demand. Like many other art historians, Um advises beginning with the objects themselves, using the time-honored analytic approach of studying visual and formal details, now stripped of their teleological armature, to identify in material terms the structures involving social practices within which they were produced – while also "acknowledging that formal features and iconographic programs may serve as convenient modes of sorting, but may not fully illuminate historical conceptions of value, aesthetic worth, or meaning" of objects whose physical movement "entailed crossings between discontinuous early modern regimes of value."[70]

Nancy Um has studied the global circulation of coffee and coffee culture beginning in Yemen, the first place where coffee cultivation was undertaken on a large scale beginning around 1570 under Ottoman rule [Figure 5.18].[71] As shown on the map reproduced in Figure 5.18, which traces the global distribution of coffee, the actual paths that commodities and other peripatetic objects travel are of greater complexity than a general map of global trade routes can indicate (compare Figure 5.2). Materials were often sourced in one place, combined, crafted, and assembled in another, and trafficked elsewhere still. Current critical global approaches emphasize not taxonomy but the circulation of objects, the mixing of signifying systems, the multivalence of objects and images. "Semantic shifts" in pre-existing types are re-purposed in many ways. Historically, we can look to the

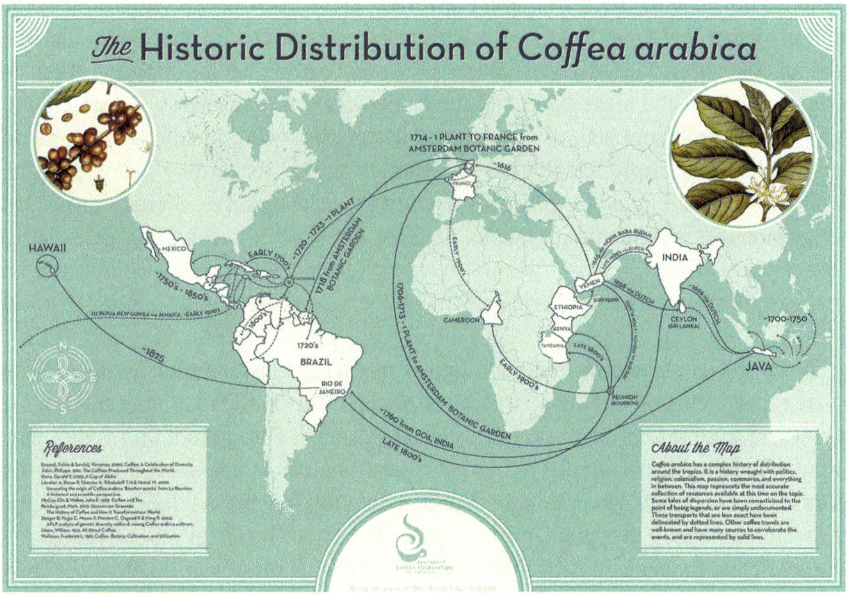

FIGURE 5.18 The historic distribution of coffee arabica. Reprinted with permission from the Speciality Coffee Association of America.

pervasive presence of print culture and other forms of mobile objects in circulating cultural models, the provisional recovery of dispossessed cultural contexts, the collecting and classification of extra-European objects in *kunstkammers* and other kinds of collections (including paper museums) in and beyond Europe, the importance of institutional settings in which objects functioned, the interaction of religion with the global exchange of objects, including networks of exchange de-centered from Europe altogether. These factors operated in multiple regional centers at various scales. Artisanal knowledge practices and other forms of technology affected processes of globalization and often promoted unequal relations of power in transcultural settings.

The field of study has become too complex, and the study of specific circumstances is at such a preliminary stage that it would be premature to decide what the main issues are or to map the field. Many art historians are currently engaged in transcultural research projects, often in collaboration to widen and deepen the knowledge necessary to pursue topics organized according to regional networks of exchange. To cite a significant example, Beate Fricke, a specialist in European medieval art and architecture, and Barry Finbarr Flood, who studies Islamic art and architecture, previewed their forthcoming collaborative study in an essay on premodern globalism in art history, commissioned by *The Art Bulletin*, published in 2022.[72] They offer a wide range of concerns and methodologies that open up when transregional connectivity is the framework for research. Their discussion of cultural exchange includes the need to specify different kinds of connections; asymmetry in the forms of knowledge that were produced in different places or circumstances; the unequal and random survival of material culture; the absence of written information about the origin, function, and meaning of circulating objects newly of interest in transcultural approaches; problems with using temporal categories such as medieval, premodern, and modern that imply teleological explanatory modes for writing history; dealing with gaps in material archives; going beyond the celebration of connectedness; and the desirability of including systems of labor beyond the recognition of expertise associated with concepts of "genius" mastery of complex techniques; and last but not least, the value of visual evidence beyond textual sources documenting histories of trade.

There are considerable methodological challenges in grappling with existing systems of inclusion/exclusion that have historically excluded a large majority of the world's cultural production from the category art. Throughout this book I have argued that the historical idea of human exceptionalism is interwoven with the discourse on art: human exceptionalism and racial thinking are two facets of the same Aristotelian legacy that gives pride of place to certain forms of inventiveness and rationality as the measures of humanness. To address these inequities, the historical discourse on art and the discourse on what it means to be fully human need to be studied together in relation to the history of environmental change and destruction. My argument has focused on effects driven by European expansionism in the Americas and beyond, but there are many other areas of research.

To encourage further discussion, I begin drawing *Writing Borderless Histories of Art* to a close by returning to three interrelated questions on economics, temporality, and positioning posed by Monica Juneja in her own dialogical questioning of global art history.[73] In shifting the focus of inquiry to South Asia, one of the most urgent questions for Juneja is whether a global art history must follow the logic of economic globalization to "effectively theorize relationships of connectivity that encompass disparities as well as contradictions and negotiate the multiple subjectivities of the actors involved." The answer is emphatically no, the connections are not limited to economic globalization, but the question is how to avoid getting trapped in the neoliberal mindset. Juneja then asks about temporality, what choices are available to "view the historical present as a simultaneity of clashing and conjoining temporalities constituted by their pre-histories?" The choices must be articulated through specific case studies. Can a "big history" emerge from such case studies without a totalizing structure? And if so, is it desirable, under what circumstances? We don't always need to think about the field or discipline as a whole. Haraway's early observations on "situated knowledge" (1988) still hold: objectivity has to derive from particular and specific embodiments. Knowledge is always partial, locatable, and critical. Objectivity is only possible through the joining of partial views into a collective subject position.[74] Positioning our heterogeneous multiplicities as mobile is key to grounding knowledge. A commitment to mobile positioning privileges contestation and "webbed connections" because the split and contradictory self is the one who can interrogate positionings and be accountable. It follows that embodiment is not about identifying a fixed location in a reified body, but about "nodes in fields, inflections in orientations, and responsibility for difference in material-semiotic fields of meaning." Bodies should be thought of as "material-semiotic generative nodes" whose "boundaries materialize in social interaction."[75]

Expanding or increasing the quantity of objects within a European/North American-centered approach to art only emphasizes the inherent risk of applying categories of analysis developed for the study of European and North American art to other histories of materiality, creativity, and objects. Different ways of making are often based on complex epistemological categories and ontologies different from the dualistic metaphysical model of Western philosophy. Elsewhere, I have written about pedagogy and offered a "borderless" curriculum as a work in progress to replace problematic national culture and period style categories and subcategories. This pedagogy, tested at my own university, initially developed from rethinking the introductory "survey" courses used in the US to introduce art history to students.[76]

Third, Juneja asks, how can the intellectual resources and insights of regional experiences beyond Euro-America be translated into globally intelligible analyses? One of the most extensively rehearsed shibboleths of "modernity" has been the idea that the past can be left behind, willed into irrelevance, de-linked and disentangled by fiat. History is *not* chronology: configuring time as a linear progression to write history is nothing more (or less) than a rhetorical strategy. History is a discourse that engages the past through the present in a wide variety of ways. In some societies, tradition does the same thing by other means. The premise of *this* book is that we can get past our past to change the relationship of humans to the rest of nature only by unpacking the epistemological structures and dualistic ontological framework of the nature/culture divide of European (or "Western" or Euro-Mediterranean) origin that still dominates eco-criticism and climate science today. The insights and resources of regional experience include the right *not* to come to the table of discussion. Isolationist strategies are a form of resistance, born of experience. The value of resistance is its ability to question structures of domination and implement change. However, isolationist attitudes, moratoriums, and cultural embargoes reinforce existing forms of domination because they do not, by themselves, encourage meaningful contestation and constructive confrontation. The concluding section of *Writing Borderless Histories of Art* recaps the question posed at the beginning of this book: Why should art history bear so much responsibility for conceiving ecologically sensitive, planetary approaches to culture?

(Un)Binding Memories: The Future of the Past

The practices and protocols by which we divide our objects of study from the present are always those of the present. It follows that history itself is not a fact of the world that is more or less accurately represented, but rather it is but one way for a society to constitute the past and establish a relation with it, a certain way to conceive of and be in the world, a certain practice of subjectivity. If history writing is to be an ethical rather than an imperial practice, writes postcolonial theorist Sanjay Seth, this understanding of history as a cultural practice needs to be recognized and its implications explored. [77] In rethinking collective identity without resorting to Western metaphysical categories, the unthought ground between the categories nature and culture, cast as an opposition between innate capacity (biology) and acquired content (culture), has become a major topic of discussion among anthropologists and sociologists in a way that bears directly on the issues discussed throughout this book. The categories of "art versus artifact," "nation," "culture," "style," "period," "canon," 'genius," "masterpiece," and so on remain entrenched not only in academe but also in the commercial world of the art and culture industry – in museum exhibitions, commercial galleries, international biennales, general education, popular culture, politics, and so on. Another model of identity and cultural memory is urgently needed, one that recognizes that multiple identities and cultural memories are simultaneously possible, that identities and diverse cultural memories can co-exist without being commensurable or reducible one into another, without being oppositional, exclusionary, or essentializing.

As evidence of the beliefs of their users, objects lead singular lives moving unpredictably from creation to destruction, sometimes persisting much longer through virtual images and written accounts. What are the pros and cons of treating artefacts as polysemic and fluid materialities, their significance never fixed, always changeable and capable of collapsing together past and present? The *intellectual* attractiveness of such an approach stems from its ability to institute a more pluralistic historical vision – an approach to history that considers different cultural traditions, signifying practices, worldviews, and contexts of use on equal footing.

Many types of objects and processes of fabrication are well-suited to this pluralistic and pluritopic framework. However, nineteenth-century assumptions about what constitutes knowledge – the epistemological foundations of the discipline – cannot be effortlessly accommodated to changing research agendas. Against an Enlightenment notion of truth as universally given is the relativist concept of partial perspectives and situated knowledge limited to its places and conditions of emergence.[78] No simple "return to the object" is adequate to the task because the materiality of the object – its significance – is fluid, capable of being interpreted otherwise and always established in relationship to other concrete factors.

As feminist studies of gender first insisted, all perspectives are partial, strategic, and vested (including the essay you are currently reading). An effective inversion of institutional authority results from practicing an anti-canonical approach to canonical texts, but inversion alone does not get rid of the values or the value system itself. Transcultural approaches to planetary culture depend on accumulating many individual case studies for comparison to build a larger picture. These can and are being conducted on the level of individual authorship but adopting a collaborative approach to research greatly enhances the speed and quality of research outcomes, while potentially integrating the efforts of local scholars and regional studies into an international network of scholarly exchange without imposing an overarching conceptual framework or a uniform methodology.

Conceiving of historical artifacts as the residues of events encourages an understanding of cultural commentary as a directly political act with the capacity to reshape the discursive ground on which cultural memory is shaped.[79] The production and exchange of cultural artifacts has been one of the primary means of social interaction for as long as humans have been around. Although the term "ecology" may be new, the relationship of art to its environment was a central concern when the discipline of art history was professionalized as a university subject and a museum practice in the nineteenth century. The critical question has always been *how* to define the relationship between culture and nature or, in the future cultural histories of the planet, "socio-becomings" that bring the social and the biological together into a single frame.

The issues of identity, inclusion/exclusion, and essentialism that I have been discussing throughout this book have also been the preoccupation of many philosophers and cultural theorists, including Giorgio Agamben and Judith Butler who insist upon "acknowledging our complicity in the law that we oppose": "there is in effect something that humans are and have to be, but this is not an essence or properly a thing: It is the simple fact of one's own existence as possibility or potentiality."[80] Being, pace Heidegger, is no longer only a matter restricted to humanity. Nor is the ethical responsibility of educators a matter of politics in the narrow sense. How far does the responsibility of producers of knowledge extend? Such fundamental questions deserve to be driving our research agendas in the context of the future of our shared planet and its rich material culture because the knowledge we produce inevitably has long-range effects far beyond the immediate contributions they are designed to make.

"Worlding" refers to processes that are going on as we rethink the European concepts of state, sovereignty, "citizen of the world," and art at the center of political questions on which the sustainability of life on Earth are articulated and institutionally constituted. Philosophical cosmopolitanism is European, "too European," Derrida argues with reference to Kant: philosophical cosmopolitanism and the European concept of international rights and law on which it draws, offer an abstract universalism that takes the history of European nations as its index and guiding thread in opposition to that of the so-called barbaric nations.[81] According to Kant, inferior nations should abandon

> a lawless state of savagery and [enter] a Society of Nations of peoples in which every state, even the smallest, could expect to derive its security and rights not from its own power or its own legal judgment, but from this great Society of Nations (i.e., of peoples: *Völkerbunde*, from the ancient Greek concept of *foedus amphyctionum*), from a united power and the law-governed decisions of a united will. [82]

The logic of this teleology, Derrida wryly reflects, is that we ought to be grateful to nature for pushing us through culture, art, artifice (*Kunst*), and reason, "to make the seeds of nature blossom."[83]

In his discussion of Kant's cosmopolitanism, Derrida also put his finger on a fundamental obstacle to treating the historical category "Art" as a transcultural critical concept at all: the widespread European colonialist practice of denigrating other societies, dispossessing their cultural practices on the basis of moral and mental deficiencies, and reconfiguring their material culture within a European system of classification with its attendant values. It denies the same status to other belief systems, epistemologies, or ontologies. Although people everywhere value certain things that are the product of artistry, "art" as a special category of things and practices is *not* recognized worldwide.[84] The epistemological regime that separates skill from knowledge is also foreign to many Indigenous societies, where practices of making and ways of living are continuous and intimately related to spiritual systems.[85] Achille Mbembe's eloquent account of "necropolitics" is apposite here: the politics of who lives and who dies. To become a museum object, "[i]t was first necessary to chase out the spirit behind the form."[86] The knowledge of craftspeople has special resonance in many Indigenous knowledge communities. From an Indigenous North

American perspective, for example, "theory" is the knowledge that is made, embedded in, and carried on through the baskets, songs, rituals, and other art forms of the native culture.[87] Many Indigenous ontologies, such as Andean cosmology, Hinduism (*Sanatana Dharma* in Sanskrit), Buddhism, to name just a few, also question the assumption that only humans have "worldmaking" capacities. Yet for the same reason, Indigenous worldviews offer many possibilities for avoiding the dualism of humans versus nature that change colonial land relations and enact other types of land relations by not viewing natural resources as commodities to be exploited.[88]

A word of caution. Critically reckoning with the broader notion that by *artistry* we might mean all that is sensible in multiple ways for diverse individuals, communities, alliances, or other bordered or borderless polities and belief systems, however these may be construed, that *mediate* between these and their realities, might *also* mean that any such understanding would confer upon art or artistry quite uncanny and extraordinary *powers* to create, sustain, and transform realities or worlds, *as well as* to suspend, destroy, or overturn given social, cultural, and epistemological systems of belief. [89] Art might then be (as it has been in the past) employed *in the guise of cosmopolitanism* to justify all manner of social, political, philosophical, and religious differences, distinctions, equalities and inequalities, and a wide variety of hierarchies, from autocracies to democracies and every nuanced order in between those realities, or worldmakings.

The challenge that the question of "worlding" poses in the twenty-first century is therefore not simply about multiculturalism or "global citizenship," a term that was appropriated by neo-liberals and has become problematic for many reasons in our era of mass migrations and statelessness driven by the climate crisis and its many collateral effects.[90] "Worlding" as understood by Cheah is a decolonial and transcultural "tactic" that "enacts openings of time and consciousness to other values and multiple modes of being."[91] Worlding functions as a creative force "with the power to create that which has not yet come into being," writes art historian Jenny Lin about contemporary Chinese artists and curators, building on Pamela Lee's argument that economic and political forces reflect and construct tenets of globalization while "perpetuating the myth of a borderless society." Lin observes that the "glimmering facades" in Shanghai and elsewhere often mask bleak realities "plagued by rising economic disparities and the eclipsing of individual freedoms."[92]

Contemporary cosmopolitan efforts insist on collaboratively re-imagining and pluralizing the "global" from "multiple geocultural perspectives in a temporally constituted and open-ended process of lived interrelations and interconnections."[93] The modern word "cosmopolitan" derives from Ancient Greek, where politês (πολίτης) refers to citizen and *kosmos* (κόσμος) refers to the entire universe or world – not just the physical geography known to ancient Greeks, but the mathematically ordered universe described by Plato in the *Timaeus* as the handiwork of a divine Craftsman (dêmiourgos, 28a6) who imposes order upon chaos in imitation of an unchanging and eternal model. The beautiful orderliness of the universe is the manifestation of Intellect (*nous*) that provides the model for rational souls to understand and emulate and it shows the ideal political arrangement of society.[94] In extending the ancient term beyond its original framework, everything hinges on how one worldview is translated into another, how such dynamic worlds intersect, how they are changed, reinterpreted, by whom and for what purpose.[95]

Who decides what this ideal arrangement is and how it is presented, to whom, for what purpose, and with what authority? Societies are in fact heterogeneous and diverse. "Worlds" are not transparent representations of society, much less of reality, a point that was emphasized in 1978 by Nelson Goodman when he introduced his concept of worldmaking: there are many possible Goodman worlds, but they are all actual ways of projecting structure onto the world with conceptualizations. When Kobena Mercer introduced the phrase "Cosmopolitan Modernisms" to art historians in his widely cited anthology of 2005, he embraced "modernism's cross-cultural past" and the recognition of multiple modernisms has since been widely accepted and practiced.[96] To grasp what is at stake regarding a responsible "worlded" approach today, I have argued that it is essential to consider a continuous history of claims emerging in the sixteenth century during the initial period of economic globalization when the issue of international human rights was first framed around Christian "cosmopolitan humanism." Debates on how to define the humanity of Indigenous peoples unrecorded in European history (were they "slaves by nature"?) introduced the idea of *degrees* of humanness based on *techne*, that is, art broadly defined in Aristotelian terms to include everything and every practice that improves nature and creates a polis ordered along the lines of the ancient Athenian city-state.

We are today participating in efforts to reimagine the study of art inherited from the nineteenth century when the evolutionary ordering of relations between peoples and cultures from primitive to civilized was commonplace in schemes of "world art." The point today is that this European cosmopolitan concept of "Art" (capital A) developed *alongside* the modern concept of "culture" and neither offers an adequate account of the devastating effects of European colonialism three centuries into the global expansion of European interests. Entrenched binaries such as art/artifact, nature/culture, human/non-human keep shifting from one context to the next while continuing to haunt our texts and practices. Both ways of defining humanness depend on the same neo-Aristotelian account of cognition that rational thought arises from sense perception, based on the model of vision. The split between making art and looking at art is another quintessentially Eurocentric binomial structure built on the same set of assumptions about the reciprocity between nature and art based on Aristotle's account that the mind is a transparent mirror of the world. Giorgio Agamben once claimed that if we really want to engage the problem of art in our time, nothing is more urgent than clearing away what is usually taken for granted about it, calling into question everything that aesthetics entails, including above all the system of relationships in which it has been embedded – framed – and which gives it its substance, namely the split between the artist as producer and the beholder that defines the way we currently use art in society.[97]

Contemporary art historians and cultural critics who associate cosmopolitanism with a global perspective that avoids servicing economic globalization rightly complain that "the absence or marginalization of the aesthetic function from the current debates on cosmopolitanism reinscribes the stigmatic chain of association that separates the ordered, consistent and steadfast truth of reason from the faulty, fleeting and flighty genius of imagination."[98] "Rationality," "imagination," and "aesthetics" are of course historical categories with problematic colonialist pedigrees far beyond the nineteenth century.

I have argued against taking a relatively short view of history in support of ongoing efforts to bring the social and the biological together beyond the twin Western dichotomies between nature and culture, and between fully rational humans and all others. In his 2012 book, *Cosmopolitanism and Culture*, Papastergiadis articulated a shift in the understanding of art and creative practices, elaborating what he termed an *aesthetic cosmopolitanism*: Art as the revelation of paradox, "world-making as a radical act of the cosmopolitan imaginary."[99] His deconstruction of the art/politics conundrum is another manifestation of the central role of art as a modality of world-making and the existence of art as a mediator. Concepts of the self in its relationships with others are inevitably posited on some methodology or tactical systems of plausibly *guaranteeing* that a given aesthetic mediation with respect to cosmopolitanism or cosmo-politics is substantive and effective, situated and rooted. At the same time, art operates in the service of the *weaponizing* of any of these issues. Cosmopolitanisms, in short, are and always have been not only epistemological technologies – arts of making meaningful worlds or "worldings" – but also politically significant practices and processes. Our "selves" are not only hybrid but composite. What agencies do composite beings have, imply, propose? Not only have we "never been modern," as Bruno Latour famously observed, we have never been entirely "human," either.[100] For what is at stake is not only what worlds and environments mean, but how, when, and where they might signify, as well as for whom and under what conditions, all in light of the transitoriness and transmissibility of palpable and impalpable phenomena, however these may be understood and applied. The radical task is reckoning – critically engaging with, for, and against all these issues.

To what extent should we as scholars, scientists, cultural critics, students, actually everyone operating in today's social networks take responsibility for the effects of the knowledge they produce? Unless we comprehensively attend to the "thought structures" that underpin our plural intellectual heritages, that which is indefensible will continue to haunt contemporary history writing in precisely the sense that Michel de Certeau defined the mnemic trace as "the return of what was forgotten, in other words, an action by a past that is now forced to disguise itself."[101] This, of course, is still the key issue and it presents a conundrum today: the need to re-imagine how art, however we construe the term, even when we intentionally abandon "art" as a category for its irredeemably Eurocentric structure, simultaneously has the power to fabricate and to problematize hegemonic power and its stagings.

Political philosophers returned to the subject of sovereignty in the late twentieth century in the context of contemporary questions of democracy and human rights, writes Étienne Balibar in an essay on citizenship (2015) that analyzes the relevance of Aristotle's exclusionary understanding of a polity in the *Politics*. *Writing Borderless Histories of Art* is a timely intervention into these discussions. Balibar did not realize that Aristotle's discussion of *techne* and "natural slavery" played a leading role in establishing the modern exclusionary discourse on human rights. Nonetheless, Balibar recognizes that the polity distributes power among all the citizens according to the "common good' but reserves citizenship to those who are "equal by nature" which Aristotle defines as capable of deliberation and decision-making. That was exactly the point in the sixteenth-century debates framed in terms of Christian humanist (aka neo-Scholastic, Thomistic) understandings of Aristotle's *Politics*. Balibar notes that the "mechanism for discrimination on the basis of anthropological difference" is built into the system.[102] What were the mechanisms and how were they built into the system? The formation and deployment of the mechanisms of race, its prequels and sequels, have been the focus of this book. The issues are inseparable from the discourse on art. Aristotle's *Politics* has been important for framing the discourse on humanness and art since the early sixteenth century.

Currently there is a disconnect on issues of human rights between contemporary political philosophers, who trace the genealogy of Aristotle's *Politics* no further back than Kant and Enlightenment philosophy, and historians who study the earlier history of natural law framed in terms of the same text interpreted according to Christian humanist universalism. Once again, disciplinary specializations have created gaps that make it difficult to grasp what has been at stake in a continuous (but emphatically non-linear) history.

Citizenship is not shared equally, Balibar continues: some are "internally excluded" such as women and civil slaves who are relegated to the domestic sphere and consigned to obey those with decision-making power for the sake of political stability. The point of discussion in contemporary debates is the tension between reciprocity and exclusion: who has a say in self-governance and how do distinct polities co-exist? Inevitably, the limitations of self-governing politeia have "irreparably collapsed as [actual] 'borders'" and it is no longer possible for any society to construct itself within such limits except in an imaginary sense. While modern states remain "stuck within the framework of the nation," civil society "is seen as extending out transnationally, across borders – a 'commercial' society." Balibar sees potential in global organizations that "are charged with protecting the collective security and the fight against unequal development," built on "universal reciprocity" but this would require a "radical democratization that still remains very distant" because it would involve international organizations like the United Nations "acquiring a cosmopolitan authority independent of that of the states."[103] Lack of commitment to shared governance at planetary scale was also Kant's unresolved dilemma in advancing the possibility of "perpetual peace" two centuries and two World Wars ago.

Beyond Balibar, I have pivoted the historical arguments taken up in earlier Fugues to the existential threat that the climate crisis/emergency/ecological disaster in our midst poses unequally to all life on Earth by focusing on the violent role of unregulated, extractive capitalism to create social inequalities. Our precariousness, while appalling, is a potential source of strength. Agency has been the subtext throughout these Fugues and Intermezzos, and the overt topic of discussion in many places has been the emancipatory potential of telling history differently. The poet Eleni Sikelianos succinctly articulated the ethical responsibility that every historian faces: "The question is how to interrogate the remains."[104] Her case at hand was intellectual and literary life in contemporary Cambodia and Vietnam, where writers manage through a system of censorship and suppression of archive and memory. Whether or not the system of handing on knowledge has been severely crippled by events too catastrophic to comprehend, the relation between archive and vision always demands imagination. Imagination, Sikelianos observes, "inserts itself and expands the real." In bringing this thought experiment full circle, I emphasize that all producers of knowledge share the ethical responsibility to understand how this knowledge shapes society. By necessity, this must be a collective endeavor. When if not now, should we make promises together and act in concert?

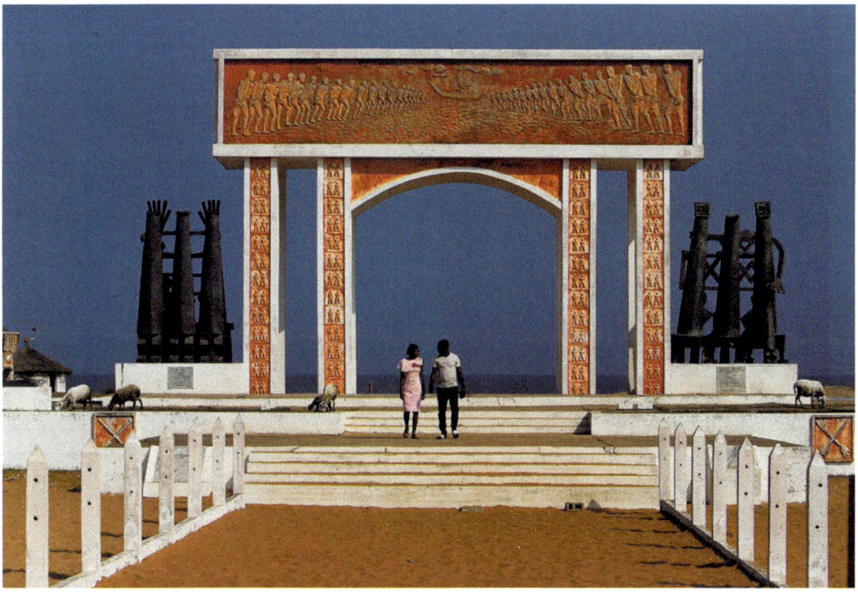

FIGURE 5.19 Yves Ahouen-Gnimon, Fortune Bandeira, Yves Kpede, and Dominque Kouas Gnonnou, *Door of No Return* memorial arch dedicated to the victims of the Atlantic slave trade, slave port of Ouidah, Benin, concrete and brass. REUTERS/Afolabi Sotunde.

Notes

1 Martin Heidegger, *Die Grundbegriffe der Metaphysik. Welt – Enlichkeit - Einsamkeit* (Frankfurt am Main, 1983); *The Fundamental Concepts of Metaphysics: World, Finitude, Solitude*, trans. William McNeill and Nicholas Walker, Bloomington, 1995). Michael Naas, *The End of the World and Other Teachable Moments: Jacques Derrida's Final Seminar*, NY: Fordham University Press, 2015.
2 Jacques Derrida, "'Genesis' and 'Structure' and Phenomenology," *Writing and Difference* (London: Routledge, 1978), 167.
3 Jacques Derrida, *The Animal That Therefore I Am*, ed. Marie-Louise Mallet, trans. David Wills (New York: Fordham University Press, 2008), 30.
4 Derrida, *The Animal That Therefore I Am*, 31 [my emphasis]. In French bête means stupid, asinine, and as a noun also refers to animals, as beasts.
5 Hans Peter Hahn and Hadas Weiss, Introduction, *Mobility, Meaning, and Transformations of Things: Shifting Contexts of Material Culture through Time and Space* (2001 German ed.; Oxford: Fordham University Press, 2013).
6 Jae Emerling, "To render time sensible: transmissibility," review of Keith Moxey, *Visual Time: The Image in History*, 2013, in *Journal of Art Historiography*, 2015; Emerling, *Transmissibility: Writing Aesthetic History* (Abingdon, Oxon: Routledge, 2024). Diagram is the term used by Foucault and described by Deleuze as "a cartography that is coextensive with the whole social field." The concept of transmissibility is indebted to Walter Benjamin's critique of the concept of social progress for the masses without revolution. Susan Buck-Morss, *The Dialectics of Seeing* (Cambridge, MA: MIT Press, 1989), 88–89.
7 See Claire Bishop, ed. and Introduction, *Participation: Documents of Contemporary Art* (London: Whitechapel Gallery & MIT Press, 2006); and by the curator/critic who introduced "relational aesthetics" in the 1990s, Nicolas Bourriaud, *Inclusions: Aesthetics of the Capitalocene*, trans. Denyse Beaulieu (Berlin: Sternberg Press, 2023).
8 Nikos Papastergiadis, *Cosmopolitanism and Culture* (Cambridge, UK–Malden, MA: Polity Press, 2012), 157.
9 Paul Carter, *The Lie of the Land* (London–Boston: Faber and Faber, 1996), 356.
10 As cited by Hetti Perkins, "Parallel universe, other worlds," in *Complex Entanglements: Art, Gobalization, and Cultural Difference*, ed. Nikos Papastergiadis (London: Rivers Oram Press, 2003), 63. Papastergiadis, *Cosmopolitanism*, 150.
11 Claire Farago, "Memory and Place from the Red Center of Australia to the Periphery of Paris: To See the Frame That Blinds Us," in *Imagined Spaces/Places*, ed. Saija Isomaa et al. (Newcastle upon Tyne: Cambridge Scholars Publishing, 2013), 3–26, from which the following discussion of Indigenous Australian cosmologies is adapted.
12 Marcia Langston, "Religion and Art from Colonial Conquest to Postcolonial Resistance," in *The Oxford Companion to Aboriginal Art and Culture*, ed. Sylvia Kleinert and Margo Neale (Melbourne: Oxford University Press), 16.
13 See further discussion in Donald Preziosi and Claire Farago, *Art Is Not What You Think It Is* (Oxford–New York: Blackwells-Wiley Publishing, 2012), 52–73.
14 Naomi Klein and Kapua'ala Sprout, "Why was there no water to fight the fires on Maui?," *The Guardian*, 17 August 2023. Stream flows can and have historically restored abundance to the islands that plantation mismanagement destroyed.
15 Terry Smith, *Iconomy: Towards a Political Economy of Images* (London–New York: Anthem Press, 2022), 58, with reference to Guy Debord's *Society of Spectacle* (1967). Debord argues that, as authentic social life is replaced with mere representation, "the commodity completes its colonization of social life" (thesis 17).
16 According to the State of Hawaii website, *Maui Recovers*, accessed on 4 May 2024: www.mauirecovers.org/water#:~:text=ABOUT%20THE%20UNSAFE%20WATER%20ADVISORIES&text=Unsafe%20Water%20Advisories%20have%20been,removed%20from%20the%20Advisory%20Area. See also T. J. Demos, "The Agency of Fire: Burning

Aesthetics," *e-flux journal* 98 (March 2019), "Welcome to the Pyrocene, the geological age of fire, matched by the overwhelming affects of fear and dread, and complicated by the very incomprehensibility of responsibility" (at p. 5 of online article, www.e-flux.com/journal/98/256882/the-agency-of-fire-burning-aesthetics/Accessed 4 October 2024).

17 Shawn Hubler, "Maui Wildfire Plaintiffs Reach $4 Billion Settlement as Anniversary Nears," *The New York Times*, 2 August 2024.

18 Gerald McMaster, "*kikway ohci mâmitonéyihtamiwewak*: What do they ask of us?," in *Postcommodity: Time Holds All the Answers*, ed. Michael Rattay (Saskatoon: Remai Modern and Wapath Centre for Indigenous Visual Knowledge, 2022), 28 [emphasis in the original]. Cited by McMaster, *Arctic/Amazon*, 89.

19 MacMaster in McMaster and Vincent, *Arctic/Amazon*, 34.

20 Vincent in McMaster and Vincent, *Arctic/Amazon*, 36.

21 On Moore, see Fugue 1. Randolph R. Resor, "Rubber in Brazil: Dominance and Collapse, 1876–1945," *The Business History Review* 51/3 (Autumn 1977): 341–366.

22 Recently, it has been shown that the islands were occupied by human settlers since the eighth century CE; see Pedro M. Raposeiro, Amrand Hernández, Sergi Pla-Rabes, Santiago Giralt, et al., "Climate change facilitated the early colonization of the Azores Archipelago during medieval times," *PNAS* 118/4 (4 October 2021), doi.org/10.1073/pnas.2108236118. Felipe Fernández-Armesto, *Before Columbus: Exploration and Colonisation from the Mediterranean to the Atlantic 1229–1492* (Philadelphia: University of Pennsylvania Press, 2007).

23 Linda Tuhiwai Smith, *Decolonizing Methodologies: Research and Indigenous Peoples*, third ed., (London–Sydney: Bloomsbury, 2022). Smith is Professor of Maori and Indigenous Studies at the University of Waikato, Aotearoa New Zealand.

24 Métis anthropologist Zoe Todd, "Indigenizing the Anthropocene," in *Art in the Anthropocene: Encounters among Aesthetics, Politics, Environments, and Epistemologies*, ed. Heather David and Etienne Turpin (London: Open Humanities Press, 2005), 241–254.

25 Vincent, in McMaster and Vincent, *Arctic/Amazon*, 94.

26 Vincent, in McMaster and Vincent, *Arctic/Amazon*, 94, cites several Indigenous thinkers who propose ways to face environmental critics with traditional knowledge, including Julie Cruikshank, *Do Glaciers Listen?: Local Knowledge, Colonial Encounters, and Social Imagination* (Vancouver: UBC Press, 2005), 3, who tells stories by Tlingit and Athapaskan people which show that "humans and nature mutually make and maintain the habitable world."

27 Isabelle Stengers, "The Cosmopolitical Proposal," in *Making Things Public: Atmospheres of Democracy*, ed. Bruno Latour and Peter Weibel (Cambridge, MA: MIT Press, 2005), 994–1003, cited by Vincent, in McMaster and Vincent, *Arctic/Amazon*, 94.

28 Alberto Acota, *El Buen Vivir: Sumak Kawsay, una opportunidad para imaginar otro mundo* (Barcelona: Icaria Editorial, 2013), cited by Vincent, in McMaster and Vincent, *Arctic/Amazon*, 56.

29 Arturo Escobar, *Territories of Difference: Place, Movements, Life, Redes* (Durham: Duke University Press, 2008), 116.

30 Gómez-Barris, T*he Extractive Zone*, 24–25. On the Forest Code (1965), see the Nature Conservatory article, www.nature.org/en-us/about-us/where-we-work/latin-america/brazil/stories-in-brazil/brazils-forest-code/.

31 Ailton Krenak, *Ideias para Adiar o Finn do Mundo* (Sao Paulo: Companhia das Letras, 2019), 12, cited by Vincent, in McMaster and Vincent, *Arctic/Amazon*, 75.

32 Krenak, *Ideias*. 13, cited by Vincent, in McMaster and Vincent, *Arctic/Amazon*, 76.

33 Vincent, in McMaster and Vincent, *Arctic/Amazon*, 85, with further references.

34 Pitseolak Pfeifer, "Becoming Intimate," in McMaster and Vincent, *Arctic/Amazon*, 162.

35 Rob Nixon, *Slow Violence and the Environmentalism of the Poor* (Cambridge, MA: Harvard University Press, 2011), 72–79. Nixon's account is based on the experiences of

Abdelrahman Munif, whose quintet of novels, entitled *Cites of Salt*, told the history of Bedouins' encounter with petroleum in the oases of Saudi Arabia beginning in 1933.

36 Naomi Klein, "Why Science Is Telling All of Us to Revolt and Change Our Lives Before We Destroy the Planet," *Alternet*, 29 October 2013, http://admin.alternet.org/environment/naomi-klein-why-science-telling-all-us-revolt-and-change-ourlives-we-destroy-planet, reporting researcher Brad Werner speaking to 24,000 earth and space scientists at the Union's annual conference in San Francisco.

37 Giorgio Agamben, *The Coming Community*, trans. Michael Hardt (Minneapolis: University of. Minnesota Press, 1993), XIX Tiananmen.

38 Naomi Klein, *No Is Not Enough: Resisting Trump's Shock Politics and Winning the World We Need* (Chicago: Haymarket Books, 2017), 233–234.

39 Laurie Parsons, *Carbon Colonialism: How Rich Countries Export Climate Breakdown* (Manchester: Manchester University Press, 2023).

40 Lisa E. Bloom, "Environment: Envisioning a More Just Future: Feminist Activist Art, Climate Change, and the Anthropocene," in *A Companion to Contemporary Art in a Global Framework*, 227–238. Lisa E. Bloom, *Climate Change and the New Polar Aesthetics: Artists Reimagine the Arctic and Antarctic* (Durham–London: Duke University Press, 2022).

41 Maja and Reuben Fowkes, *Art and Climate Change* (London: Thames & Hudson Ltd, 2022), 7–8.

42 Birgit Hopfener and Karin Zitewitz, Introduction, *Towards a Multi-Temporal Pluriverse of Art: Decolonizing Universalized Historiographic and Temporal Frameworks*, Special issue of *21: Inquiries into Art, History, and the Visual*, No. 1 (2024): https://doi.org/10.11588/xxi.2024.1. Another theoretically informed, multidisciplinary anthology is *Deep Horizons: A Multisensory Archive of Ecological Affects and Prospects*, ed. Brianne Cohen and Erin Espelie (Amherst College Press, 2023). The editors describe their project in the introduction as investigating "intersectional questions of how the changing planet affects specific peoples, communities, wildlife species, and ecosystems in varying and inequitable ways. . . . We take our title in part from the Deepwater Horizon oil spill in 2010 in the Gulf of Mexico, an event that epitomizes the deleterious ways in which an environmental disaster can unfold."

43 For use of the term "pluriverse," see Walter Mignolo, "Foreword, On Pluriversality and Multipolarity," in: *Constructing the Pluriverse: The Geopolitics of Knowledge*, ed. Bernd Reiter (Durham: Duke University Press, 2018), ix–xvi, and Arturo Escobar, *Pluriversal Politics. The Real and the Possible*, trans. David Frye (Durham: Duke University Press, 2020).

44 They cite the comparative literary scholar Shu-mei Shih and philosopher Yuk Hui, both of whom advocate pluriversal thinking, the latter focusing on Chinese thought traditions that take issue with the "omnipresence of Western science and technology" as "the root of our present dilemmas." Yuk Hui, *The Question Concerning Technology in China: An Essay in Cosmotechnics* (Falmouth: Urbanomic, 2016/2019); and Hui, *Art and Cosmotechnics* (Minneapolis: University of Minnesota Press, 2021).

45 T. J. Demos, Emily Eliza Scott, and Subhankar Banerjee, "Introduction," *The Routledge Companion to Contemporary Art, Visual Culture, and Climate Change*, ed. T. J. Demos, Emily Eliza Scott, and Subhankar Banerjee (New York–London: Routledge, 2021), 6. See also, T. J. Demos, *Decolonizing Nature: Contemporary Art and the Politics of Ecology* (Sternberg Press, Berlin, 2016); and Vesna's emancipatory *Atmosphere of Sound: Sonic Art in Times of Climate Disruption*, ed. Victoria Vesna and Anuradha Vikram (Los Angeles: UCLA Art/Sci Center, 2024).

46 Derrida, *The Animal That Therefore I Am*, 30–31.

47 Hans Peter Hahn and Hadas Weiss, Introduction, *Mobility, Meaning, and Transformations of Things: Shifting Contexts of Material Culture through Time and Space* (2001 German ed., Oxford: Oxbow Books, 2013).

48 Dipesh Chakrabarty, "The Climate of History: Four Theses," *Critical Inquiry 35*(2) (Winter 2009): 197–222; Chakrabarty, "Climate and Capital: On Conjoined Histories,"

Critical Inquiry 41 (Autumn 2014): 1–23; Chakrabarty, *The Climate of History in a Planetary Age* (Chicago: University of Chicago Press, 2021), 40–41, discusses the links between fossil fuels and climate on the scale of geological time. Chakrabarty has doubled down on his claim that economic globalization since the sixteenth century is not relevant, in the foreword to a book edited by Julia Thomas, *Altered Earth: Getting the Anthropocene Right* (Cambridge: Cambridge University Press, 2022), xi–xiii. Chakrabarty "cannot overemphasize the importance of this stance," because there is one criticism that is not helpful, "the reluctance of many humanistic and social scientists to even consider whether a transformed planet might transform our questions and narratives about the human past." These debates are sometimes acrimonious and divisive (evidently he doesn't see his own arguments in such a way) whereas the volume *Altered Earth* states "generative conversations across disciplines in a spirit of mutual respect." Chakrabarty and *Altered Earth* as it is framed in his foreword are caught in the logical bind of either/or regarding a both/and situation. Attention to deep history does not necessarily exclude attention to the effects wrought by humans in the past five hundred years.

49 J. Victor Moreno-Mayar, B. Potter, L. Vinner, et al., "Terminal Pleistocene Alaskan Genome Reveals First Founding Population of Native Americans," *Nature* 553 (2018): 203–207. https://doi.org/10.1038/nature25173

50 The international team was led by Professor Tom Higham, Director of the University of Oxford Radiocarbon Accelerator Unit. "The Earliest Americans Arrived in the New World 30,000 years ago," *University of Oxford News and Events* 22 July 2020. www.ox.ac.uk/news/2020-07-22-earliest-americans-arrived-new-world-30000-years-ago

51 Steven R. Holen et al., "A Thirty-thousand Year Old Archaeological Site in Southern California, USA," *Nature* 544 (27 April 2017): 479–483 [updated 8 May 2017]. https://doi.org/10.1038/nature22065

52 Vine Deloria, Jr., *Red Earth, White Lies: Native Americans and the Myth of Scientific Fact* (New York–Singapore: Scribner, 1995).

53 TARA (Trust for African Art), https://africanrockart.org/south-africa/. *The Oxford Handbook of the Archaeology and Anthropology of Rock Art*, ed. Bruno David and Ian J. McNiven (Oxford: Oxford University Press, 2018).

54 L. Barham, G. A. T. Duller, I. Candy, et al., "Evidence for the earliest structural use of wood at least 476,000 years ago," *Nature* 622 (20 September 2023): 107–111. https://doi.org/10.1038/s41586-023-06557-9. The authors report that an even older wooden artifact is a polished plank found in Israel's northern Jordan Valley in 1991, dating about 780,000 years ago. When the present book was in press, a much older find was announced: Ignacio de la Torre et al., "Systematic bone tool production at 1.5 million years ago," *Nature 640* (2025): 130–134, an assemblage of 27 bone tools shaped by knapping discovered in East Africa.

55 Known as the Milankovitch (Orbital) cycles after their discoverer, Milutin Milankovitch, they cannot explain the Earth's current warming. Lawrence Guy Straus, "The World at the End of the Last Ice Age," in *Humans at the End of the Ice Age: The Archaeology of the Pleistocene–Holocene Transition*, ed. Lawrence Guy Straus et al. (New York: Plenum, 1996), 5, cited by Chakrabarty, *The Climate of History*, 41.

56 Kristian Kristiansen, *Europe Before History* (Cambridge: Cambridge University Press, 1998), 1.

57 Kristiansen, *Europe before History*, 3.

58 Flemming Kaul, "The Xenia Concept of Guest-friendship – Providing an Elucidatory Model for Bronze Age Communication," in *North Meets South: Theoretical Aspects on the Northern and Southern Rock Art Traditions in Scandinavia*, ed. Peter Skoglund, Johan Ling, and Ulf Bertilsson (Oxford: Oxbow Books, 2017), 172–198. My brief overview also draws from the introduction to the same volume by Peter Skoglund and Johan Ling. See also Flemming Kaul, "The Nordic Razor as a Medium of Creativity," in *Considering Creativity: Creativity, Knowledge and Practice in Bronze Age Europe*, ed.

Joanna Sofaer (Oxford: Archaeopress Publishing, 2018), 105–115, reproduced here Fig. 7.1 (p. 107); Kaul, "Middle Bronze Age Long Distance Exchange: Early Glass, Amber, and Guest-Friendship, *Xenia*," in *Bronzezeitlicher Transport: Akteure, Mittel, und Wege*, ed. Bianka Nessel, Daniel Neumann, and Martin Bertelheim (Tübingen: Tübingen University Press, 2018), 189–212.

59 Flemming Kaul, "The Eternal Voyage of the Sun and the Perpetual, Cyclical Advance of Time, Seen from a Nordic Bronze Age Perspective. Movement Is Time – Time Is Movement," in *Zeit Is Macht. Wer macht Zeit. Time Is Power. Who Makes Time?*, ed. Harald Meller, Alfred Reischenberger, and Roberto Risch (Halle [Saale]: Tagungen des Landesmuseum für Vorgeschichte 24, 2021), 165–180; Kaul, "The Chariot of the Sun and Other Sun Horses of the Nordic Bronze Age – Including Some Interesting Anatomical Details," in *Giving the Past a Future: Essays in Archaeology and Rock Art Studies in Honour of Dr. Phil. h.c. Gerhard Milstreu*, ed. James Dodd and Ellen Meijer (Oxford: Archaeopress Publishing Ltd, 2018), 58–69.

60 Jeanette Varberg, Flemming Kaul, and Bernard Gratuze, "Bronze Age Glass and Amber: Evidence of Bronze Age Long Distance Exchange," *Adoranten* 2019: 5–29. https://www.researchgate.net/publication/342787189; Varberg, Gratuze, and Kaul, "Between Egypt, Mesopotamia and Scandinavia: Late Bronze Age Glass Beads Found in Denmark," *Journal of Archaeological Science* 64 (2015): 168–181; Kaul, "The *Xenia* Concept." The dynamic movement of people and materials documented in Danish Bronze Age burial mounds also took place at smaller scale. Karin Frei et al., "A matter of months: High precision migration chronology of a Bronze Age female," PLOS One June 5, 2017, accessed at https://doi.org/10.1371/journal.pone.0178834

61 Janet L. Abu-Lughod, *Before European Hegemony: The World System A.D. 1250–1350* (New York, 1989).

62 This trade system was not global in the sense that all parts were evenly articulated with one another – a situation which does not exist even today; Abu-Lughod, *Before European Hegemony*, 32.

63 Roxanna M. Brown, "Shipwreck Evidence for the China–Manila Ceramics Trade," in *Asia & Spanish America: Trans-Pacific Artistic and Cultural Exchange, 1500–1850*, ed. Donna Pierce and Ronald Otsuka (Denver: Denver Art Museum, 2009), 59–68.

64 Other commodities were exported: cotton textiles in exchange for silk and other luxury fabrics; iron, steel, stone vessles, gold, ivory, tortoiseshell, rhino horn, frankincense, myrrh, ebony and other hardwoods, and slaves. G. Pwiti, "Trade and Economies in Southern Africa: The Archaeological Evidence," *Zambezia* 18/2 (1991): 119–129.

65 Peregrine Horden and Nicholas Purcell, T*he Corrupting Sea: A Study of Mediterranean History* (Oxford: Blackwell Publishers, 2000); Horden and Purcell, "The Mediterranean and the New Thalassology," AHR Forum, *The American Historical Review* 111/3 (2006), accessed online at www.historycoperative.org. My description of regions is indebted to Hoffman, *Remapping the Art of the Mediterranean.*

66 *The Oxford Companion to the Decorative Arts*, ed. Harold Osborne (Oxford: Oxford University Press, 1975), 331; Jack Ogden, "Metals," in Ancient Egyptian Materials and Technology, ed. Paul T. Nicholson and Ian Shaw (Cambridge: Cambridge University Press, 2000), 149–176.

67 The term "object itineraries" is a revision of the widely adopted concept of "object biographies" introduced by Igor Kopytoff, "The Cultural Biography of Things: Commoditization as Process," in *The Social Life of Things*, ed. Arjun Appadurai (Cambridge: Cambridge University Press,1986), 64–91. See Hahn and Weiss, "Biographies, Travels, and Itineraries of Things."

68 Sussan Babaie, "The Mercantile Effect: On Art and Exchange in the Islamicate World," in *The Mercantile Effect: Art and Exchange in the Islamicate World during the 17th and 18th Centuries*, ed. Sussan Babaie and Melanie Gibson (London: Gingko Library, 2019), 9–12, citing studies by historians Peter Francopan, Sanjay Subrahmanyan, and Marshall G. S. Hodgson.

69 Martin W. Lewis and Kären E. Wigen, *The Myth of Continents: A Critique of Metageopgrahy* (Berkeley: University of California Press, 1997), which includes an excellent historical critique of shifting ideas of East and West.
70 Nancy Um, "The Mechanics of Cultivating Desire: Connecting Early Modern Objects, Artisans, and Workshops," *Routledge Companion to Global Renaissance Art*, ed. Stephen J. Campbell and Stephanie Porras (Oxford: Routledge, 2024), 17–20. DOI: 10.4324/9781003294986-3; Um, "Silver: Mutability and Materiality across Seventeenth-Century Networks of Trade and Plunder in the Indian and Atlantic Oceans," Annual Hammer Art History Lecture, Center for Early Global Studies, University of California Los Angeles, 8 May 2024.
71 Nancy Um, "Aromatics, Stimulants, and their Vessels: The Material Culture and Rites of Merchant Interaction in Eighteenth-Century Mocha," in *The Mercantile Effect*, 63–73. A review of the Eurasian maritime literature is beyond the scope of the present study, but see the foundational study by Sanjay Subrahmanyam, "Connected Histories: Notes towards a Reconfiguration of Early Modern Eurasia," *Modern Asian Studies 31/3 (July 1997): Special Issue: The Eurasian Context of the Early Modern History of Mainland South East Asia, 1400–1800,* 735–762. Recently, Subrahmanyam, *Across the Green Sea: Histories from the Western Indian Ocean, 1440–1640 (Austin:* University of Texas Press, 2024).
72 Beate Fricke and Barry Finbarr Flood, *Archives of Flotsam: Objects and Early Globalism*, forthcoming from Princeton University Press, reported in "Premodern Globalism in Art History: A Conversation," *The Art Bulletin*, December 2022, 6–18.
73 Juneja, *Can Art History Be Made Global?*, Introduction.
74 Donna Haraway, "Situated Knowledges: The Science Question in Feminism and the Privilege of Partial Perspective," *Feminist Studies* 14, n. 3 (Autumn 1988), 575–599.
75 Donna Haraway, *Simians, Cyborgs, and Women: The Reinvention of Nature* (New York: Routledge, 1991), 201.
76 Claire Farago, "Imagining Art History Otherwise," in *Global and World Art in the Practice of the University Museum*, ed. Jane Chin Davidson and Sandra Esslinger (London–New York: Routledge, 2017), 115–130; Farago, "What Comes After World Art? Taking a Creative Commons Approach to Pedagogy," in *Worlding Syllabi*, ed. Eva Bentcheva, Birgit Hopfener, Franziska Koch, Miriam Oesterreich, and Ming Tiampo, Worlding Public Cultures (Berlin: ICI Berlin Press, 2025).
77 Sanjay Seth, "Reason of Reasoning? Clio or Siva?," *Postcolonial Traces*, ed. Brent Hayes Edwards, special issue of *Social Text* 78 (Spring 2004): 84–101.
78 Clifford Geertz, *Local Knowledge: Further Essays in Interpretive Anthropology (*New York: Basic Books, 1983).
79 Tony Bennett, *Making Culture, Changing Society* (London–New York: Routledge, 2013), drawing on Foucault and Deleuze, regards culture as a "historically specific set of knowledge practices [that] . . . are the products of specific forms of expertise performed in particular institutional settings" whose interactions comprise a "culture complex." (p. 2).
80 Judith Butler, *The Psychic Life of Power: Theories in Subjection* (Stanford: Stanford University Press, 1997), 131, citing Giorgio Agamben, *The Coming Community*, trans. Michael Hardt (Minneapolis: University of Minnesota Press, 1993), 42.
81 Jacques Derrida, "The Right to Philosophy from the Cosmopolitical Point of View (the Example of an International Institution)," *Ethics, Institutions, and the Right to Philosophy*, trans. and ed. Peter Pericles Trifonas (Lanham/Oxford: Rowman & Littlefield Publishers, Inc, 2002), 1–18.
82 Derrida, *The Right to Philosophy*, 7, citing Kant, *Philosophie de l'histoire*, trans. Stéphanie Piobetta (Paris: Aubier, 1947), 69–70, translation modified by Derrida.
83 Derrida, *The Right To Philosophy*, 8.
84 Carolyn Dean, "The Trouble with (the Term) Art," *Art Journal* 65/2 (2006): 24–32.
85 Sabine MacCormack, "Cultural Histories of the Material World: Whose Material World?," in *Cultural Histories of the Material World*, 74–80.

86 Achille Mbembe, *Necropolitics*, trans. S. Corcoran (Durham, NC: Duke University Press, 2019), 171, as cited by Dan Hicks, *The Brutish Museums*, 178. See discussion of the Benin Bronzes in Fugue 2.
87 Alexander Watkins, "Teaching Inclusive Authorities: Indigenous Ways of Knowing and the Framework for Information Literacy in Native Art." In *Disciplinary Applications of Information Literacy Threshold Concepts*. ACRL. He draws from Linda Tuhiwai Smith, *Decolonizing Methodologies.*
88 Max Liboiron, *Pollution is Colonialism* (Durham: Duke University Press, 2021), 14 and 23.
89 Donald Preziosi and Claire Farago, "Art and the Question of Cosmopolitanism," January 2023, unpublished manuscript.
90 Debra D. Chapman, Tania Ruiz-Chapman, and Peter Eglin, "Global Citizenship as Neoliberal Propaganda: A Political-Economic and Postcolonial Critique," *Alternate Routes: A Journal of Critical Social Research* 29 (February 2018): 142–166.https://alternateroutes.ca/index.php/ar/article/view/22450
91 Rob Wilson, "Afterword: Worlding as Future Tactic," in *The Worlding Project: Doing Cultural Studies in the Era of Globalization*, ed. Rob Wilson and Christopher Leigh Connery (Berkeley: North Atlantic Books, 2007).
92 Jenny Lin, *Above Sea: Contemporary Art, Urban Culture, and the Fashioning of Global Shanghai* (Manchester: University of Manchester Press, 2019), 118.
93 Vincenzo Cicchelli, Sylvie Octobre, and Viviane Riegl, "Introduction: How Aesthetic Cosmopolitan Is Our Global World?," in *Aesthetic Cosmopolitanism and Global Culture*, ed. Vincenzo Cicchelli, Sylvie Octobre, and Viviane Riegl (Leiden: Brill, 2020), 56.
94 Pauline Kleingeld and Eric Brown, "Cosmopolitanism," *The Stanford Encyclopedia of Philosophy* (Winter 2019 Edition), ed. Edward N. Zalta, https://plato.stanford.edu/archives/win2019/entries/cosmopolitanism/
95 Nelson Goodman, *Ways of Worldmaking* (Indianapolis: Hackett Publishing Co.,1978), 57–70.
96 Kobena Mercer, "Introduction," in *Cosmopolitan Modernisms*, ed. Kobena Mercer (London: Institute of International Visual Arts and the MIT Press, 2005), 7.
97 Giorgio Agamben, *The Man Without Content* [1994 Italian ed.], trans. Georgia Albert (Stanford: Stanford University Press, 1999). See also Luc Ferry, *Homo Aestheticus: The Invention of Taste in the Democratic Age* [1990, French ed.], trans. Robert de Loaiza (Chicago: Chicago University Press, 1993). Donald Preziosi and I have developed the argument further in the Introduction to *Art Is Not What You Think It Is*.
98 Papastergiadis, *Cosmopolitanism and Culture*, 88; Papastergiadis, "Aesethetic Cosmopolitanism," in *Routledge International Handbook in Cosmopolitan Studies*, ed. Gerard Delanty (Routledge, 2018), 198–310, at 209. www.routledgehandbooks.com/doi/10.4324/9781351028905-18. See also Marsha Meskimmon, *Contemporary Art and the Cosmopolitan Imagination* (London–New York: Routledge, 2011).
99 Papastergiadis, *Cosmopolitanism and Culture*, 91.
100 Bruno Latour, *We Have Never Been Modern* [1991], trans. Catherine Porter (Cambridge: Harvard University Press, 1993). See discussion in Fugue 4.
101 Michel De Certeau, "Psychoanalysis and its History," *Heterologies: Discourse on the Other*, trans. Brian Massumi (Minneapolis–London: University of Minnesota Press, 1986), 3.
102 Étienne Balibar, *Citizenship*, trans. Thomas Scott-Railton (Malden: Polity Press, 2015).
103 Balibar, *Citizenship*, 27.
104 Eleni Sikelianos, "The Question Is How to Interrogate the Remains," in *Cross Worlds: Transcultural Poetics, an Anthology*, ed. Anne Waldman and Laura Wright (Minneapolis: Coffee House Press, 2014), 319–320.

INDEX

References in *italics* are to figures. References of the form "XnY" refer to footnote Y on page X.

For Product Safety Concerns and Information please contact our EU representative GPSR@taylorandfrancis.com Taylor & Francis Verlag GmbH, Kaufingerstraße 24, 80331 München, Germany

* 9 7 8 1 1 3 8 4 9 5 8 2 1 *

T - #0133 - 180625 - C79 - 234/156/15 - PB - 9781138495821 - Matt Lamination